VOLUME
8

Silver Spoon

HIROMU ARAKAWA

STORY & CHARACTERS

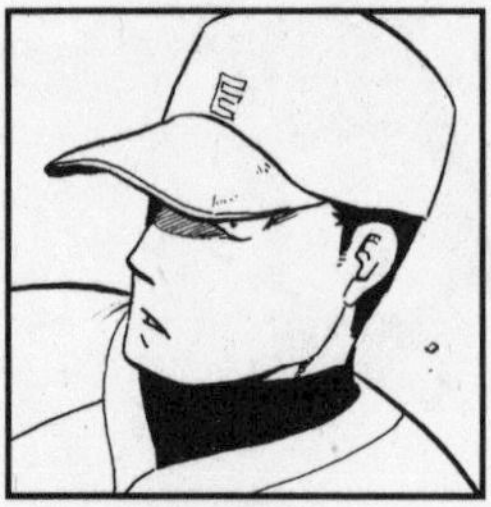

ICHIROU KOMABA

A first-year student at Ooezo Agricultural High School, enrolled in the Dairy Science Program. Pitcher for the baseball team with the potential to be their next ace player. Plans on taking over the family farm after graduation.

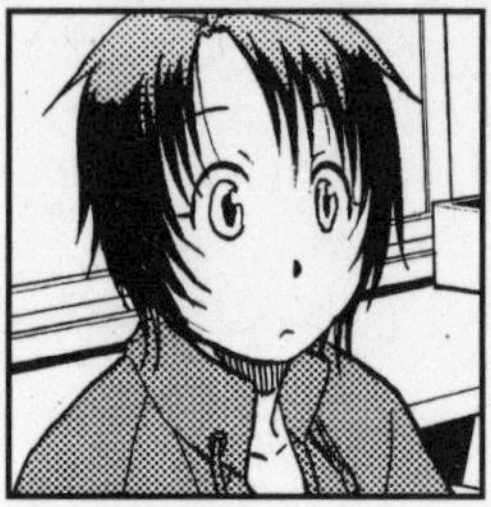

AKI MIKAGE

A first-year student at Ooezo Agricultural High School, enrolled in the Dairy Science Program. Her family keeps cows and horses, and she's expected to carry on the family business. Deep down, though, she wants to work with horses...

YUUGO HACHIKEN

A first-year student at Ooezo Agricultural High School, enrolled in the Dairy Science Program. A city kid from Sapporo who got in through the general entrance exam. Now he's vice president of the Equestrian Club.

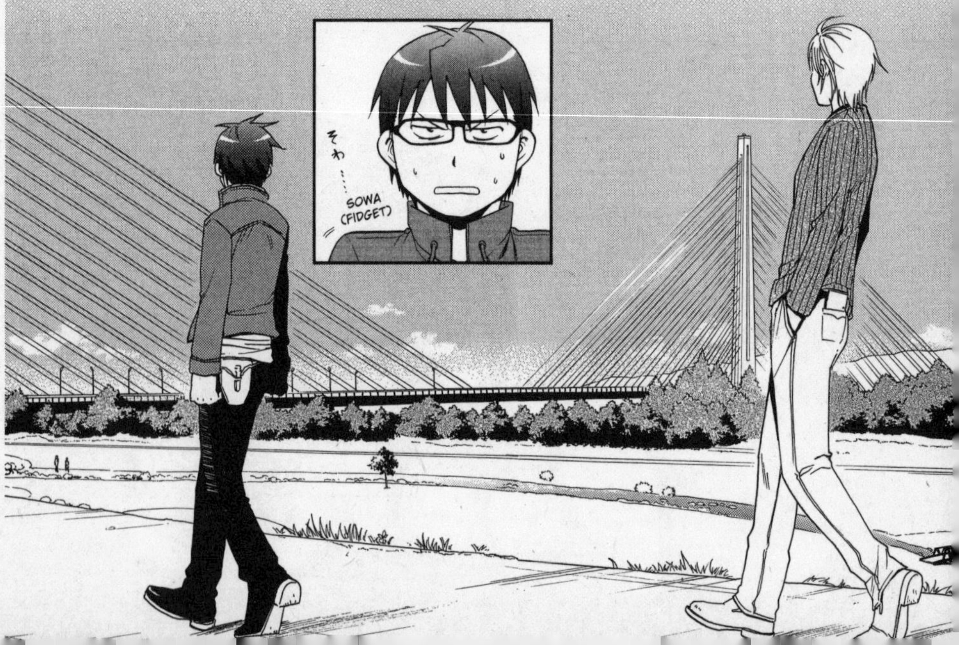
そわ…
SOWA (FIDGET)

AYAME MINAMIKUJOU

Aki's childhood friend. Started an Equestrian Club at Shimizu West High School to compete with Aki. Sees Hachiken as a rival...for some reason.

TAMAKO INADA

A first-year student at Ooezo Agricultural High School, enrolled in the Dairy Science Program. Her family runs the megafarm. A complete enigma.

The Story Thus Far:

It was all for nothing... These words run round and round in Hachiken's head. After days spent scurrying frantically between club and hands-ons and juggling a mountain of prep work for the Ezo Ag Festival, Hachiken faints the morning the festival is due to begin... An unwanted encounter with his father leaves Hachiken with a hurting heart, but the thoughtfulness of his friends soon sets it to right. However, one of those friends, Ichirou Komaba, stands at a crossroads in his own life. When Komaba's hopes and dreams, which had been held together only by the ongoing success of the baseball team, are cut short by a loss, what can Hachiken do?

SHINNOSUKE AIKAWA

A first-year student at Ooezo Agricultural High School, enrolled in the Dairy Science Program. His dream is to become a veterinarian, but he can't handle blood.

KEIJI TOKIWA

A first-year student at Ooezo Agricultural High School, enrolled in the Dairy Science Program. Son of chicken farmers. Awful at academics.

CONTENTS

Silver Spoon

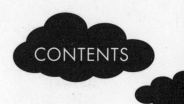

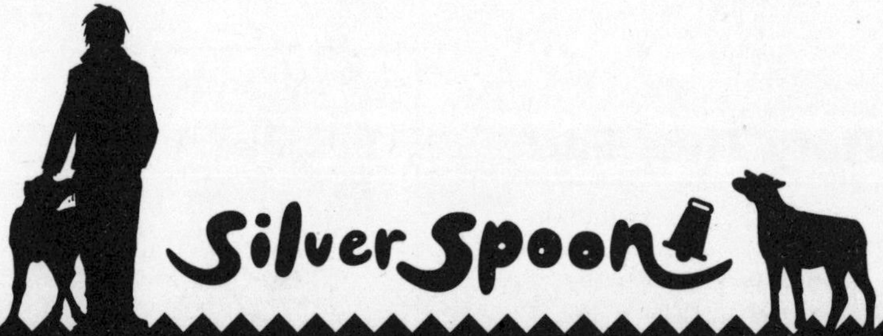

Chapter 62:
Tale of Autumn ㉛

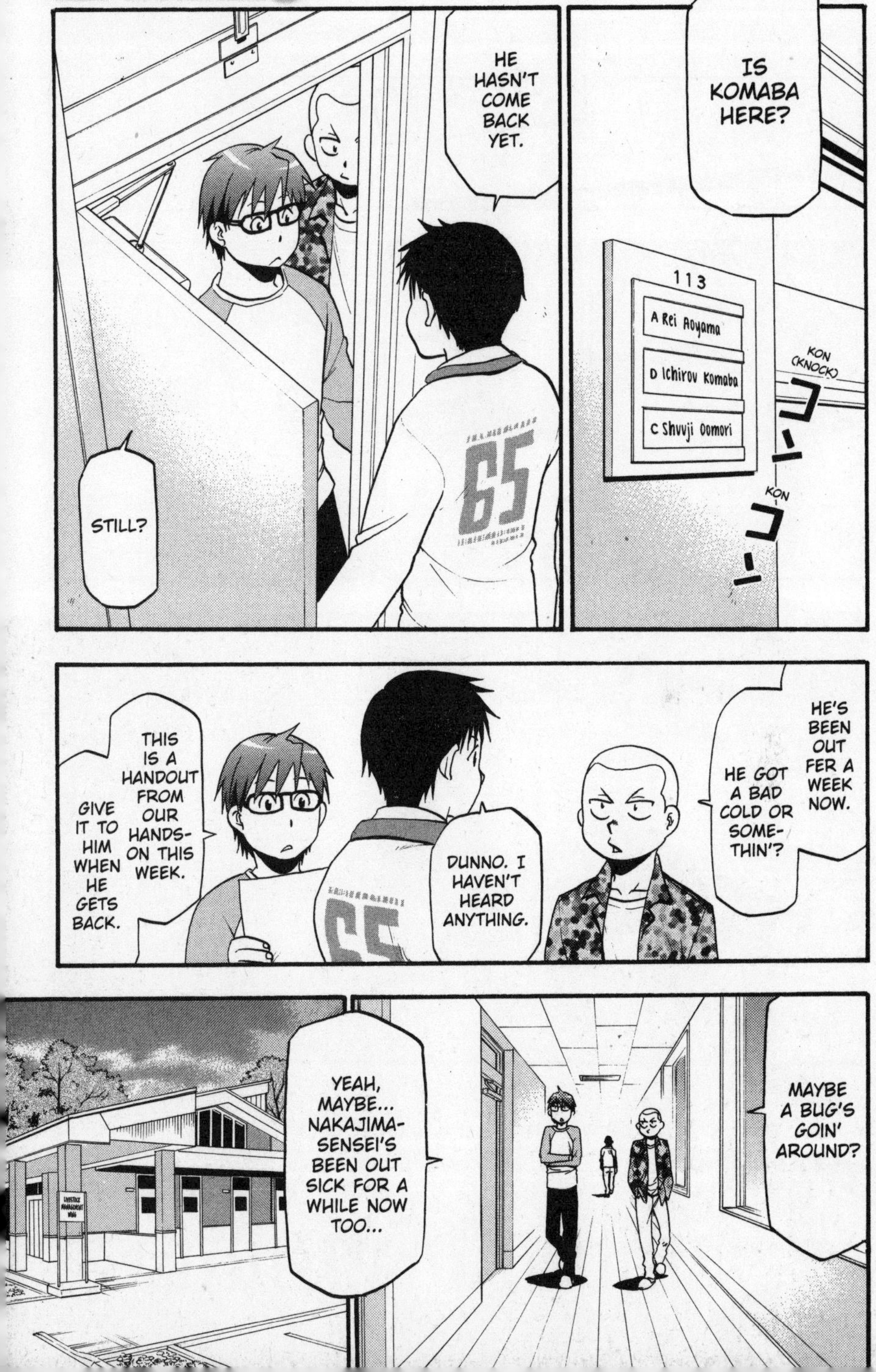
IS KOMABA HERE?
113
A Rei Aoyama
D Ichirou Komaba
C Shuuji Oomori
KON (KNOCK)
KON
HE HASN'T COME BACK YET.
STILL?
HE'S BEEN OUT FER A WEEK NOW.
HE GOT A BAD COLD OR SOME-THIN'?
DUNNO. I HAVEN'T HEARD ANYTHING.
THIS IS A HANDOUT FROM OUR HANDS-ON THIS WEEK.
GIVE IT TO HIM WHEN HE GETS BACK.
MAYBE A BUG'S GOIN' AROUND?
YEAH, MAYBE... NAKAJIMA-SENSEI'S BEEN OUT SICK FOR A WHILE NOW TOO...

CHEESEMAKING LAB

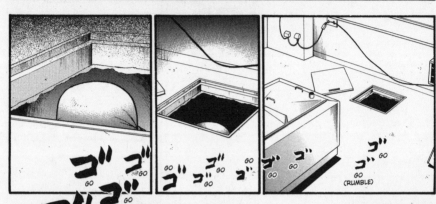

ゴ
GO
ゴ
GO
ゴ
GO
ゴ
GO
ゴ
GO
ゴ
GO
ゴ
GO
ゴ
GO
ゴ
GO
ゴ
GO
(RUMBLE)

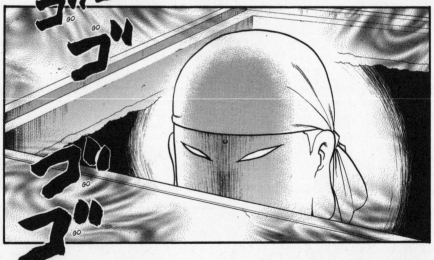

ゴ
GO
ゴ
GO
ゴ
GO
ゴ
GO
ゴ
GO
ゴ
GO

Chapter 62:
Tale of Autumn ㉛

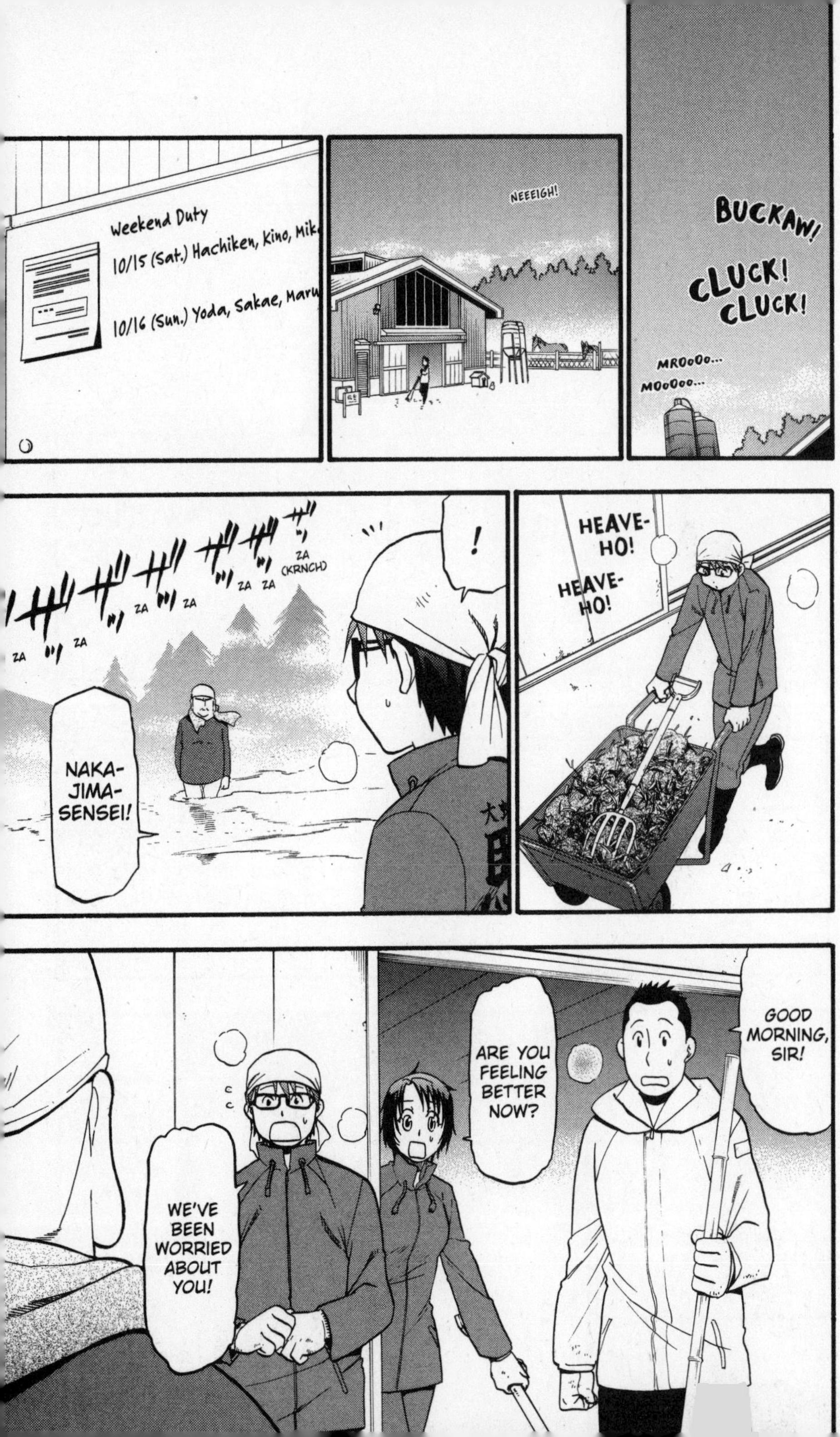
BUCKAW!
CLUCK! CLUCK!
MROoOo...
MOoOoo...
NEEEIGH!
Weekend Duty
10/15 (Sat.) Hachiken, Kino, Mik
10/16 (Sun.) Yoda, Sakae, Maru
HEAVE-HO!
HEAVE-HO!
!
ZA ZA ZA ZA ZA ZA
ZA (KRNCH)
NAKAJIMA-SENSEI!
GOOD MORNING, SIR!
ARE YOU FEELING BETTER NOW?
WE'VE BEEN WORRIED ABOUT YOU!

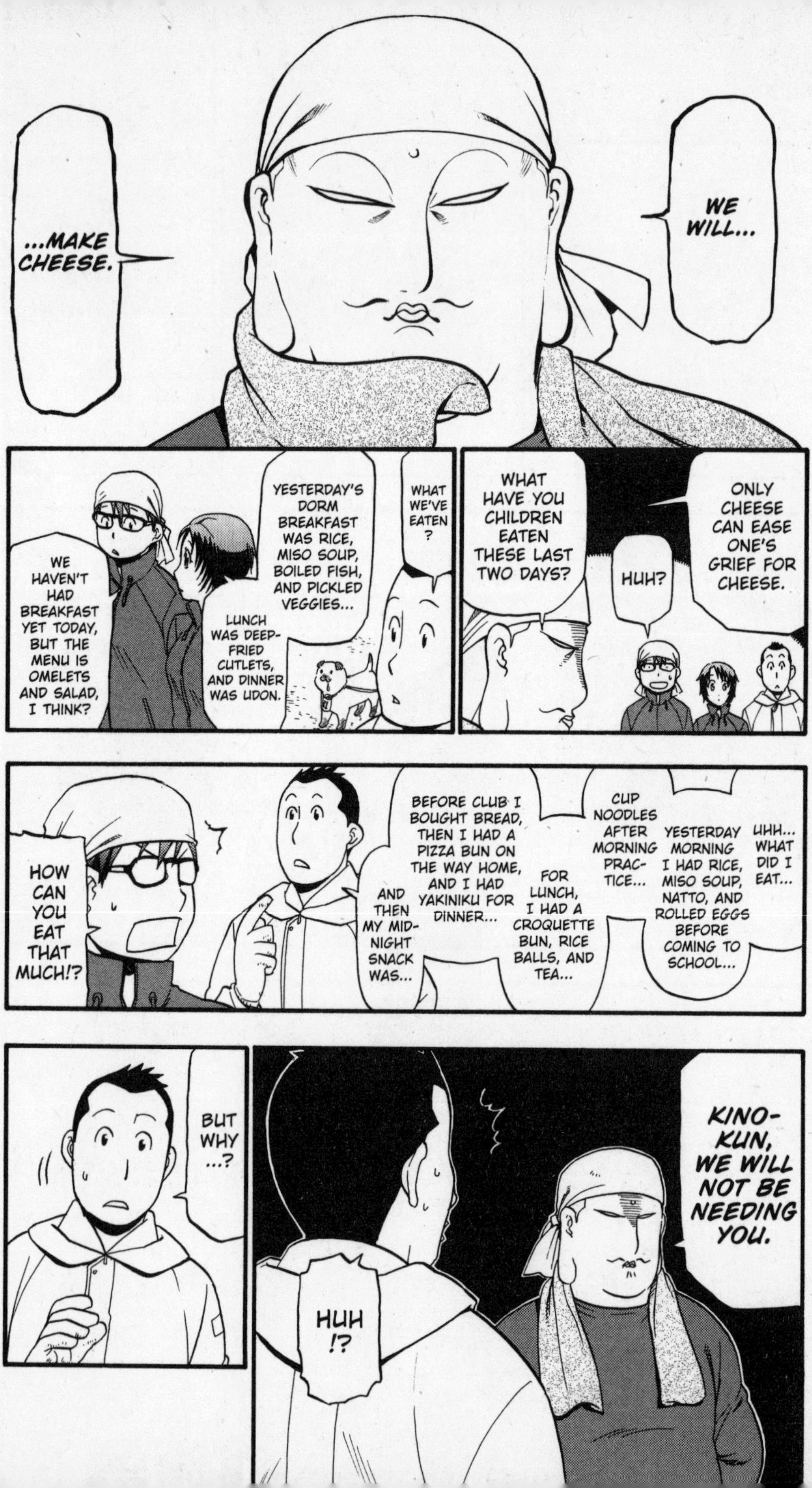
WE WILL...
...MAKE CHEESE.
ONLY CHEESE CAN EASE ONE'S GRIEF FOR CHEESE.
HUH?
WHAT HAVE YOU CHILDREN EATEN THESE LAST TWO DAYS?
WHAT WE'VE EATEN?
YESTERDAY'S DORM BREAKFAST WAS RICE, MISO SOUP, BOILED FISH, AND PICKLED VEGGIES...
LUNCH WAS DEEP-FRIED CUTLETS, AND DINNER WAS UDON.
WE HAVEN'T HAD BREAKFAST YET TODAY, BUT THE MENU IS OMELETS AND SALAD, I THINK?
UHH... WHAT DID I EAT...
YESTERDAY MORNING I HAD RICE, MISO SOUP, NATTO, AND ROLLED EGGS BEFORE COMING TO SCHOOL...
CUP NOODLES AFTER MORNING PRAC-TICE...
FOR LUNCH, I HAD A CROQUETTE BUN, RICE BALLS, AND TEA...
BEFORE CLUB I BOUGHT BREAD, THEN I HAD A PIZZA BUN ON THE WAY HOME, AND I HAD YAKINIKU FOR DINNER...
AND THEN MY MID-NIGHT SNACK WAS...
HOW CAN YOU EAT THAT MUCH!?
KINO-KUN, WE WILL NOT BE NEEDING YOU.
HUH!?
BUT WHY...?

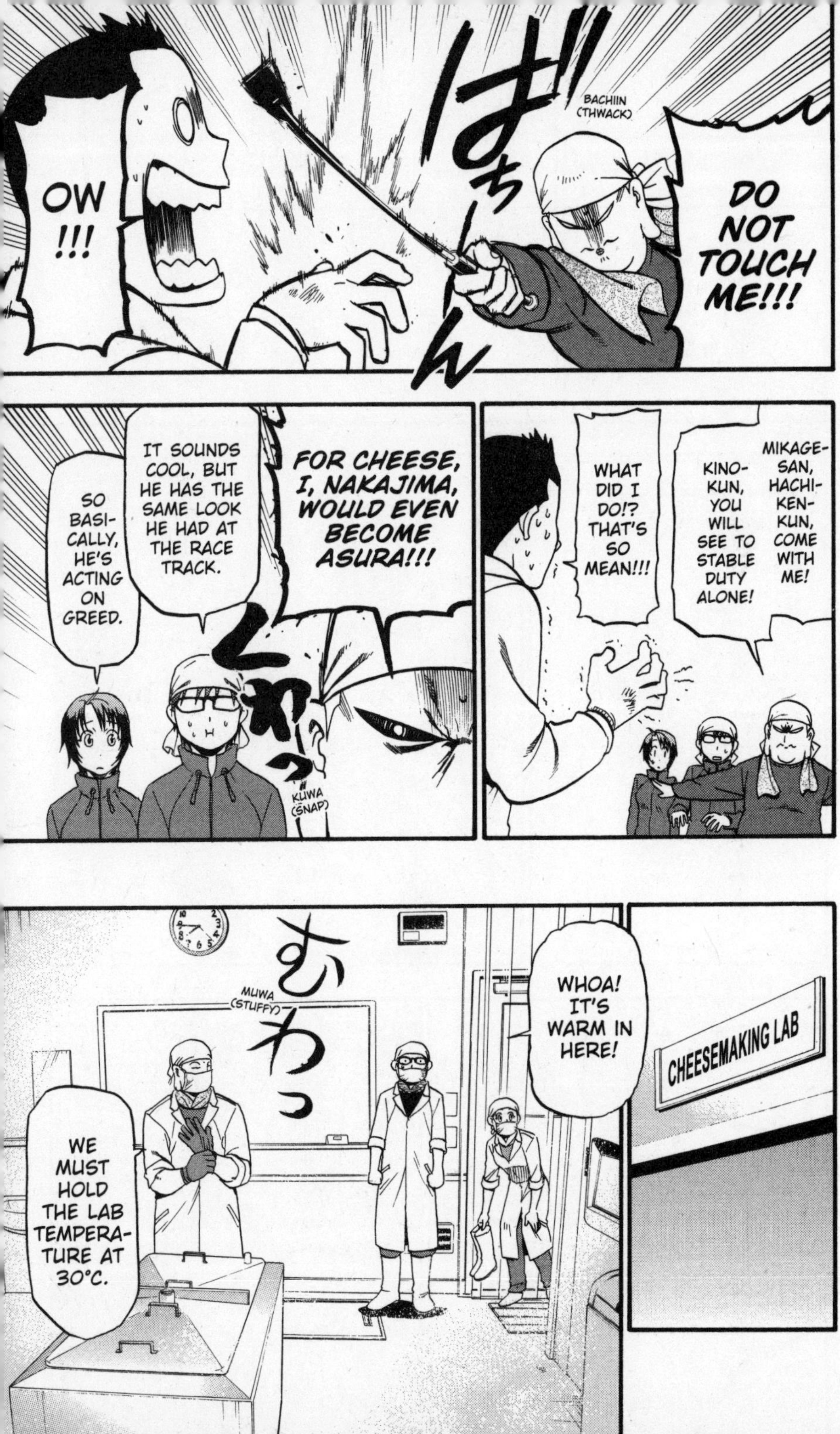
DO NOT TOUCH ME!!!
BACHIIN (THWACK)
OW !!!
MIKAGE-SAN, HACHIKEN-KUN, COME WITH ME!
KINO-KUN, YOU WILL SEE TO STABLE DUTY ALONE!
WHAT DID I DO!? THAT'S SO MEAN!!!
FOR CHEESE, I, NAKAJIMA, WOULD EVEN BECOME ASURA!!!
KUWA (SNAP)
IT SOUNDS COOL, BUT HE HAS THE SAME LOOK HE HAD AT THE RACE TRACK.
SO BASICALLY, HE'S ACTING ON GREED.
CHEESEMAKING LAB
WHOA! IT'S WARM IN HERE!
MUWA (STUFFY)
WE MUST HOLD THE LAB TEMPERATURE AT 30°C.

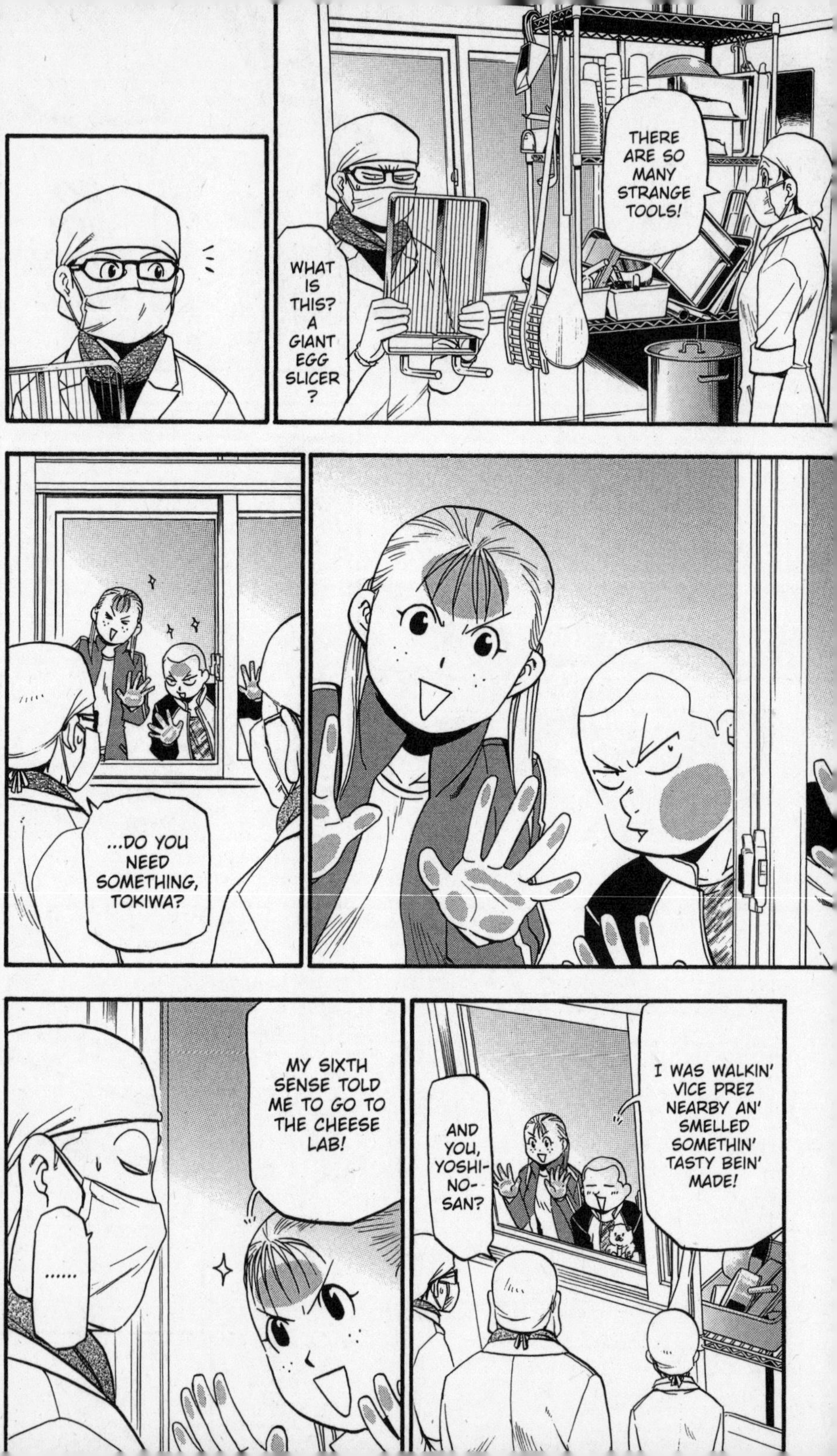
THERE ARE SO MANY STRANGE TOOLS!
WHAT IS THIS? A GIANT EGG SLICER?
...DO YOU NEED SOMETHING, TOKIWA?
I WAS WALKIN' VICE PREZ NEARBY AN' SMELLED SOMETHIN' TASTY BEIN' MADE!
AND YOU, YOSHI-NO-SAN?
MY SIXTH SENSE TOLD ME TO GO TO THE CHEESE LAB!
......

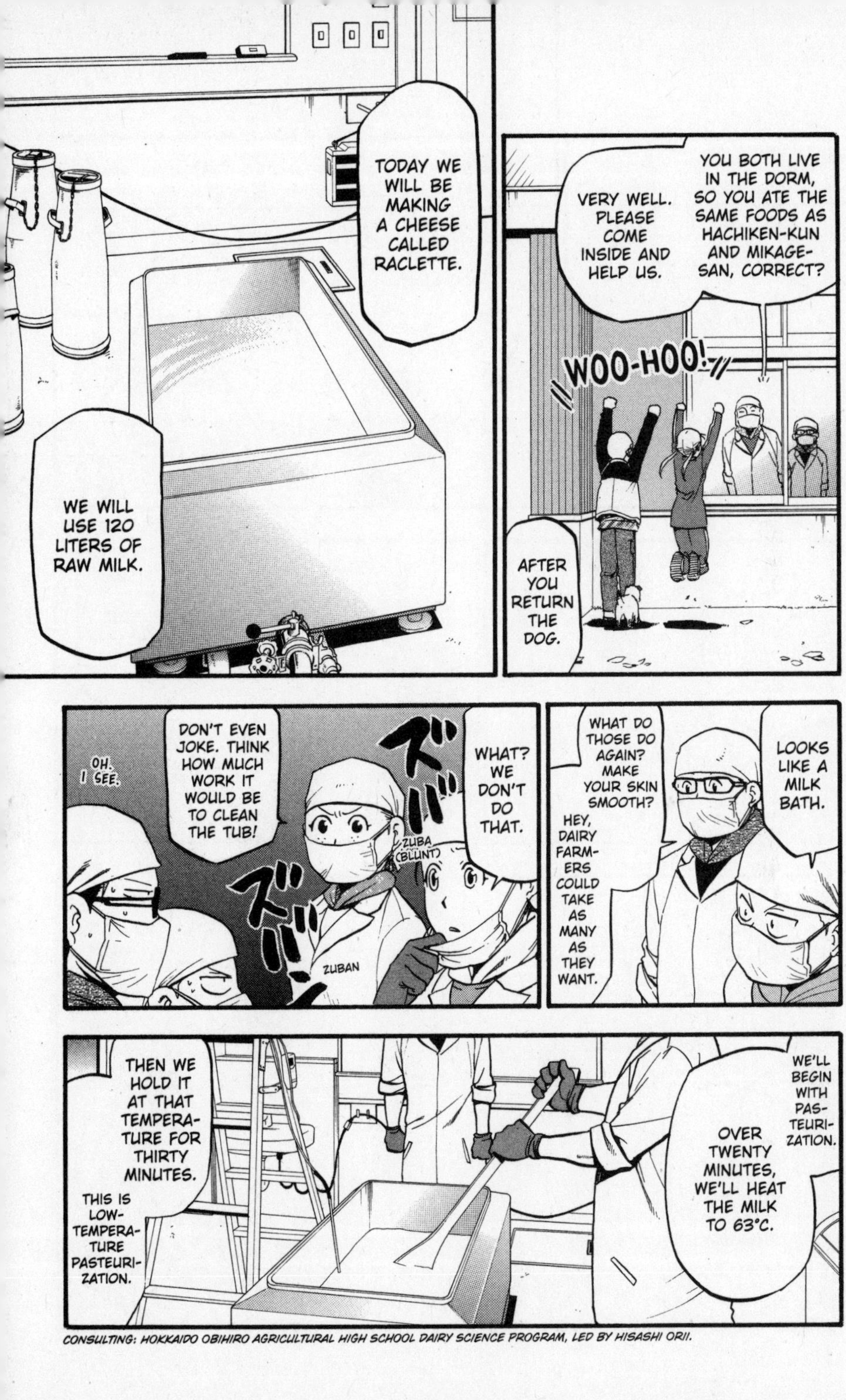
YOU BOTH LIVE IN THE DORM, SO YOU ATE THE SAME FOODS AS HACHIKEN-KUN AND MIKAGE-SAN, CORRECT?
VERY WELL. PLEASE COME INSIDE AND HELP US.
WOO-HOO!
AFTER YOU RETURN THE DOG.
TODAY WE WILL BE MAKING A CHEESE CALLED RACLETTE.
WE WILL USE 120 LITERS OF RAW MILK.
LOOKS LIKE A MILK BATH.
WHAT DO THOSE DO AGAIN? MAKE YOUR SKIN SMOOTH?
HEY, DAIRY FARMERS COULD TAKE AS MANY AS THEY WANT.
WHAT? WE DON'T DO THAT.
ZUBA (BLUNT)
DON'T EVEN JOKE. THINK HOW MUCH WORK IT WOULD BE TO CLEAN THE TUB!
ZUBAN
OH. I SEE.
WE'LL BEGIN WITH PASTEURIZATION.
OVER TWENTY MINUTES, WE'LL HEAT THE MILK TO 63°C.
THEN WE HOLD IT AT THAT TEMPERATURE FOR THIRTY MINUTES.
THIS IS LOW-TEMPERATURE PASTEURIZATION.

CONSULTING: HOKKAIDO OBIHIRO AGRICULTURAL HIGH SCHOOL DAIRY SCIENCE PROGRAM, LED BY HISASHI ORII.

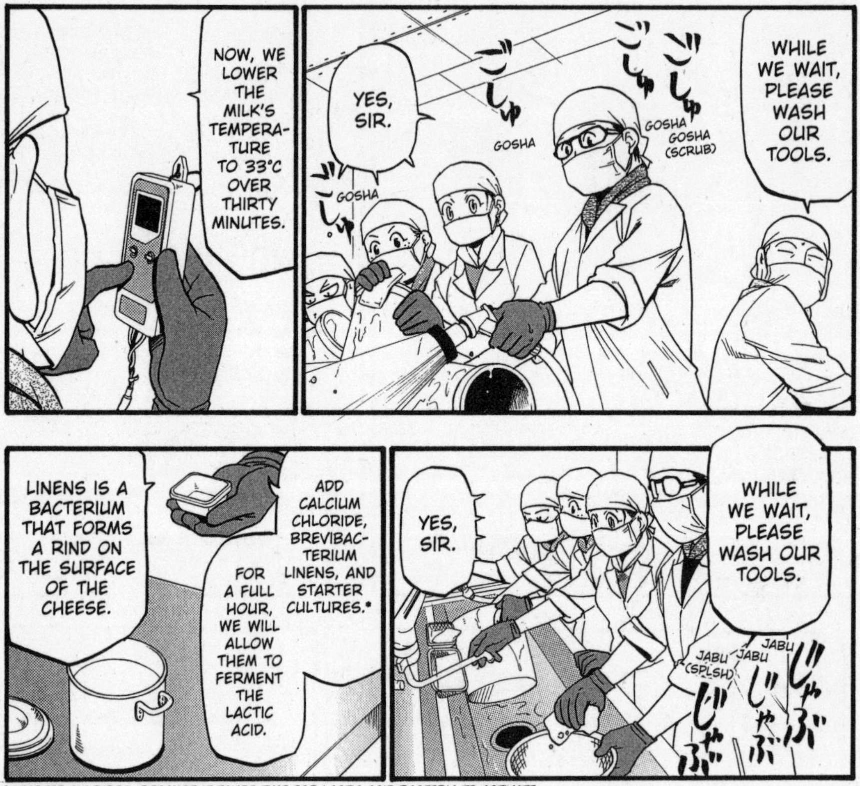
WHILE WE WAIT, PLEASE WASH OUR TOOLS.
YES, SIR.
ごしゅ ごしゅ
GOSHA GOSHA (SCRUB)
ごしゅ
GOSHA
ごしゅ
GOSHA
NOW, WE LOWER THE MILK'S TEMPERA-TURE TO 33°C OVER THIRTY MINUTES.
WHILE WE WAIT, PLEASE WASH OUR TOOLS.
YES, SIR.
じゃぶ じゃぶ じゃぶ
JABU JABU JABU (SPLSH)
ADD CALCIUM CHLORIDE, BREVIBAC-TERIUM LINENS, AND STARTER CULTURES.*
FOR A FULL HOUR, WE WILL ALLOW THEM TO FERMENT THE LACTIC ACID.
LINENS IS A BACTERIUM THAT FORMS A RIND ON THE SURFACE OF THE CHEESE.

*STARTER CULTURES: BECAUSE IT TAKES TIME FOR LACTIC ACID BACTERIA TO ACTIVATE, PRE-FERMENTED BACTERIA ARE ADDED TO SPEED UP THE FERMENTATION PROCESS.

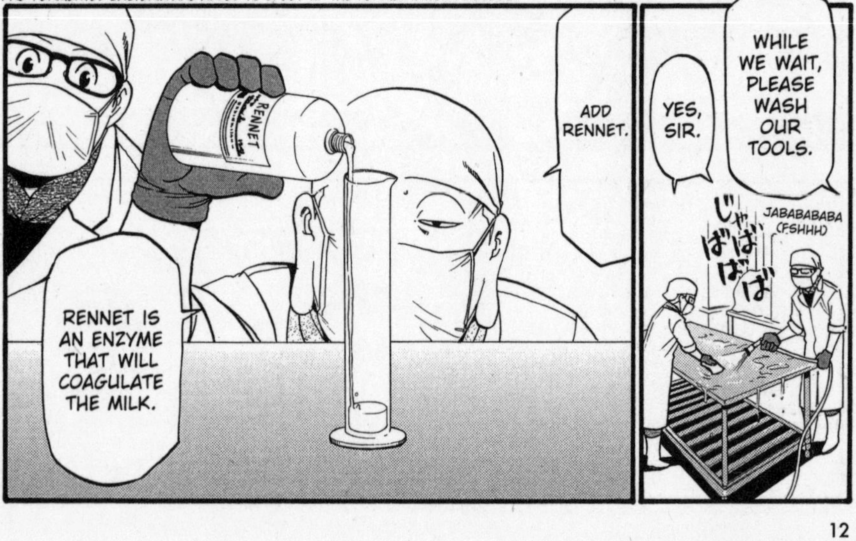
WHILE WE WAIT, PLEASE WASH OUR TOOLS.
YES, SIR.
じゃばばばば
JABABABABA (FSHHH)
ADD RENNET.
RENNET
RENNET IS AN ENZYME THAT WILL COAGULATE THE MILK.

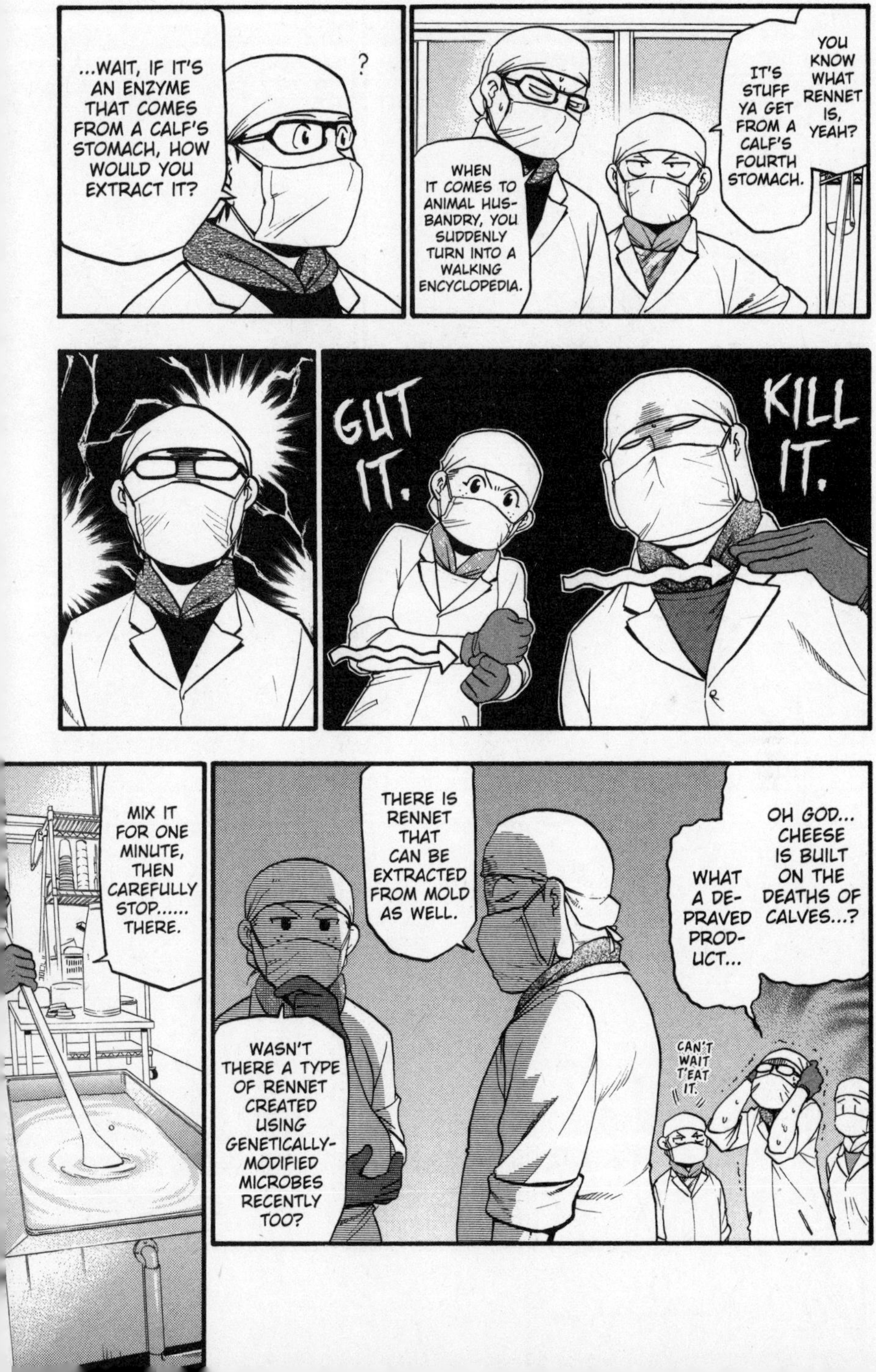
YOU KNOW WHAT RENNET IS, YEAH?
IT'S STUFF YA GET FROM A CALF'S FOURTH STOMACH.
WHEN IT COMES TO ANIMAL HUS-BANDRY, YOU SUDDENLY TURN INTO A WALKING ENCYCLOPEDIA.
?
...WAIT, IF IT'S AN ENZYME THAT COMES FROM A CALF'S STOMACH, HOW WOULD YOU EXTRACT IT?
KILL IT.
GUT IT.
OH GOD... CHEESE IS BUILT ON THE DEATHS OF CALVES...?
WHAT A DE-PRAVED PROD-UCT...
THERE IS RENNET THAT CAN BE EXTRACTED FROM MOLD AS WELL.
CAN'T WAIT T'EAT IT.
WASN'T THERE A TYPE OF RENNET CREATED USING GENETICALLY-MODIFIED MICROBES RECENTLY TOO?
MIX IT FOR ONE MINUTE, THEN CAREFULLY STOP...... THERE.

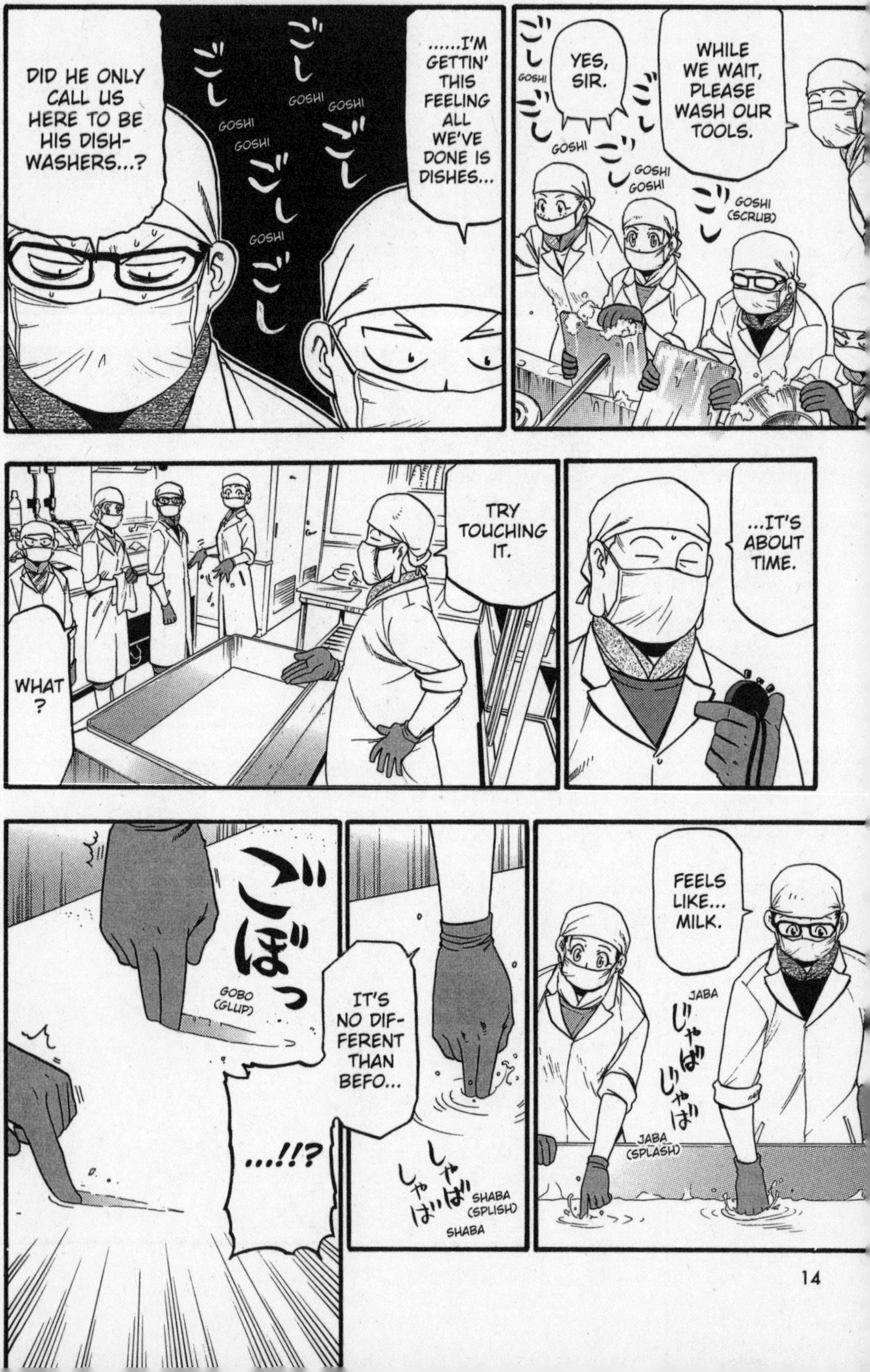

WHILE WE WAIT, PLEASE WASH OUR TOOLS.
YES, SIR.
ごしごし
GOSHI
ごしごし
GOSHI GOSHI
ごし
GOSHI (SCRUB)
......I'M GETTIN' THIS FEELING ALL WE'VE DONE IS DISHES...
ごしごし
GOSHI GOSHI
ごしごし
GOSHI GOSHI
ごし
GOSHI
DID HE ONLY CALL US HERE TO BE HIS DISH-WASHERS...?
...IT'S ABOUT TIME.
TRY TOUCHING IT.
WHAT?
FEELS LIKE... MILK.
じゃばじゃば
JABA
JABA (SPLASH)
IT'S NO DIF-FERENT THAN BEFO...
しゃばしゃば
SHABA (SPLISH)
SHABA
ごぼっ
GOBO (GLUP)
...!!?

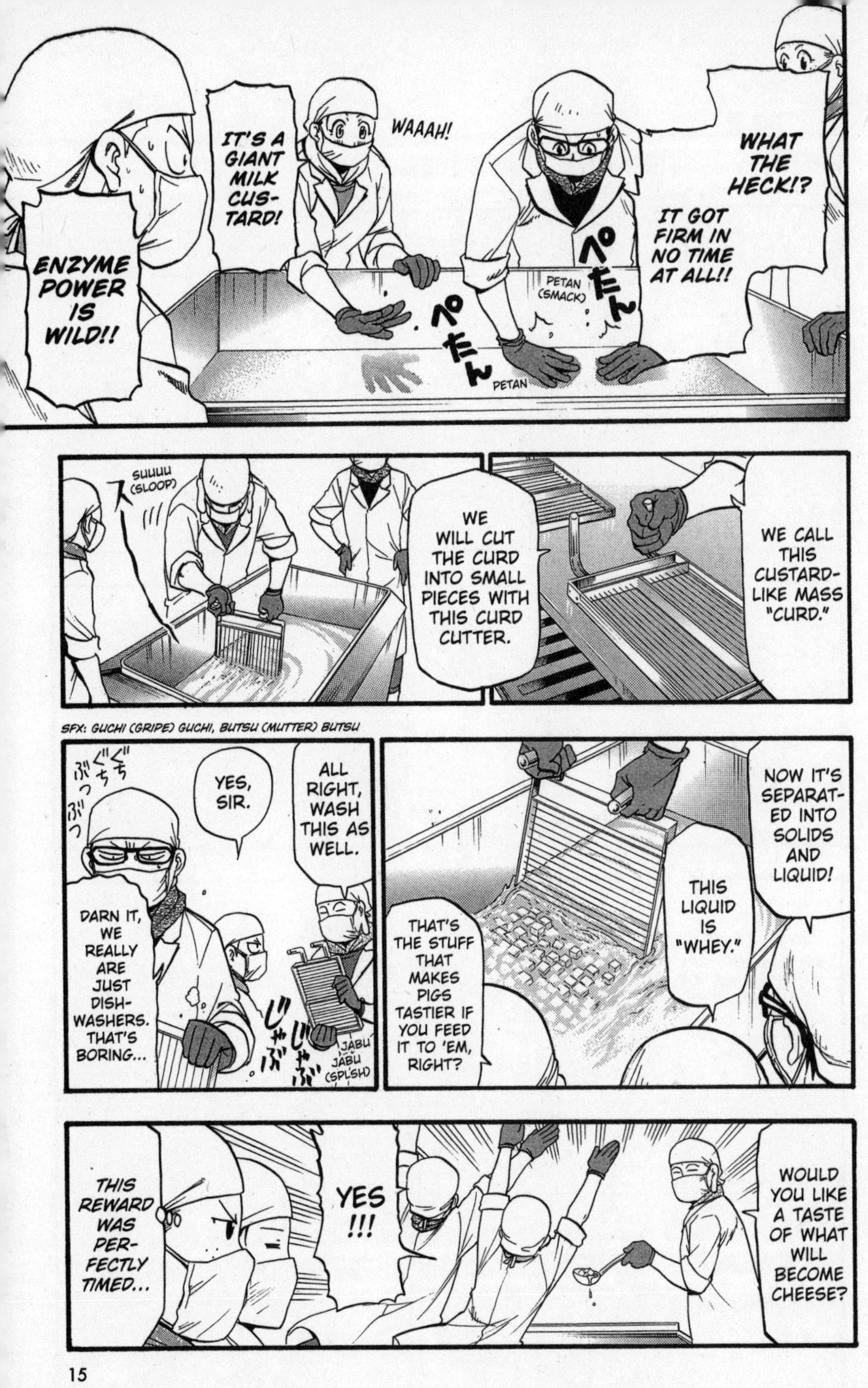
WHAT THE HECK!?
IT GOT FIRM IN NO TIME AT ALL!!
PETAN (SMACK)
WAAAH!
IT'S A GIANT MILK CUS-TARD!
ENZYME POWER IS WILD!!
PETAN
WE CALL THIS CUSTARD-LIKE MASS "CURD."
WE WILL CUT THE CURD INTO SMALL PIECES WITH THIS CURD CUTTER.
SUUUU (SLOOP)
SFX: GUCHI (GRIPE) GUCHI, BUTSU (MUTTER) BUTSU
NOW IT'S SEPARAT-ED INTO SOLIDS AND LIQUID!
THIS LIQUID IS "WHEY."
THAT'S THE STUFF THAT MAKES PIGS TASTIER IF YOU FEED IT TO 'EM, RIGHT?
ALL RIGHT, WASH THIS AS WELL.
YES, SIR.
DARN IT, WE REALLY ARE JUST DISH-WASHERS. THAT'S BORING...
JABU JABU (SPL'SH)
WOULD YOU LIKE A TASTE OF WHAT WILL BECOME CHEESE?
YES !!!
THIS REWARD WAS PER-FECTLY TIMED...

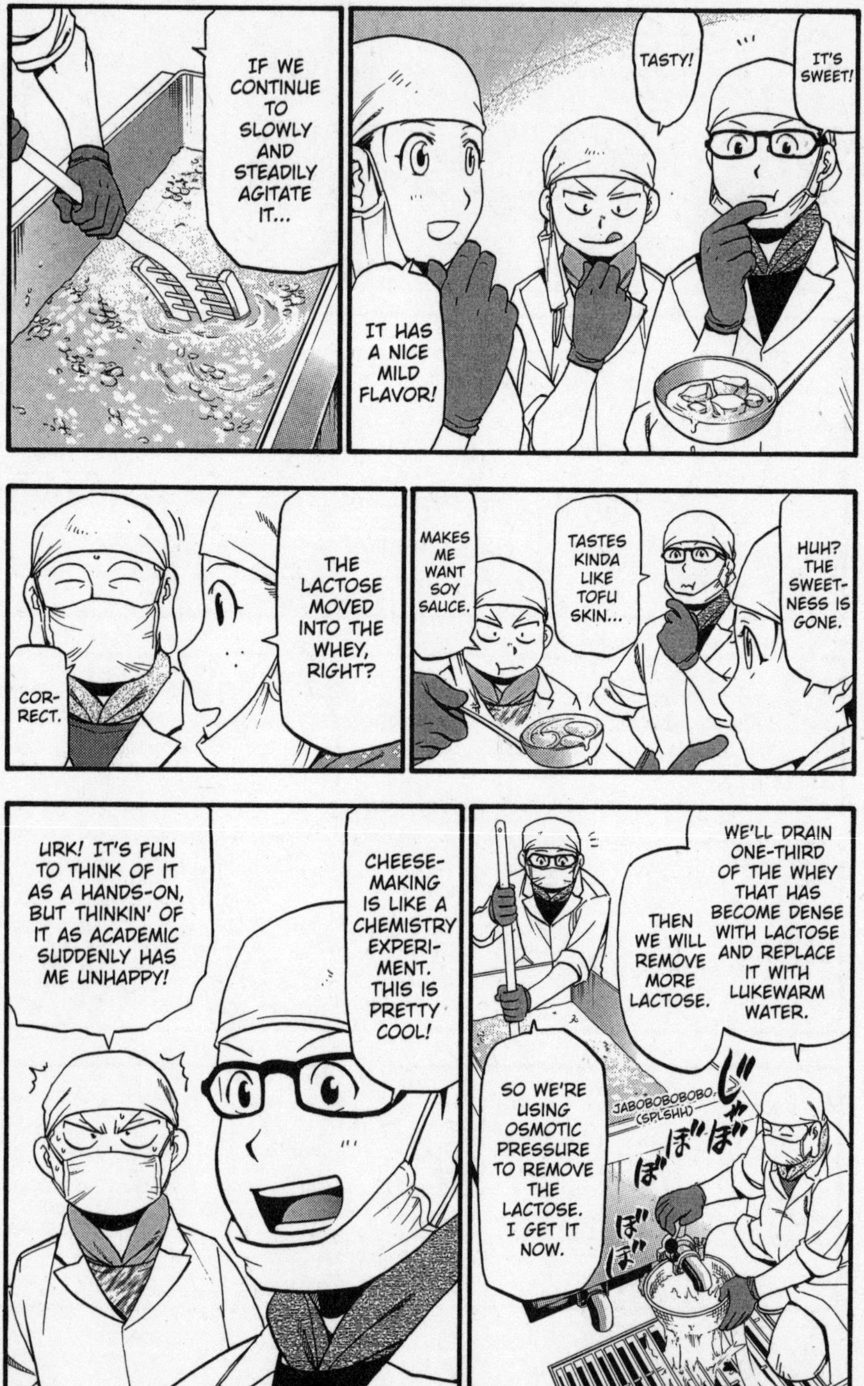
IT'S SWEET!
TASTY!
IT HAS A NICE MILD FLAVOR!
IF WE CONTINUE TO SLOWLY AND STEADILY AGITATE IT...
HUH? THE SWEETNESS IS GONE.
TASTES KINDA LIKE TOFU SKIN...
MAKES ME WANT SOY SAUCE.
THE LACTOSE MOVED INTO THE WHEY, RIGHT?
CORRECT.
WE'LL DRAIN ONE-THIRD OF THE WHEY THAT HAS BECOME DENSE WITH LACTOSE AND REPLACE IT WITH LUKEWARM WATER.
THEN WE WILL REMOVE MORE LACTOSE.
JABOBOBOBO (SPLSHH)
SO WE'RE USING OSMOTIC PRESSURE TO REMOVE THE LACTOSE. I GET IT NOW.
CHEESE-MAKING IS LIKE A CHEMISTRY EXPERIMENT. THIS IS PRETTY COOL!
URK! IT'S FUN TO THINK OF IT AS A HANDS-ON, BUT THINKIN' OF IT AS ACADEMIC SUDDENLY HAS ME UNHAPPY!

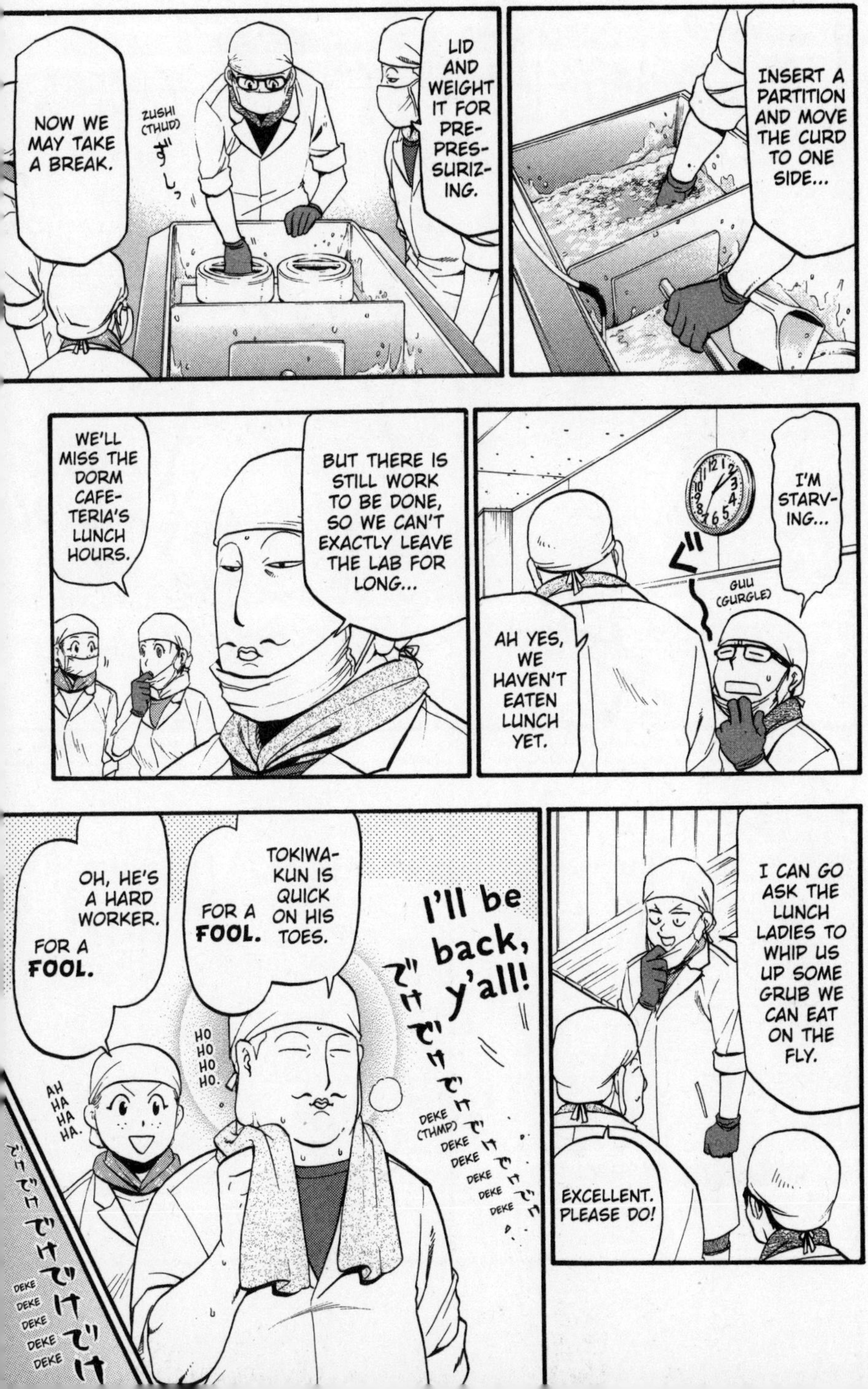
INSERT A PARTITION AND MOVE THE CURD TO ONE SIDE...
LID AND WEIGHT IT FOR PRE-PRESSURIZING.
ZUSHI (THUD)
ずしっ
NOW WE MAY TAKE A BREAK.
I'M STARVING...
GUU (GURGLE)
ぐ
AH YES, WE HAVEN'T EATEN LUNCH YET.
BUT THERE IS STILL WORK TO BE DONE, SO WE CAN'T EXACTLY LEAVE THE LAB FOR LONG...
WE'LL MISS THE DORM CAFETERIA'S LUNCH HOURS.
I CAN GO ASK THE LUNCH LADIES TO WHIP US UP SOME GRUB WE CAN EAT ON THE FLY.
EXCELLENT. PLEASE DO!
I'll be back, y'all!
でけでけでけでけでけでけでけ
DEKE (THMP) DEKE DEKE DEKE DEKE DEKE
TOKIWA-KUN IS QUICK ON HIS TOES.
FOR A **FOOL.**
HO HO HO HO.
OH, HE'S A HARD WORKER.
FOR A **FOOL.**
AH HA HA HA.
でけでけでけでけでけ
DEKE DEKE DEKE DEKE DEKE

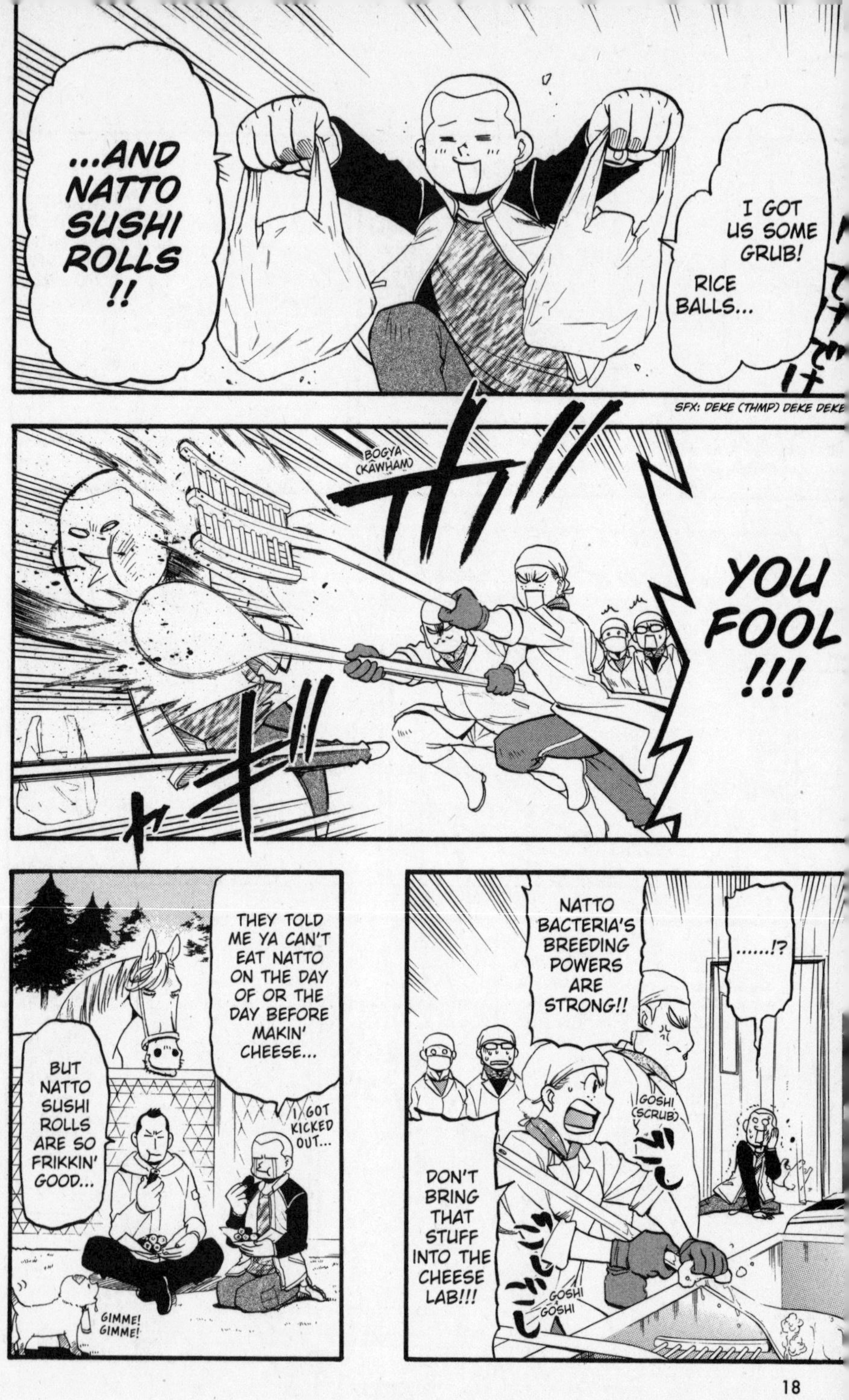
I GOT US SOME GRUB!
RICE BALLS...
...AND NATTO SUSHI ROLLS!!
SFX: DEKE (THMP) DEKE DEKE
YOU FOOL!!!
BOGYA (KAWHAM)
......!?
NATTO BACTERIA'S BREEDING POWERS ARE STRONG!!
GOSHI (SCRUB)
DON'T BRING THAT STUFF INTO THE CHEESE LAB!!!
GOSHI GOSHI
THEY TOLD ME YA CAN'T EAT NATTO ON THE DAY OF OR THE DAY BEFORE MAKIN' CHEESE...
I GOT KICKED OUT...
BUT NATTO SUSHI ROLLS ARE SO FRIKKIN' GOOD...
GIMME! GIMME!

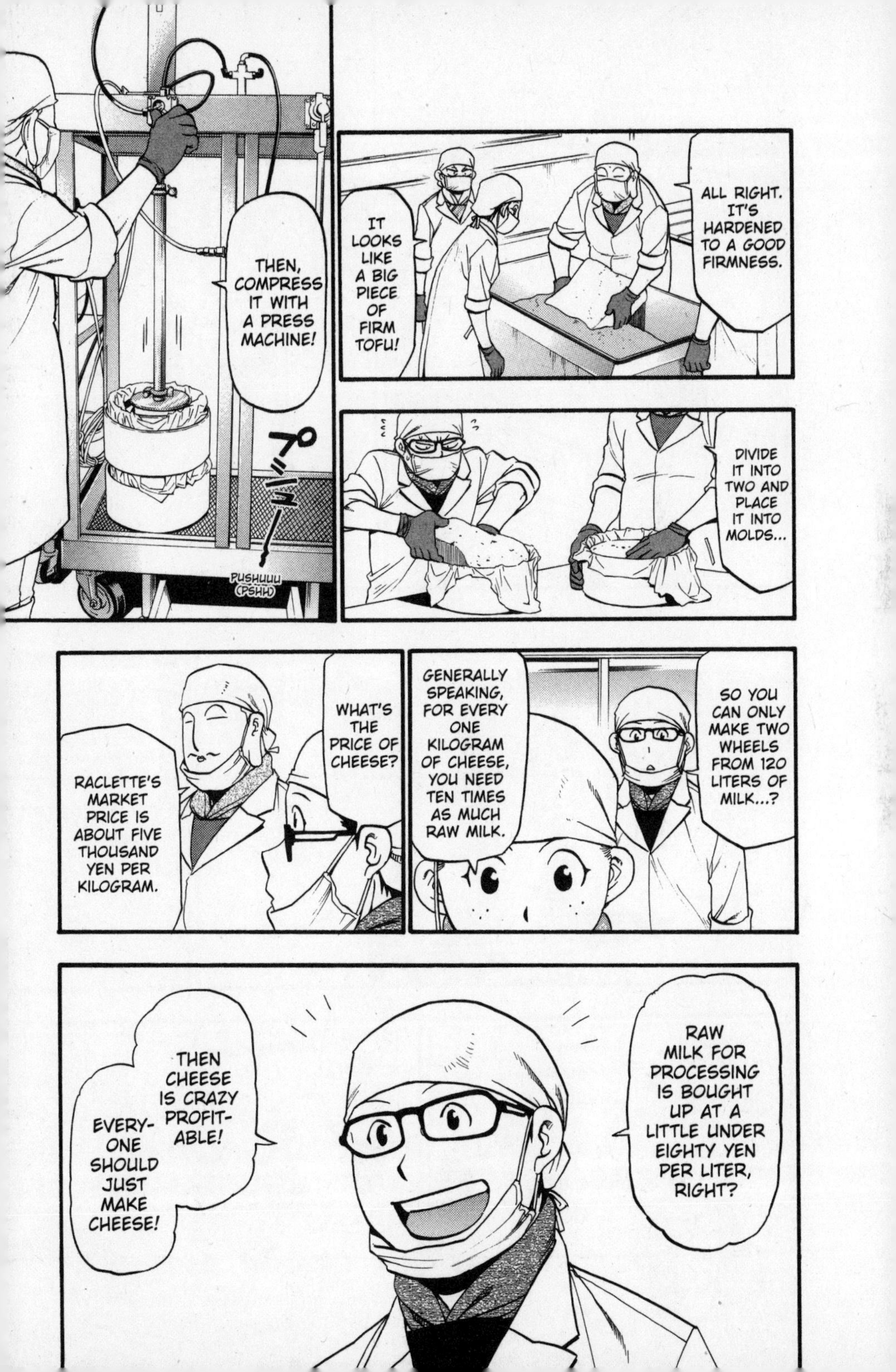
ALL RIGHT. IT'S HARDENED TO A GOOD FIRMNESS.
IT LOOKS LIKE A BIG PIECE OF FIRM TOFU!
DIVIDE IT INTO TWO AND PLACE IT INTO MOLDS...
THEN, COMPRESS IT WITH A PRESS MACHINE!
PUSHUUU (PSHH)
SO YOU CAN ONLY MAKE TWO WHEELS FROM 120 LITERS OF MILK...?
GENERALLY SPEAKING, FOR EVERY ONE KILOGRAM OF CHEESE, YOU NEED TEN TIMES AS MUCH RAW MILK.
WHAT'S THE PRICE OF CHEESE?
RACLETTE'S MARKET PRICE IS ABOUT FIVE THOUSAND YEN PER KILOGRAM.
RAW MILK FOR PROCESSING IS BOUGHT UP AT A LITTLE UNDER EIGHTY YEN PER LITER, RIGHT?
THEN CHEESE IS CRAZY PROFIT-ABLE!
EVERY-ONE SHOULD JUST MAKE CHEESE!

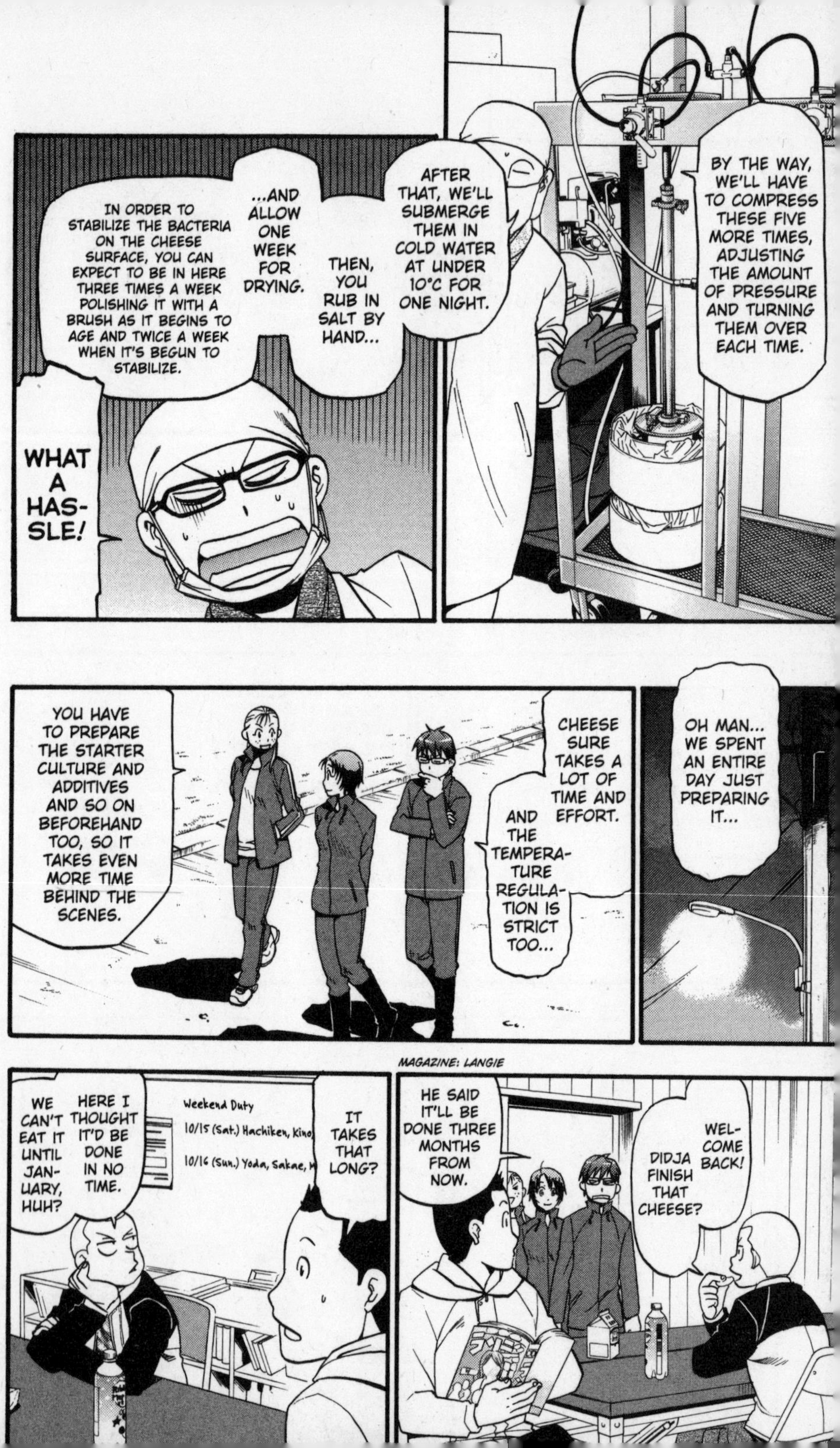
BY THE WAY, WE'LL HAVE TO COMPRESS THESE FIVE MORE TIMES, ADJUSTING THE AMOUNT OF PRESSURE AND TURNING THEM OVER EACH TIME.
AFTER THAT, WE'LL SUBMERGE THEM IN COLD WATER AT UNDER 10°C FOR ONE NIGHT.
THEN, YOU RUB IN SALT BY HAND...
...AND ALLOW ONE WEEK FOR DRYING.
IN ORDER TO STABILIZE THE BACTERIA ON THE CHEESE SURFACE, YOU CAN EXPECT TO BE IN HERE THREE TIMES A WEEK POLISHING IT WITH A BRUSH AS IT BEGINS TO AGE AND TWICE A WEEK WHEN IT'S BEGUN TO STABILIZE.
WHAT A HAS-SLE!
OH MAN... WE SPENT AN ENTIRE DAY JUST PREPARING IT...
CHEESE SURE TAKES A LOT OF TIME AND EFFORT.
AND THE TEMPERA-TURE REGULA-TION IS STRICT TOO...
YOU HAVE TO PREPARE THE STARTER CULTURE AND ADDITIVES AND SO ON BEFOREHAND TOO, SO IT TAKES EVEN MORE TIME BEHIND THE SCENES.
MAGAZINE: LANGIE
WEL-COME BACK!
DIDJA FINISH THAT CHEESE?
HE SAID IT'LL BE DONE THREE MONTHS FROM NOW.
IT TAKES THAT LONG?
Weekend Duty
10/15 (Sat.) Hachiken, Kino
10/16 (Sun.) Yoda, Sakae,
HERE I THOUGHT IT'D BE DONE IN NO TIME.
WE CAN'T EAT IT UNTIL JAN-UARY, HUH?

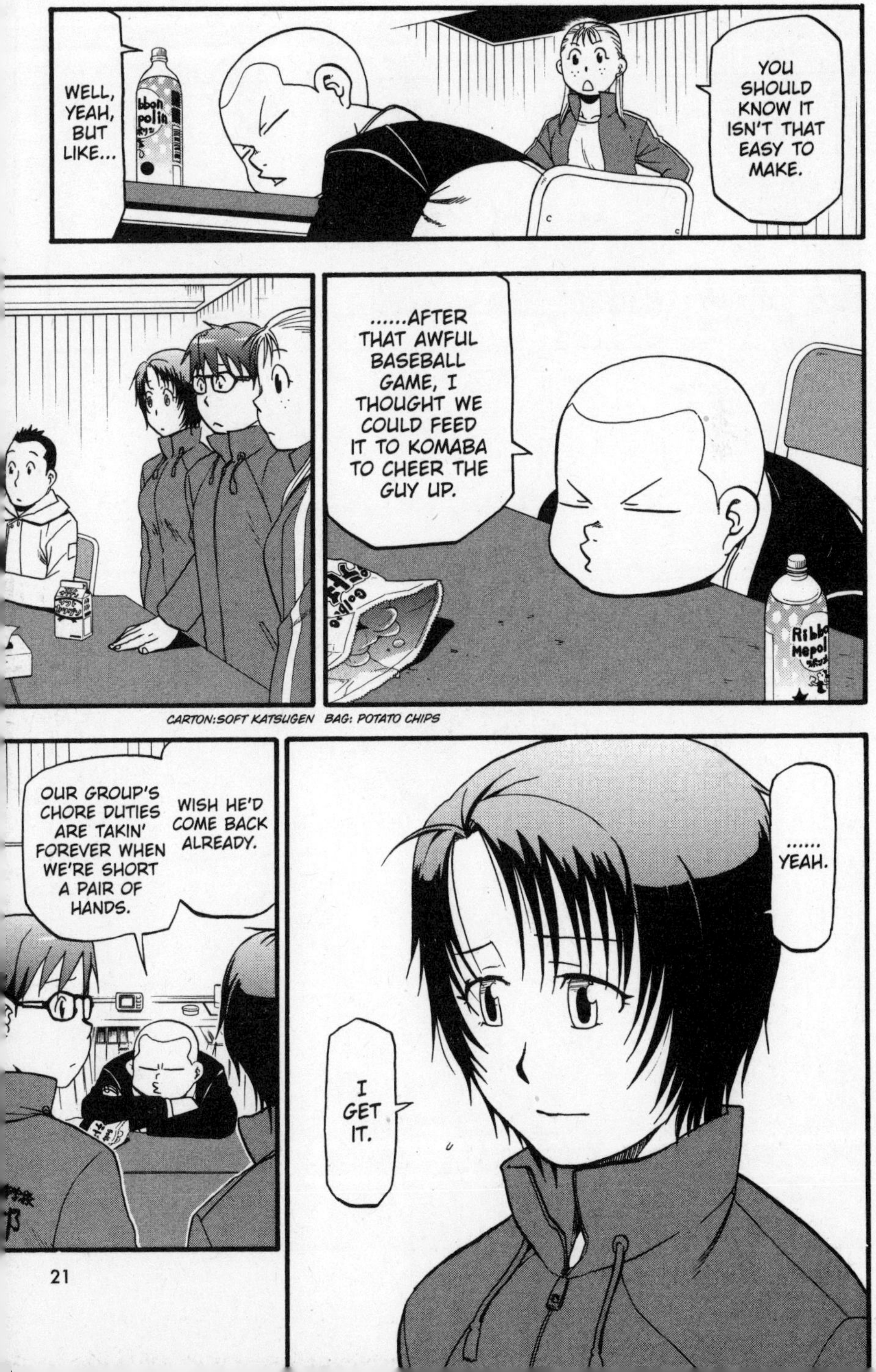
YOU SHOULD KNOW IT ISN'T THAT EASY TO MAKE.
WELL, YEAH, BUT LIKE...
......AFTER THAT AWFUL BASEBALL GAME, I THOUGHT WE COULD FEED IT TO KOMABA TO CHEER THE GUY UP.
CARTON:SOFT KATSUGEN BAG: POTATO CHIPS
......YEAH.
I GET IT.
WISH HE'D COME BACK ALREADY.
OUR GROUP'S CHORE DUTIES ARE TAKIN' FOREVER WHEN WE'RE SHORT A PAIR OF HANDS.

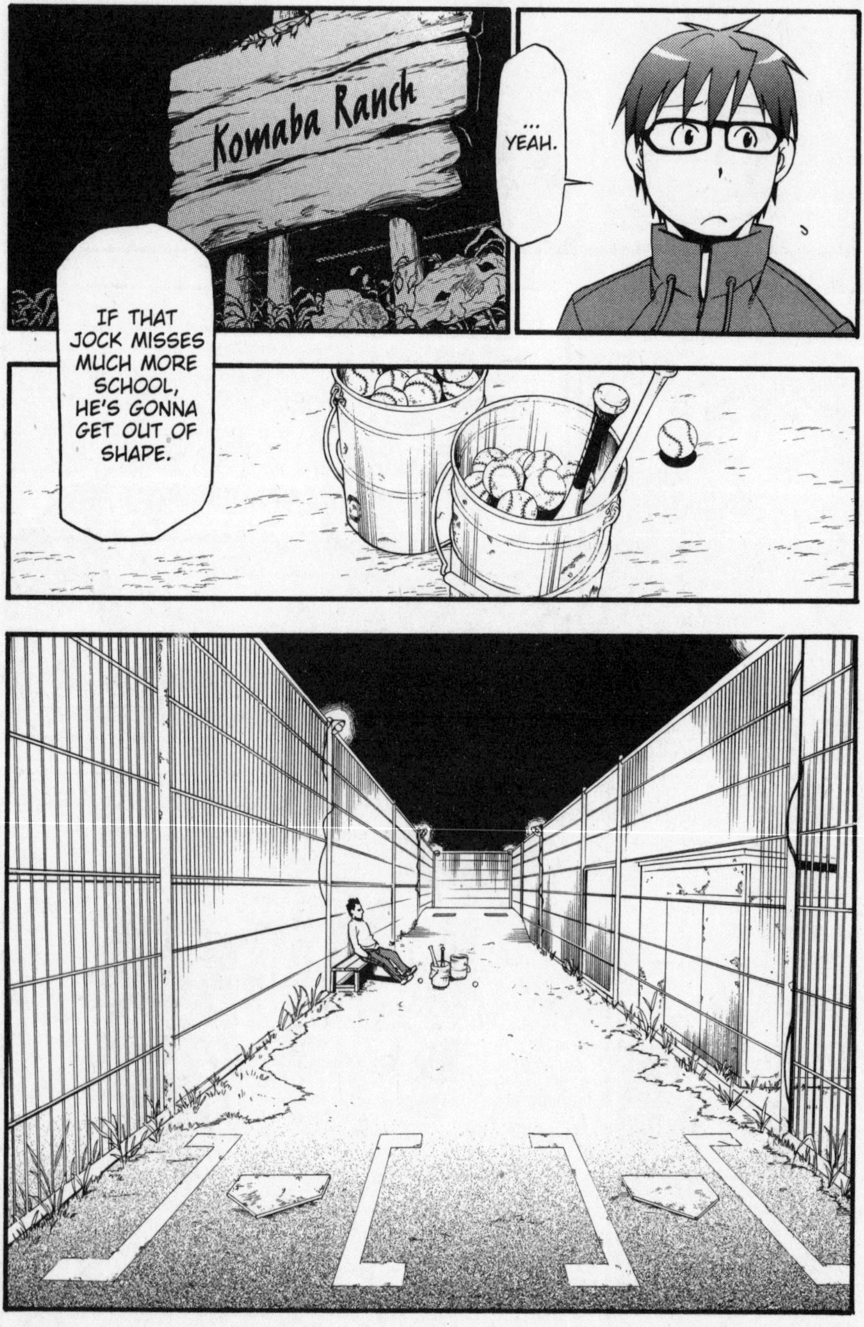
... YEAH.
Komaba Ranch
IF THAT JOCK MISSES MUCH MORE SCHOOL, HE'S GONNA GET OUT OF SHAPE.

Silver Spoon

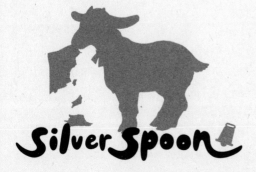

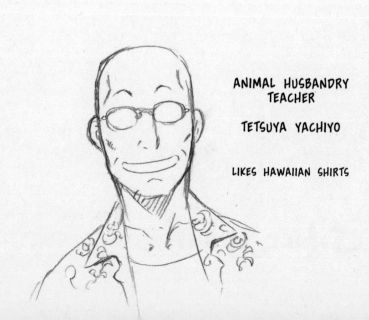

ANIMAL HUSBANDRY
TEACHER

TETSUYA YACHIYO

LIKES HAWAIIAN SHIRTS

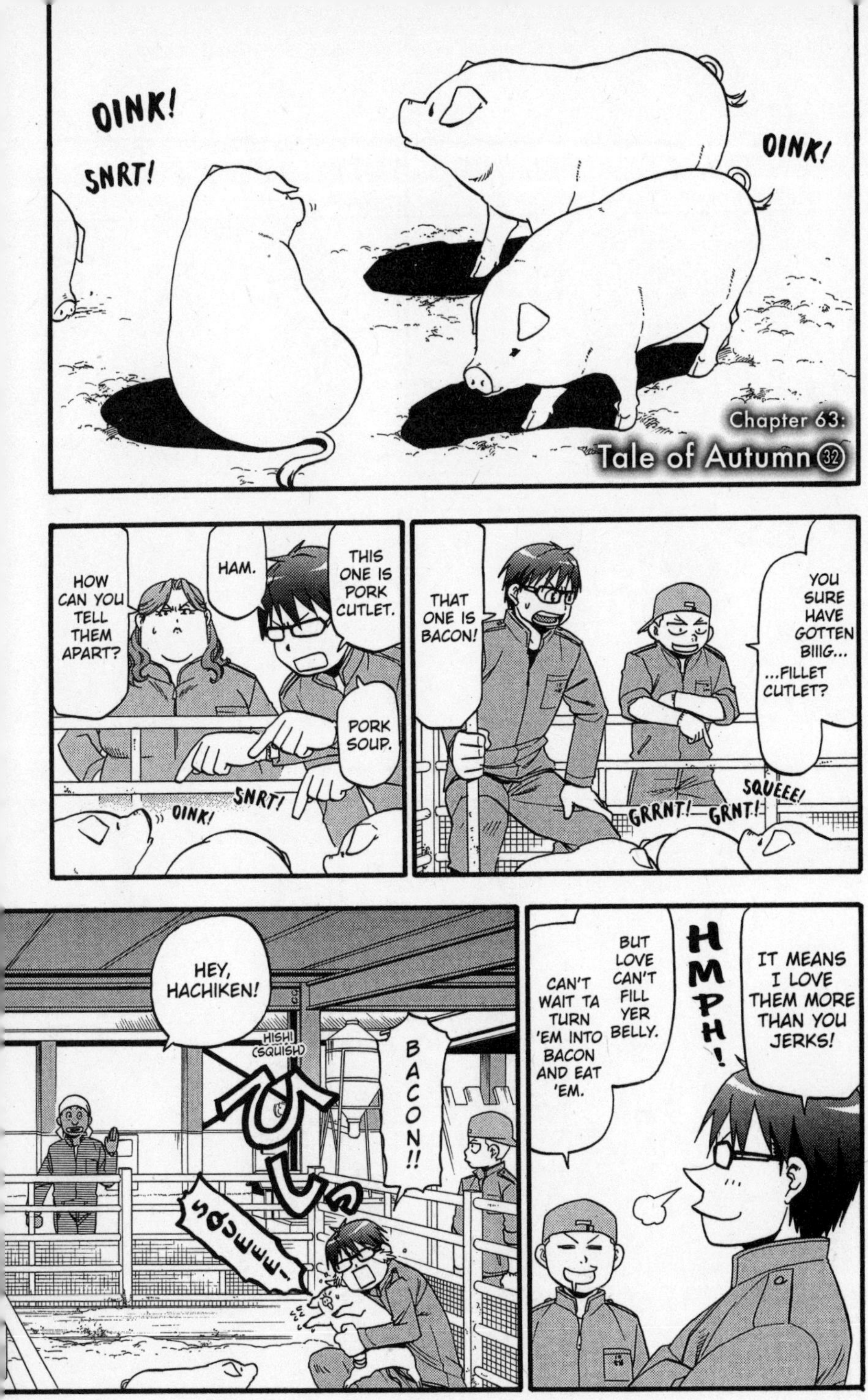
OINK!
Chapter 63:
Tale of Autumn ㉜
OINK!
SNRT!
YOU SURE HAVE GOTTEN BIIIG... ...FILLET CUTLET?
THAT ONE IS BACON!
SQUEEE!
GRNT!
GRRNT!
THIS ONE IS PORK CUTLET.
HAM.
HOW CAN YOU TELL THEM APART?
PORK SOUP.
SNRT!
OINK!
IT MEANS I LOVE THEM MORE THAN YOU JERKS!
HMPH!
BUT LOVE CAN'T FILL YER BELLY.
CAN'T WAIT TA TURN 'EM INTO BACON AND EAT 'EM.
BACON!!
HISHI (SQUISH)
HEY, HACHIKEN!
SQUEEEE-

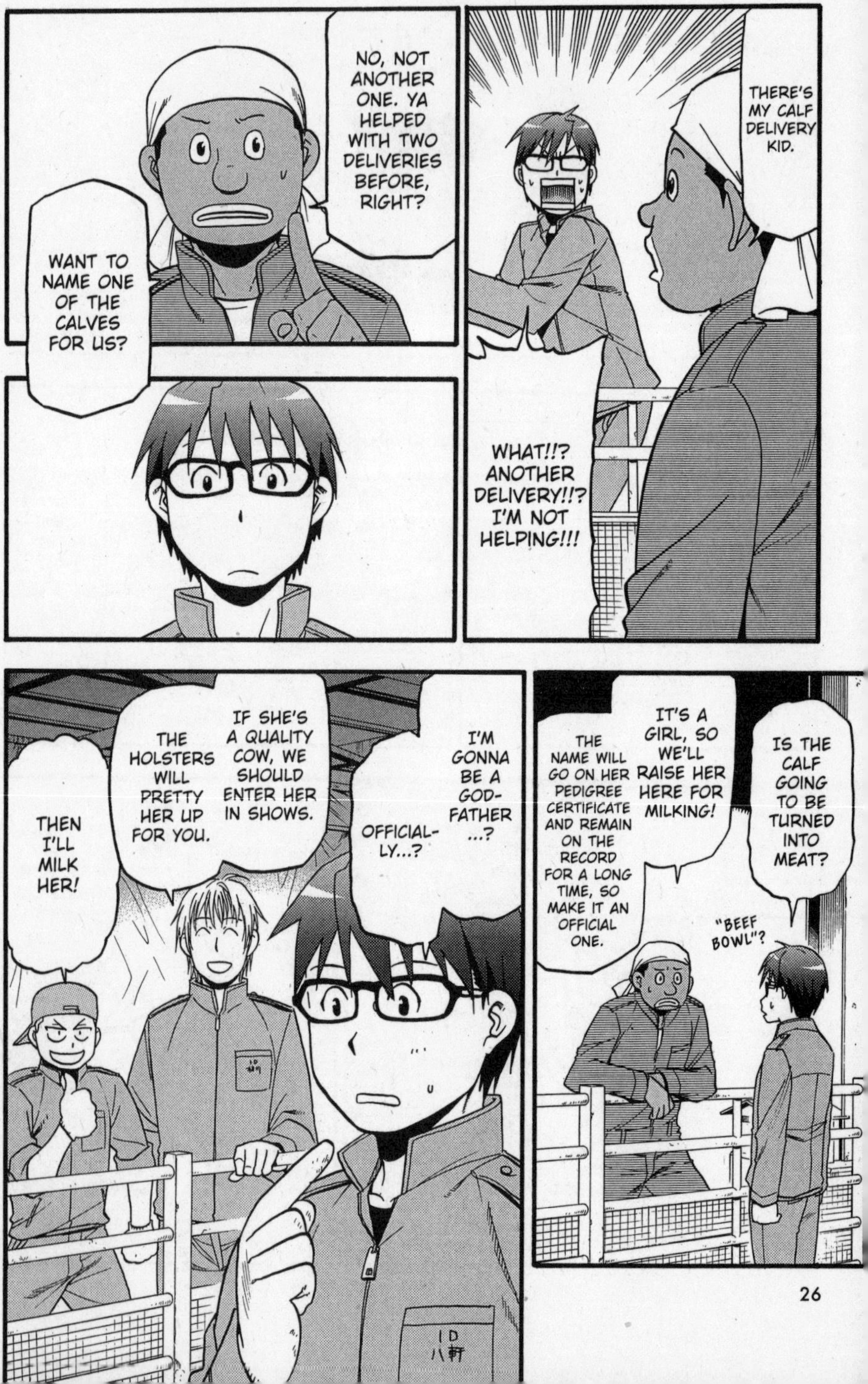
THERE'S MY CALF DELIVERY KID.
WHAT!!? ANOTHER DELIVERY!!? I'M NOT HELPING!!!
NO, NOT ANOTHER ONE. YA HELPED WITH TWO DELIVERIES BEFORE, RIGHT?
WANT TO NAME ONE OF THE CALVES FOR US?
IS THE CALF GOING TO BE TURNED INTO MEAT?
IT'S A GIRL, SO WE'LL RAISE HER HERE FOR MILKING!
THE NAME WILL GO ON HER PEDIGREE CERTIFICATE AND REMAIN ON THE RECORD FOR A LONG TIME, SO MAKE IT AN OFFICIAL ONE.
"BEEF BOWL"?
I'M GONNA BE A GOD-FATHER ...?
OFFICIAL-LY...?
IF SHE'S A QUALITY COW, WE SHOULD ENTER HER IN SHOWS.
THE HOLSTERS WILL PRETTY HER UP FOR YOU.
THEN I'LL MILK HER!

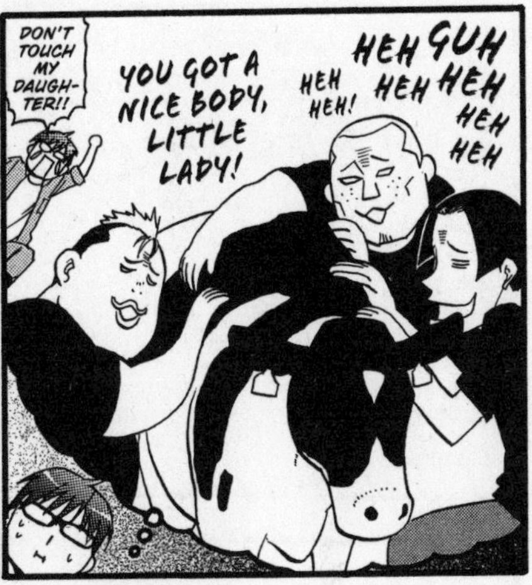
GUH HEH HEH HEH
HEH HEH
HEH HEH!
YOU GOT A NICE BODY, LITTLE LADY!
DON'T TOUCH MY DAUGHTER!!

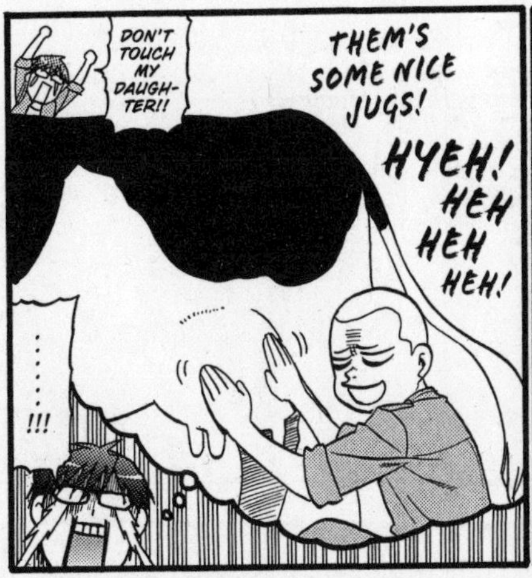
THEM'S SOME NICE JUGS!
HYEH! HEH HEH HEH!
DON'T TOUCH MY DAUGHTER!!
......!!!

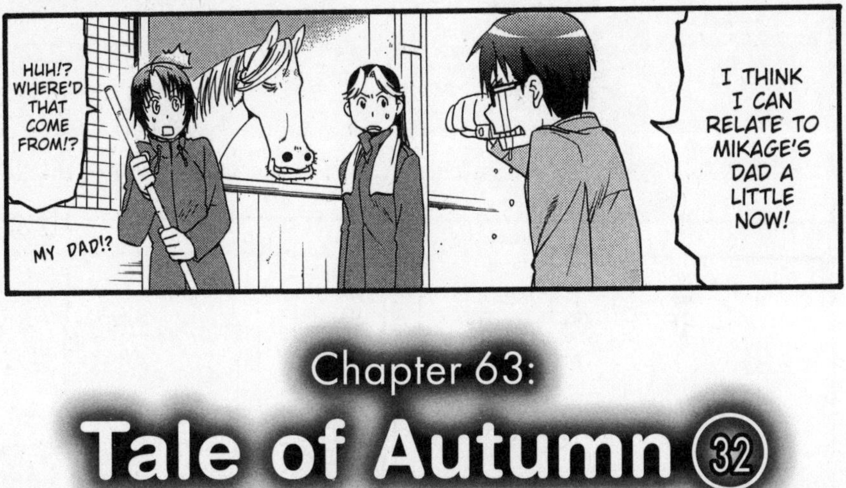
I THINK I CAN RELATE TO MIKAGE'S DAD A LITTLE NOW!
HUH!? WHERE'D THAT COME FROM!?
MY DAD!?

Chapter 63:
Tale of Autumn ㉜

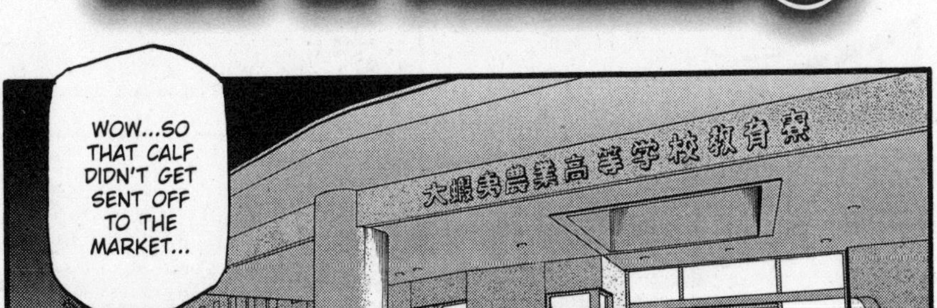
WOW...SO THAT CALF DIDN'T GET SENT OFF TO THE MARKET...

SIGN: OOEZO AGRICULTURAL HIGH SCHOOL STUDENT DORMS

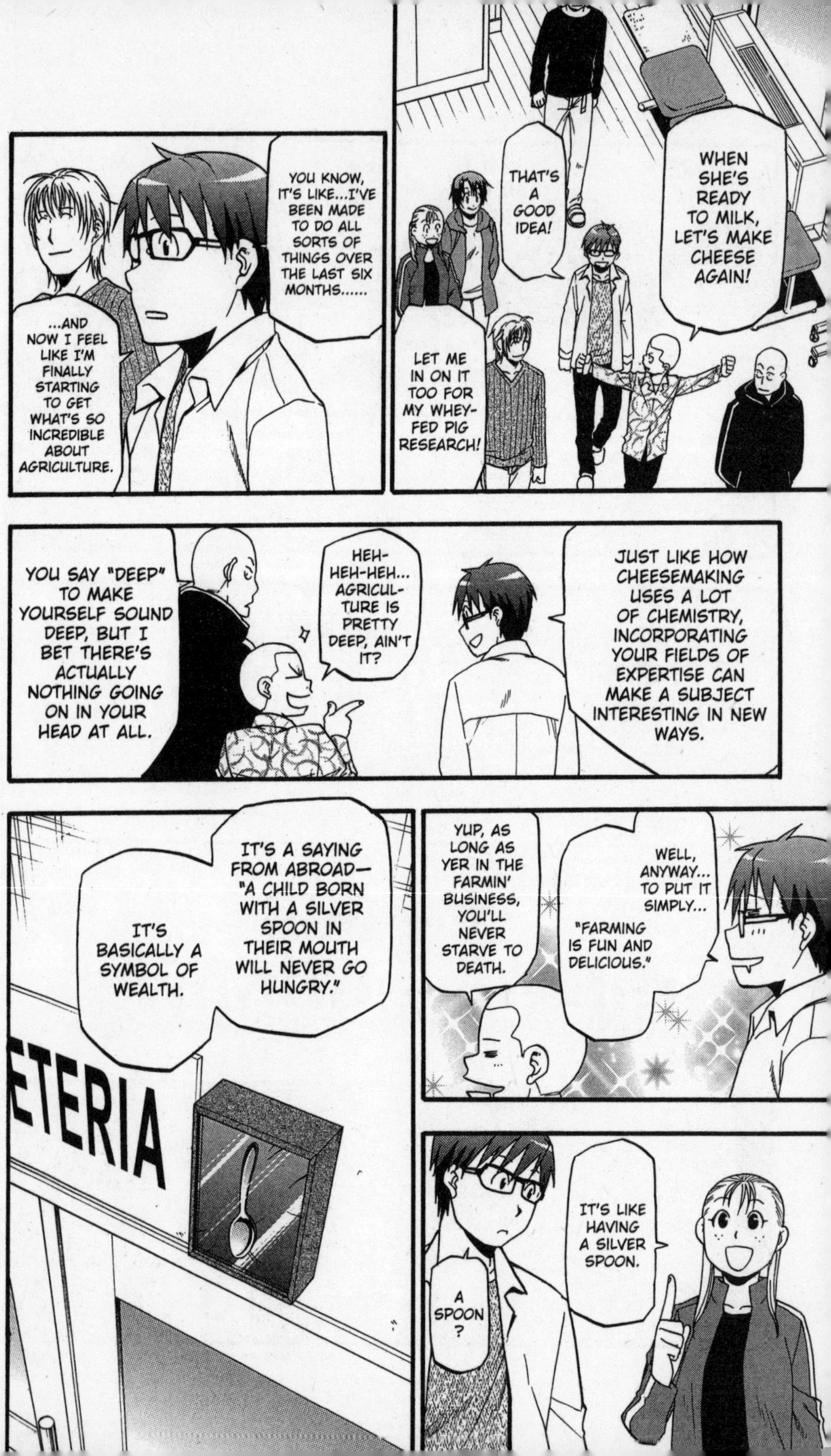
WHEN SHE'S READY TO MILK, LET'S MAKE CHEESE AGAIN!
THAT'S A GOOD IDEA!
LET ME IN ON IT TOO FOR MY WHEY-FED PIG RESEARCH!
YOU KNOW, IT'S LIKE...I'VE BEEN MADE TO DO ALL SORTS OF THINGS OVER THE LAST SIX MONTHS......
...AND NOW I FEEL LIKE I'M FINALLY STARTING TO GET WHAT'S SO INCREDIBLE ABOUT AGRICULTURE.
JUST LIKE HOW CHEESEMAKING USES A LOT OF CHEMISTRY, INCORPORATING YOUR FIELDS OF EXPERTISE CAN MAKE A SUBJECT INTERESTING IN NEW WAYS.
HEH-HEH-HEH... AGRICULTURE IS PRETTY DEEP, AIN'T IT?
YOU SAY "DEEP" TO MAKE YOURSELF SOUND DEEP, BUT I BET THERE'S ACTUALLY NOTHING GOING ON IN YOUR HEAD AT ALL.
WELL, ANYWAY... TO PUT IT SIMPLY...
"FARMING IS FUN AND DELICIOUS."
YUP, AS LONG AS YER IN THE FARMIN' BUSINESS, YOU'LL NEVER STARVE TO DEATH.
IT'S LIKE HAVING A SILVER SPOON.
A SPOON?
IT'S A SAYING FROM ABROAD— "A CHILD BORN WITH A SILVER SPOON IN THEIR MOUTH WILL NEVER GO HUNGRY."
IT'S BASICALLY A SYMBOL OF WEALTH.
ETERIA

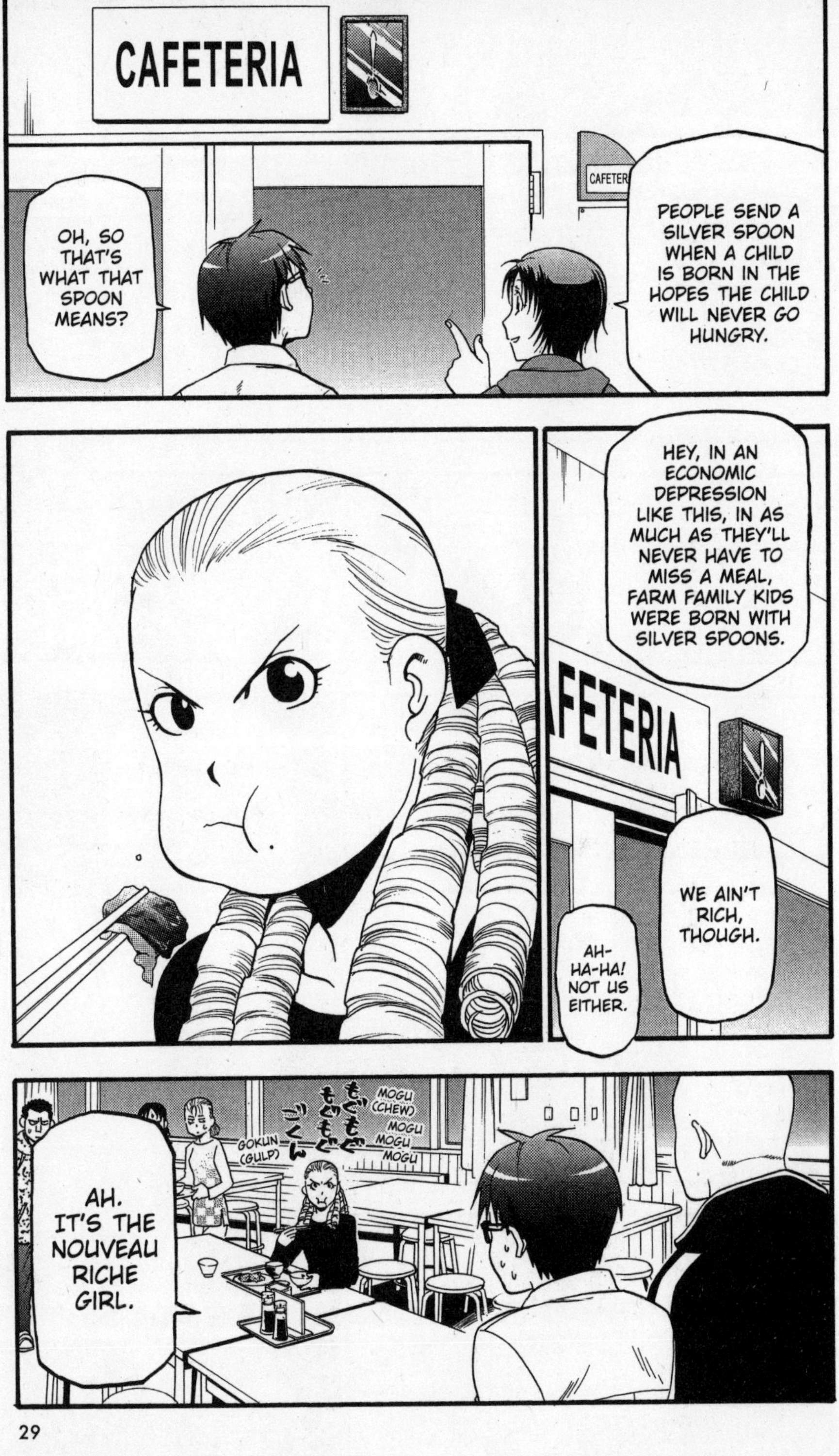
CAFETERIA
PEOPLE SEND A SILVER SPOON WHEN A CHILD IS BORN IN THE HOPES THE CHILD WILL NEVER GO HUNGRY.
OH, SO THAT'S WHAT THAT SPOON MEANS?
HEY, IN AN ECONOMIC DEPRESSION LIKE THIS, IN AS MUCH AS THEY'LL NEVER HAVE TO MISS A MEAL, FARM FAMILY KIDS WERE BORN WITH SILVER SPOONS.
WE AIN'T RICH, THOUGH.
AH-HA-HA! NOT US EITHER.
もぐもぐもぐもぐ
MOGU (CHEW) MOGU MOGU MOGU
ごくん
GOKUN (GULP)
AH. IT'S THE NOUVEAU RICHE GIRL.

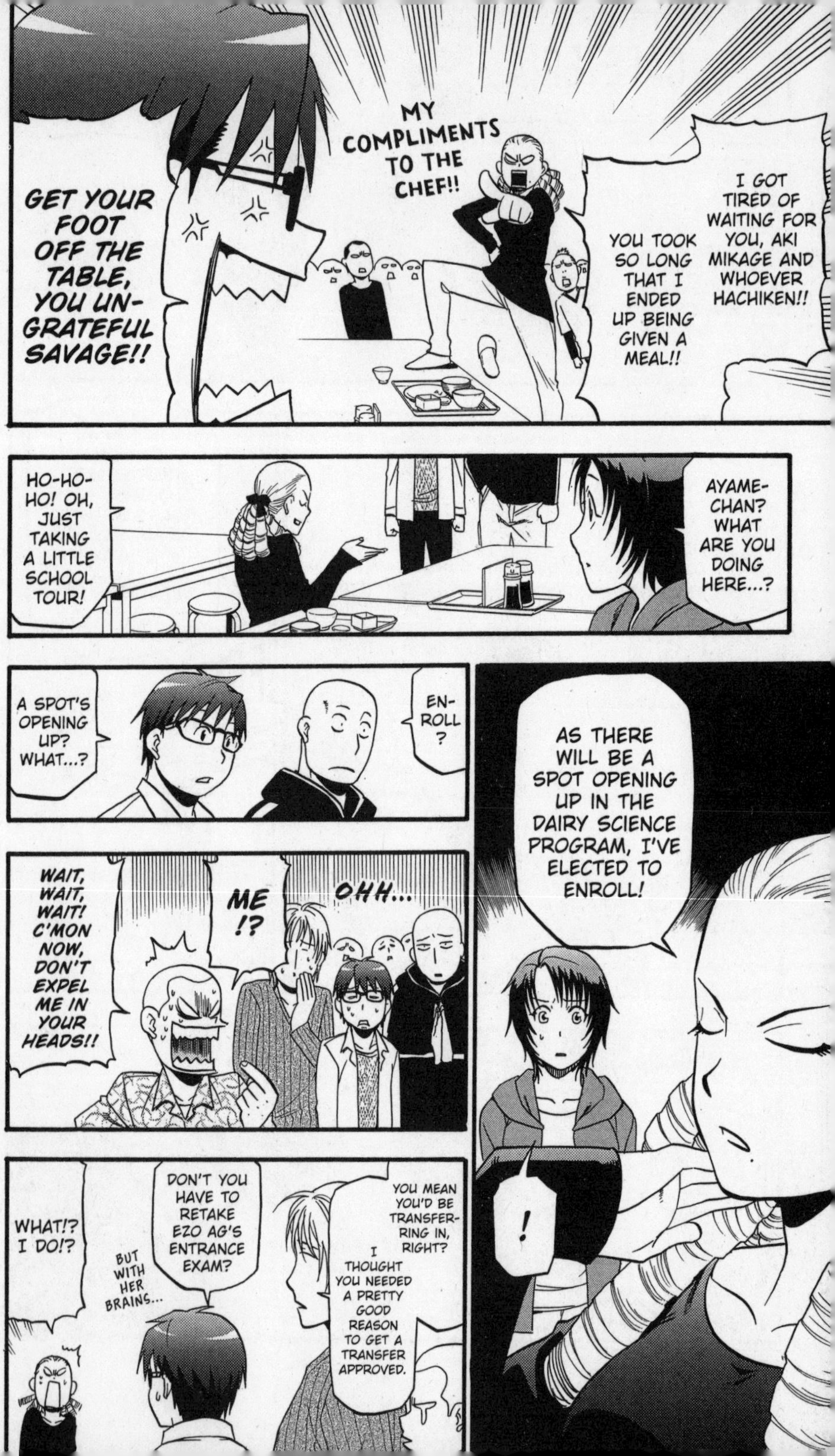

I GOT TIRED OF WAITING FOR YOU, AKI MIKAGE AND WHOEVER HACHIKEN!!
YOU TOOK SO LONG THAT I ENDED UP BEING GIVEN A MEAL!!
MY COMPLIMENTS TO THE CHEF!!
GET YOUR FOOT OFF THE TABLE, YOU UN-GRATEFUL SAVAGE!!
AYAME-CHAN? WHAT ARE YOU DOING HERE...?
HO-HO-HO! OH, JUST TAKING A LITTLE SCHOOL TOUR!
AS THERE WILL BE A SPOT OPENING UP IN THE DAIRY SCIENCE PROGRAM, I'VE ELECTED TO ENROLL!
!
EN-ROLL?
A SPOT'S OPENING UP? WHAT...?
OHH...
ME!?
WAIT, WAIT, WAIT! C'MON NOW, DON'T EXPEL ME IN YOUR HEADS!!
YOU MEAN YOU'D BE TRANSFER-RING IN, RIGHT?
I THOUGHT YOU NEEDED A PRETTY GOOD REASON TO GET A TRANSFER APPROVED.
DON'T YOU HAVE TO RETAKE EZO AG'S ENTRANCE EXAM?
BUT WITH HER BRAINS...
WHAT!? I DO!?

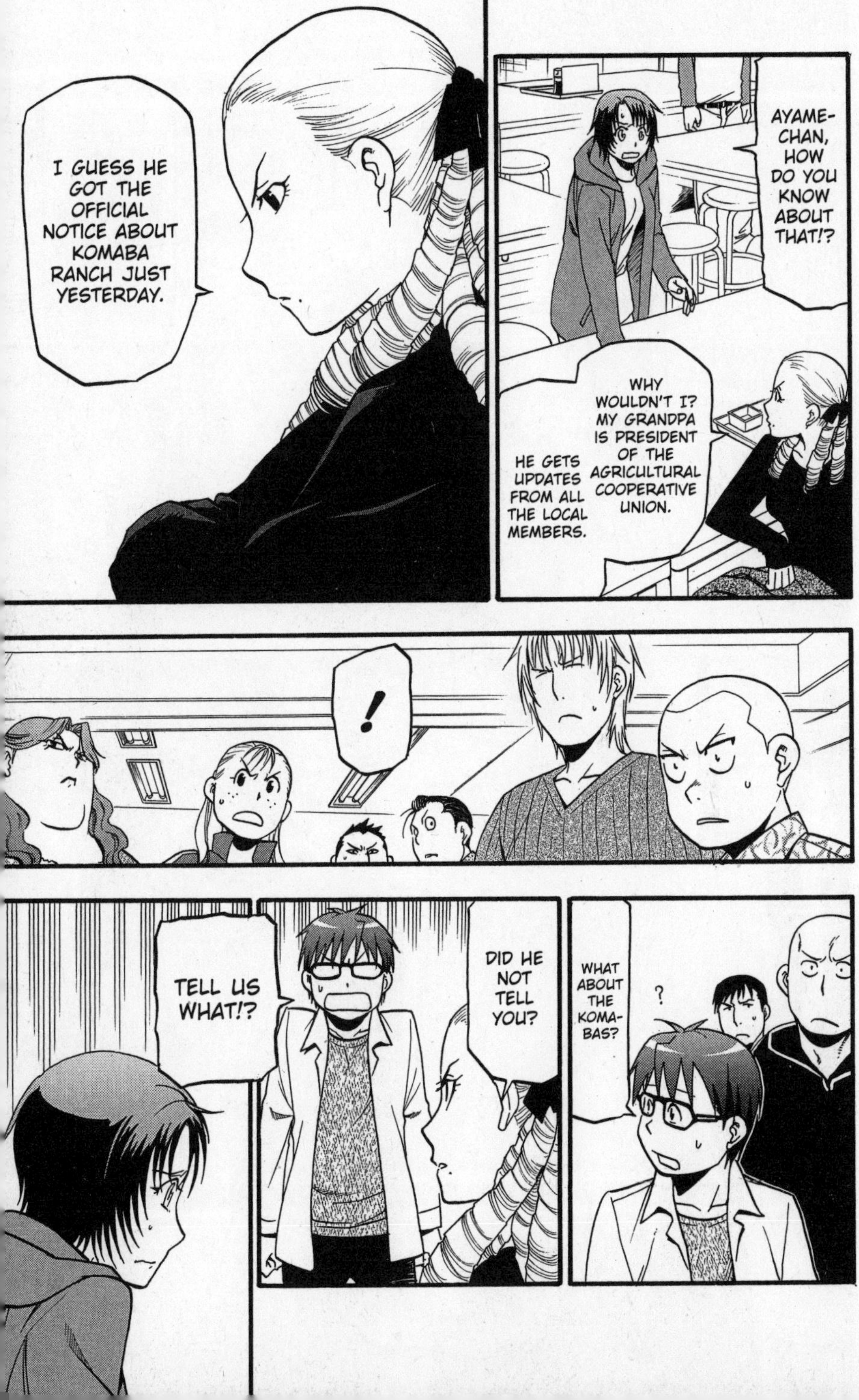
AYAME-CHAN, HOW DO YOU KNOW ABOUT THAT!?
WHY WOULDN'T I? MY GRANDPA IS PRESIDENT OF THE AGRICULTURAL COOPERATIVE UNION.
HE GETS UPDATES FROM ALL THE LOCAL MEMBERS.
I GUESS HE GOT THE OFFICIAL NOTICE ABOUT KOMABA RANCH JUST YESTERDAY.
!
WHAT ABOUT THE KOMA-BAS?
?
DID HE NOT TELL YOU?
TELL US WHAT!?

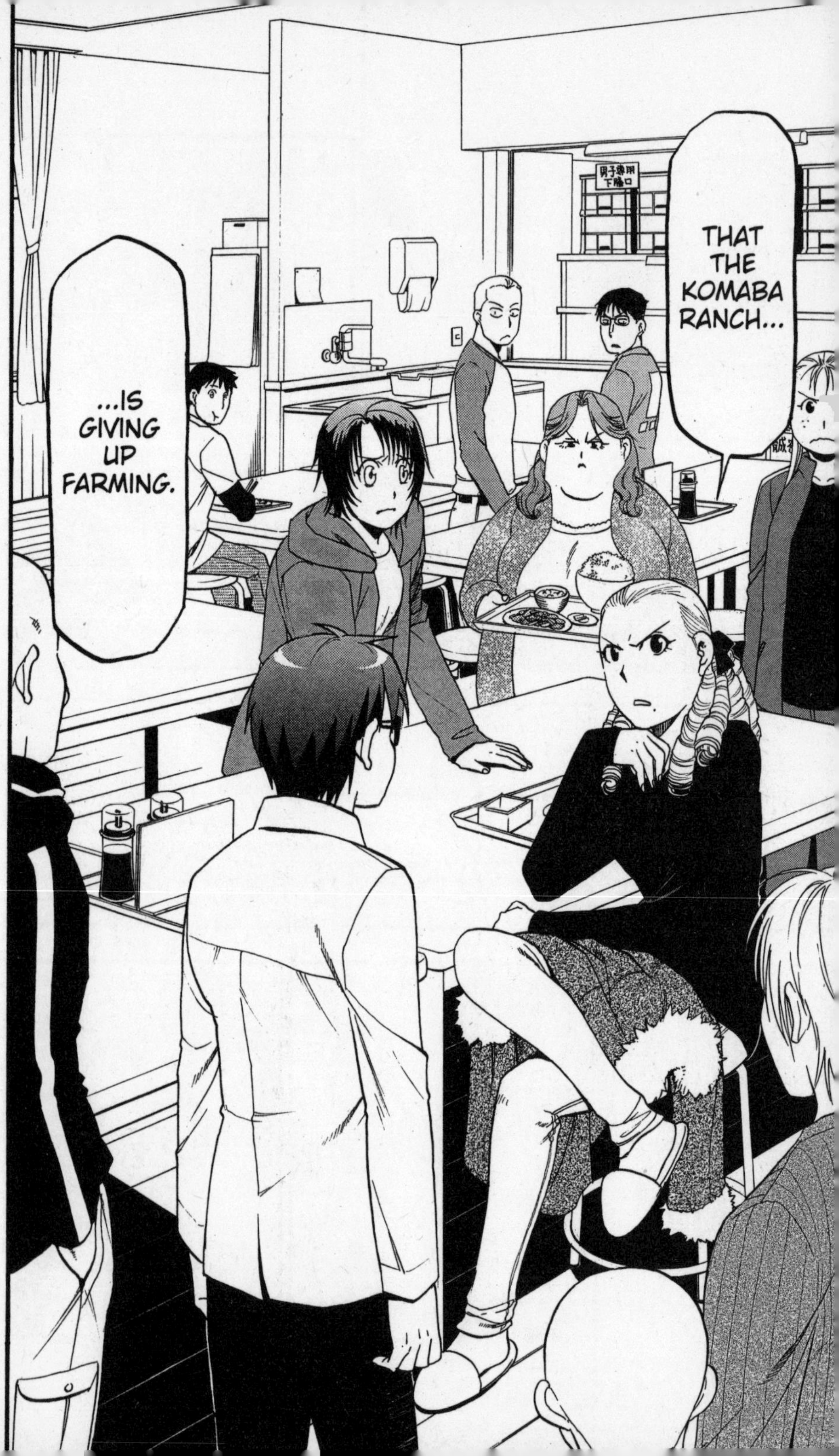
THAT THE KOMABA RANCH...
...IS GIVING UP FARMING.

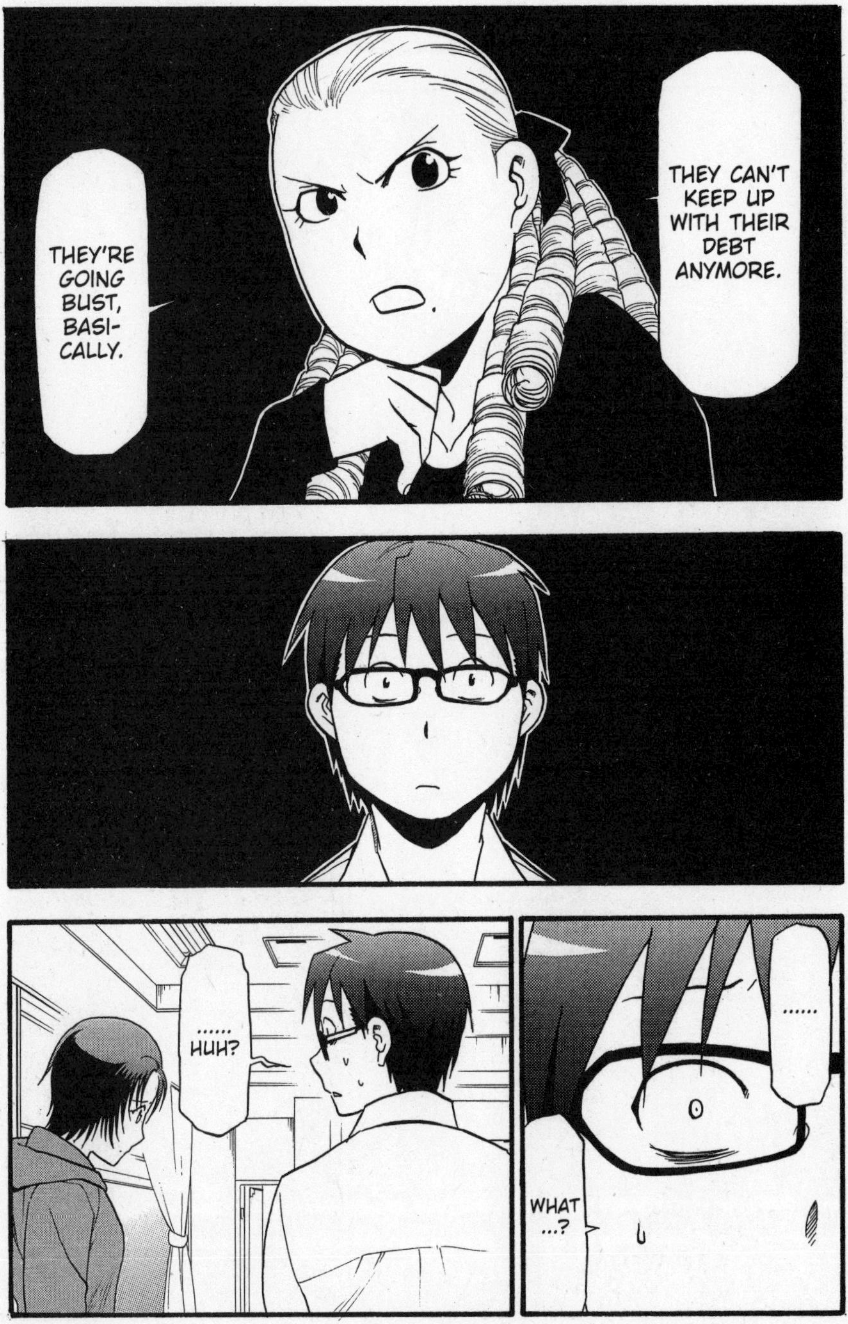
THEY CAN'T KEEP UP WITH THEIR DEBT ANYMORE.
THEY'RE GOING BUST, BASI-CALLY.
......
WHAT ...?
...... HUH?

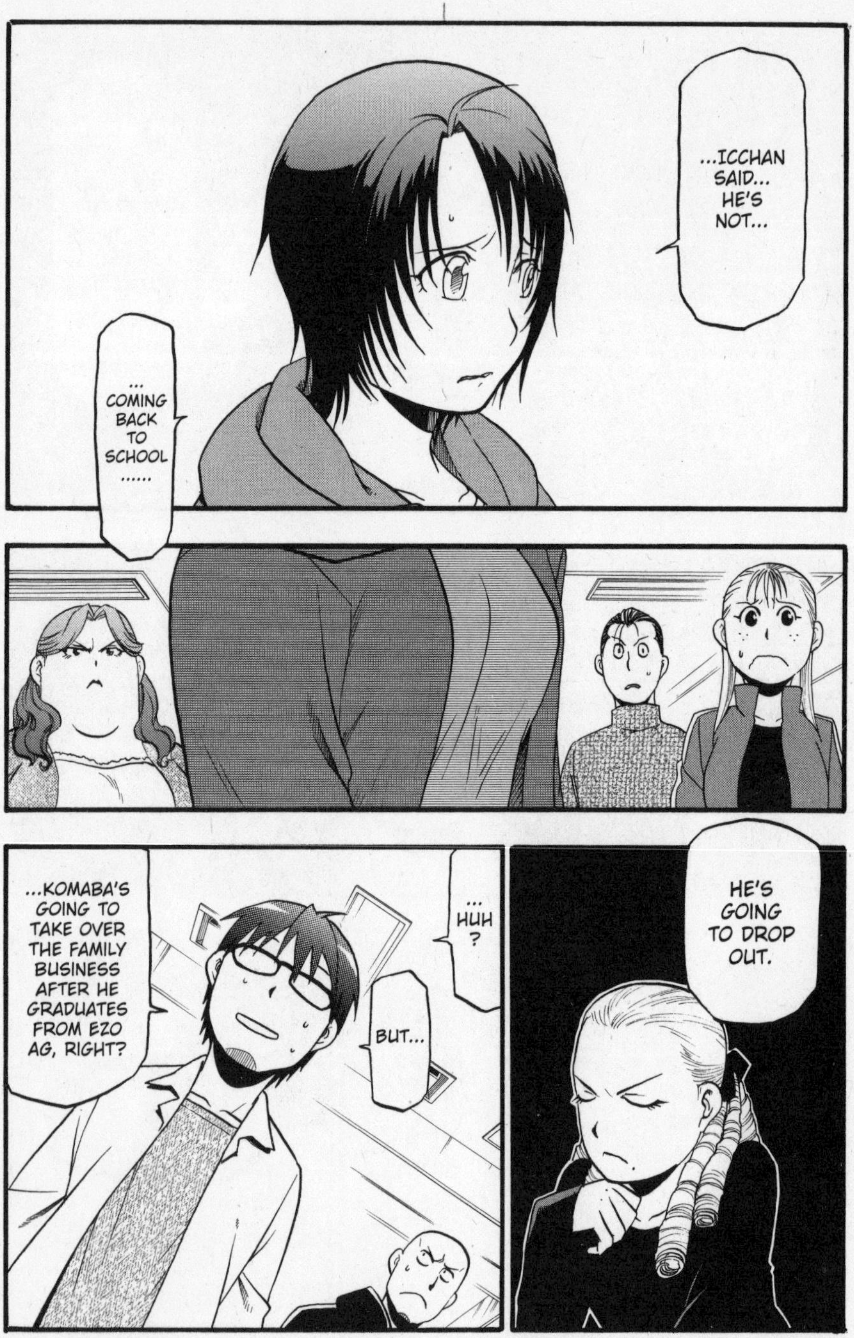
...ICCHAN SAID... HE'S NOT...
...COMING BACK TO SCHOOL ......
HE'S GOING TO DROP OUT.
...HUH?
BUT...
...KOMABA'S GOING TO TAKE OVER THE FAMILY BUSINESS AFTER HE GRADUATES FROM EZO AG, RIGHT?

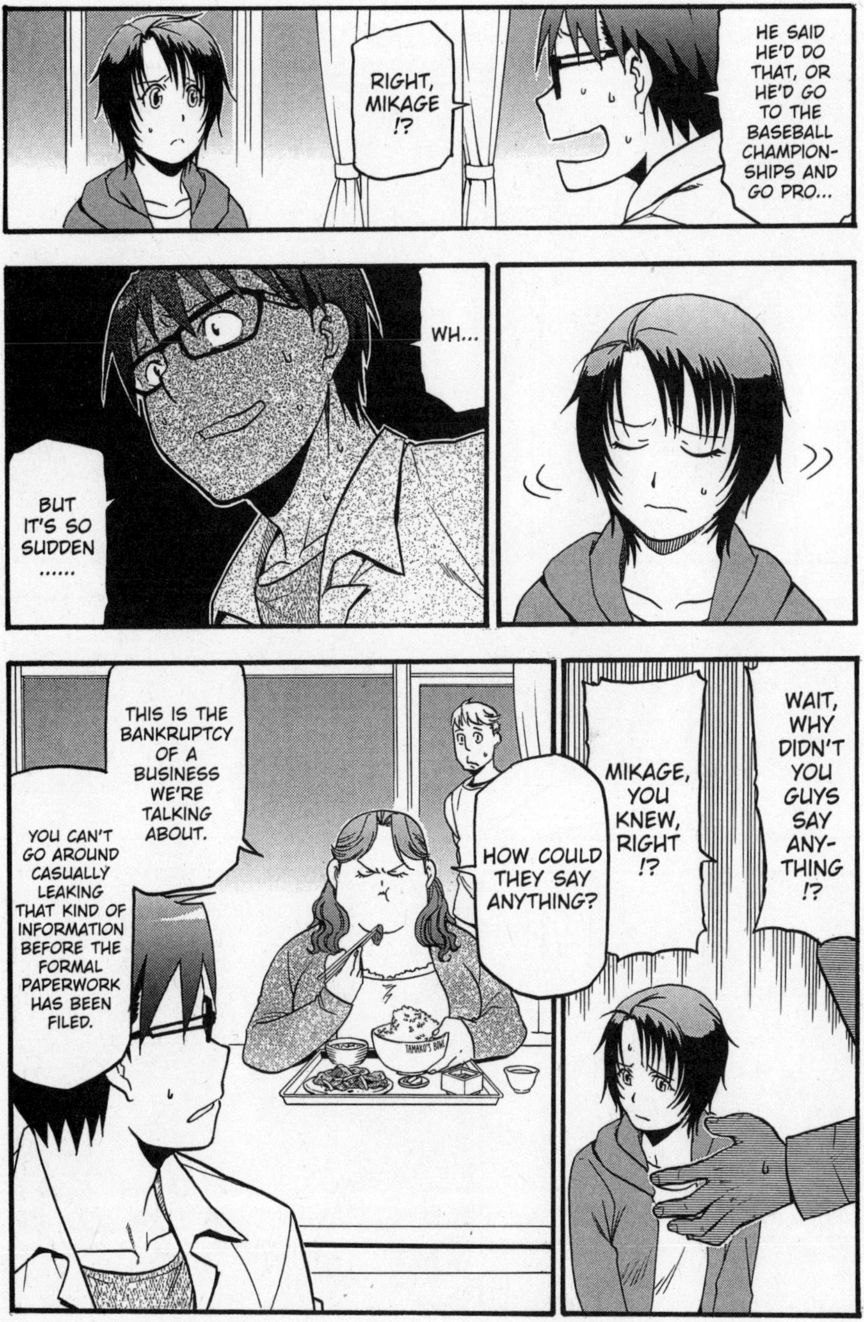
HE SAID HE'D DO THAT, OR HE'D GO TO THE BASEBALL CHAMPIONSHIPS AND GO PRO...
RIGHT, MIKAGE !?
WH...
BUT IT'S SO SUDDEN......
WAIT, WHY DIDN'T YOU GUYS SAY ANYTHING !?
MIKAGE, YOU KNEW, RIGHT !?
HOW COULD THEY SAY ANYTHING?
THIS IS THE BANKRUPTCY OF A BUSINESS WE'RE TALKING ABOUT.
YOU CAN'T GO AROUND CASUALLY LEAKING THAT KIND OF INFORMATION BEFORE THE FORMAL PAPERWORK HAS BEEN FILED.
TAMAKO'S BOWL

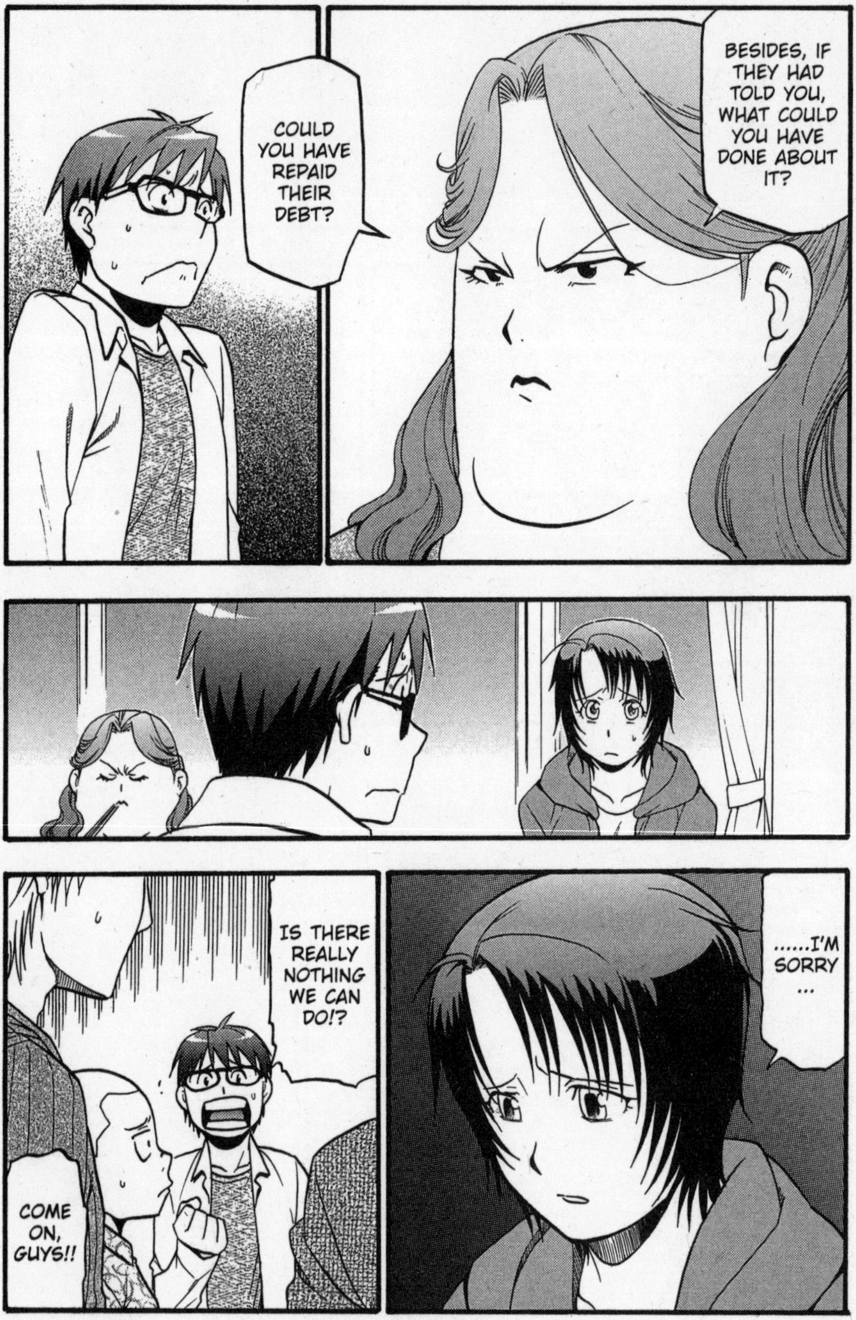
BESIDES, IF THEY HAD TOLD YOU, WHAT COULD YOU HAVE DONE ABOUT IT?
COULD YOU HAVE REPAID THEIR DEBT?
......I'M SORRY ...
IS THERE REALLY NOTHING WE CAN DO!?
COME ON, GUYS!!

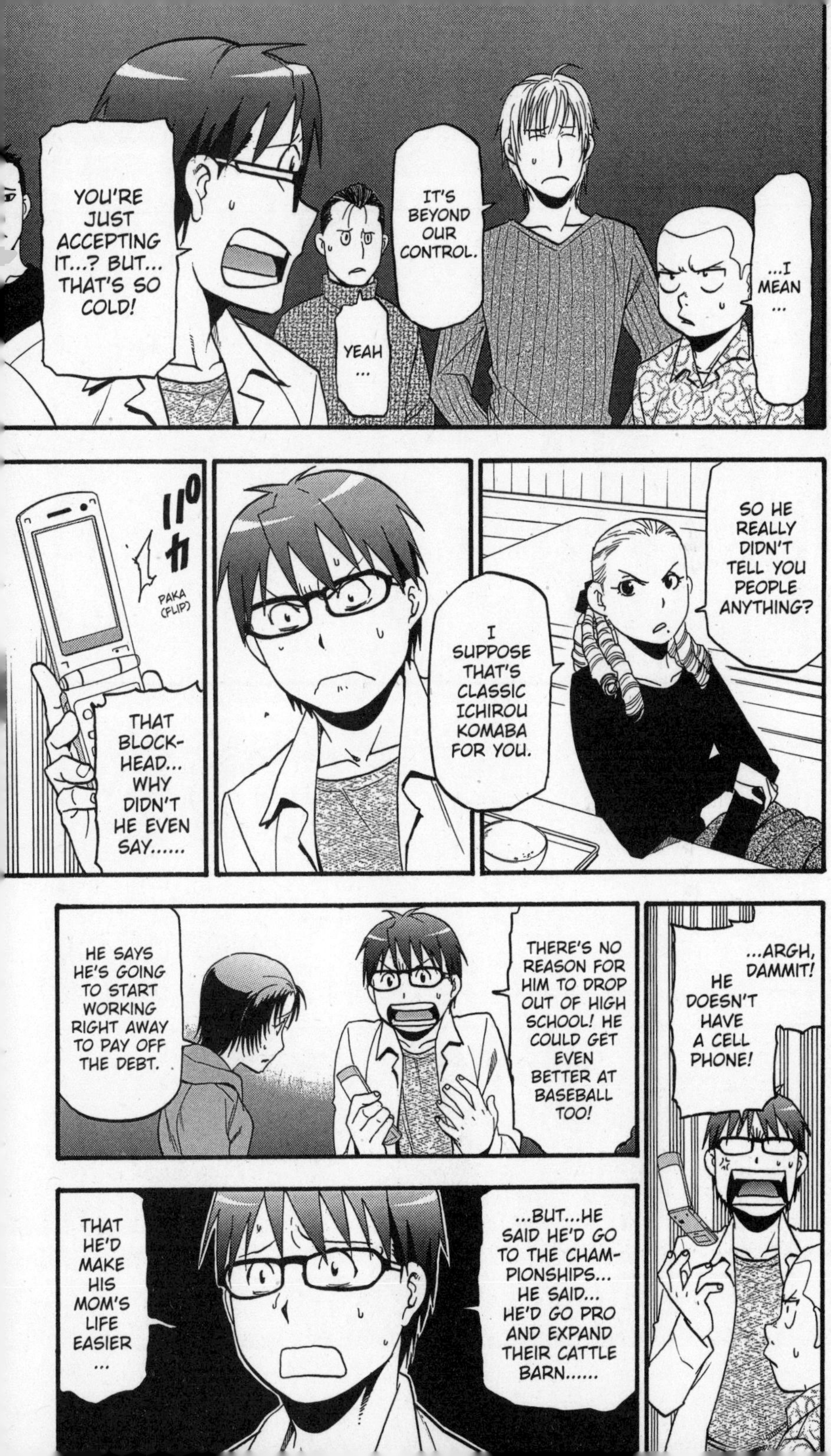
...I MEAN...
IT'S BEYOND OUR CONTROL.
YEAH...
YOU'RE JUST ACCEPTING IT...? BUT... THAT'S SO COLD!
SO HE REALLY DIDN'T TELL YOU PEOPLE ANYTHING?
I SUPPOSE THAT'S CLASSIC ICHIROU KOMABA FOR YOU.
PAKA (FLIP)
THAT BLOCKHEAD... WHY DIDN'T HE EVEN SAY......
...ARGH, DAMMIT!
HE DOESN'T HAVE A CELL PHONE!
THERE'S NO REASON FOR HIM TO DROP OUT OF HIGH SCHOOL! HE COULD GET EVEN BETTER AT BASEBALL TOO!
HE SAYS HE'S GOING TO START WORKING RIGHT AWAY TO PAY OFF THE DEBT.
...BUT...HE SAID HE'D GO TO THE CHAMPIONSHIPS... HE SAID... HE'D GO PRO AND EXPAND THEIR CATTLE BARN......
THAT HE'D MAKE HIS MOM'S LIFE EASIER...

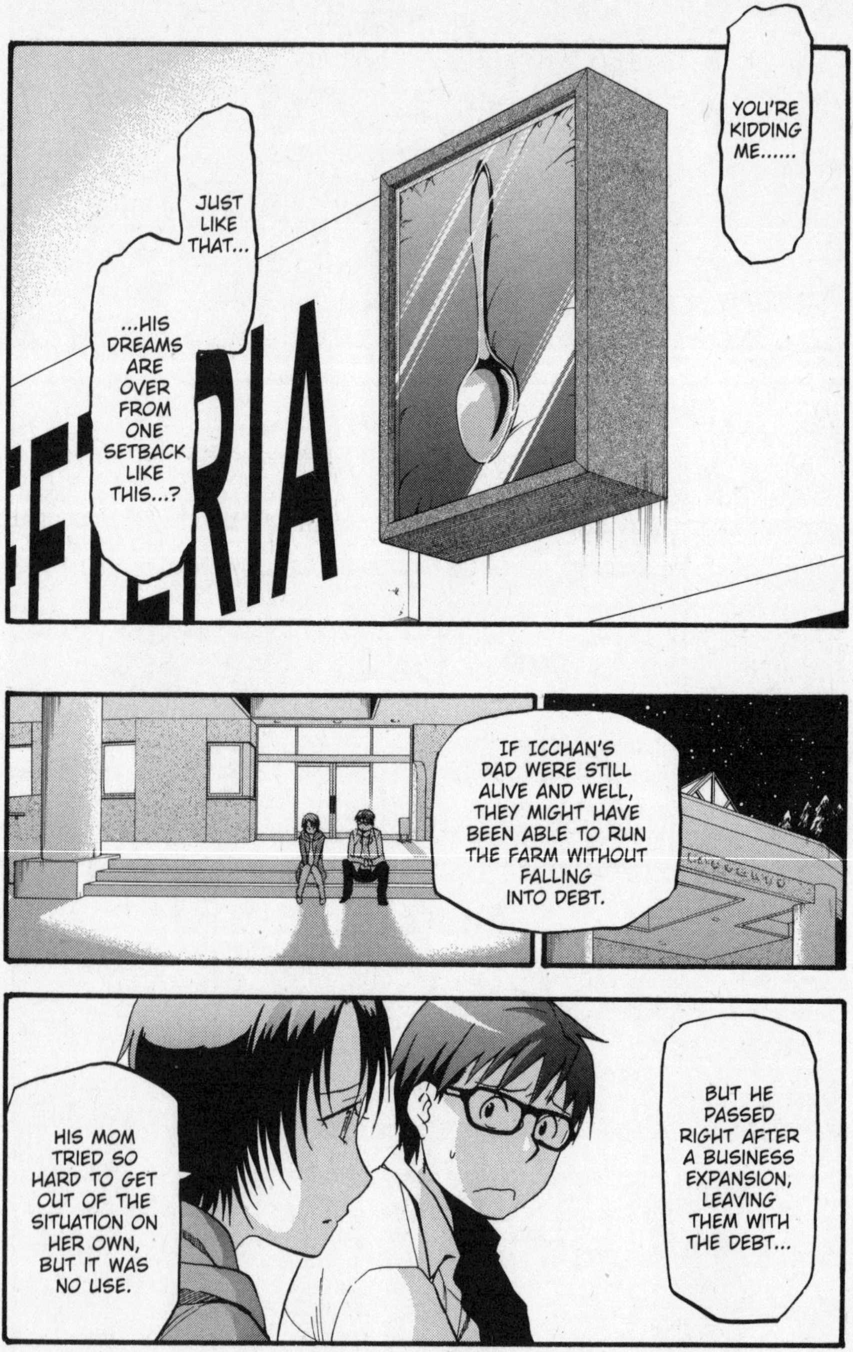
YOU'RE KIDDING ME......
JUST LIKE THAT...
...HIS DREAMS ARE OVER FROM ONE SETBACK LIKE THIS...?
IF ICCHAN'S DAD WERE STILL ALIVE AND WELL, THEY MIGHT HAVE BEEN ABLE TO RUN THE FARM WITHOUT FALLING INTO DEBT.
BUT HE PASSED RIGHT AFTER A BUSINESS EXPANSION, LEAVING THEM WITH THE DEBT...
HIS MOM TRIED SO HARD TO GET OUT OF THE SITUATION ON HER OWN, BUT IT WAS NO USE.

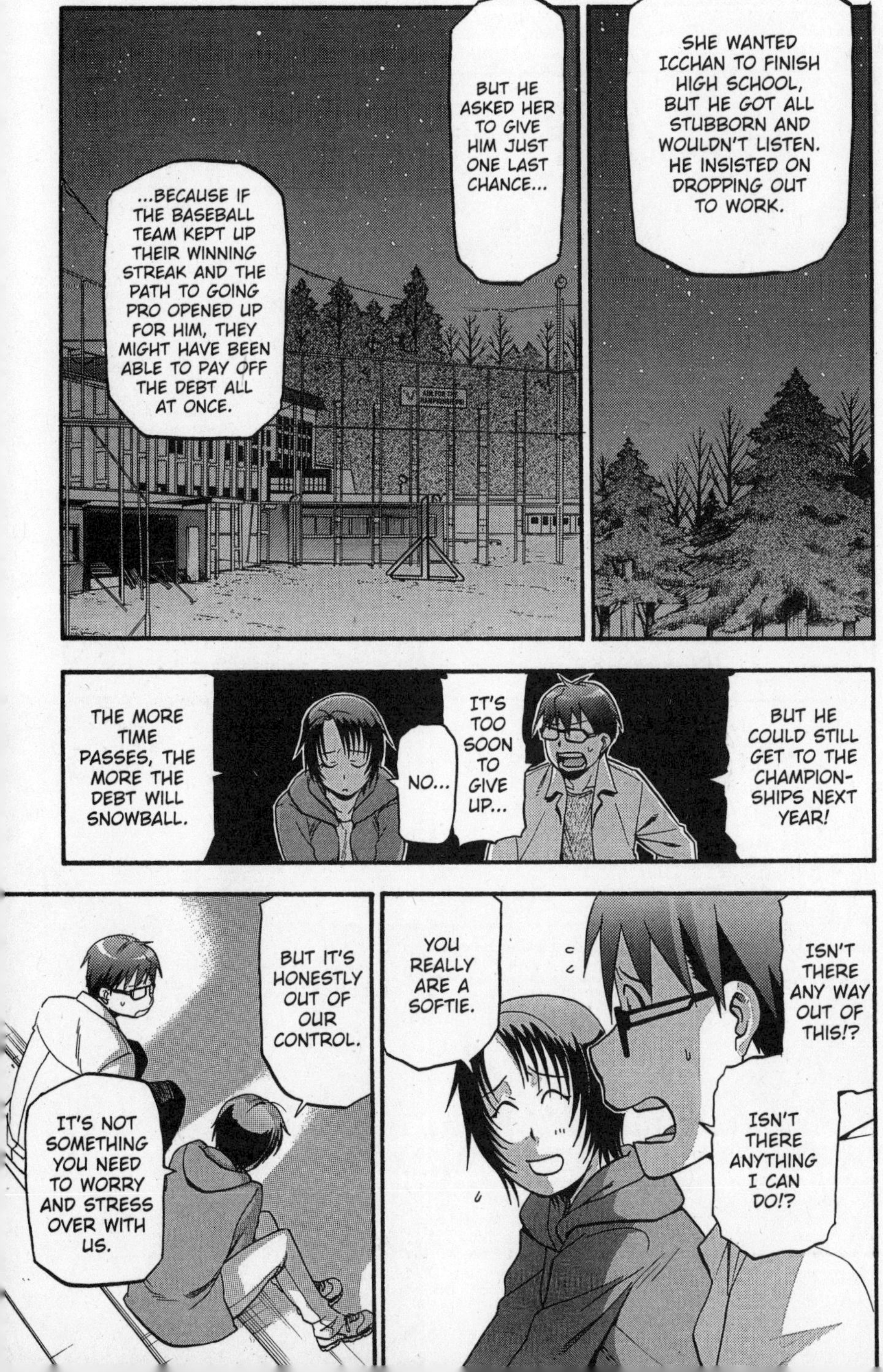
SHE WANTED ICCHAN TO FINISH HIGH SCHOOL, BUT HE GOT ALL STUBBORN AND WOULDN'T LISTEN. HE INSISTED ON DROPPING OUT TO WORK.
BUT HE ASKED HER TO GIVE HIM JUST ONE LAST CHANCE...
...BECAUSE IF THE BASEBALL TEAM KEPT UP THEIR WINNING STREAK AND THE PATH TO GOING PRO OPENED UP FOR HIM, THEY MIGHT HAVE BEEN ABLE TO PAY OFF THE DEBT ALL AT ONCE.
BUT HE COULD STILL GET TO THE CHAMPION-SHIPS NEXT YEAR!
IT'S TOO SOON TO GIVE UP...
NO...
THE MORE TIME PASSES, THE MORE THE DEBT WILL SNOWBALL.
ISN'T THERE ANY WAY OUT OF THIS!?
YOU REALLY ARE A SOFTIE.
ISN'T THERE ANYTHING I CAN DO!?
BUT IT'S HONESTLY OUT OF OUR CONTROL.
IT'S NOT SOMETHING YOU NEED TO WORRY AND STRESS OVER WITH US.

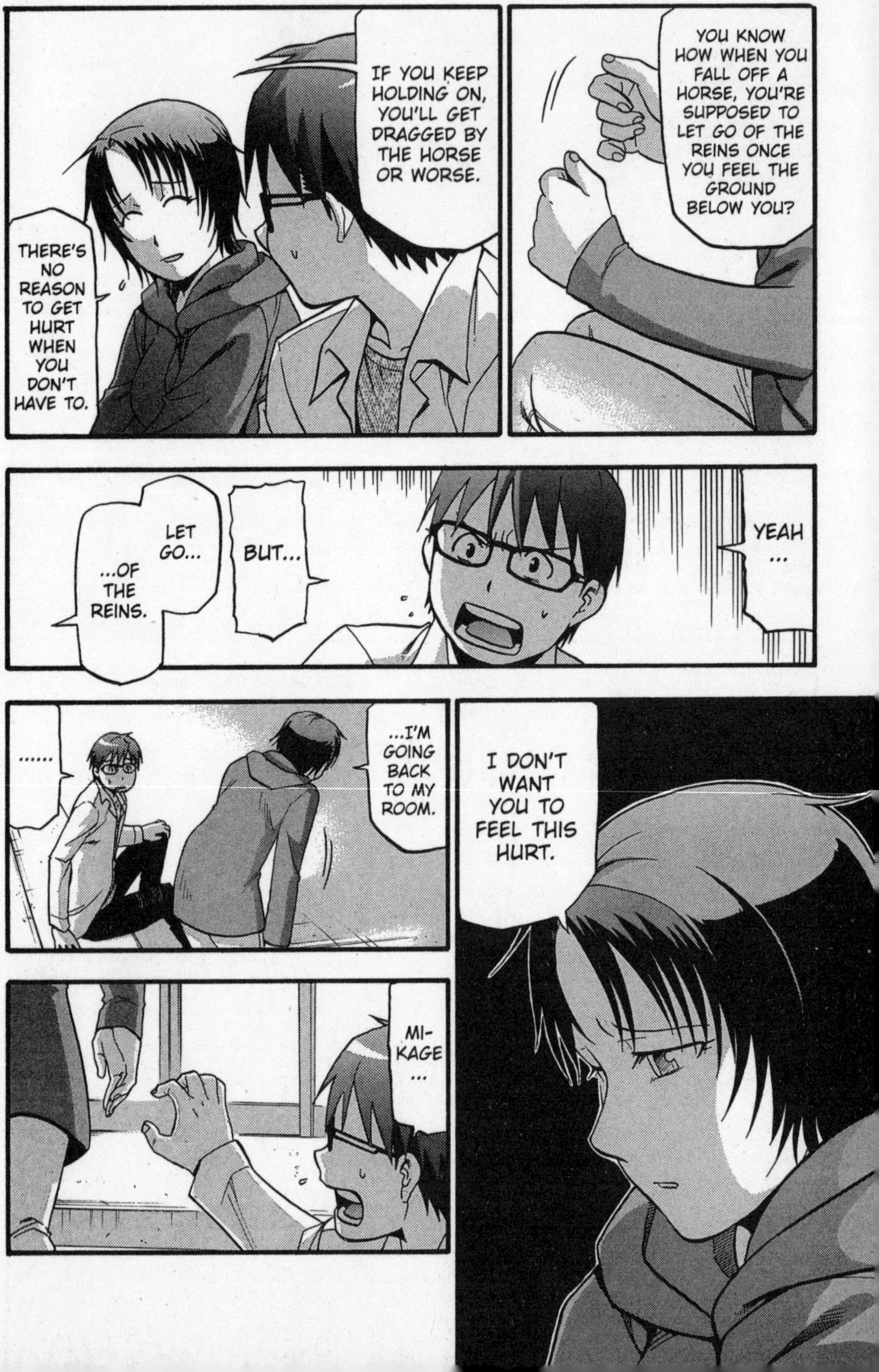
YOU KNOW HOW WHEN YOU FALL OFF A HORSE, YOU'RE SUPPOSED TO LET GO OF THE REINS ONCE YOU FEEL THE GROUND BELOW YOU?
IF YOU KEEP HOLDING ON, YOU'LL GET DRAGGED BY THE HORSE OR WORSE.
THERE'S NO REASON TO GET HURT WHEN YOU DON'T HAVE TO.
YEAH ...
BUT...
LET GO...
...OF THE REINS.
I DON'T WANT YOU TO FEEL THIS HURT.
...I'M GOING BACK TO MY ROOM.
......
MI-KAGE ...

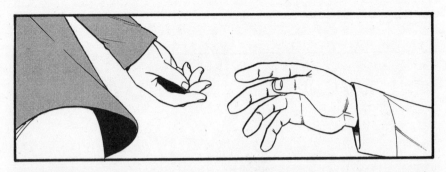

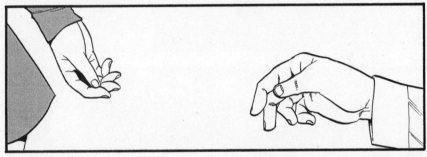

GARA
(RATTLE)

ガラ

ガラ
GARA

ガラ
GARA

YOU OUGHTA
QUIT MINDIN'
OTHER PEOPLE
ALL THE TIME
AND DO YOUR
OWN THINGS.

PATAN
(SHUT)

パタン

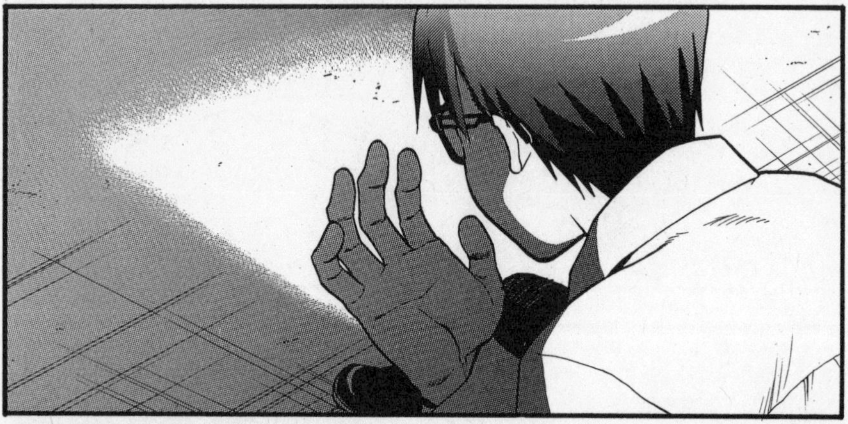

SIGN: OOEZO AGRICULTURAL HIGH SCHOOL STUDENT DORMS

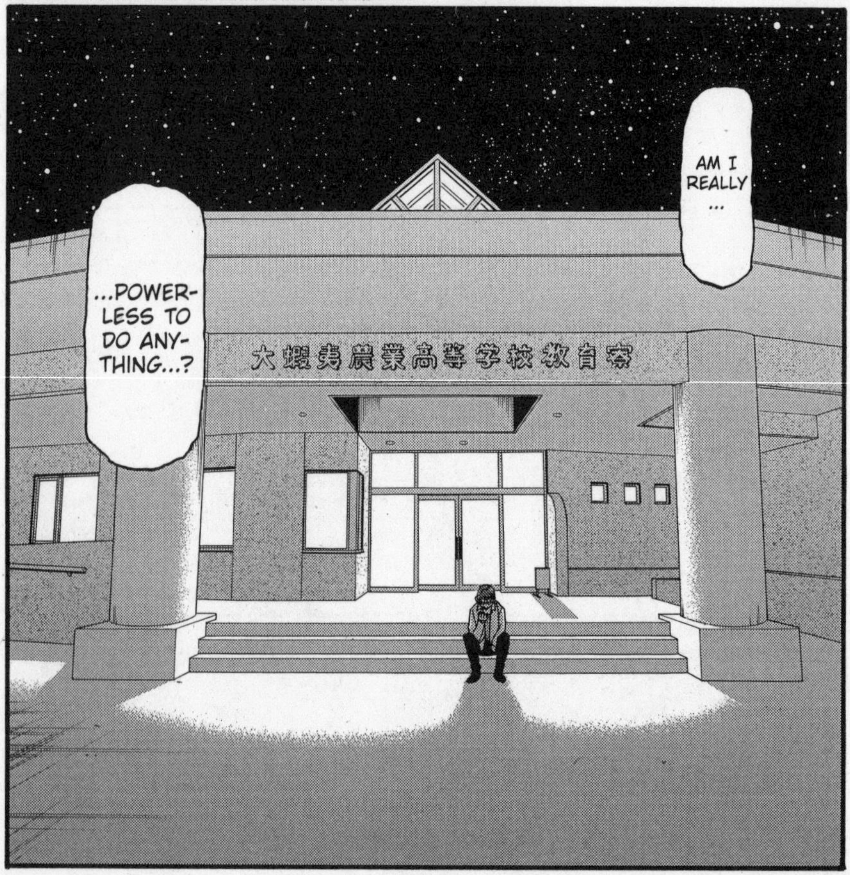
AM I REALLY ...
...POWER-LESS TO DO ANY-THING...?
大蝦夷農業高等学校教育寮

Silver Spoon

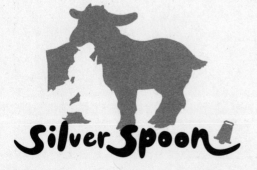

PIG BARN
TEACHER

ICHIKO FUJI

HAS A HUNTING
LICENSE

Chapter 64:
Tale of Winter ①

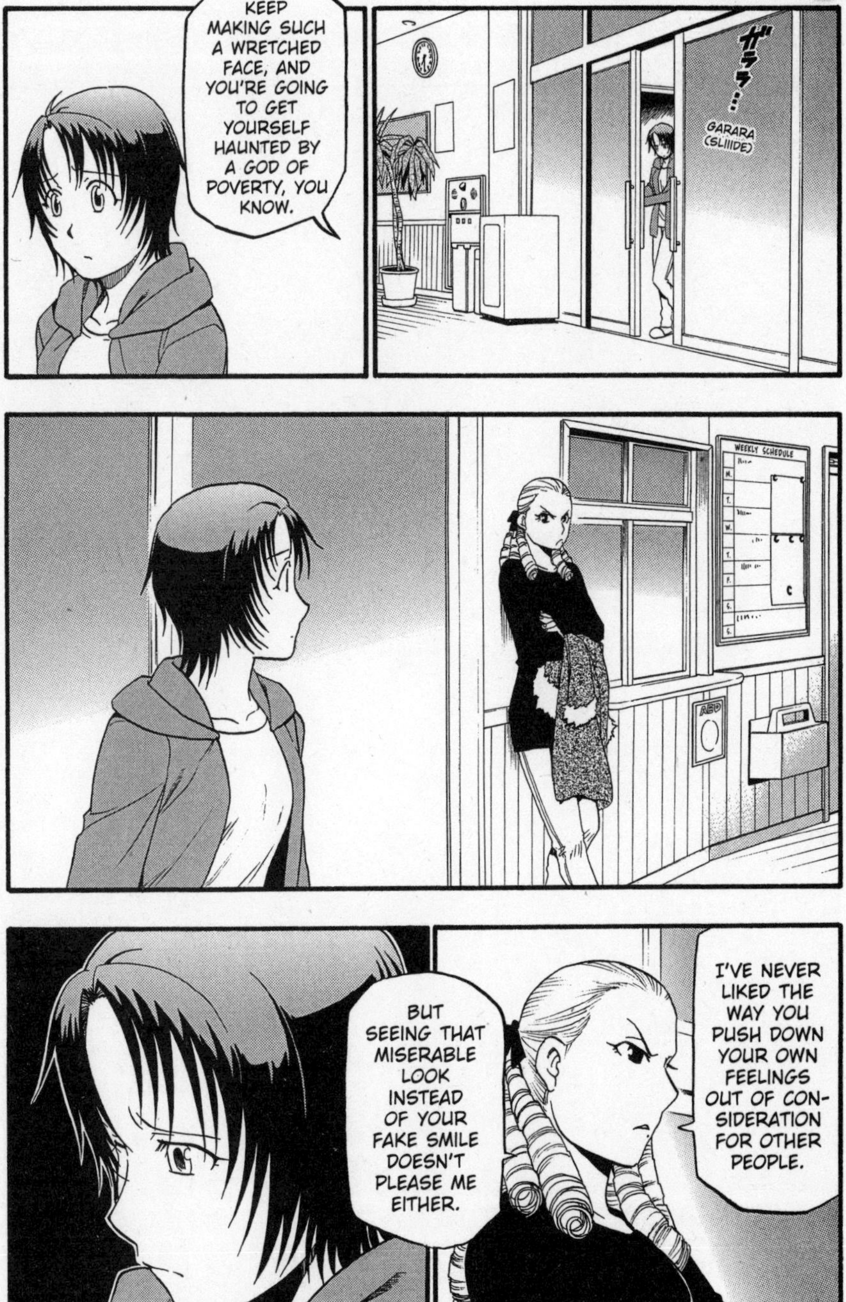
ガラ…
GARARA (SLIIIDE)
KEEP MAKING SUCH A WRETCHED FACE, AND YOU'RE GOING TO GET YOURSELF HAUNTED BY A GOD OF POVERTY, YOU KNOW.
WEEKLY SCHEDULE
AED
I'VE NEVER LIKED THE WAY YOU PUSH DOWN YOUR OWN FEELINGS OUT OF CON-SIDERATION FOR OTHER PEOPLE.
BUT SEEING THAT MISERABLE LOOK INSTEAD OF YOUR FAKE SMILE DOESN'T PLEASE ME EITHER.

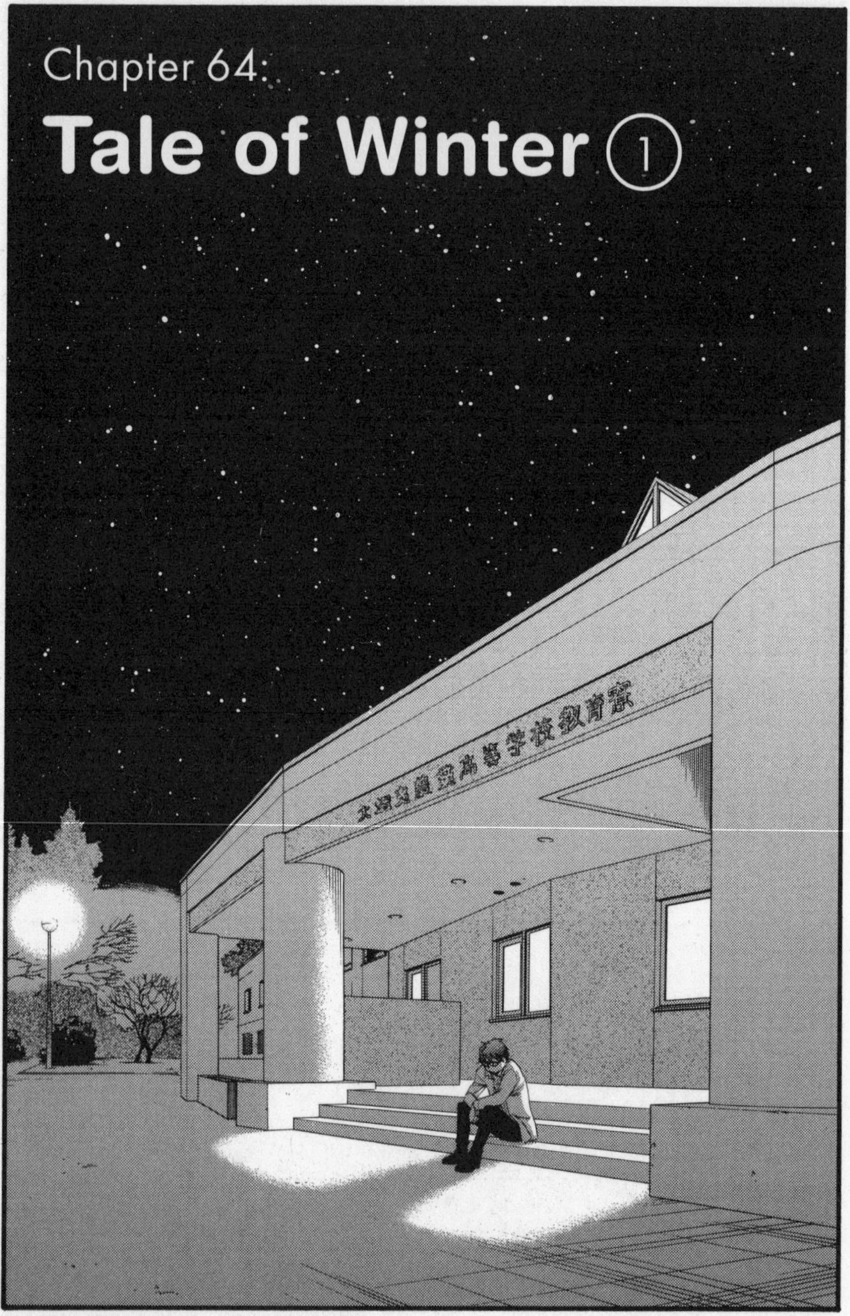
Chapter 64:
Tale of Winter ①

SIGN: OOEZO AGRICULTURAL HIGH SCHOOL STUDENT DORMS

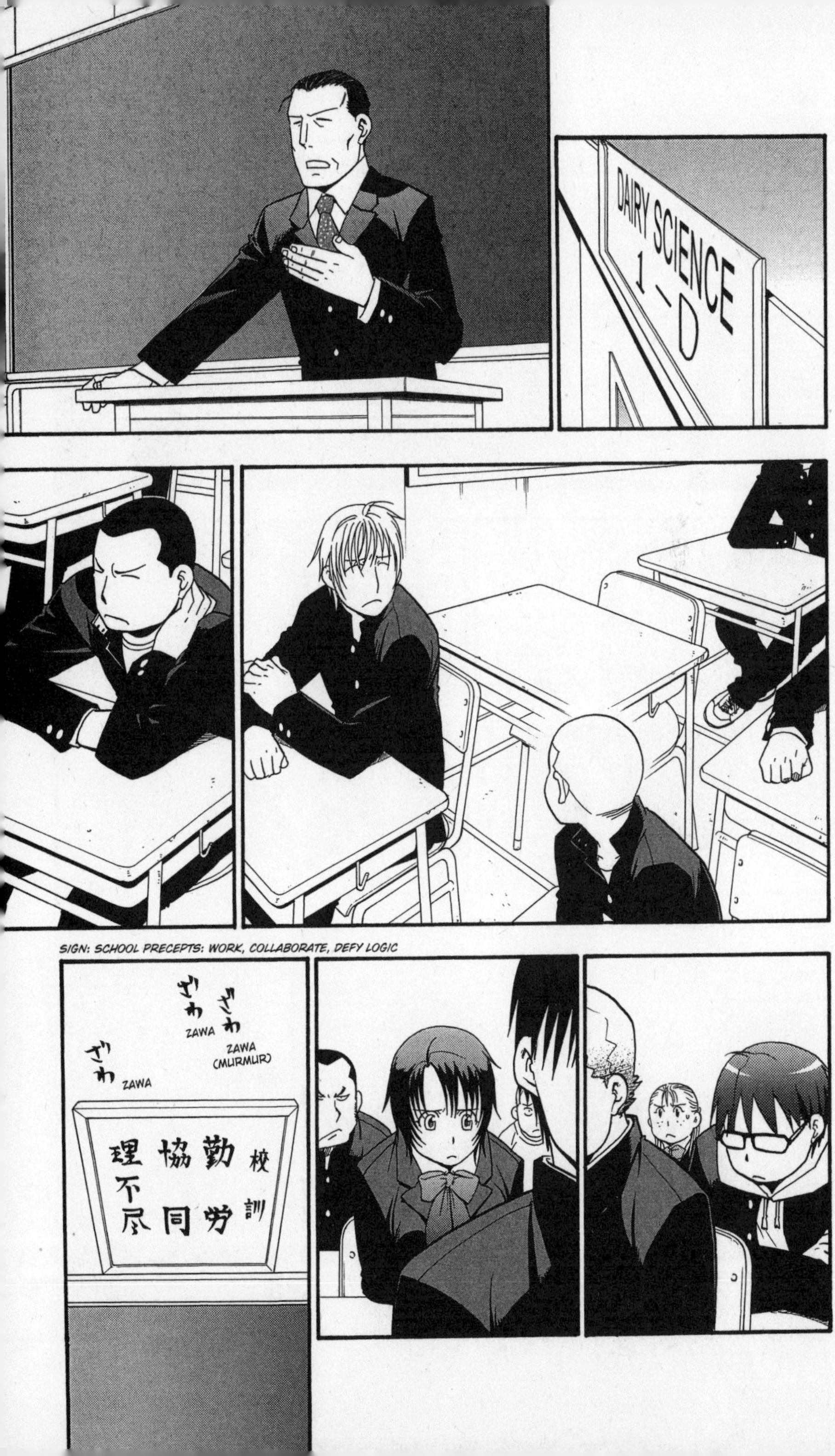
DAIRY SCIENCE
1-D
SIGN: SCHOOL PRECEPTS: WORK, COLLABORATE, DEFY LOGIC
ざわ
ZAWA
ざわ
ZAWA
(MURMUR)
ざわ
ZAWA
校訓
勤労
協同
理不尽

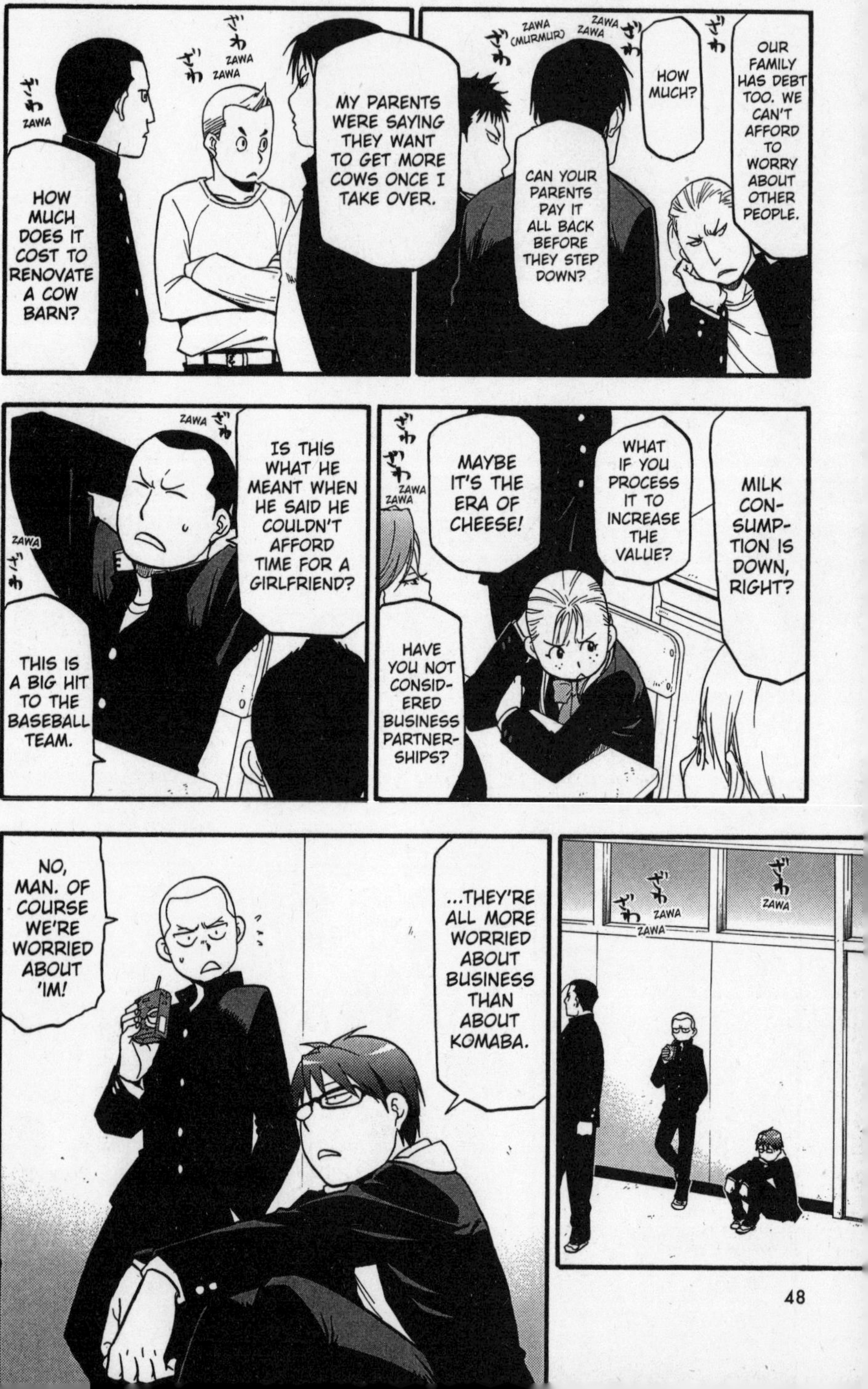
ZAWA (MURMUR)
ZAWA ZAWA
OUR FAMILY HAS DEBT TOO. WE CAN'T AFFORD TO WORRY ABOUT OTHER PEOPLE.
HOW MUCH?
CAN YOUR PARENTS PAY IT ALL BACK BEFORE THEY STEP DOWN?
ZAWA ZAWA
MY PARENTS WERE SAYING THEY WANT TO GET MORE COWS ONCE I TAKE OVER.
ZAWA
HOW MUCH DOES IT COST TO RENOVATE A COW BARN?
MILK CON-SUMP-TION IS DOWN, RIGHT?
WHAT IF YOU PROCESS IT TO INCREASE THE VALUE?
MAYBE IT'S THE ERA OF CHEESE!
ZAWA ZAWA
HAVE YOU NOT CONSID-ERED BUSINESS PARTNER-SHIPS?
ZAWA
IS THIS WHAT HE MEANT WHEN HE SAID HE COULDN'T AFFORD TIME FOR A GIRLFRIEND?
ZAWA
THIS IS A BIG HIT TO THE BASEBALL TEAM.
ZAWA
ZAWA ZAWA
...THEY'RE ALL MORE WORRIED ABOUT BUSINESS THAN ABOUT KOMABA.
NO, MAN. OF COURSE WE'RE WORRIED ABOUT 'IM!

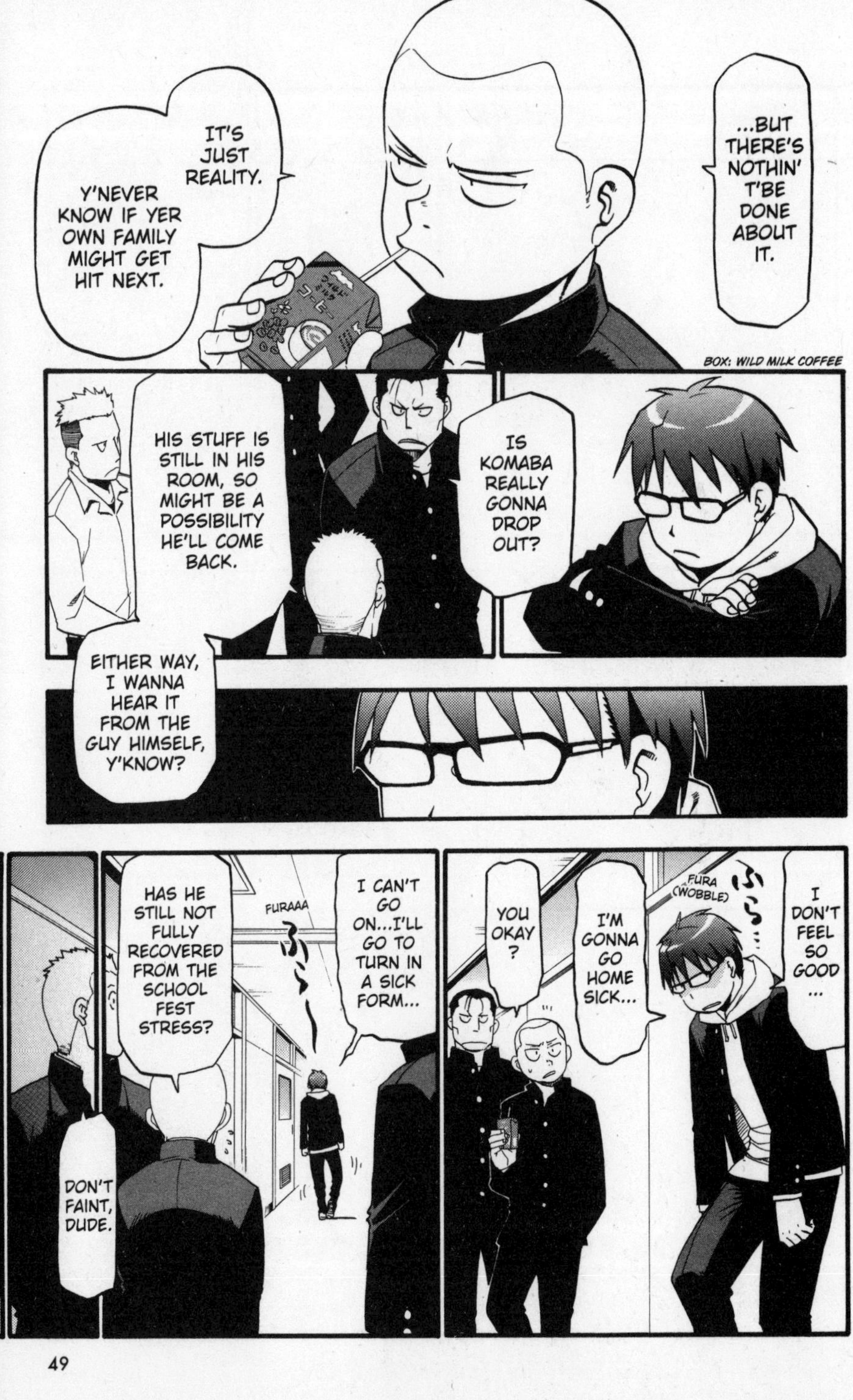
...BUT THERE'S NOTHIN' T'BE DONE ABOUT IT.
IT'S JUST REALITY.
Y'NEVER KNOW IF YER OWN FAMILY MIGHT GET HIT NEXT.
BOX: WILD MILK COFFEE
IS KOMABA REALLY GONNA DROP OUT?
HIS STUFF IS STILL IN HIS ROOM, SO MIGHT BE A POSSIBILITY HE'LL COME BACK.
EITHER WAY, I WANNA HEAR IT FROM THE GUY HIMSELF, Y'KNOW?
ふら…
FURA (WOBBLE)
I DON'T FEEL SO GOOD ...
I'M GONNA GO HOME SICK...
YOU OKAY ?
I CAN'T GO ON...I'LL GO TO TURN IN A SICK FORM...
ふら〜
FURAAA
HAS HE STILL NOT FULLY RECOVERED FROM THE SCHOOL FEST STRESS?
DON'T FAINT, DUDE.

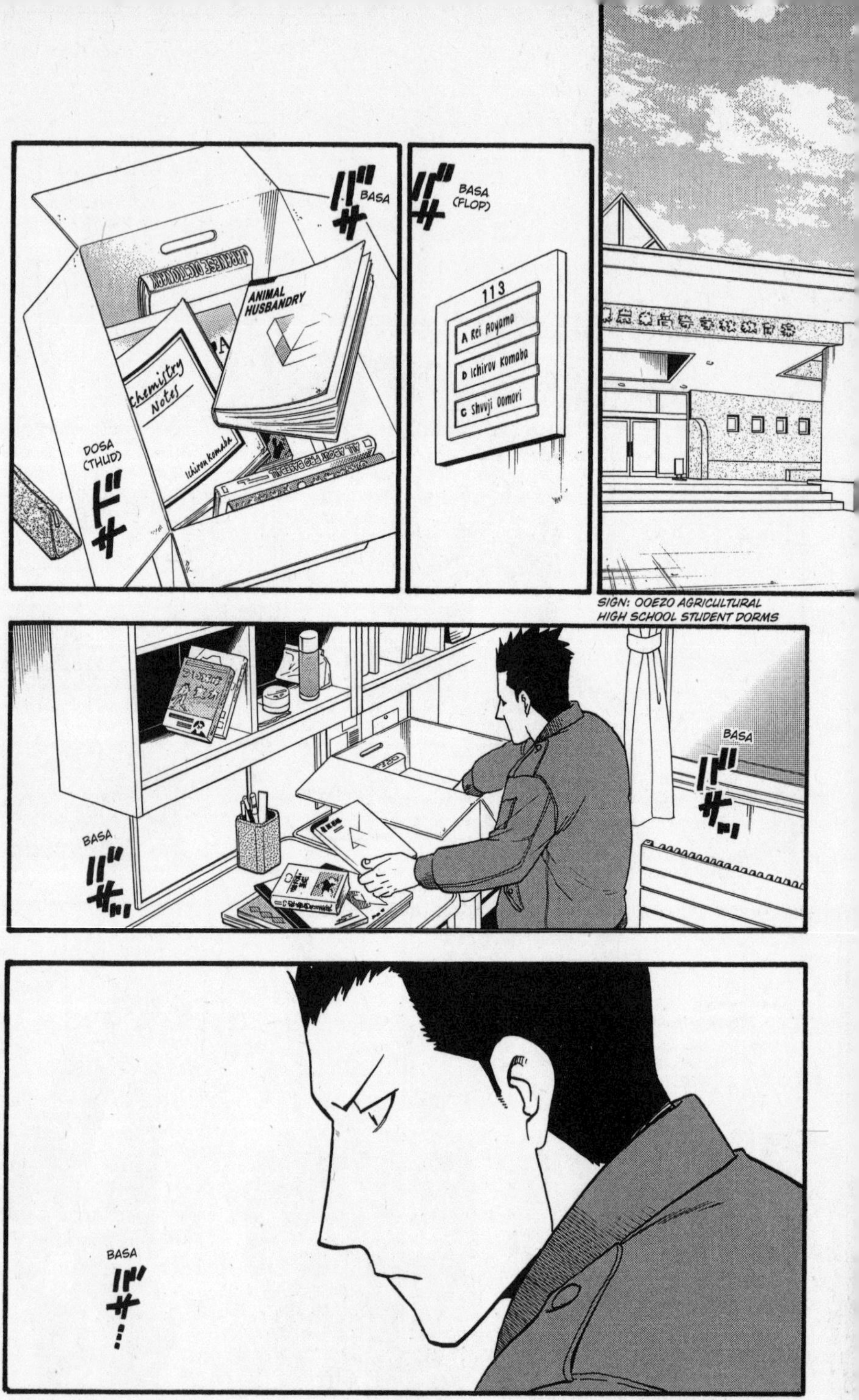
SIGN: OOEZO AGRICULTURAL HIGH SCHOOL STUDENT DORMS
113
A Rei Aoyama
B Ichirou Komaba
C Shuuji Oomori
BASA (FLOP)
BASA
ANIMAL HUSBANDRY
Chemistry Notes
Ichirou Komaba
ALL ABOUT PRO BASEBALL
DOSA (THUD)
BASA
BASA
BASA

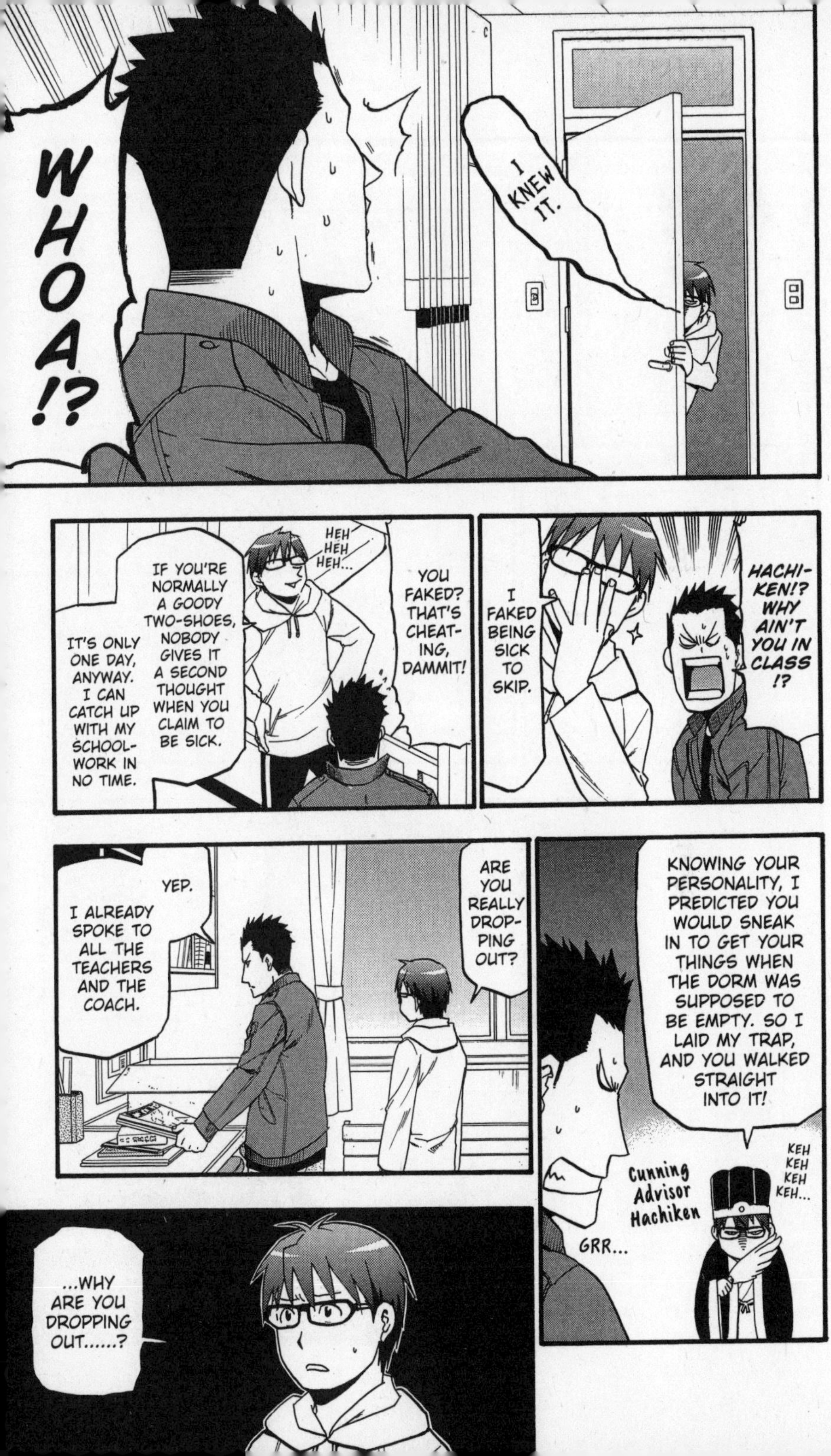
I KNEW IT.
WHOA!?
HACHIKEN!? WHY AIN'T YOU IN CLASS!?
I FAKED BEING SICK TO SKIP.
YOU FAKED? THAT'S CHEATING, DAMMIT!
HEH HEH HEH...
IF YOU'RE NORMALLY A GOODY TWO-SHOES, NOBODY GIVES IT A SECOND THOUGHT WHEN YOU CLAIM TO BE SICK.
IT'S ONLY ONE DAY, ANYWAY. I CAN CATCH UP WITH MY SCHOOLWORK IN NO TIME.
KNOWING YOUR PERSONALITY, I PREDICTED YOU WOULD SNEAK IN TO GET YOUR THINGS WHEN THE DORM WAS SUPPOSED TO BE EMPTY. SO I LAID MY TRAP, AND YOU WALKED STRAIGHT INTO IT!
KEH KEH KEH KEH...
Cunning Advisor Hachiken
GRR...
ARE YOU REALLY DROPPING OUT?
YEP.
I ALREADY SPOKE TO ALL THE TEACHERS AND THE COACH.
...WHY ARE YOU DROPPING OUT......?

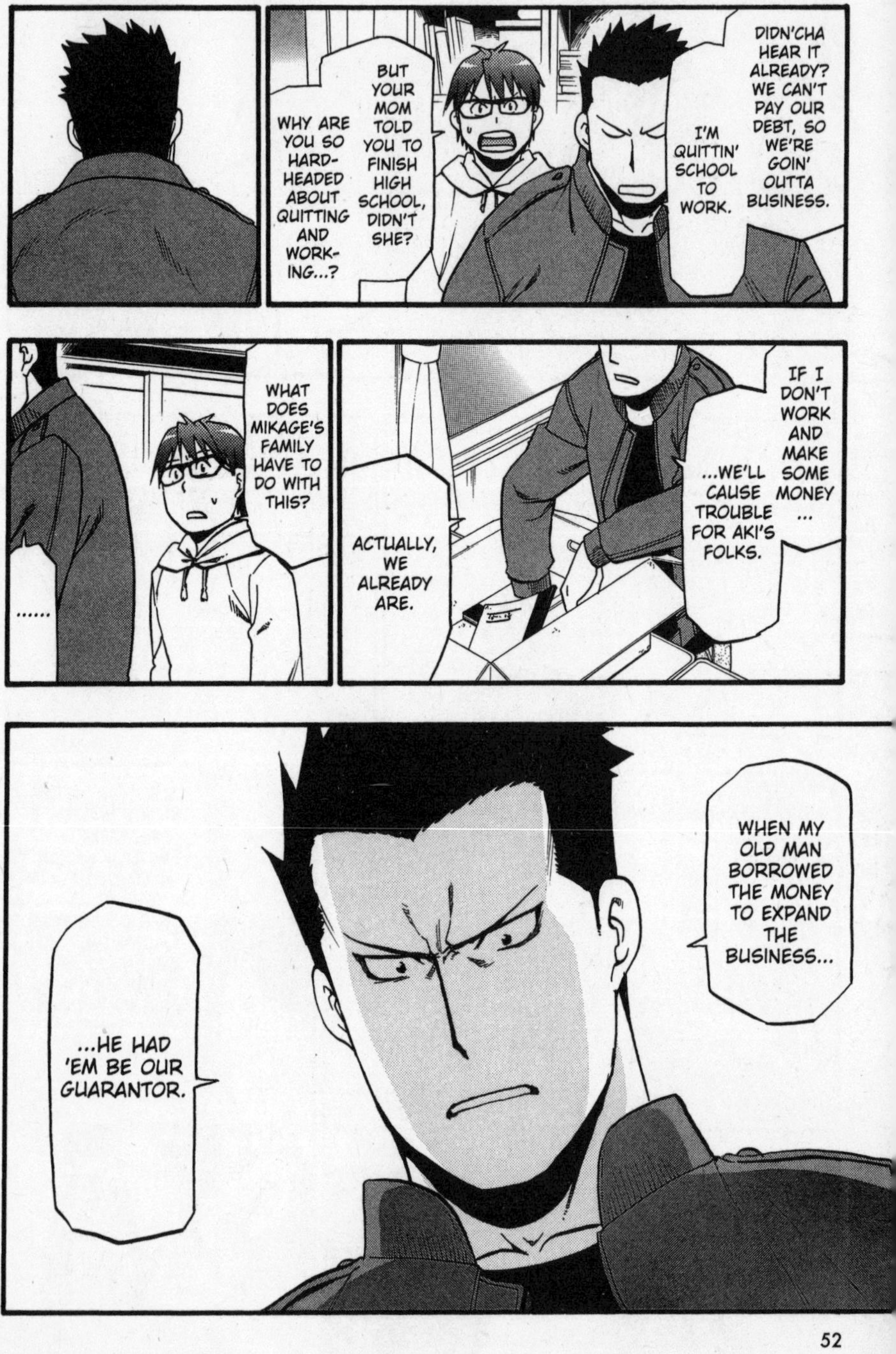
DIDN'CHA HEAR IT ALREADY? WE CAN'T PAY OUR DEBT, SO WE'RE GOIN' OUTTA BUSINESS.
I'M QUITTIN' SCHOOL TO WORK.
BUT YOUR MOM TOLD YOU TO FINISH HIGH SCHOOL, DIDN'T SHE?
WHY ARE YOU SO HARD-HEADED ABOUT QUITTING AND WORKING...?
IF I DON'T WORK AND MAKE SOME MONEY ...
...WE'LL CAUSE TROUBLE FOR AKI'S FOLKS.
ACTUALLY, WE ALREADY ARE.
WHAT DOES MIKAGE'S FAMILY HAVE TO DO WITH THIS?
......
WHEN MY OLD MAN BORROWED THE MONEY TO EXPAND THE BUSINESS...
...HE HAD 'EM BE OUR GUARANTOR.

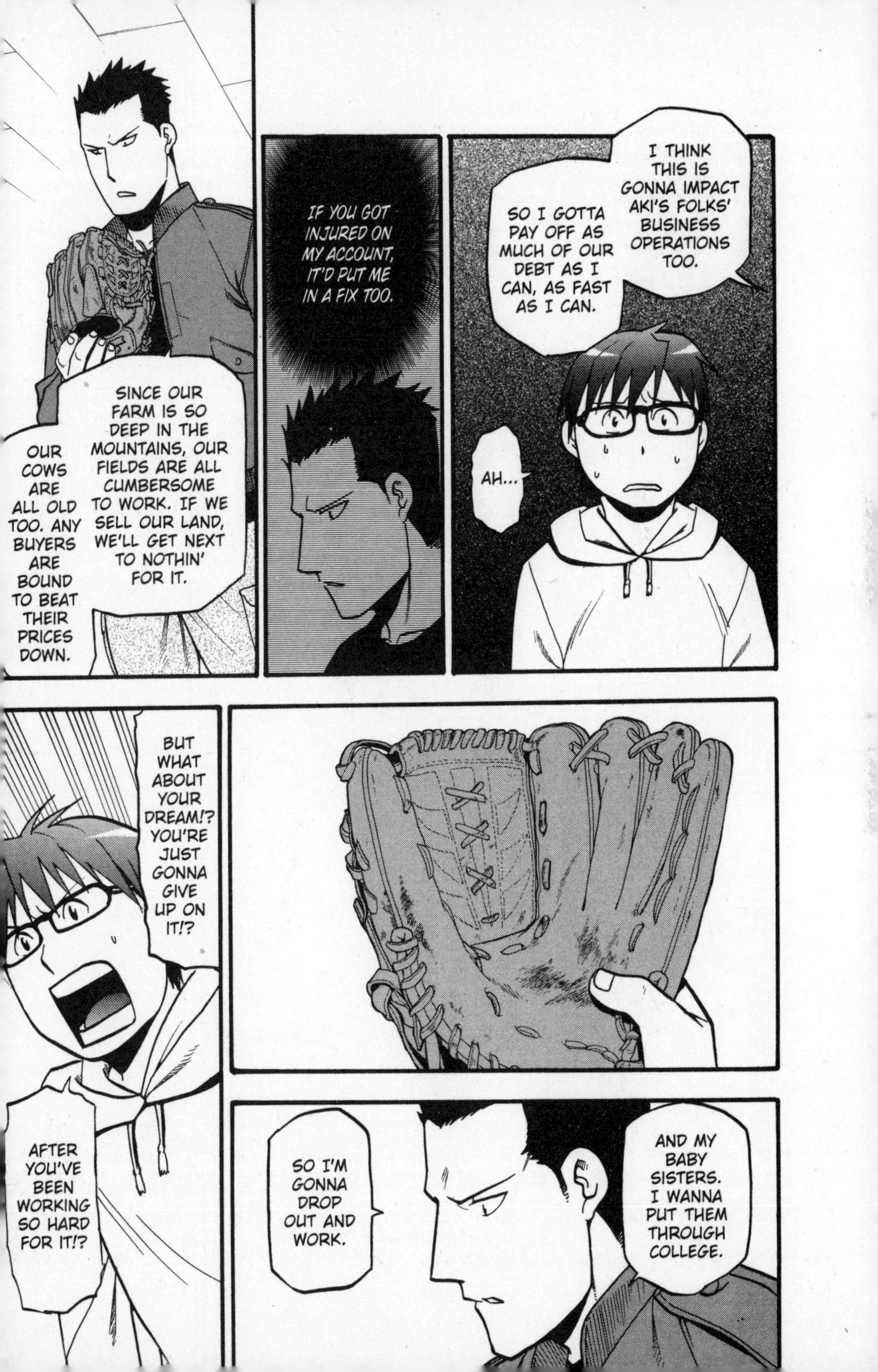
I THINK THIS IS GONNA IMPACT AKI'S FOLKS' BUSINESS OPERATIONS TOO.
SO I GOTTA PAY OFF AS MUCH OF OUR DEBT AS I CAN, AS FAST AS I CAN.
AH...
IF YOU GOT INJURED ON MY ACCOUNT, IT'D PUT ME IN A FIX TOO.
SINCE OUR FARM IS SO DEEP IN THE MOUNTAINS, OUR FIELDS ARE ALL CUMBERSOME TO WORK. IF WE SELL OUR LAND, WE'LL GET NEXT TO NOTHIN' FOR IT.
OUR COWS ARE ALL OLD TOO. ANY BUYERS ARE BOUND TO BEAT THEIR PRICES DOWN.
AND MY BABY SISTERS. I WANNA PUT THEM THROUGH COLLEGE.
SO I'M GONNA DROP OUT AND WORK.
BUT WHAT ABOUT YOUR DREAM!? YOU'RE JUST GONNA GIVE UP ON IT!?
AFTER YOU'VE BEEN WORKING SO HARD FOR IT!?

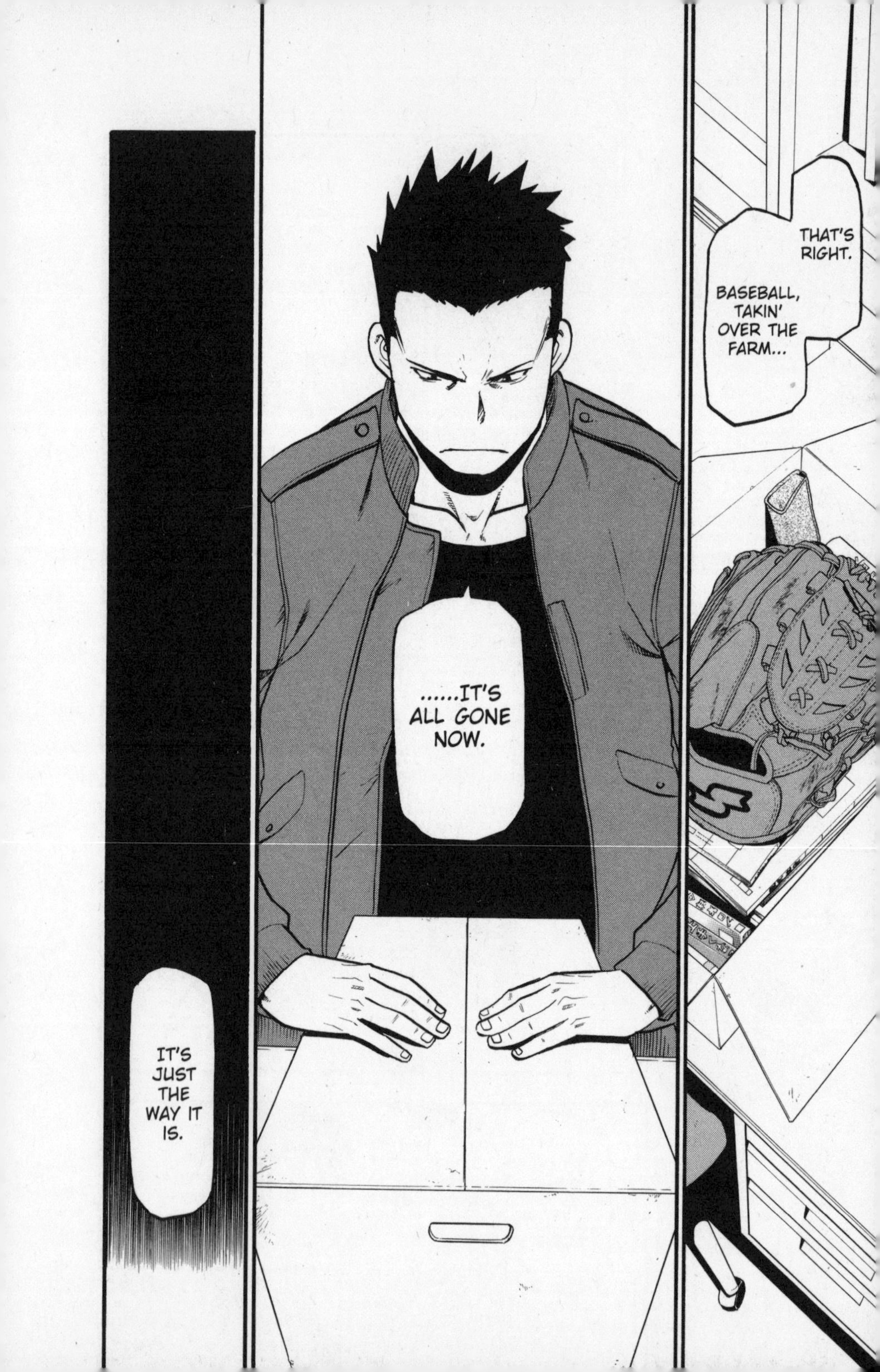
THAT'S RIGHT.
BASEBALL, TAKIN' OVER THE FARM...
......IT'S ALL GONE NOW.
IT'S JUST THE WAY IT IS.

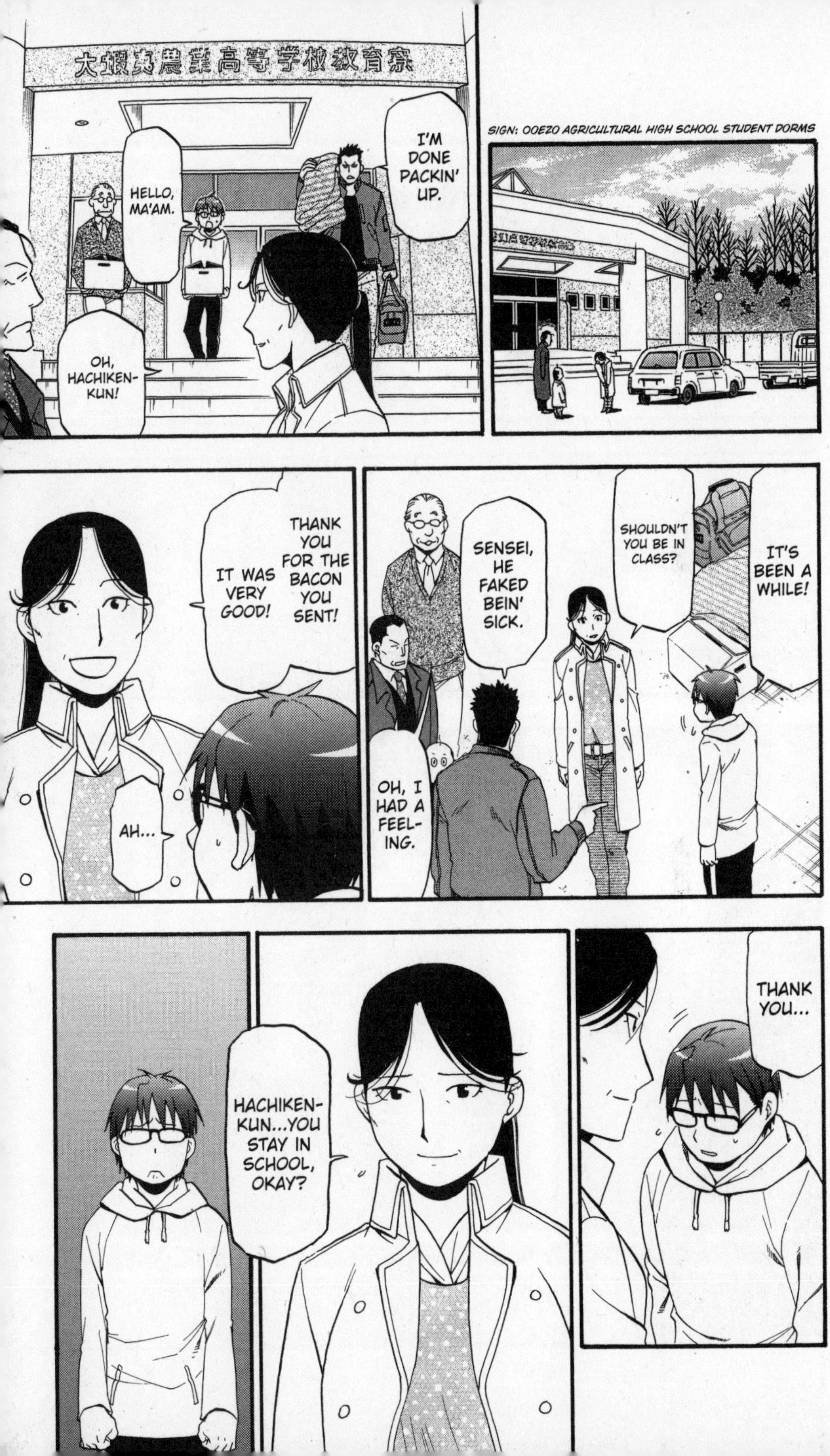
SIGN: OOEZO AGRICULTURAL HIGH SCHOOL STUDENT DORMS
大蝦夷農業高等学校教育寮
I'M DONE PACKIN' UP.
HELLO, MA'AM.
OH, HACHIKEN-KUN!
IT'S BEEN A WHILE!
SHOULDN'T YOU BE IN CLASS?
SENSEI, HE FAKED BEIN' SICK.
OH, I HAD A FEEL-ING.
THANK YOU FOR THE BACON YOU SENT!
IT WAS VERY GOOD!
AH...
THANK YOU...
HACHIKEN-KUN...YOU STAY IN SCHOOL, OKAY?

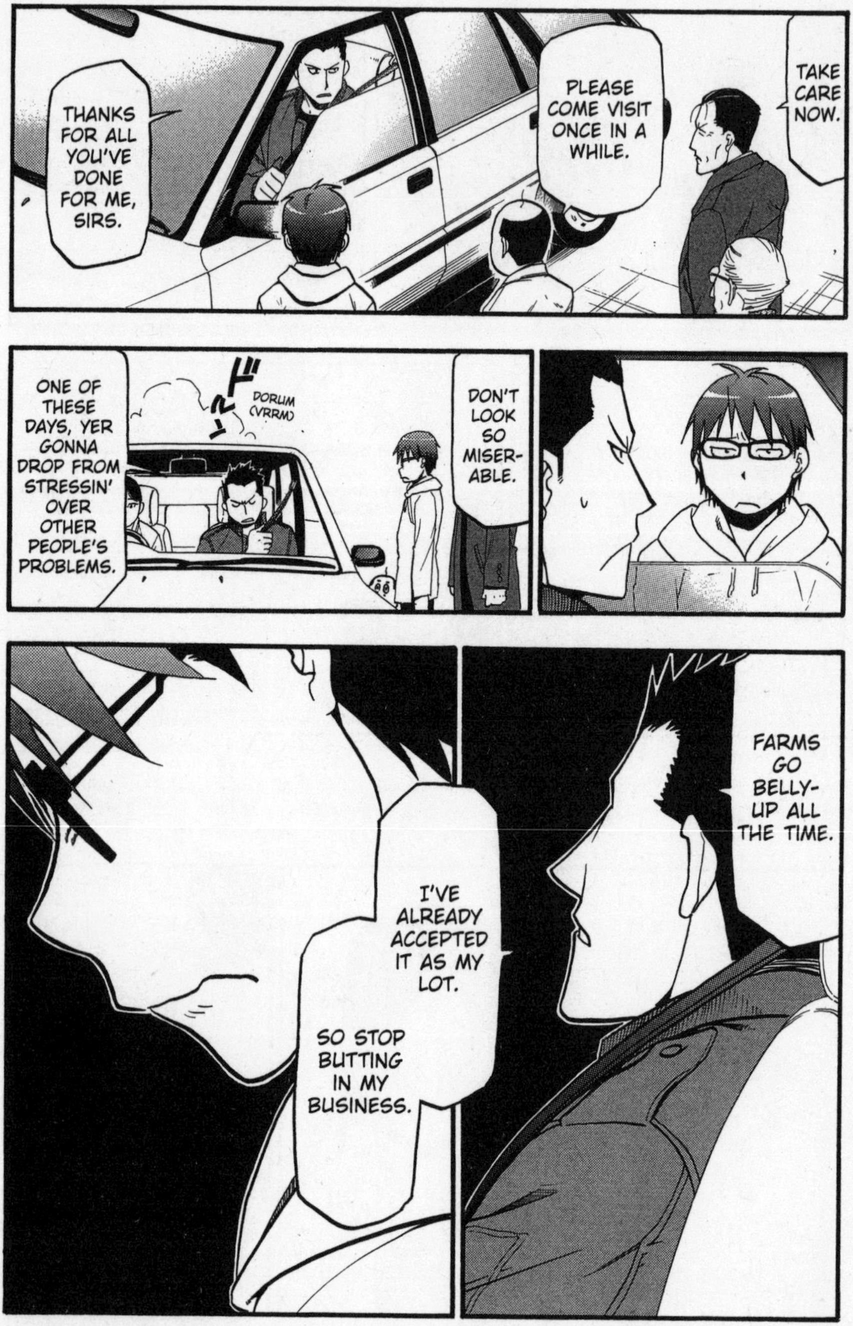
TAKE CARE NOW.
PLEASE COME VISIT ONCE IN A WHILE.
THANKS FOR ALL YOU'VE DONE FOR ME, SIRS.
DON'T LOOK SO MISER-ABLE.
DORUM (VRRM)
ONE OF THESE DAYS, YER GONNA DROP FROM STRESSIN' OVER OTHER PEOPLE'S PROBLEMS.
FARMS GO BELLY-UP ALL THE TIME.
I'VE ALREADY ACCEPTED IT AS MY LOT.
SO STOP BUTTING IN MY BUSINESS.

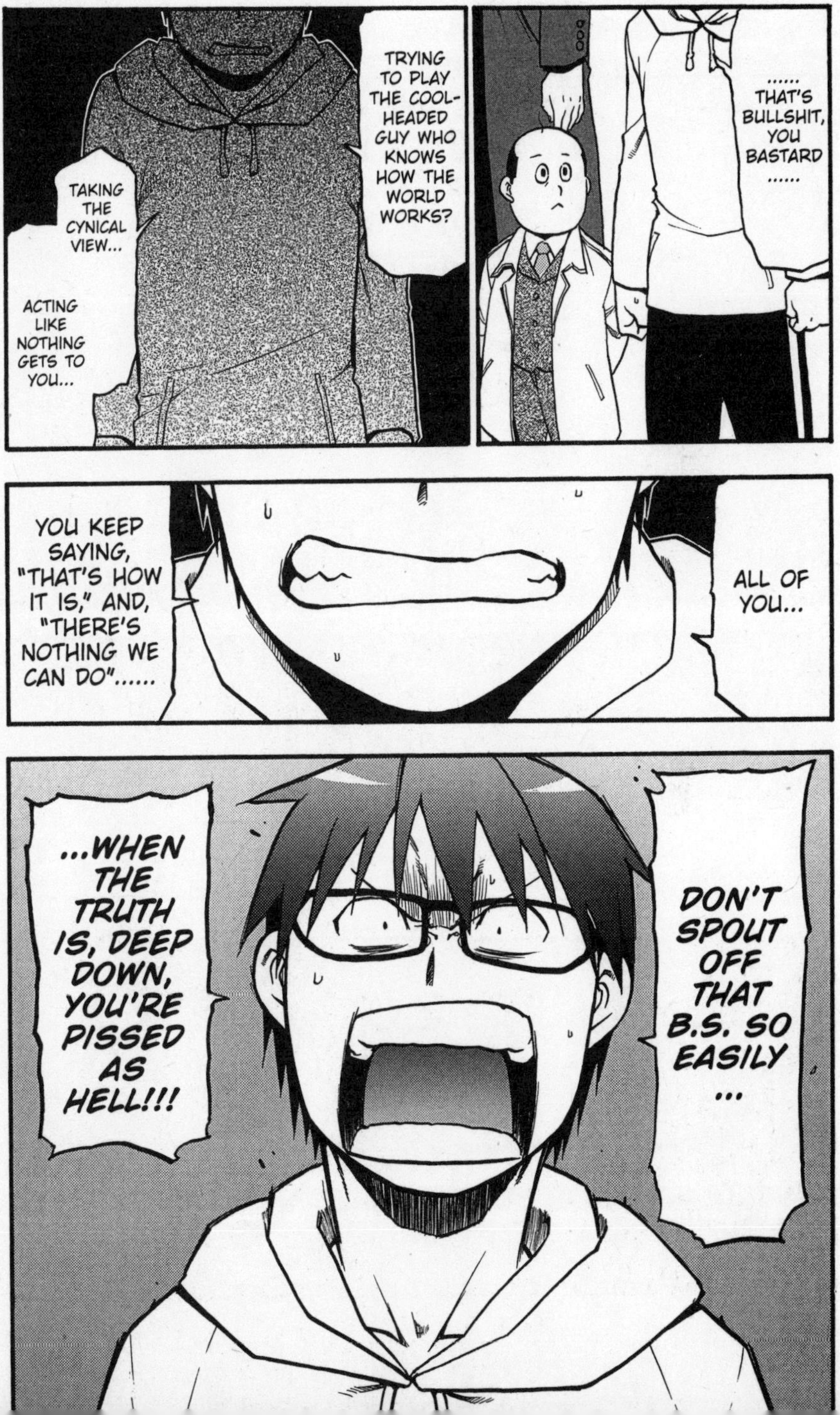
...... THAT'S BULLSHIT, YOU BASTARD ......
TRYING TO PLAY THE COOL-HEADED GUY WHO KNOWS HOW THE WORLD WORKS?
TAKING THE CYNICAL VIEW...
ACTING LIKE NOTHING GETS TO YOU...
ALL OF YOU...
YOU KEEP SAYING, "THAT'S HOW IT IS," AND, "THERE'S NOTHING WE CAN DO"......
DON'T SPOUT OFF THAT B.S. SO EASILY ...
...WHEN THE TRUTH IS, DEEP DOWN, YOU'RE PISSED AS HELL!!!

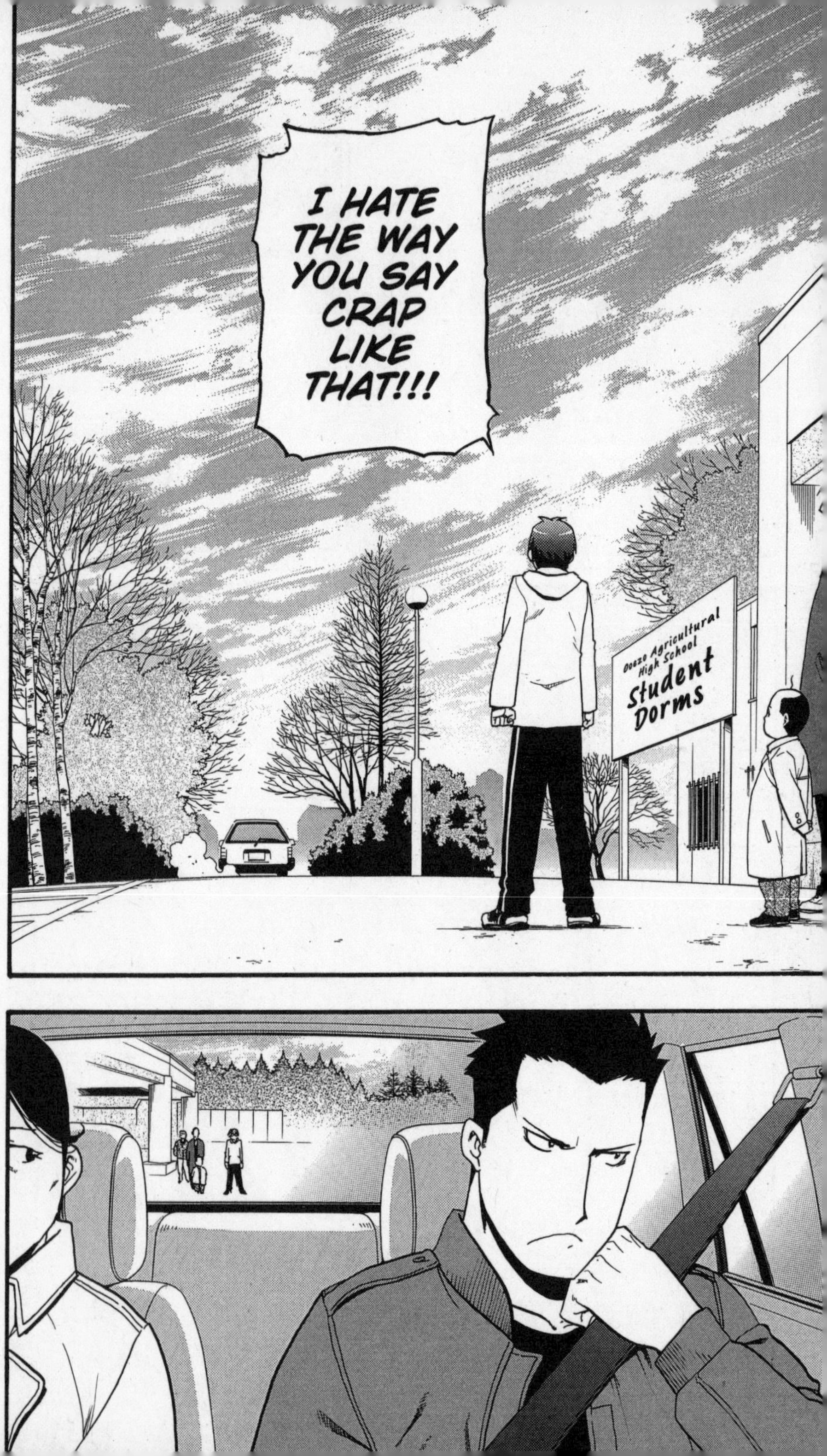
I HATE THE WAY YOU SAY CRAP LIKE THAT!!!
Ooezo Agricultural High School Student Dorms

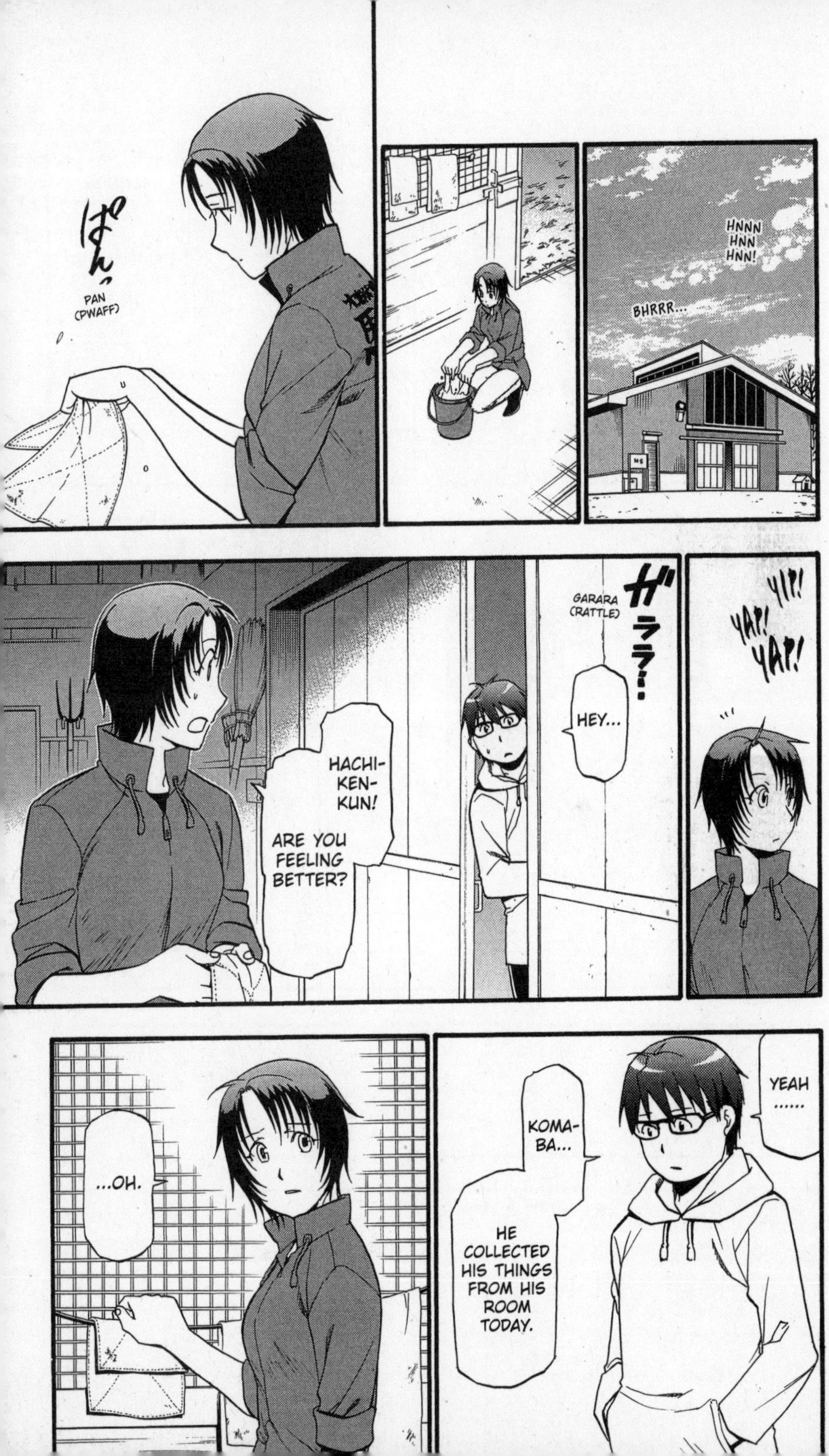
HNNN HNN HNN!
BHRRR...
ぱん
PAN (PWAFF)
YIP! YAP! YAP!
ガララ
GARARA (RATTLE)
HEY...
HACHI-KEN-KUN!
ARE YOU FEELING BETTER?
YEAH ......
KOMA-BA...
HE COLLECTED HIS THINGS FROM HIS ROOM TODAY.
...OH.

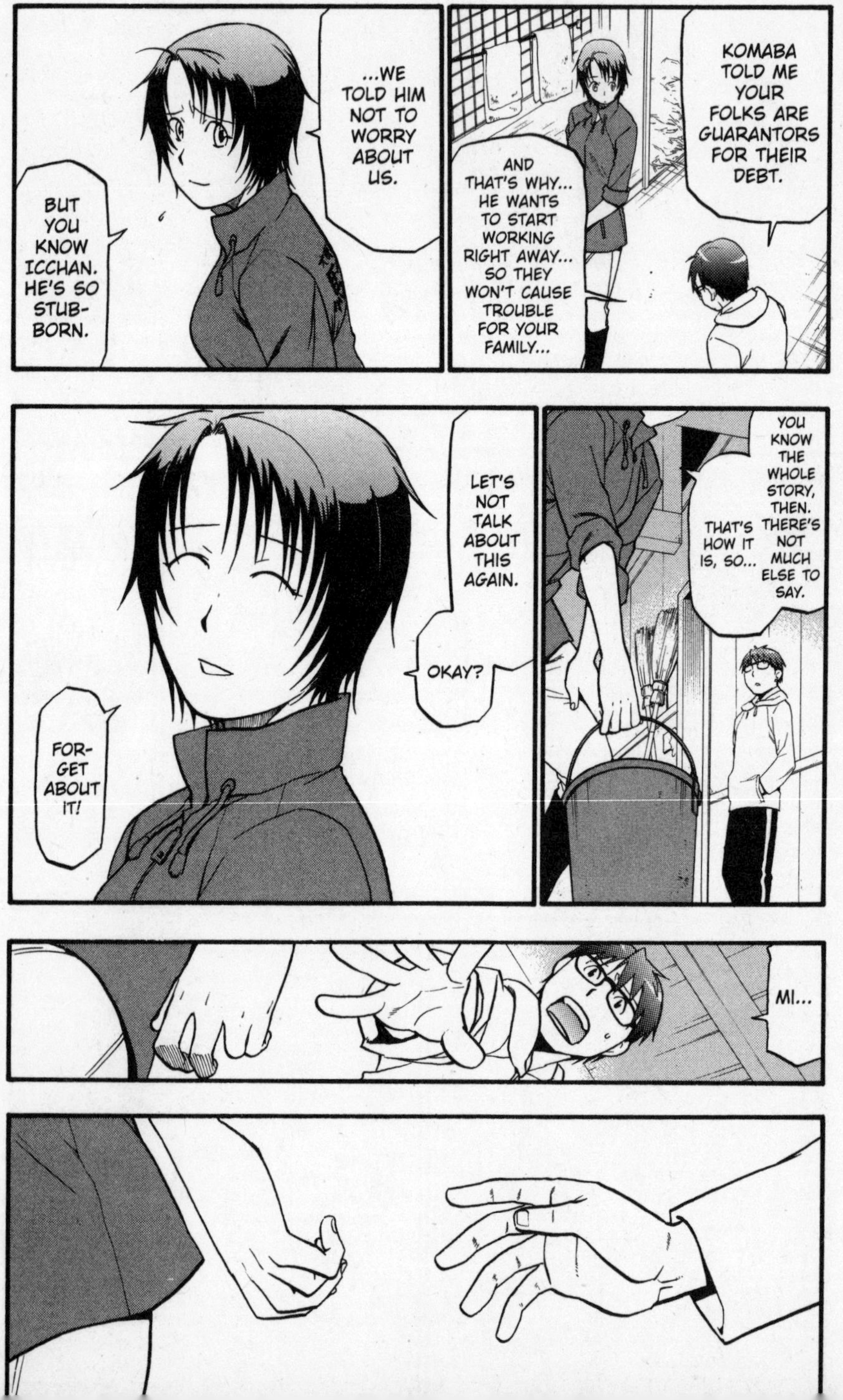
KOMABA TOLD ME YOUR FOLKS ARE GUARANTORS FOR THEIR DEBT.
AND THAT'S WHY... HE WANTS TO START WORKING RIGHT AWAY... SO THEY WON'T CAUSE TROUBLE FOR YOUR FAMILY...
...WE TOLD HIM NOT TO WORRY ABOUT US.
BUT YOU KNOW ICCHAN. HE'S SO STUBBORN.
YOU KNOW THE WHOLE STORY, THEN. THERE'S NOT MUCH ELSE TO SAY.
THAT'S HOW IT IS, SO...
LET'S NOT TALK ABOUT THIS AGAIN.
OKAY?
FORGET ABOUT IT!
MI...

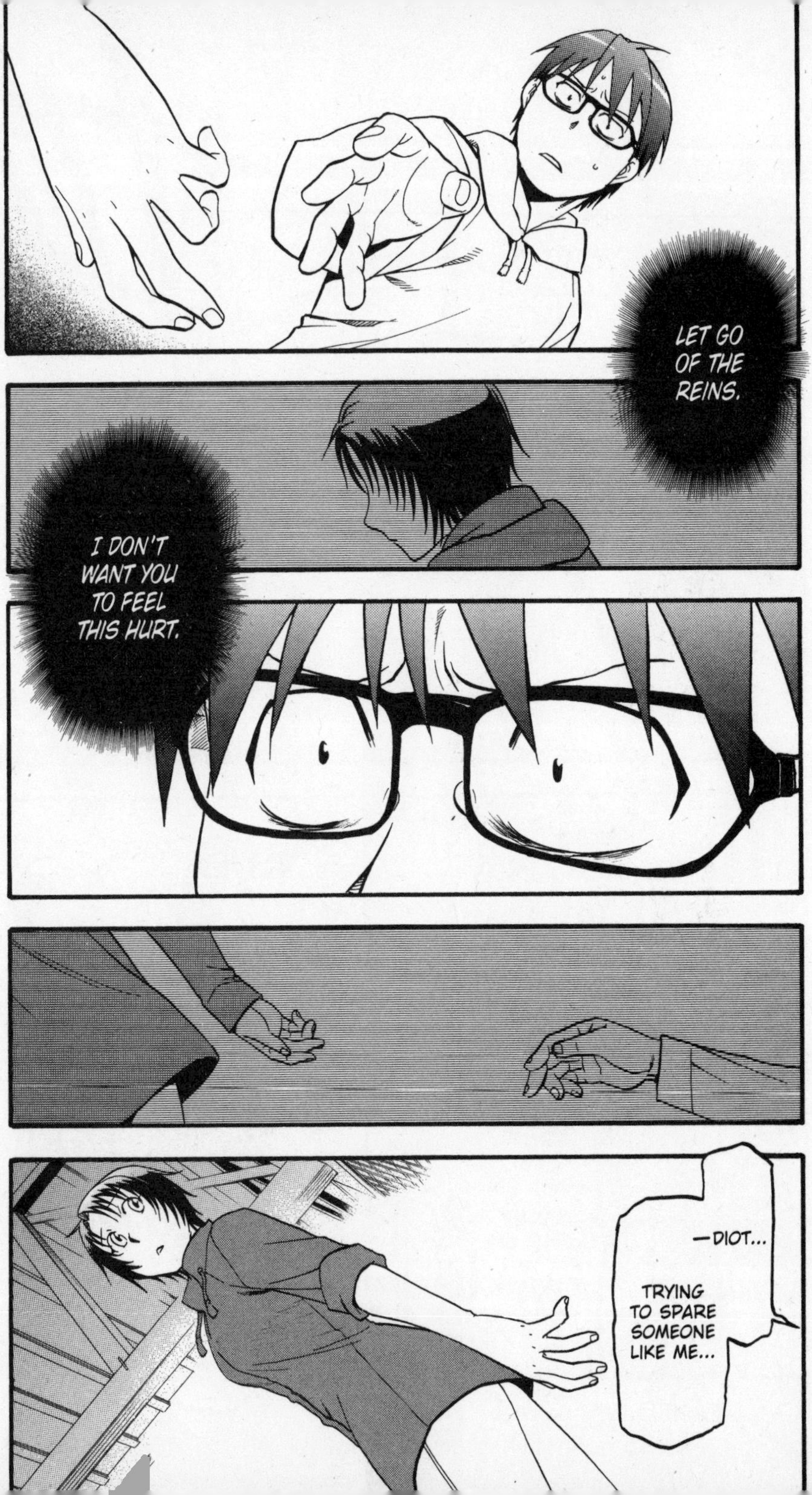
LET GO OF THE REINS.
I DON'T WANT YOU TO FEEL THIS HURT.
—DIOT...
TRYING TO SPARE SOMEONE LIKE ME...

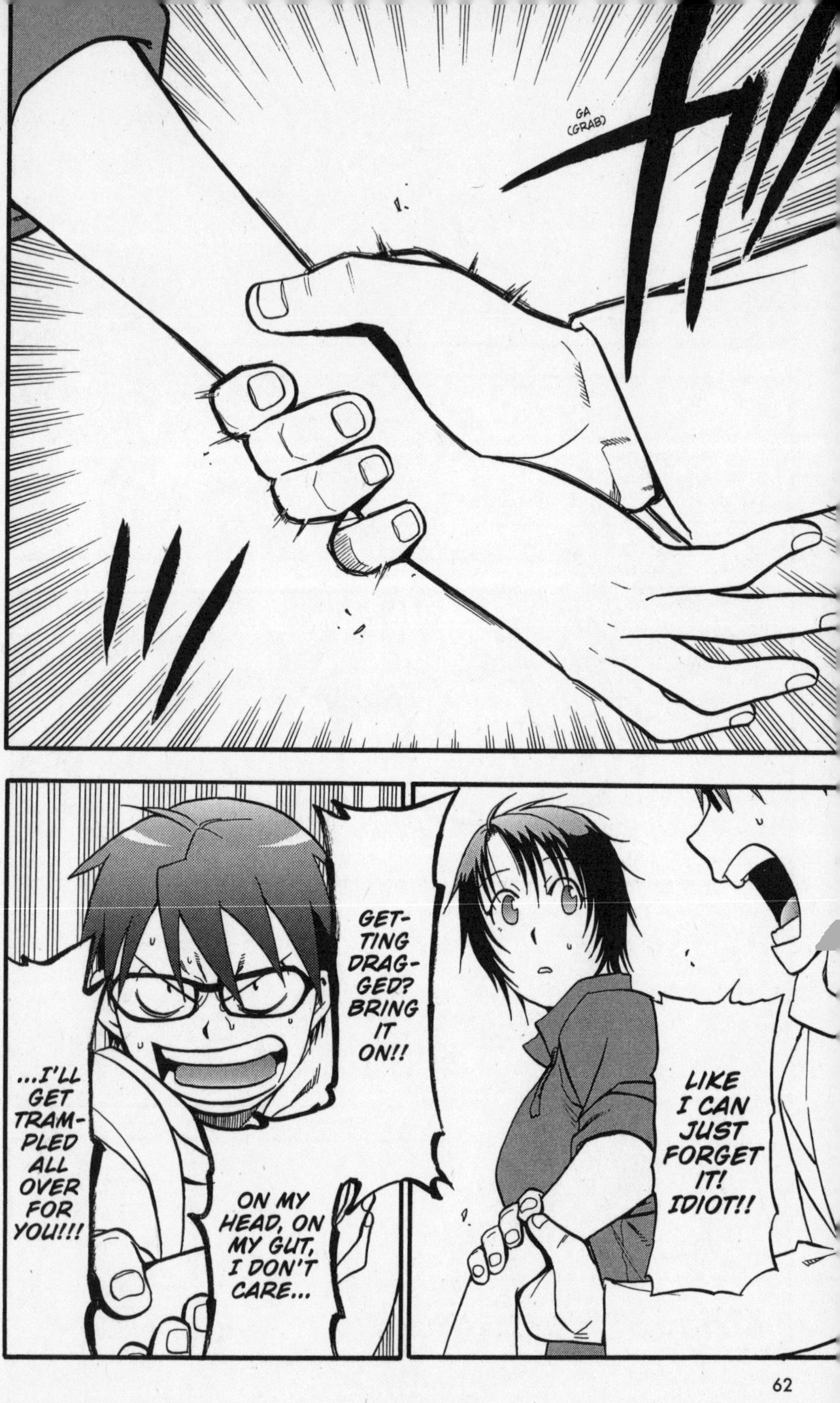
GA (GRAB)
LIKE I CAN JUST FORGET IT! IDIOT!!
GETTING DRAGGED? BRING IT ON!!
ON MY HEAD, ON MY GUT, I DON'T CARE...
...I'LL GET TRAMPLED ALL OVER FOR YOU!!!

Silver Spoon

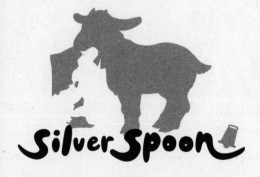

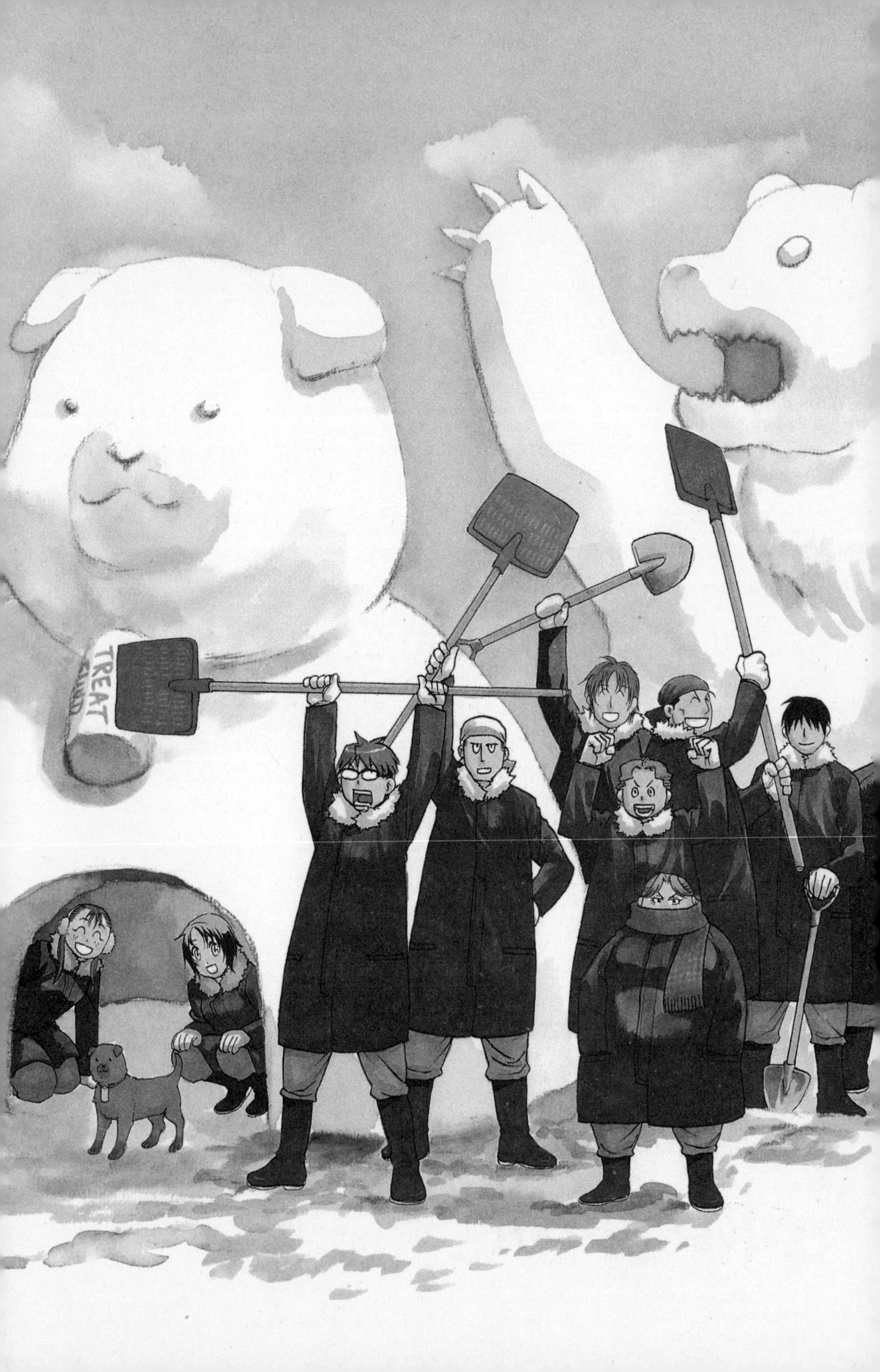
TREAT

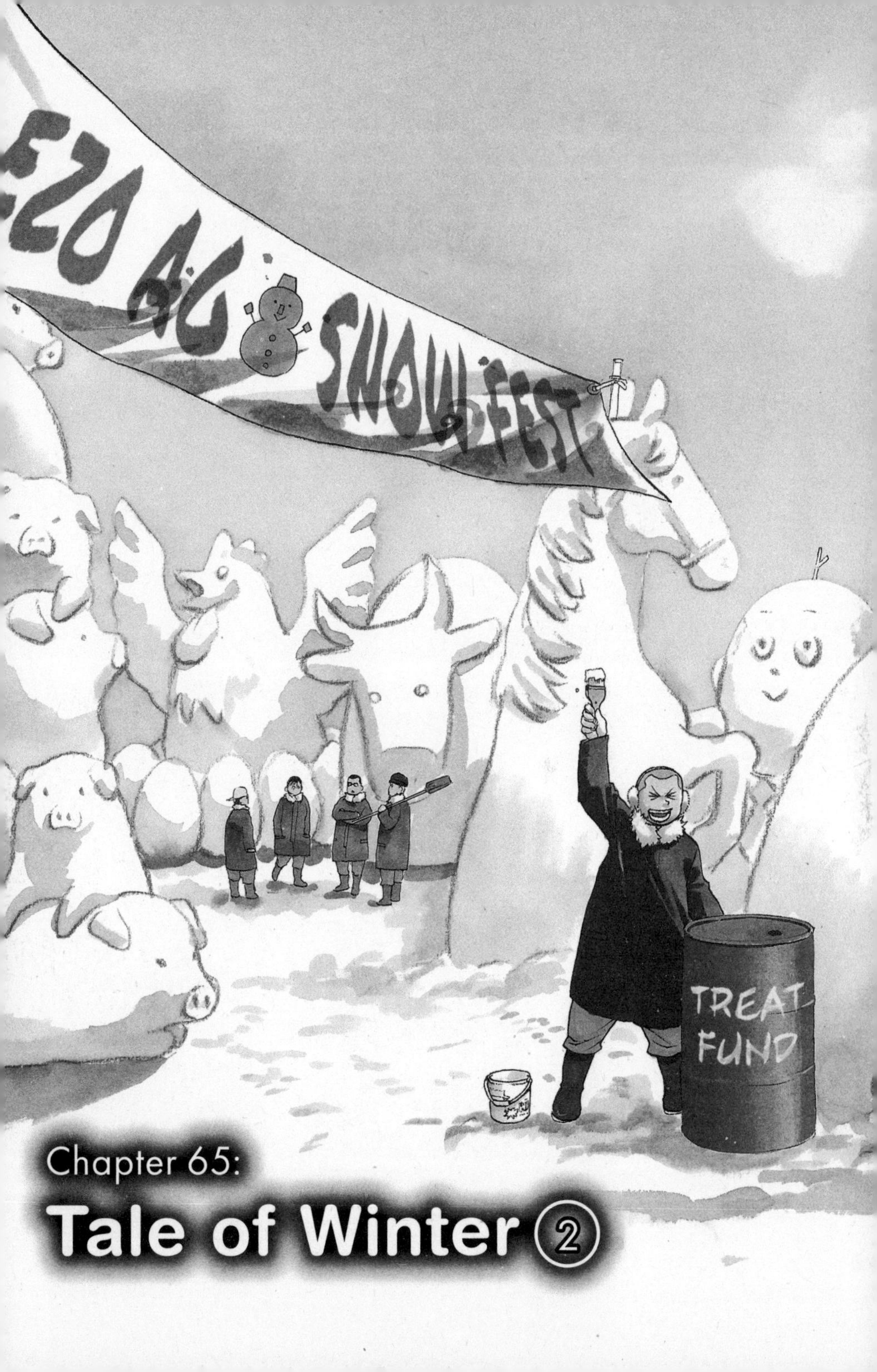
EZO AG SNOW FEST
TREAT FUND

Chapter 65:
Tale of Winter ②

CHICKEN BARN
TEACHER

ITSUKI SHIRAKABA

THEY CALL HIM
"CHICKEN-SENSEI"

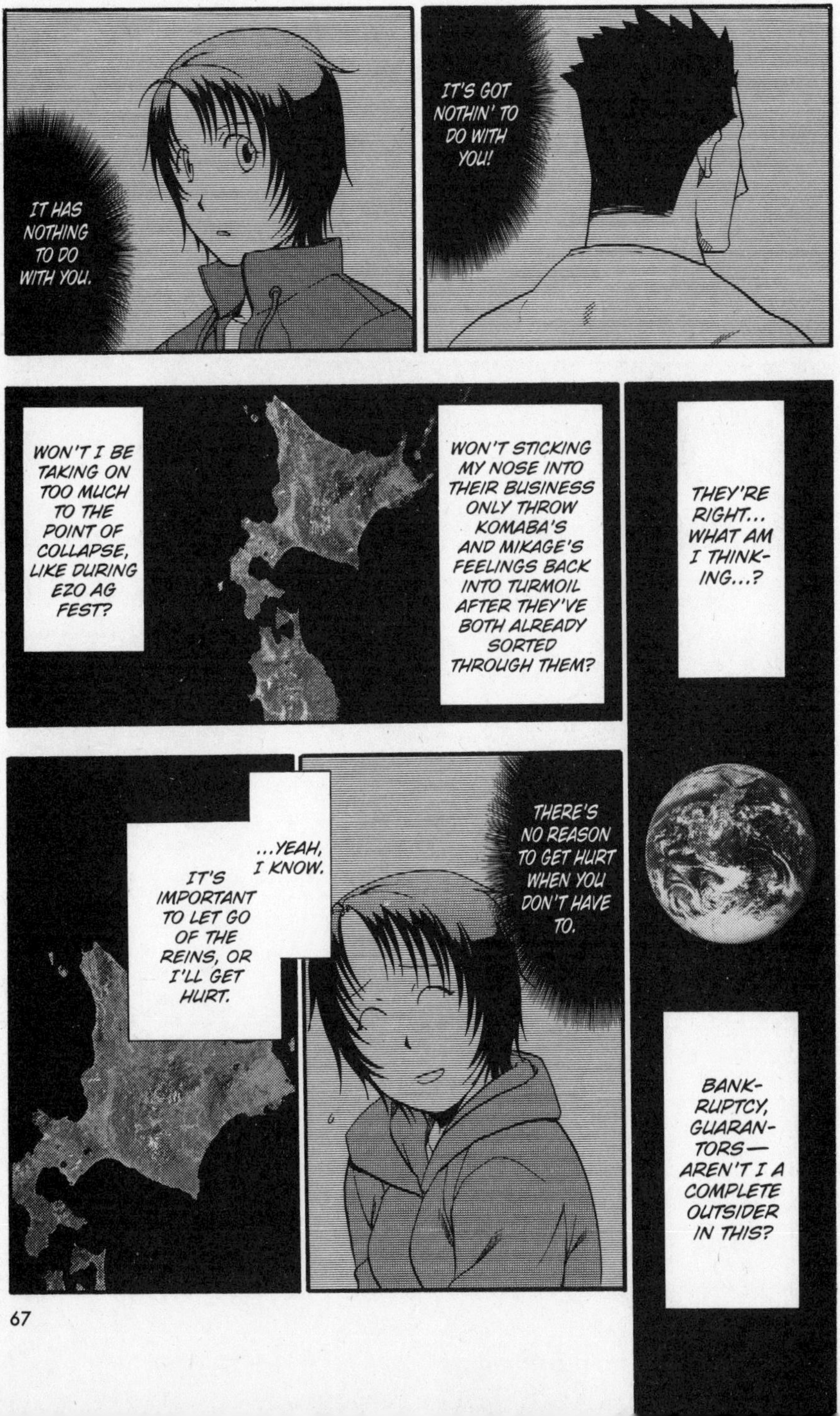
IT'S GOT NOTHIN' TO DO WITH YOU!
IT HAS NOTHING TO DO WITH YOU.
THEY'RE RIGHT... WHAT AM I THINK-ING...?
BANK-RUPTCY, GUARAN-TORS— AREN'T I A COMPLETE OUTSIDER IN THIS?
WON'T STICKING MY NOSE INTO THEIR BUSINESS ONLY THROW KOMABA'S AND MIKAGE'S FEELINGS BACK INTO TURMOIL AFTER THEY'VE BOTH ALREADY SORTED THROUGH THEM?
WON'T I BE TAKING ON TOO MUCH TO THE POINT OF COLLAPSE, LIKE DURING EZO AG FEST?
THERE'S NO REASON TO GET HURT WHEN YOU DON'T HAVE TO.
...YEAH, I KNOW.
IT'S IMPORTANT TO LET GO OF THE REINS, OR I'LL GET HURT.

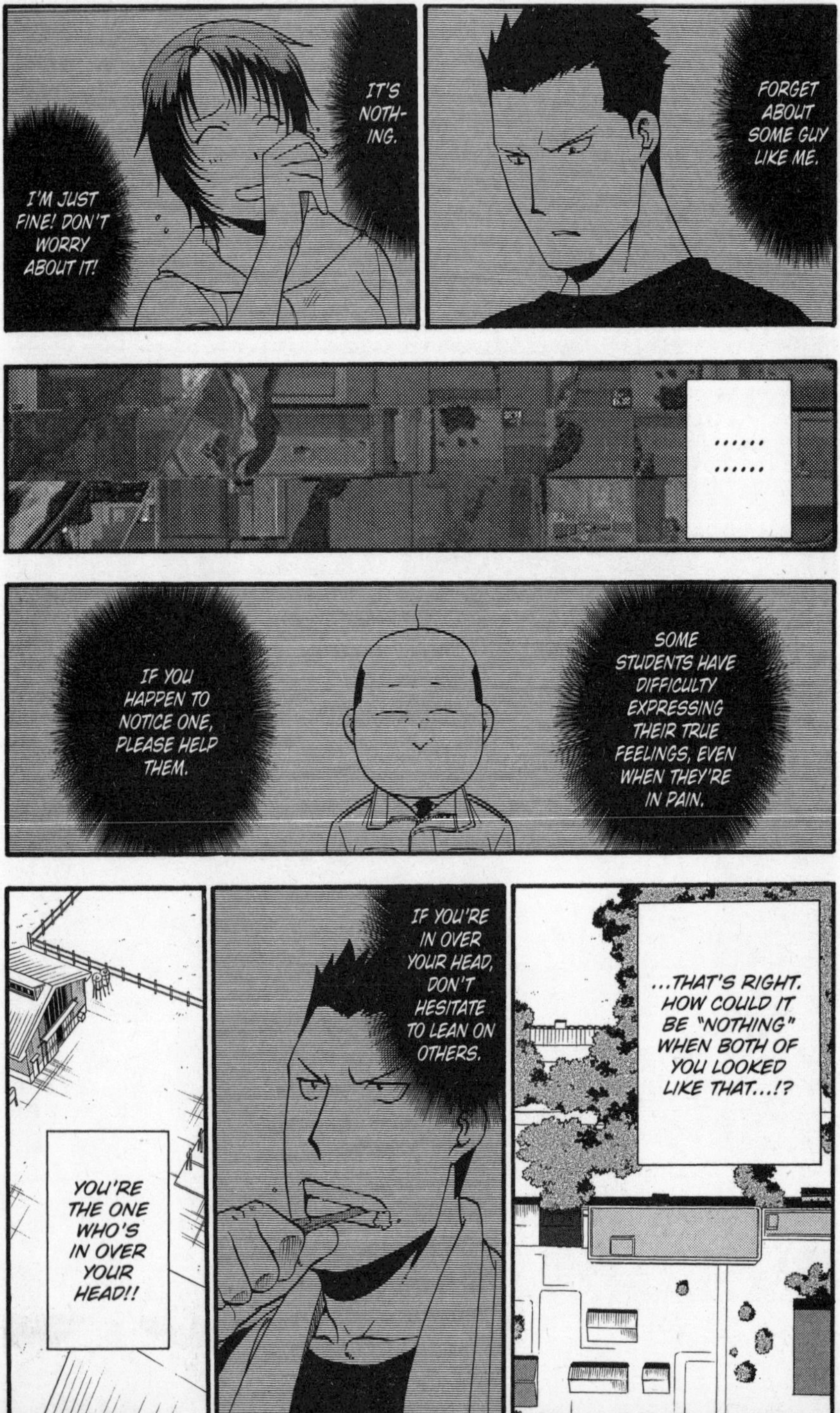
FORGET ABOUT SOME GUY LIKE ME.
IT'S NOTH-ING.
I'M JUST FINE! DON'T WORRY ABOUT IT!
......
......
SOME STUDENTS HAVE DIFFICULTY EXPRESSING THEIR TRUE FEELINGS, EVEN WHEN THEY'RE IN PAIN.
IF YOU HAPPEN TO NOTICE ONE, PLEASE HELP THEM.
...THAT'S RIGHT. HOW COULD IT BE "NOTHING" WHEN BOTH OF YOU LOOKED LIKE THAT...!?
IF YOU'RE IN OVER YOUR HEAD, DON'T HESITATE TO LEAN ON OTHERS.
YOU'RE THE ONE WHO'S IN OVER YOUR HEAD!!

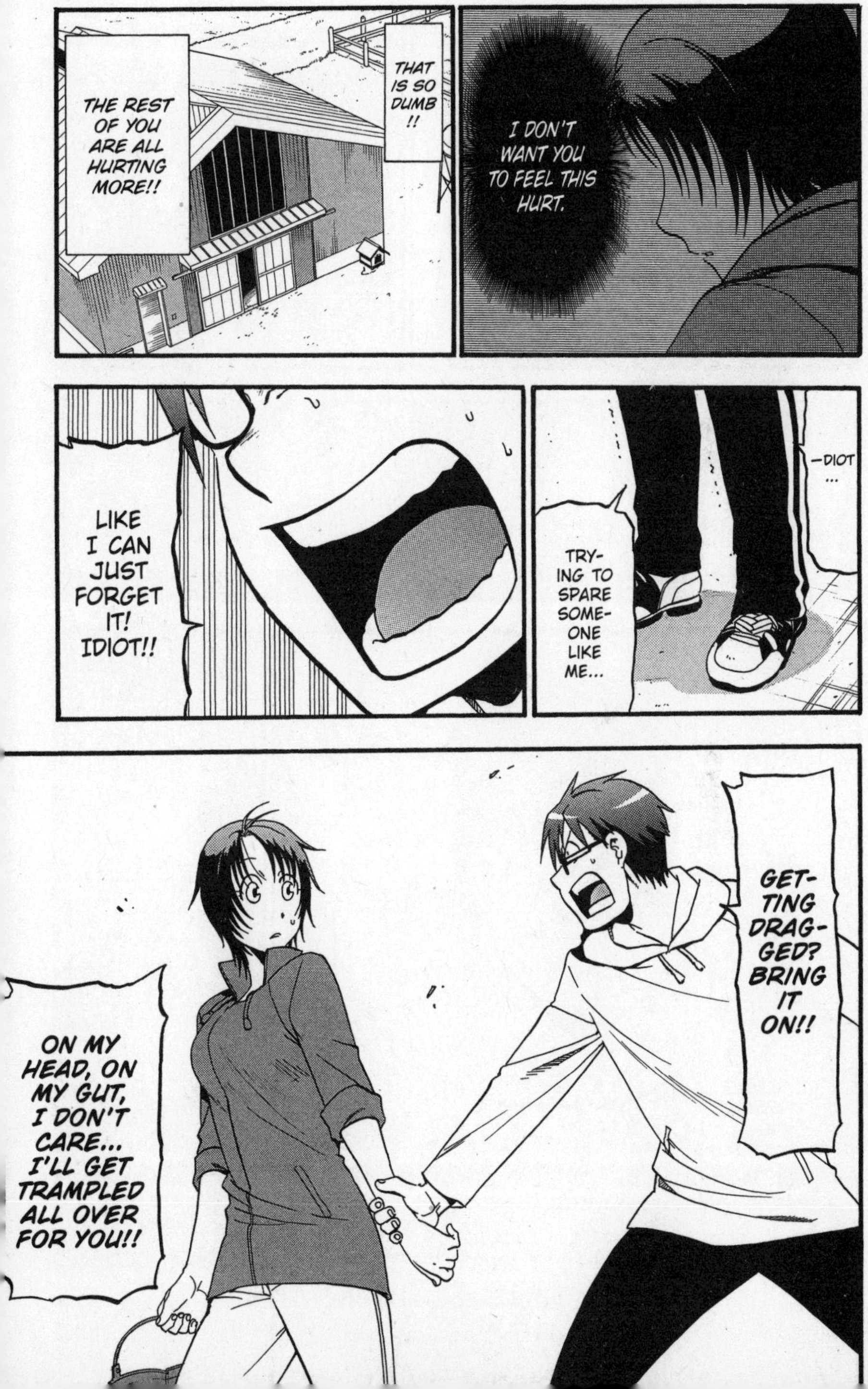
I DON'T WANT YOU TO FEEL THIS HURT.
THAT IS SO DUMB!!
THE REST OF YOU ARE ALL HURTING MORE!!
—DIOT...
TRYING TO SPARE SOMEONE LIKE ME...
LIKE I CAN JUST FORGET IT! IDIOT!!
GETTING DRAGGED? BRING IT ON!!
ON MY HEAD, ON MY GUT, I DON'T CARE... I'LL GET TRAMPLED ALL OVER FOR YOU!!

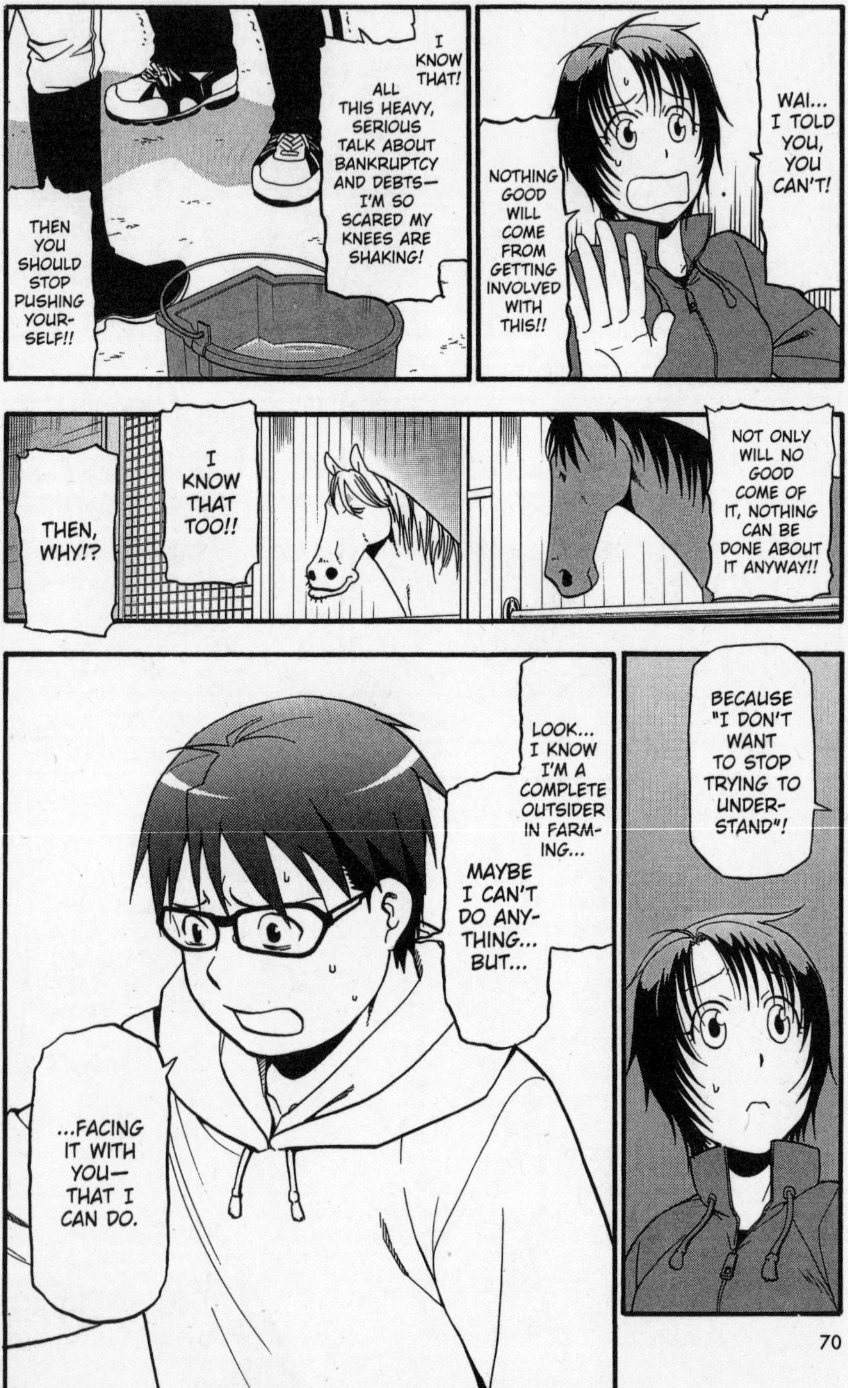
WAI... I TOLD YOU, YOU CAN'T!
NOTHING GOOD WILL COME FROM GETTING INVOLVED WITH THIS!!
I KNOW THAT!
ALL THIS HEAVY, SERIOUS TALK ABOUT BANKRUPTCY AND DEBTS—I'M SO SCARED MY KNEES ARE SHAKING!
THEN YOU SHOULD STOP PUSHING YOUR-SELF!!
NOT ONLY WILL NO GOOD COME OF IT, NOTHING CAN BE DONE ABOUT IT ANYWAY!!
I KNOW THAT TOO!!
THEN, WHY!?
BECAUSE "I DON'T WANT TO STOP TRYING TO UNDER-STAND"!
LOOK... I KNOW I'M A COMPLETE OUTSIDER IN FARM-ING...
MAYBE I CAN'T DO ANY-THING... BUT...
...FACING IT WITH YOU—THAT I CAN DO.

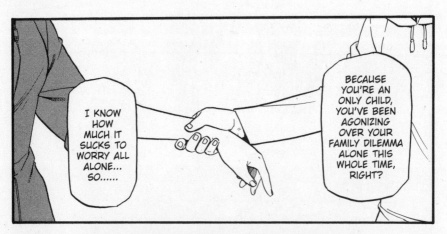

BECAUSE YOU'RE AN ONLY CHILD, YOU'VE BEEN AGONIZING OVER YOUR FAMILY DILEMMA ALONE THIS WHOLE TIME, RIGHT?
I KNOW HOW MUCH IT SUCKS TO WORRY ALL ALONE... SO......
......THIS IS WHY I DIDN'T WANT TO...
YOU'VE GOT A GOOD HEART, SO EVEN IF YOU KNEW IT WAS SOMETHIN' DOWNRIGHT AWFUL, YA COULDN'T JUS' LEAVE US BE, COULD YA?

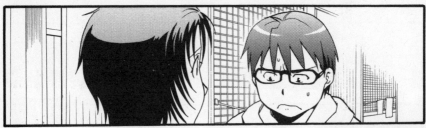

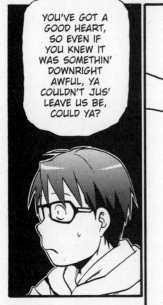

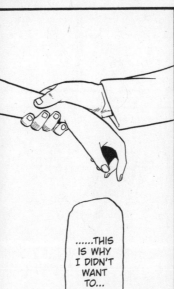

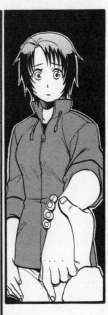

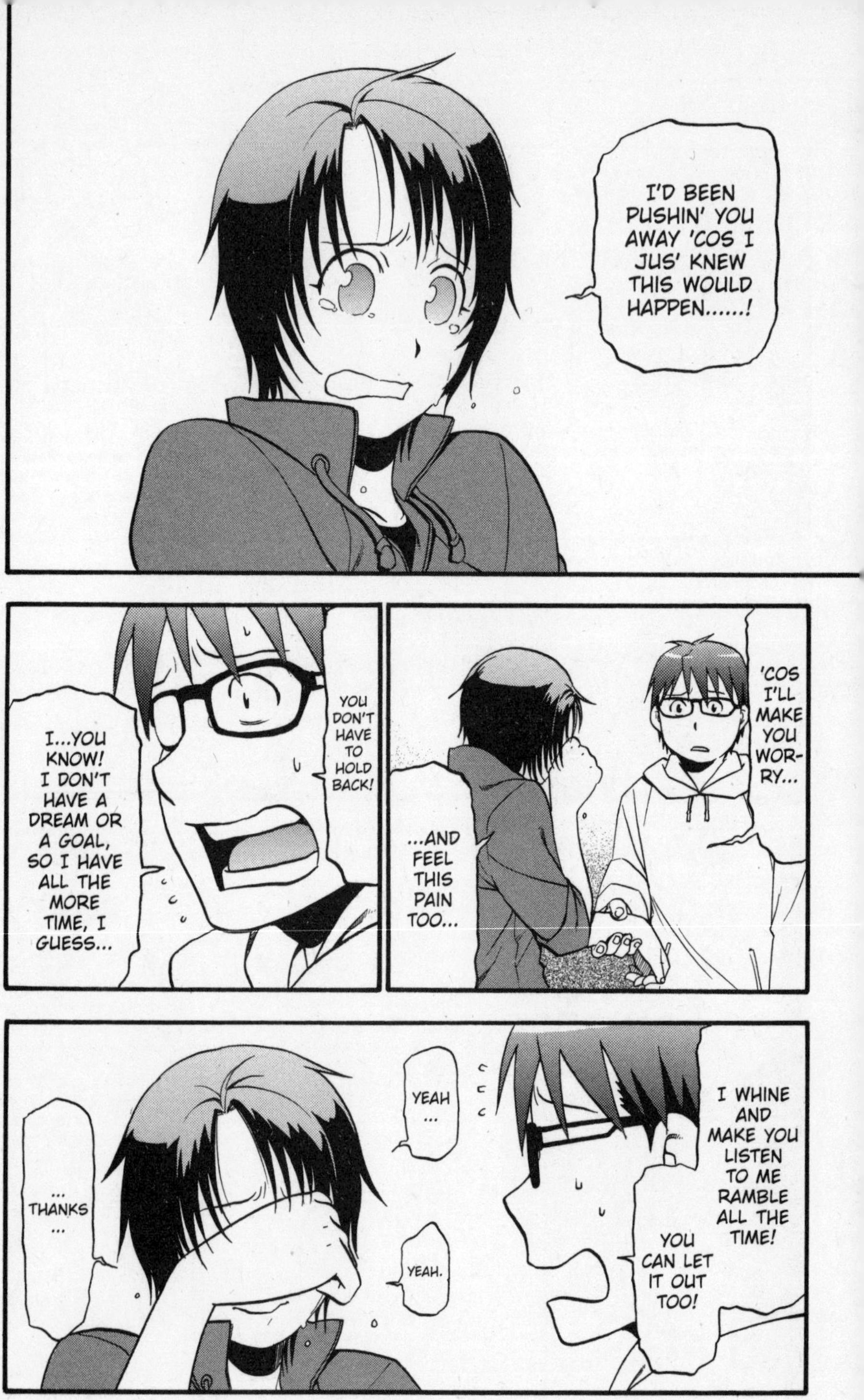
I'D BEEN PUSHIN' YOU AWAY 'COS I JUS' KNEW THIS WOULD HAPPEN......!
'COS I'LL MAKE YOU WORRY...
...AND FEEL THIS PAIN TOO...
YOU DON'T HAVE TO HOLD BACK!
I...YOU KNOW! I DON'T HAVE A DREAM OR A GOAL, SO I HAVE ALL THE MORE TIME, I GUESS...
I WHINE AND MAKE YOU LISTEN TO ME RAMBLE ALL THE TIME!
YOU CAN LET IT OUT TOO!
YEAH...
YEAH.
...THANKS...

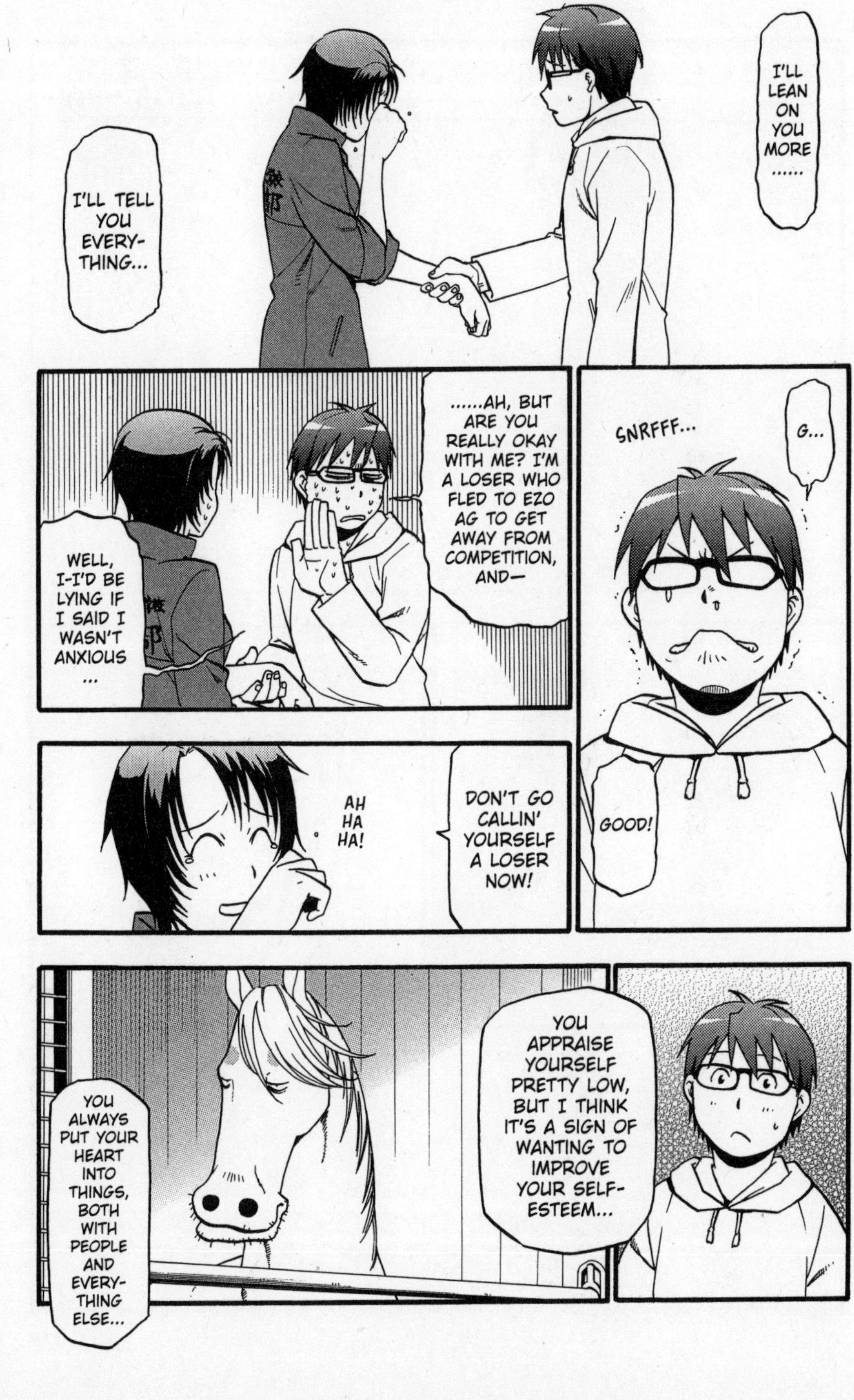
I'LL LEAN ON YOU MORE......
I'LL TELL YOU EVERY-THING...
SNRFFF...
G...
GOOD!
......AH, BUT ARE YOU REALLY OKAY WITH ME? I'M A LOSER WHO FLED TO EZO AG TO GET AWAY FROM COMPETITION, AND—
WELL, I-I'D BE LYING IF I SAID I WASN'T ANXIOUS...
DON'T GO CALLIN' YOURSELF A LOSER NOW!
AH HA HA!
YOU APPRAISE YOURSELF PRETTY LOW, BUT I THINK IT'S A SIGN OF WANTING TO IMPROVE YOUR SELF-ESTEEM...
YOU ALWAYS PUT YOUR HEART INTO THINGS, BOTH WITH PEOPLE AND EVERY-THING ELSE...

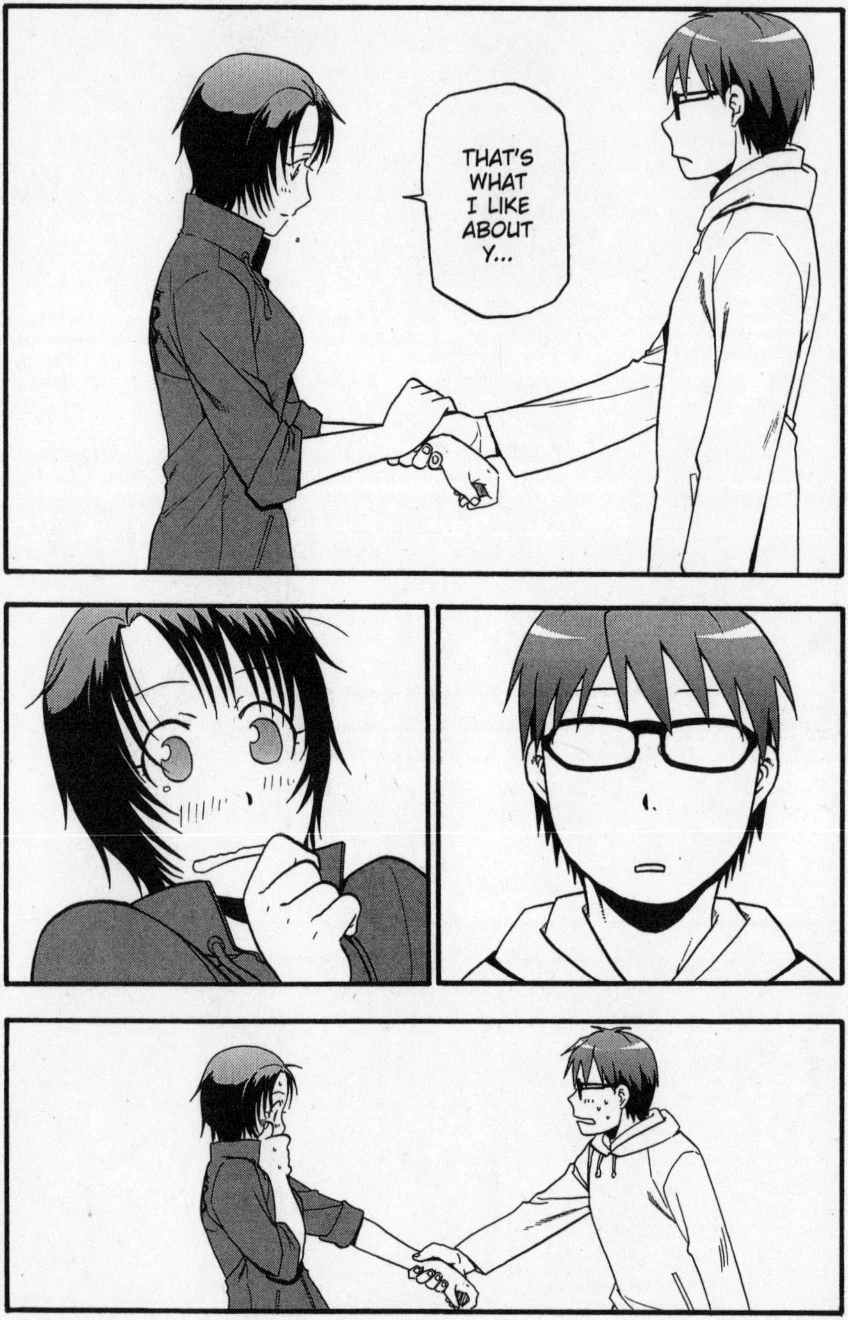
THAT'S WHAT I LIKE ABOUT Y...

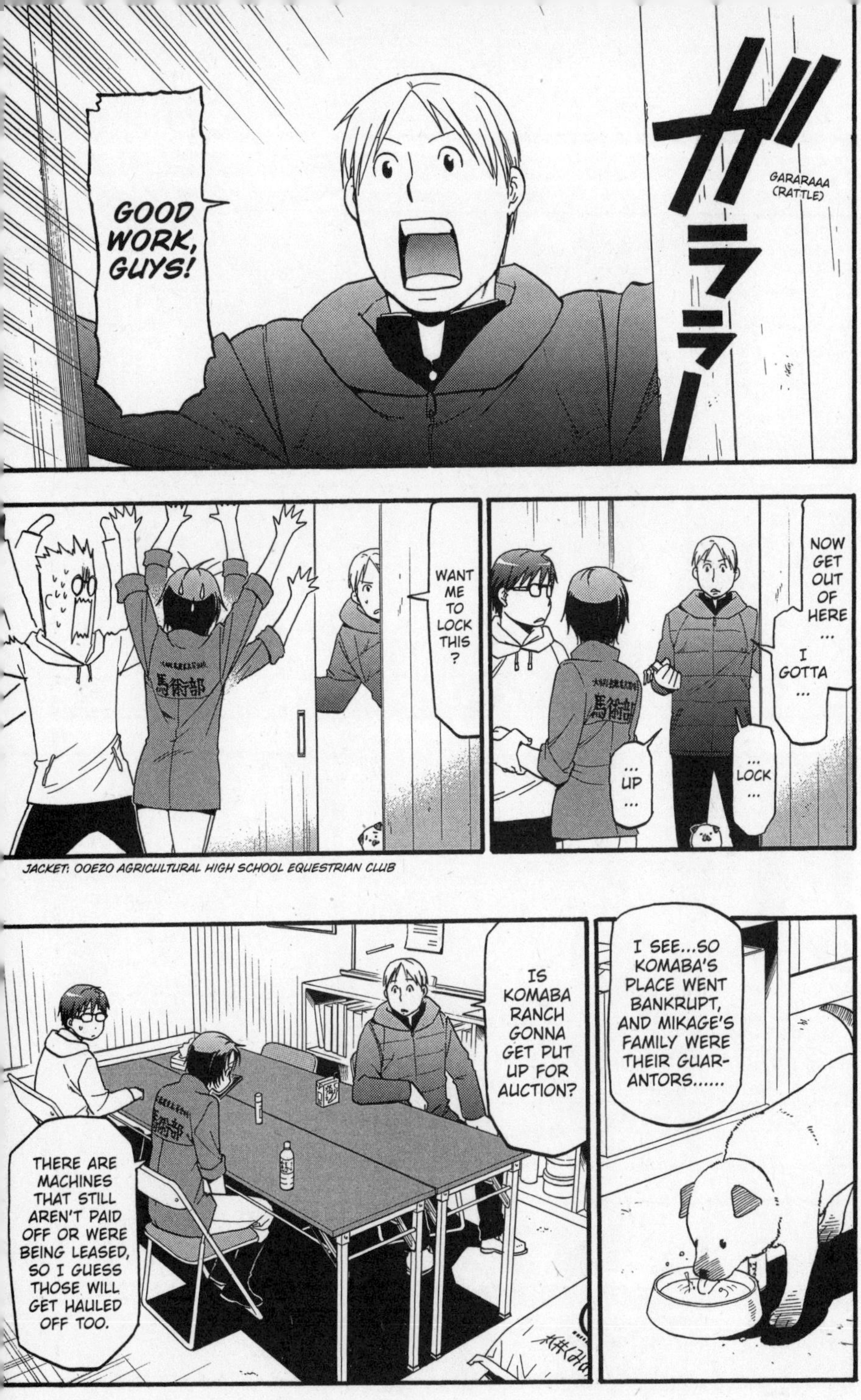
GARARAAA (RATTLE)
GOOD WORK, GUYS!
NOW GET OUT OF HERE... I GOTTA...
...LOCK...
...UP...
WANT ME TO LOCK THIS?
JACKET: OOEZO AGRICULTURAL HIGH SCHOOL EQUESTRIAN CLUB
I SEE...SO KOMABA'S PLACE WENT BANKRUPT, AND MIKAGE'S FAMILY WERE THEIR GUAR-ANTORS......
IS KOMABA RANCH GONNA GET PUT UP FOR AUCTION?
THERE ARE MACHINES THAT STILL AREN'T PAID OFF OR WERE BEING LEASED, SO I GUESS THOSE WILL GET HAULED OFF TOO.

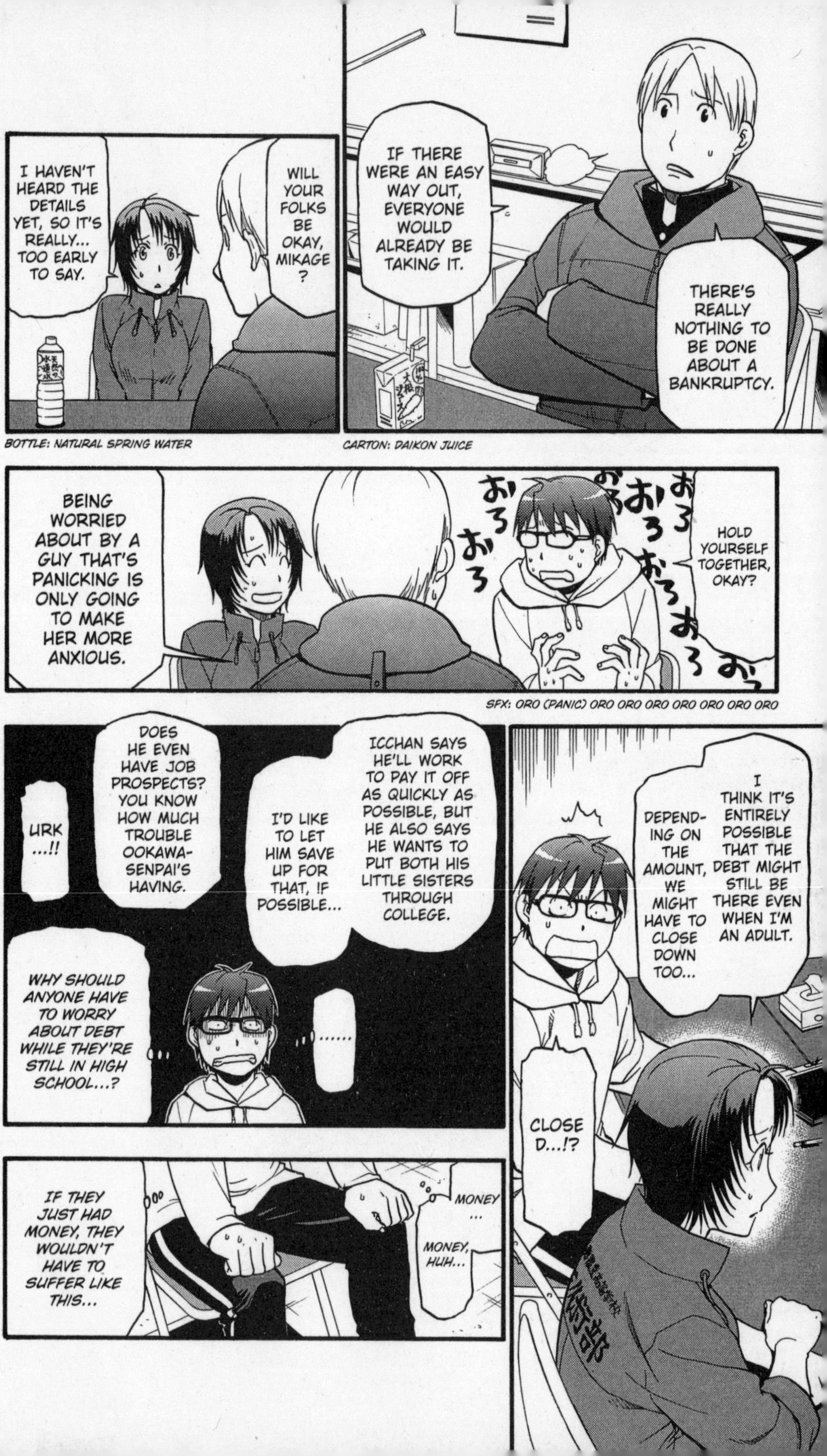
THERE'S REALLY NOTHING TO BE DONE ABOUT A BANKRUPTCY.
IF THERE WERE AN EASY WAY OUT, EVERYONE WOULD ALREADY BE TAKING IT.
CARTON: DAIKON JUICE
WILL YOUR FOLKS BE OKAY, MIKAGE?
I HAVEN'T HEARD THE DETAILS YET, SO IT'S REALLY... TOO EARLY TO SAY.
BOTTLE: NATURAL SPRING WATER
HOLD YOURSELF TOGETHER, OKAY?
BEING WORRIED ABOUT BY A GUY THAT'S PANICKING IS ONLY GOING TO MAKE HER MORE ANXIOUS.
SFX: ORO (PANIC) ORO ORO ORO ORO ORO ORO ORO
I THINK IT'S ENTIRELY POSSIBLE THAT THE DEBT MIGHT STILL BE THERE EVEN WHEN I'M AN ADULT.
DEPENDING ON THE AMOUNT, WE MIGHT HAVE TO CLOSE DOWN TOO...
CLOSE D...!?
ICCHAN SAYS HE'LL WORK TO PAY IT OFF AS QUICKLY AS POSSIBLE, BUT HE ALSO SAYS HE WANTS TO PUT BOTH HIS LITTLE SISTERS THROUGH COLLEGE.
I'D LIKE TO LET HIM SAVE UP FOR THAT, IF POSSIBLE...
DOES HE EVEN HAVE JOB PROSPECTS? YOU KNOW HOW MUCH TROUBLE OOKAWA-SENPAI'S HAVING.
URK ...!!
......
WHY SHOULD ANYONE HAVE TO WORRY ABOUT DEBT WHILE THEY'RE STILL IN HIGH SCHOOL...?
MONEY...
MONEY, HUH...
IF THEY JUST HAD MONEY, THEY WOULDN'T HAVE TO SUFFER LIKE THIS...

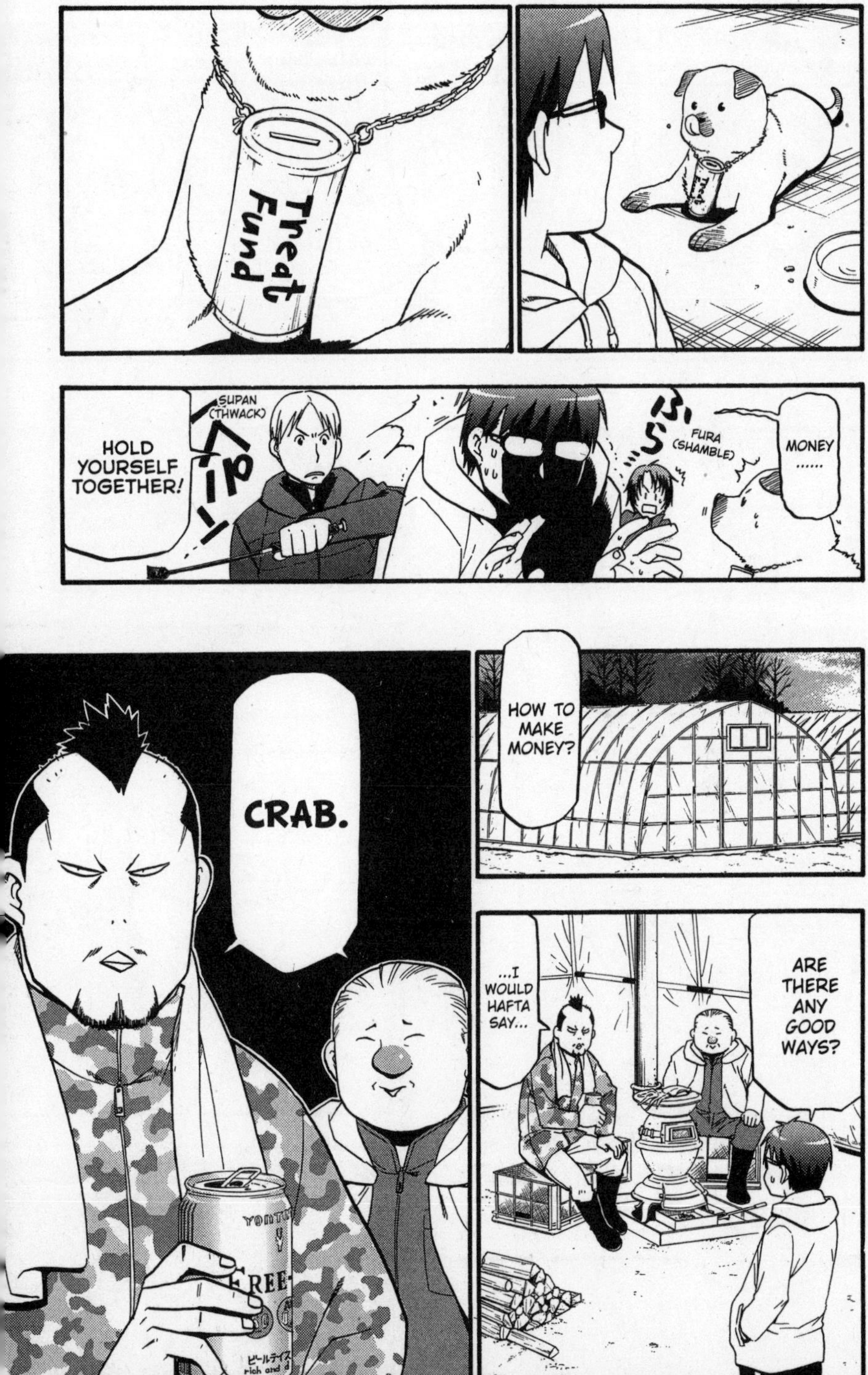
Treat Fund
MONEY ......
ふら
FURA (SHAMBLE)
HOLD YOURSELF TOGETHER!
スパーン
SUPAN (THWACK)
HOW TO MAKE MONEY?
ARE THERE ANY GOOD WAYS?
...I WOULD HAFTA SAY...
CRAB.

MAKE NICE WITH THE RUSSIAN MAFIA'S SHIPS, THEN PAY A LIIIITTLE VISIT INTO THEIR WATERS...

THANK YOU FOR YOUR TIME.

ピシャーン

PISHAN (SHUT)

MAKING MONEY... MAKING MONEY, HMM...

WELL, THERE IS A SIMPLE WAY TO INCREASE PROFITS.

REALLY, SIR!? HOW!?

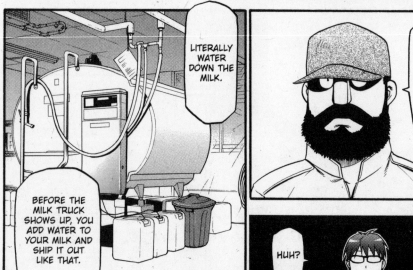

WATER IT DOWN.

LITERALLY WATER DOWN THE MILK.

BEFORE THE MILK TRUCK SHOWS UP, YOU ADD WATER TO YOUR MILK AND SHIP IT OUT LIKE THAT.

HUH?

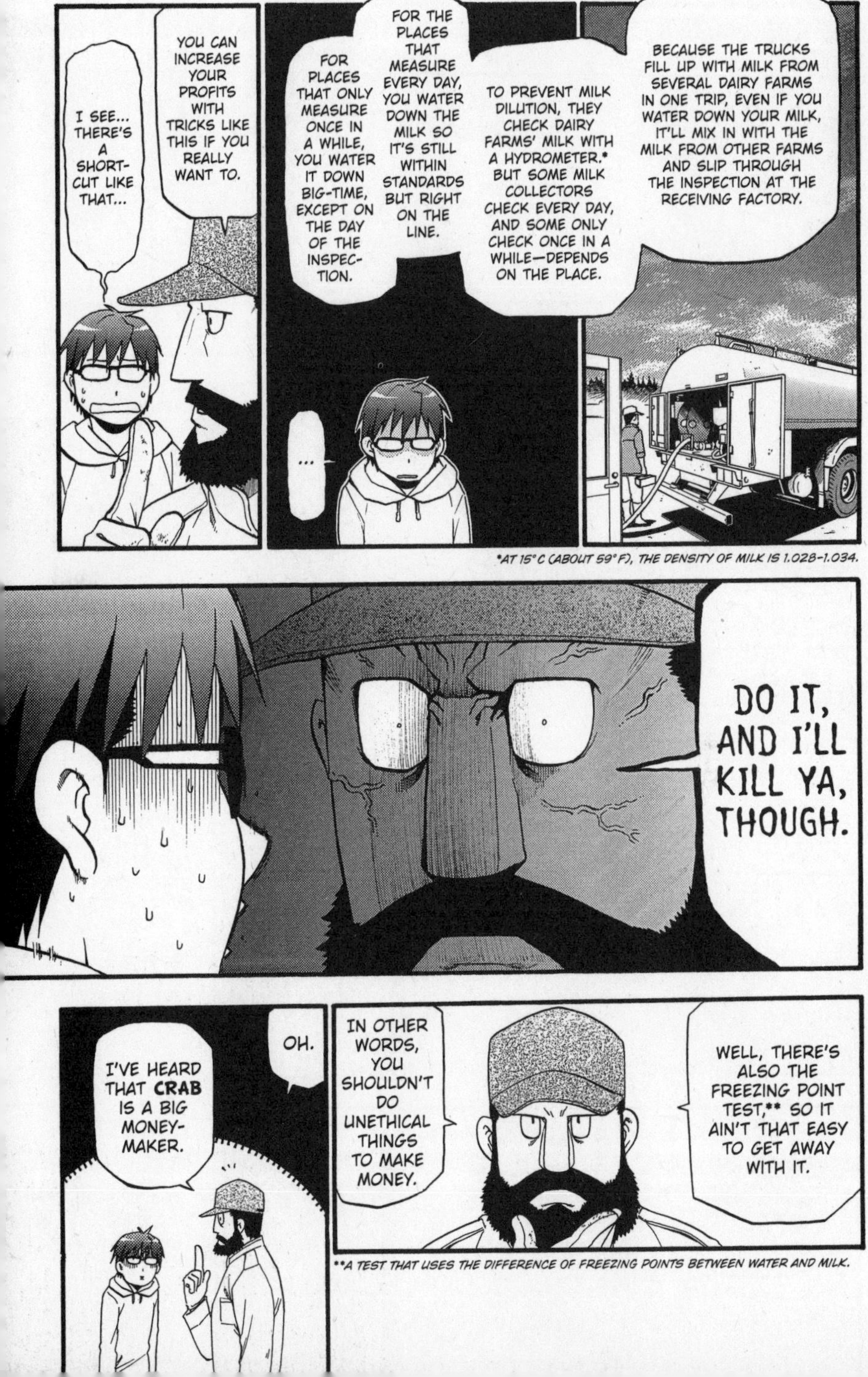
BECAUSE THE TRUCKS FILL UP WITH MILK FROM SEVERAL DAIRY FARMS IN ONE TRIP, EVEN IF YOU WATER DOWN YOUR MILK, IT'LL MIX IN WITH THE MILK FROM OTHER FARMS AND SLIP THROUGH THE INSPECTION AT THE RECEIVING FACTORY.
TO PREVENT MILK DILUTION, THEY CHECK DAIRY FARMS' MILK WITH A HYDROMETER.* BUT SOME MILK COLLECTORS CHECK EVERY DAY, AND SOME ONLY CHECK ONCE IN A WHILE—DEPENDS ON THE PLACE.
FOR THE PLACES THAT MEASURE EVERY DAY, YOU WATER DOWN THE MILK SO IT'S STILL WITHIN STANDARDS BUT RIGHT ON THE LINE.
FOR PLACES THAT ONLY MEASURE ONCE IN A WHILE, YOU WATER IT DOWN BIG-TIME, EXCEPT ON THE DAY OF THE INSPECTION.
...
YOU CAN INCREASE YOUR PROFITS WITH TRICKS LIKE THIS IF YOU REALLY WANT TO.
I SEE... THERE'S A SHORTCUT LIKE THAT...
DO IT, AND I'LL KILL YA, THOUGH.
WELL, THERE'S ALSO THE FREEZING POINT TEST,** SO IT AIN'T THAT EASY TO GET AWAY WITH IT.
IN OTHER WORDS, YOU SHOULDN'T DO UNETHICAL THINGS TO MAKE MONEY.
OH.
I'VE HEARD THAT **CRAB** IS A BIG MONEY-MAKER.

*AT 15° C (ABOUT 59° F), THE DENSITY OF MILK IS 1.028–1.034.

**A TEST THAT USES THE DIFFERENCE OF FREEZING POINTS BETWEEN WATER AND MILK.

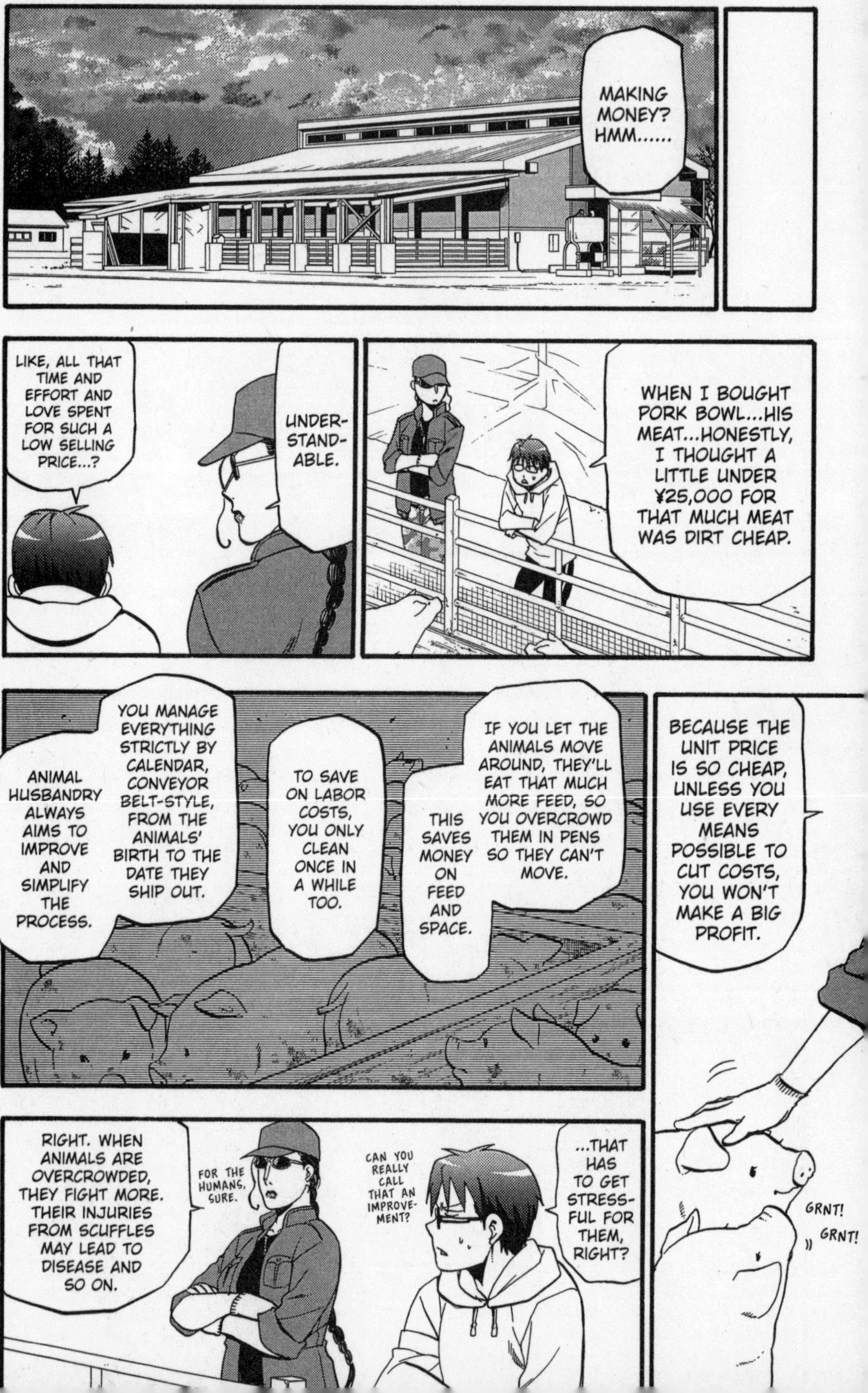
MAKING MONEY? HMM......
WHEN I BOUGHT PORK BOWL...HIS MEAT...HONESTLY, I THOUGHT A LITTLE UNDER ¥25,000 FOR THAT MUCH MEAT WAS DIRT CHEAP.
UNDER-STANDABLE.
LIKE, ALL THAT TIME AND EFFORT AND LOVE SPENT FOR SUCH A LOW SELLING PRICE...?
BECAUSE THE UNIT PRICE IS SO CHEAP, UNLESS YOU USE EVERY MEANS POSSIBLE TO CUT COSTS, YOU WON'T MAKE A BIG PROFIT.
GRNT!
GRNT!
IF YOU LET THE ANIMALS MOVE AROUND, THEY'LL EAT THAT MUCH MORE FEED, SO YOU OVERCROWD THEM IN PENS SO THEY CAN'T MOVE.
THIS SAVES MONEY ON FEED AND SPACE.
TO SAVE ON LABOR COSTS, YOU ONLY CLEAN ONCE IN A WHILE TOO.
YOU MANAGE EVERYTHING STRICTLY BY CALENDAR, CONVEYOR BELT-STYLE, FROM THE ANIMALS' BIRTH TO THE DATE THEY SHIP OUT.
ANIMAL HUSBANDRY ALWAYS AIMS TO IMPROVE AND SIMPLIFY THE PROCESS.
...THAT HAS TO GET STRESS-FUL FOR THEM, RIGHT?
CAN YOU REALLY CALL THAT AN IMPROVE-MENT?
FOR THE HUMANS, SURE.
RIGHT. WHEN ANIMALS ARE OVERCROWDED, THEY FIGHT MORE. THEIR INJURIES FROM SCUFFLES MAY LEAD TO DISEASE AND SO ON.

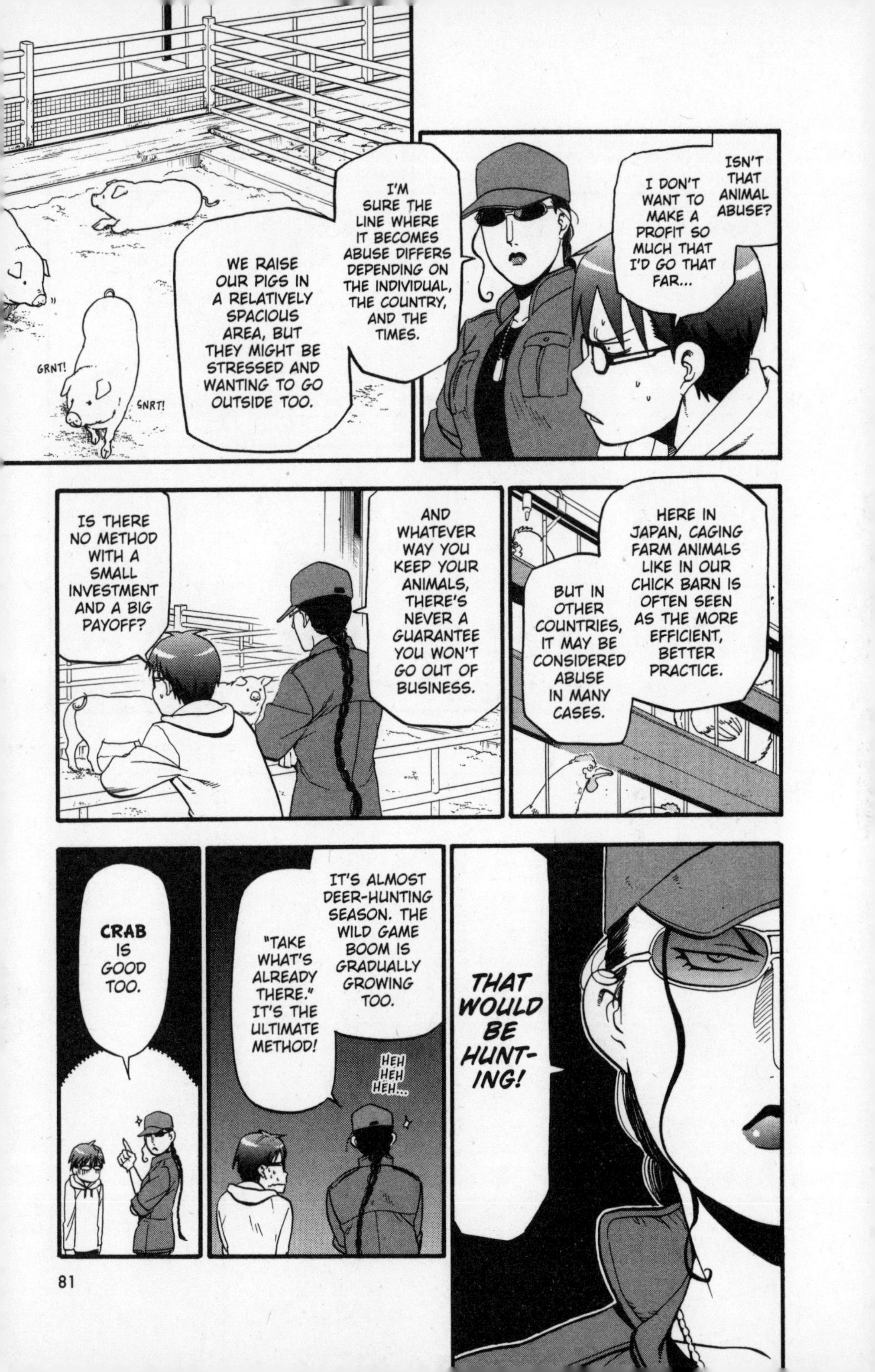
ISN'T THAT ANIMAL ABUSE?
I DON'T WANT TO MAKE A PROFIT SO MUCH THAT I'D GO THAT FAR...
I'M SURE THE LINE WHERE IT BECOMES ABUSE DIFFERS DEPENDING ON THE INDIVIDUAL, THE COUNTRY, AND THE TIMES.
WE RAISE OUR PIGS IN A RELATIVELY SPACIOUS AREA, BUT THEY MIGHT BE STRESSED AND WANTING TO GO OUTSIDE TOO.
GRNT!
SNRT!
HERE IN JAPAN, CAGING FARM ANIMALS LIKE IN OUR CHICK BARN IS OFTEN SEEN AS THE MORE EFFICIENT, BETTER PRACTICE.
BUT IN OTHER COUNTRIES, IT MAY BE CONSIDERED ABUSE IN MANY CASES.
AND WHATEVER WAY YOU KEEP YOUR ANIMALS, THERE'S NEVER A GUARANTEE YOU WON'T GO OUT OF BUSINESS.
IS THERE NO METHOD WITH A SMALL INVESTMENT AND A BIG PAYOFF?
THAT WOULD BE HUNT-ING!
IT'S ALMOST DEER-HUNTING SEASON. THE WILD GAME BOOM IS GRADUALLY GROWING TOO.
"TAKE WHAT'S ALREADY THERE." IT'S THE ULTIMATE METHOD!
HEH HEH HEH...
CRAB IS GOOD TOO.

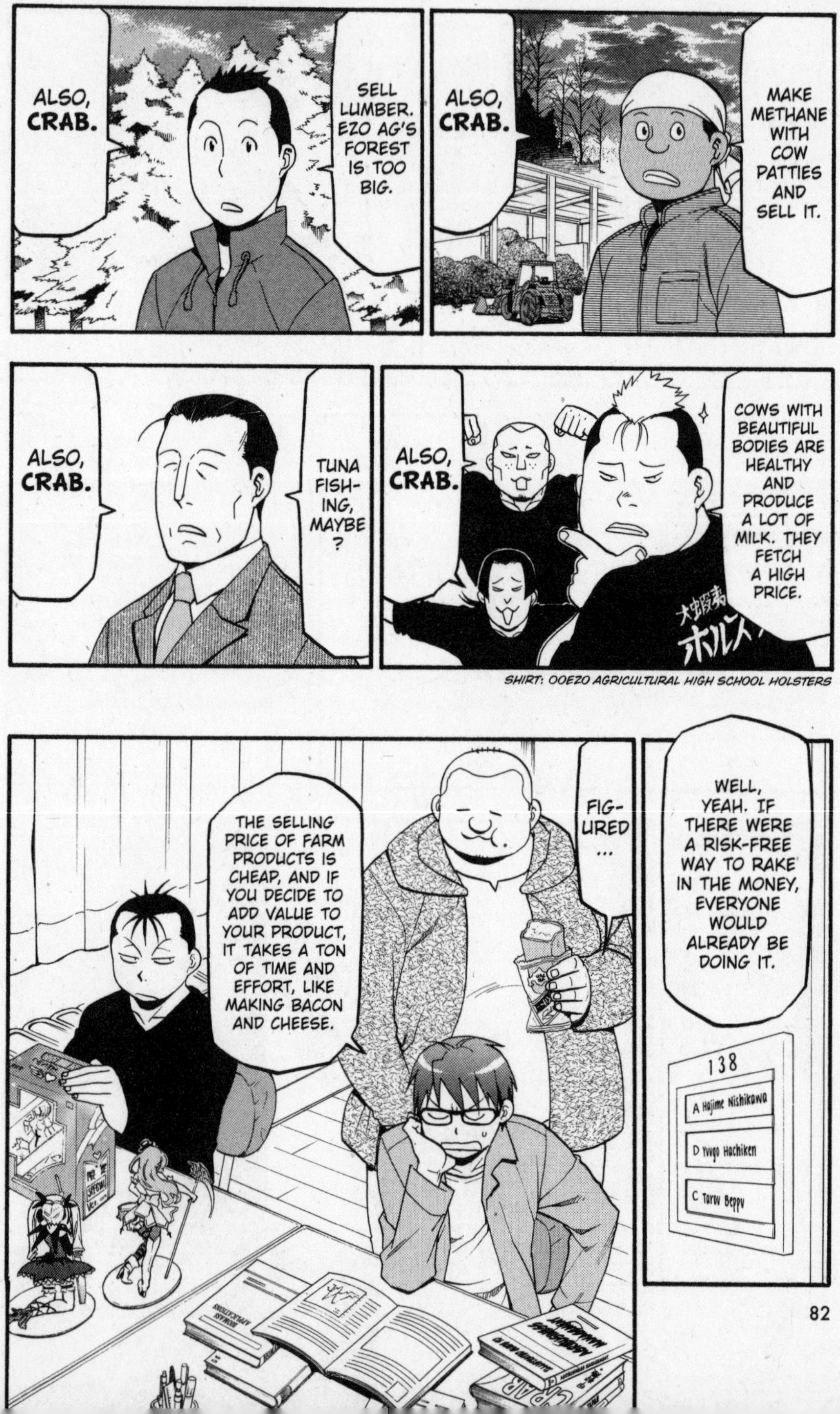
MAKE METHANE WITH COW PATTIES AND SELL IT.
ALSO, CRAB.
SELL LUMBER. EZO AG'S FOREST IS TOO BIG.
ALSO, CRAB.
COWS WITH BEAUTIFUL BODIES ARE HEALTHY AND PRODUCE A LOT OF MILK. THEY FETCH A HIGH PRICE.
ALSO, CRAB.
TUNA FISHING, MAYBE?
ALSO, CRAB.
SHIRT: OOEZO AGRICULTURAL HIGH SCHOOL HOLSTERS
WELL, YEAH. IF THERE WERE A RISK-FREE WAY TO RAKE IN THE MONEY, EVERYONE WOULD ALREADY BE DOING IT.
138
A Hajime Nishikawa
D Yuugo Hachiken
C Tarou Beppu
FIGURED...
THE SELLING PRICE OF FARM PRODUCTS IS CHEAP, AND IF YOU DECIDE TO ADD VALUE TO YOUR PRODUCT, IT TAKES A TON OF TIME AND EFFORT, LIKE MAKING BACON AND CHEESE.

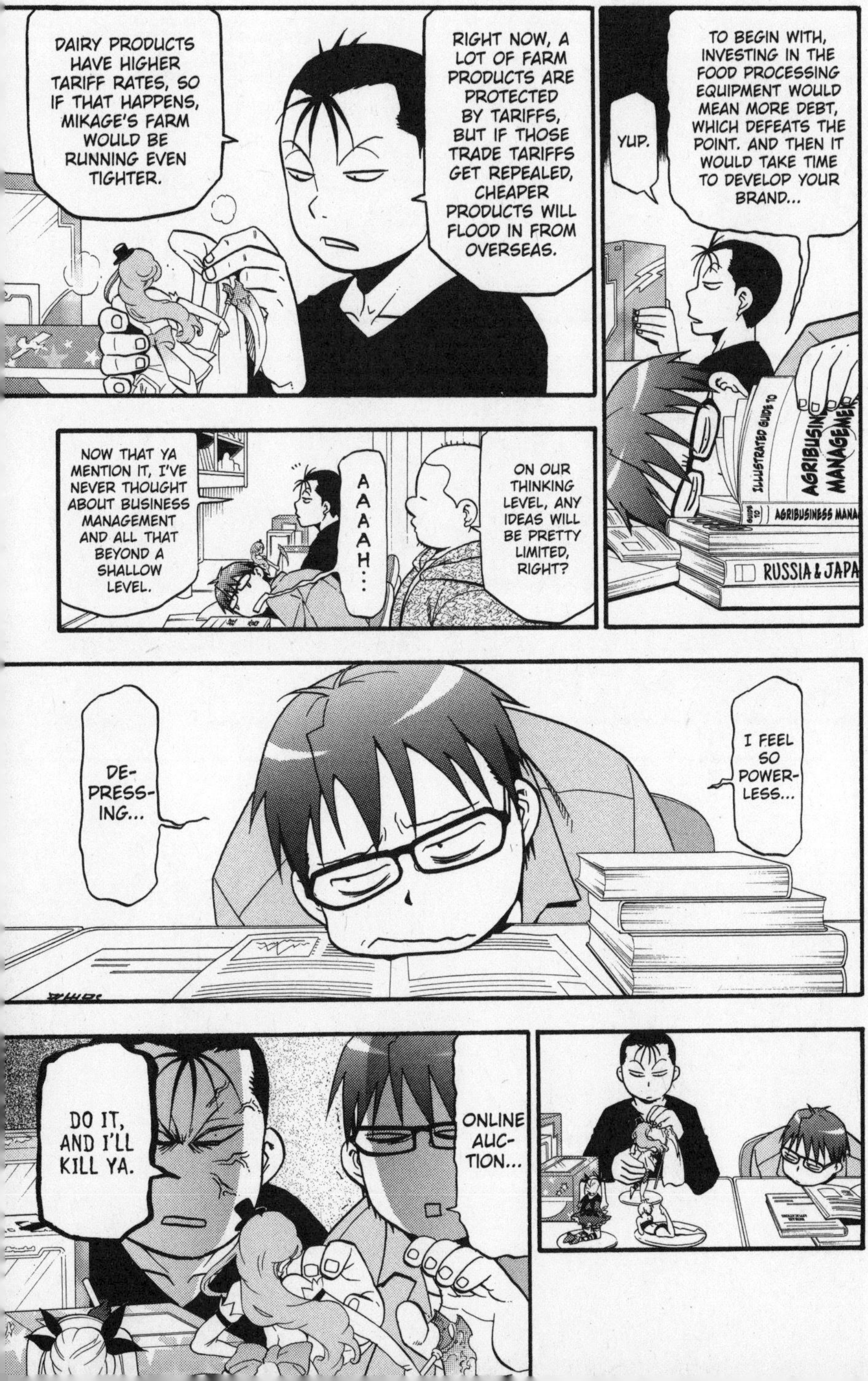
TO BEGIN WITH, INVESTING IN THE FOOD PROCESSING EQUIPMENT WOULD MEAN MORE DEBT, WHICH DEFEATS THE POINT. AND THEN IT WOULD TAKE TIME TO DEVELOP YOUR BRAND...
YUP.
ILLUSTRATED GUIDE TO AGRIBUSINESS MANAGEMEN
AGRIBUSINESS MANA
RUSSIA & JAPA
RIGHT NOW, A LOT OF FARM PRODUCTS ARE PROTECTED BY TARIFFS, BUT IF THOSE TRADE TARIFFS GET REPEALED, CHEAPER PRODUCTS WILL FLOOD IN FROM OVERSEAS.
DAIRY PRODUCTS HAVE HIGHER TARIFF RATES, SO IF THAT HAPPENS, MIKAGE'S FARM WOULD BE RUNNING EVEN TIGHTER.
ON OUR THINKING LEVEL, ANY IDEAS WILL BE PRETTY LIMITED, RIGHT?
AAAAH...
NOW THAT YA MENTION IT, I'VE NEVER THOUGHT ABOUT BUSINESS MANAGEMENT AND ALL THAT BEYOND A SHALLOW LEVEL.
I FEEL SO POWER-LESS...
DE-PRESS-ING...
ONLINE AUC-TION...
DO IT, AND I'LL KILL YA.

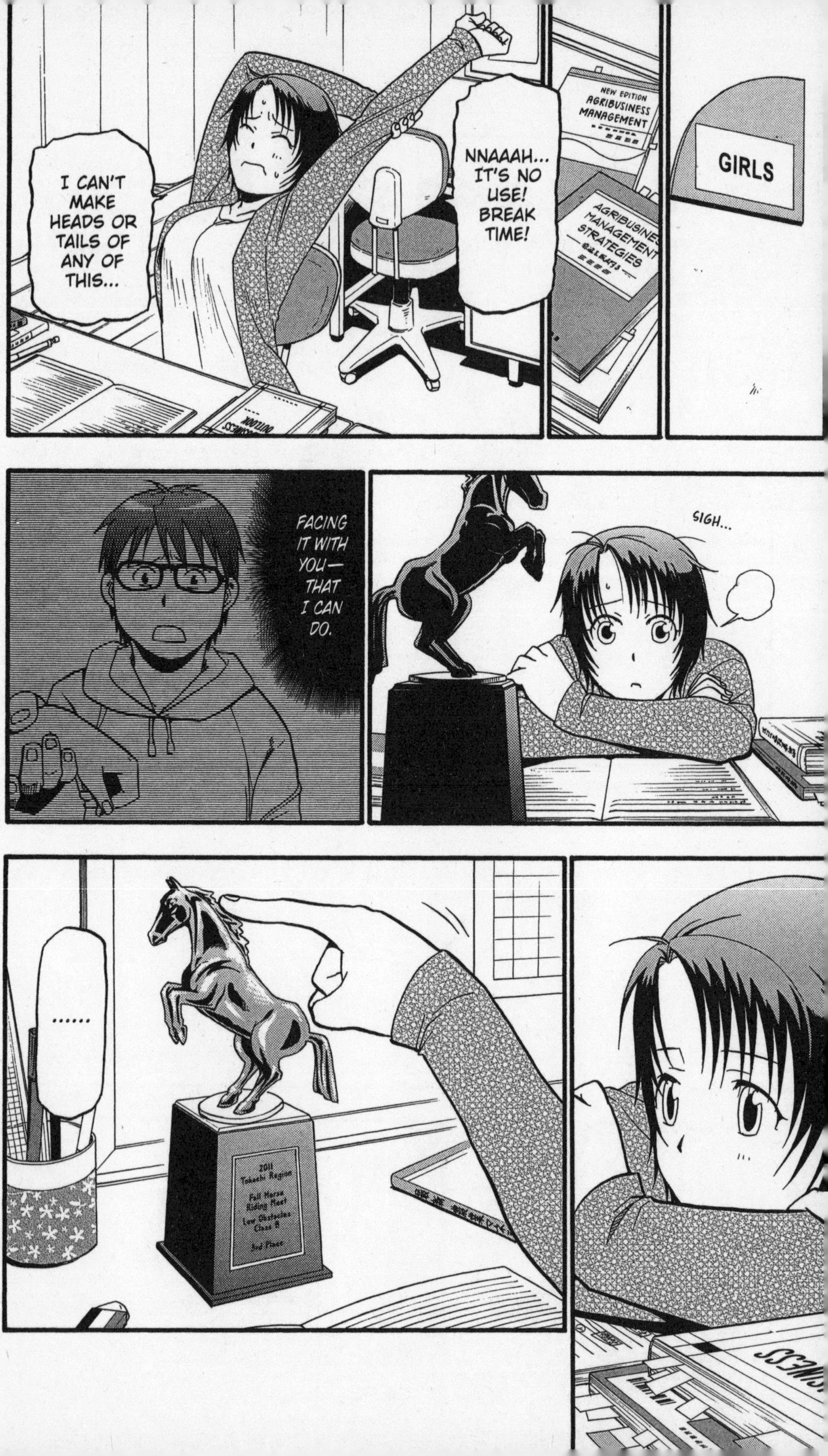
GIRLS
NEW EDITION AGRIBUSINESS MANAGEMENT
AGRIBUSINESS MANAGEMENT STRATEGIES
NNAAAH... IT'S NO USE! BREAK TIME!
I CAN'T MAKE HEADS OR TAILS OF ANY OF THIS...
SIGH...
FACING IT WITH YOU—THAT I CAN DO.
......
2011 Tokachi Region
Fall Horse Riding Meet
Low Obstacles Class B
3rd Place

Silver Spoon

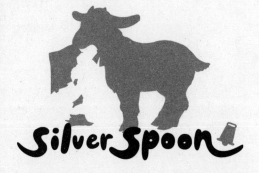

COW BARN TEACHER
MASATAKA MINAMI

Chapter 66:
Tale of Winter ③

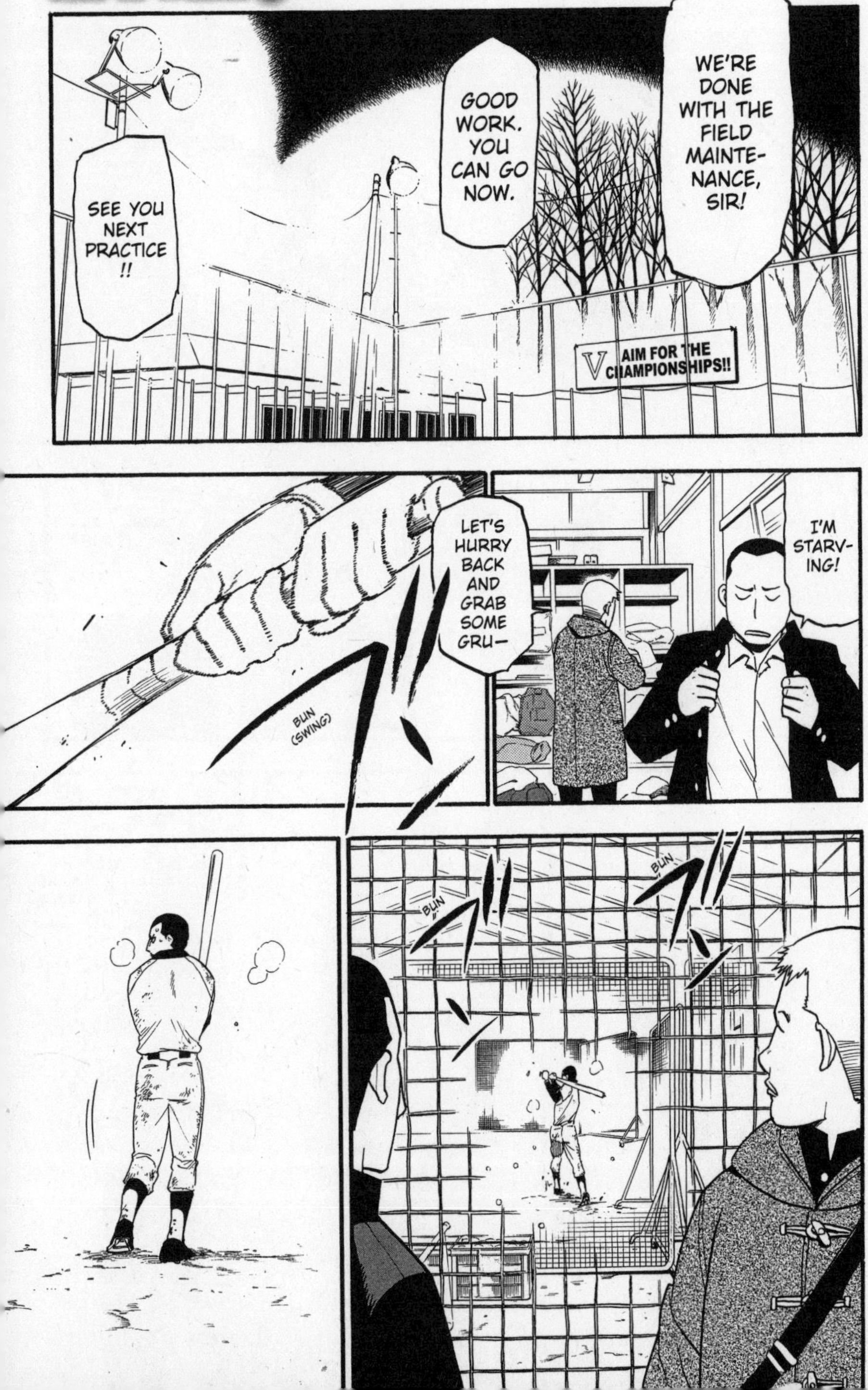
WE'RE DONE WITH THE FIELD MAINTE-NANCE, SIR!
GOOD WORK. YOU CAN GO NOW.
SEE YOU NEXT PRACTICE !!
V AIM FOR THE CHAMPIONSHIPS!!
I'M STARV-ING!
LET'S HURRY BACK AND GRAB SOME GRU—
BUN (SWING)
BUN
BUN

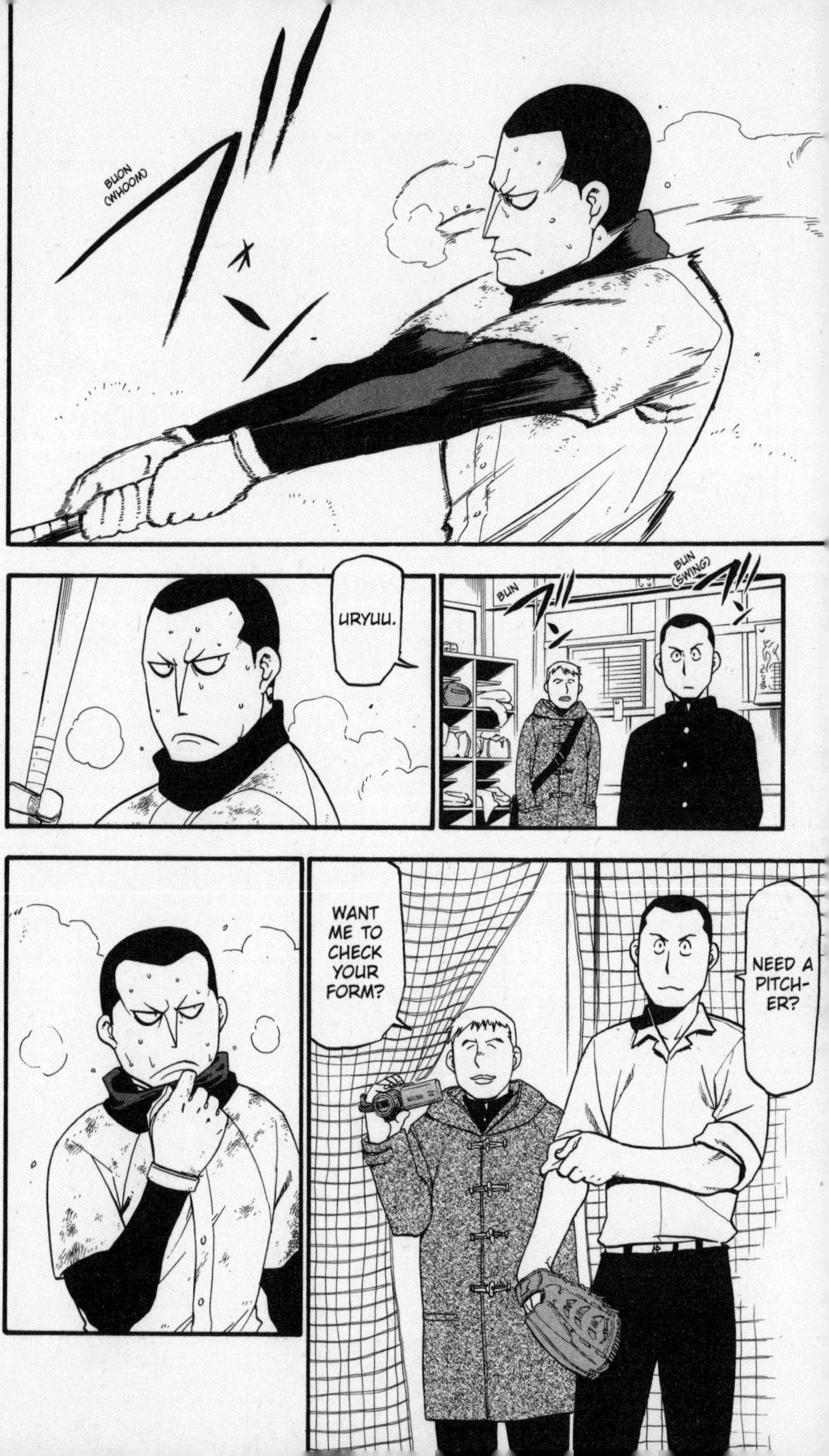
BUON (WHOOM)
BUN (SWING)
BUN
URYUU.
NEED A PITCH-ER?
WANT ME TO CHECK YOUR FORM?

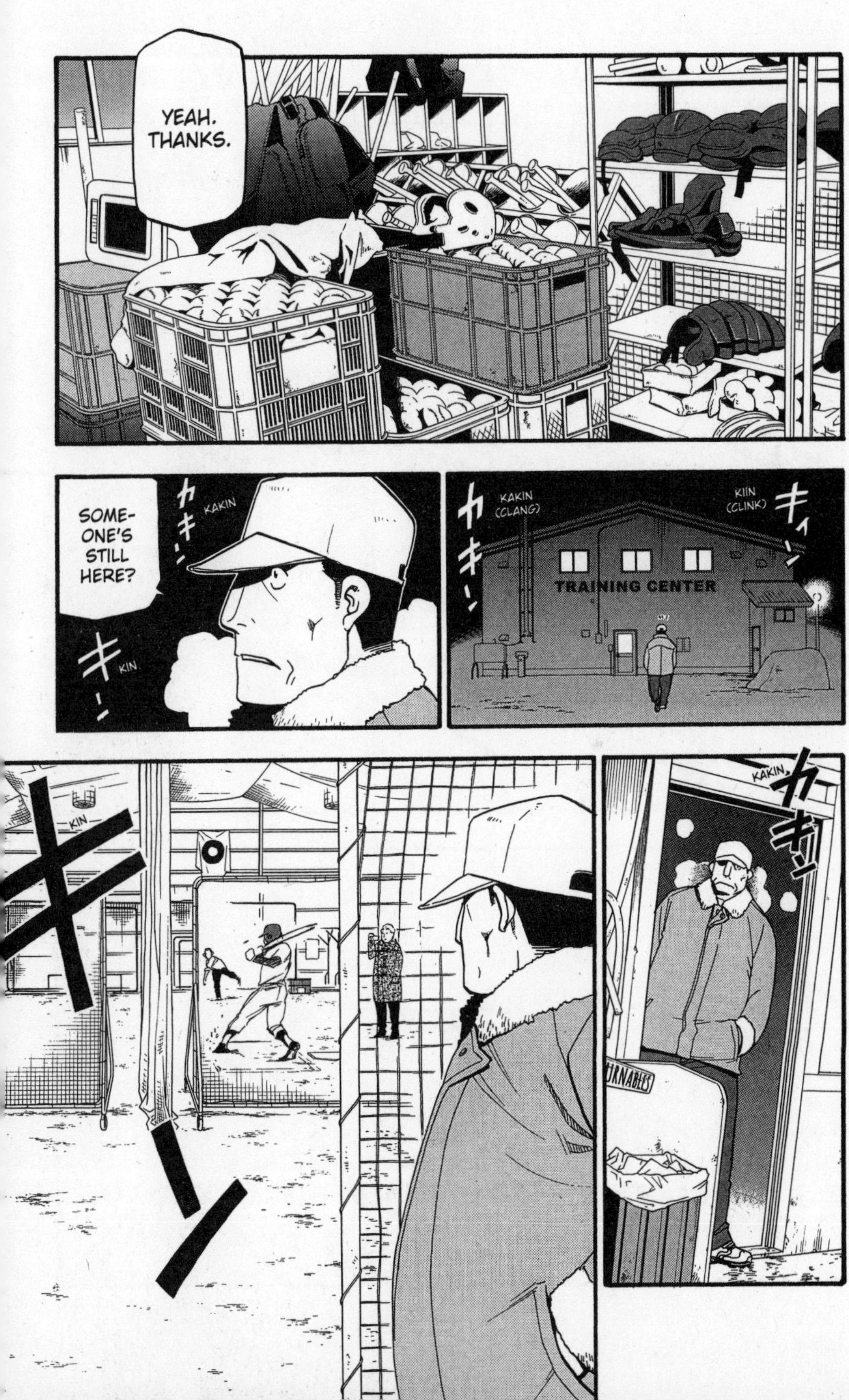
YEAH. THANKS.
KAKIN (CLANG)
KIIN (CLINK)
TRAINING CENTER
KAKIN
SOME-ONE'S STILL HERE?
KIN
KAKIN
KIN

URYUU. TURN IN.
OH.
SO THE BAT COMES MORE FROM THE INSIDE.
WAS I OPEN?
WIDE OPEN.
THIS ONE WAS A GOOD HIT.
YEAH, THAT ONE FELT LIKE A CLEAN SWING.
キーン
KIN (CLINK)
キーン
KIN
カキーン
KAKIN (KACLINK)
キイーン
KIIN

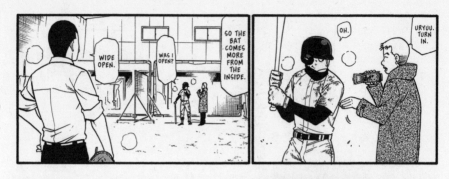

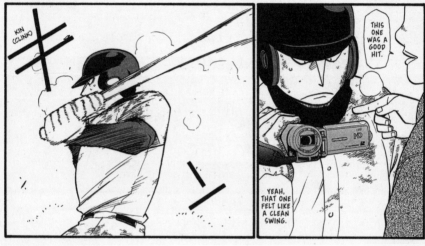

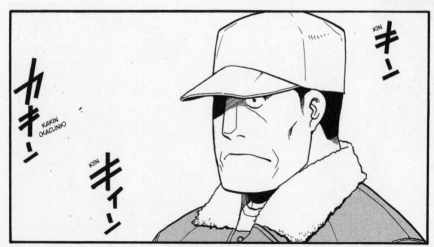

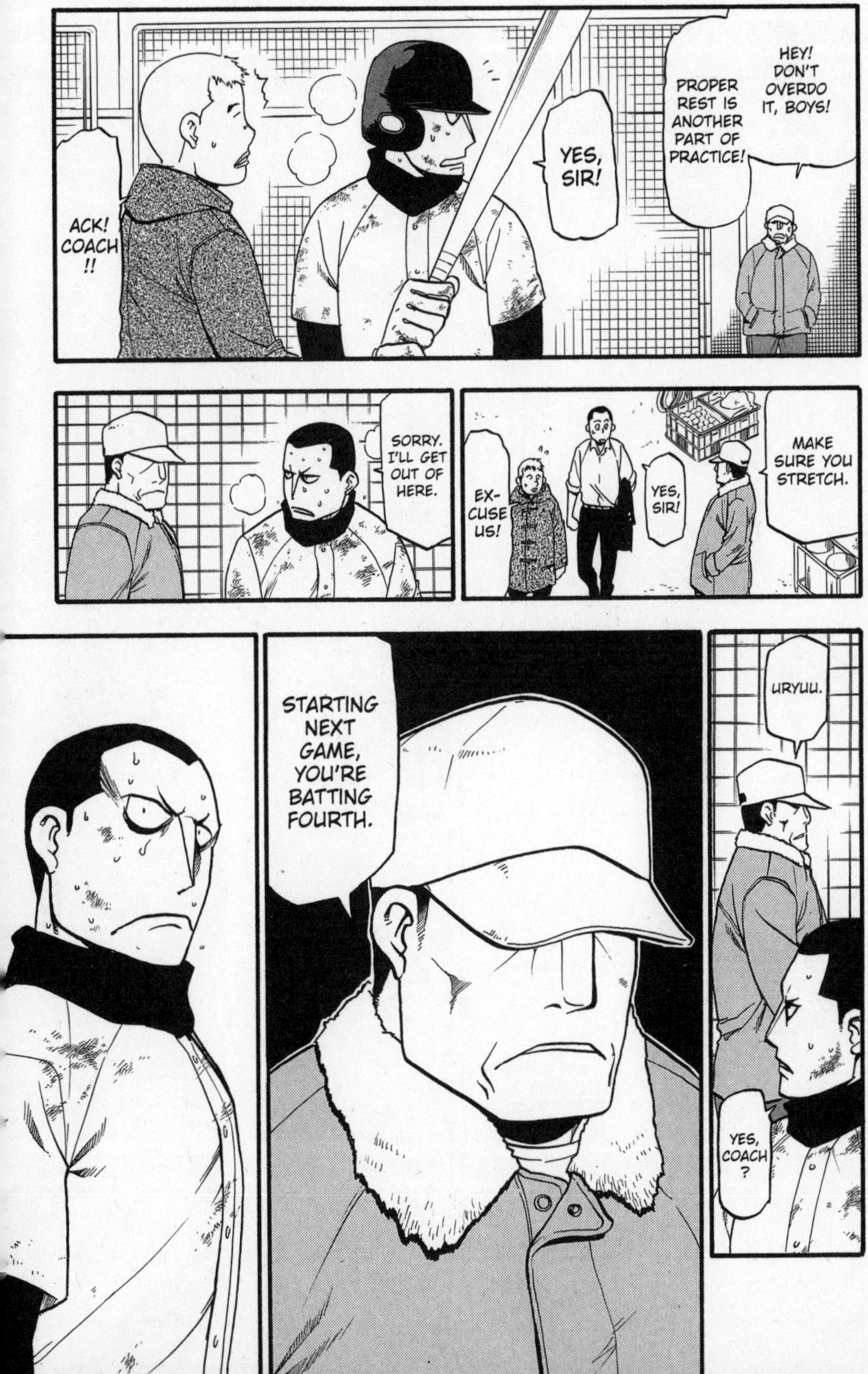
HEY! DON'T OVERDO IT, BOYS!
PROPER REST IS ANOTHER PART OF PRACTICE!
YES, SIR!
ACK! COACH !!
MAKE SURE YOU STRETCH.
YES, SIR!
EX-CUSE US!
SORRY. I'LL GET OUT OF HERE.
URYUU.
YES, COACH?
STARTING NEXT GAME, YOU'RE BATTING FOURTH.

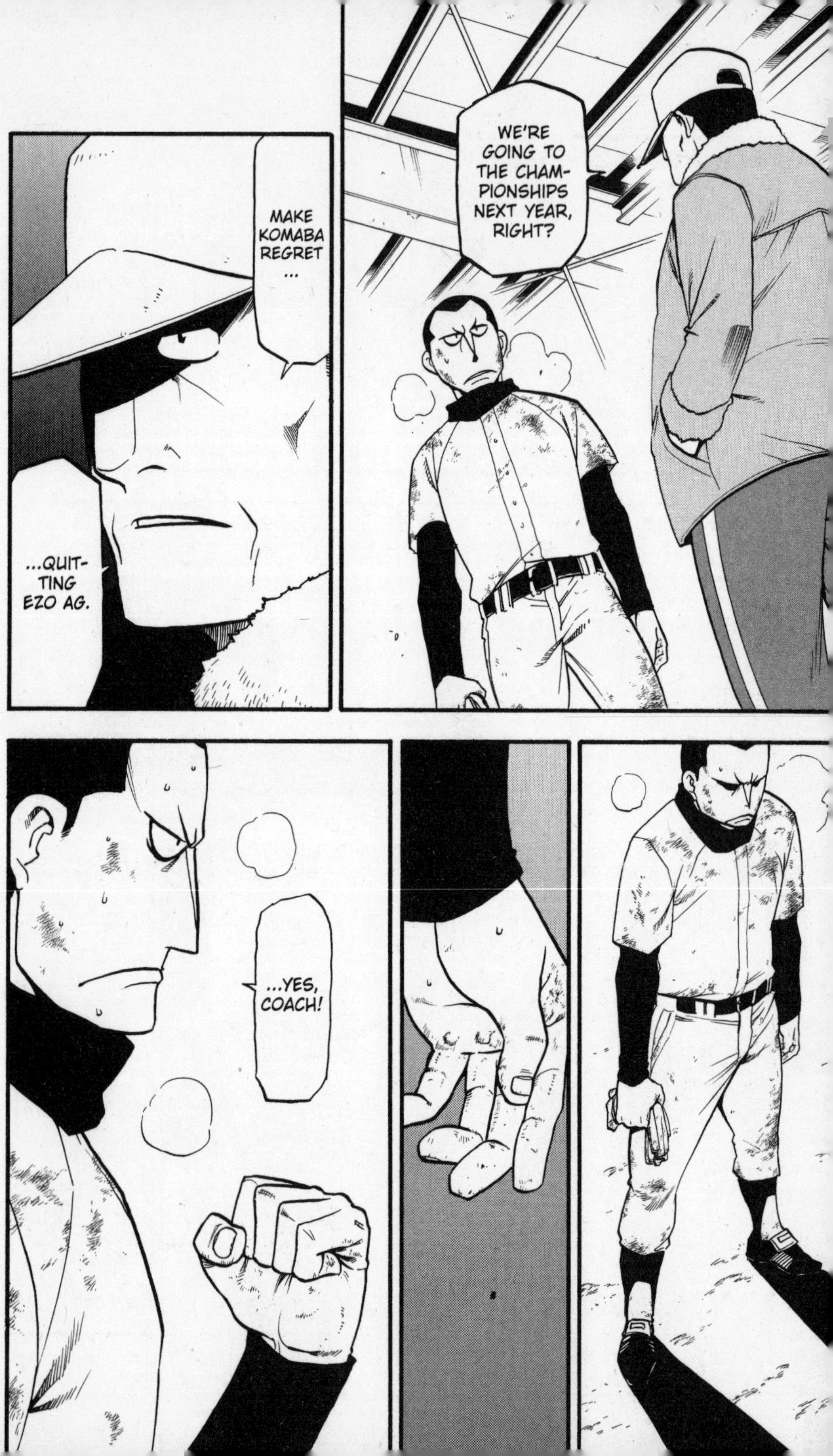
WE'RE GOING TO THE CHAMPIONSHIPS NEXT YEAR, RIGHT?
MAKE KOMABA REGRET ...
...QUITTING EZO AG.
...YES, COACH!

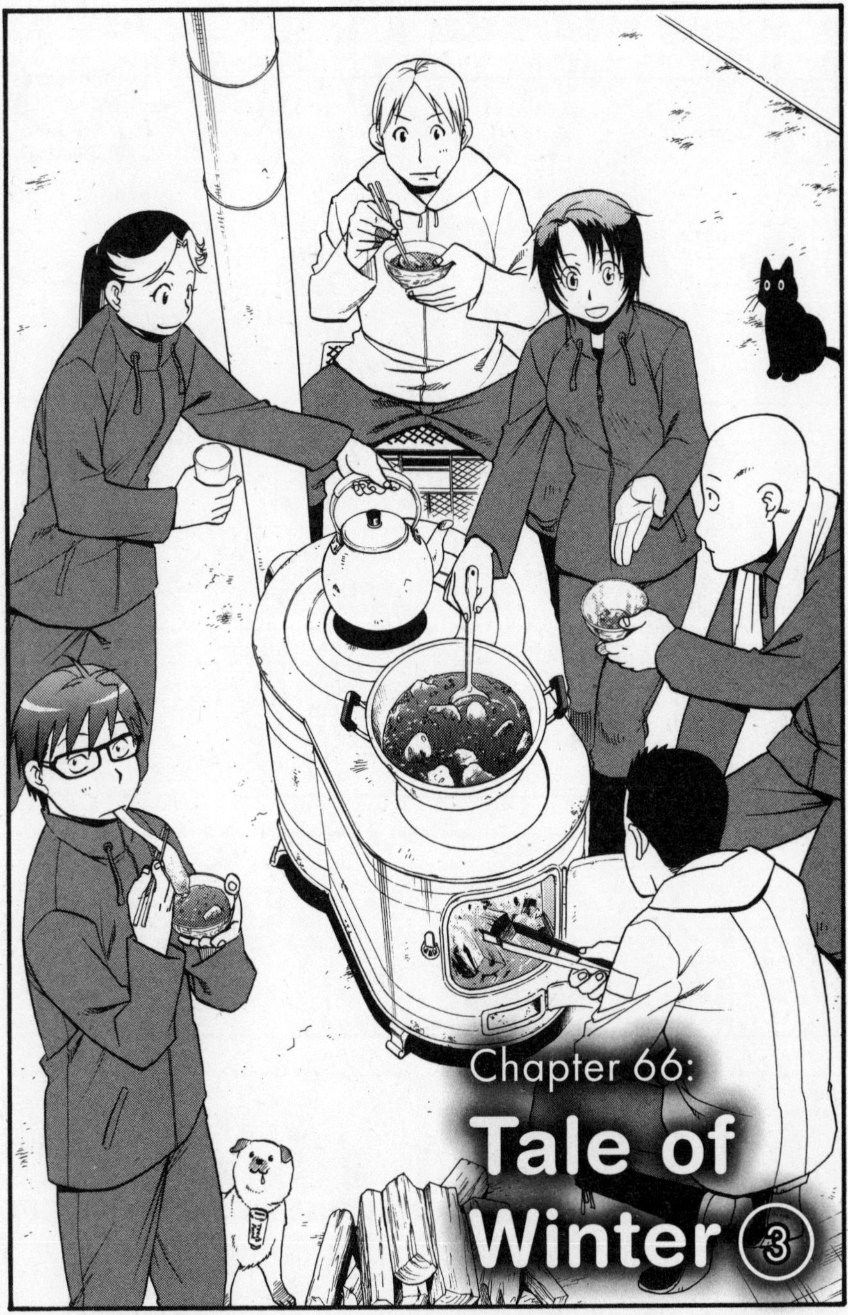
Chapter 66:
Tale of
Winter ③

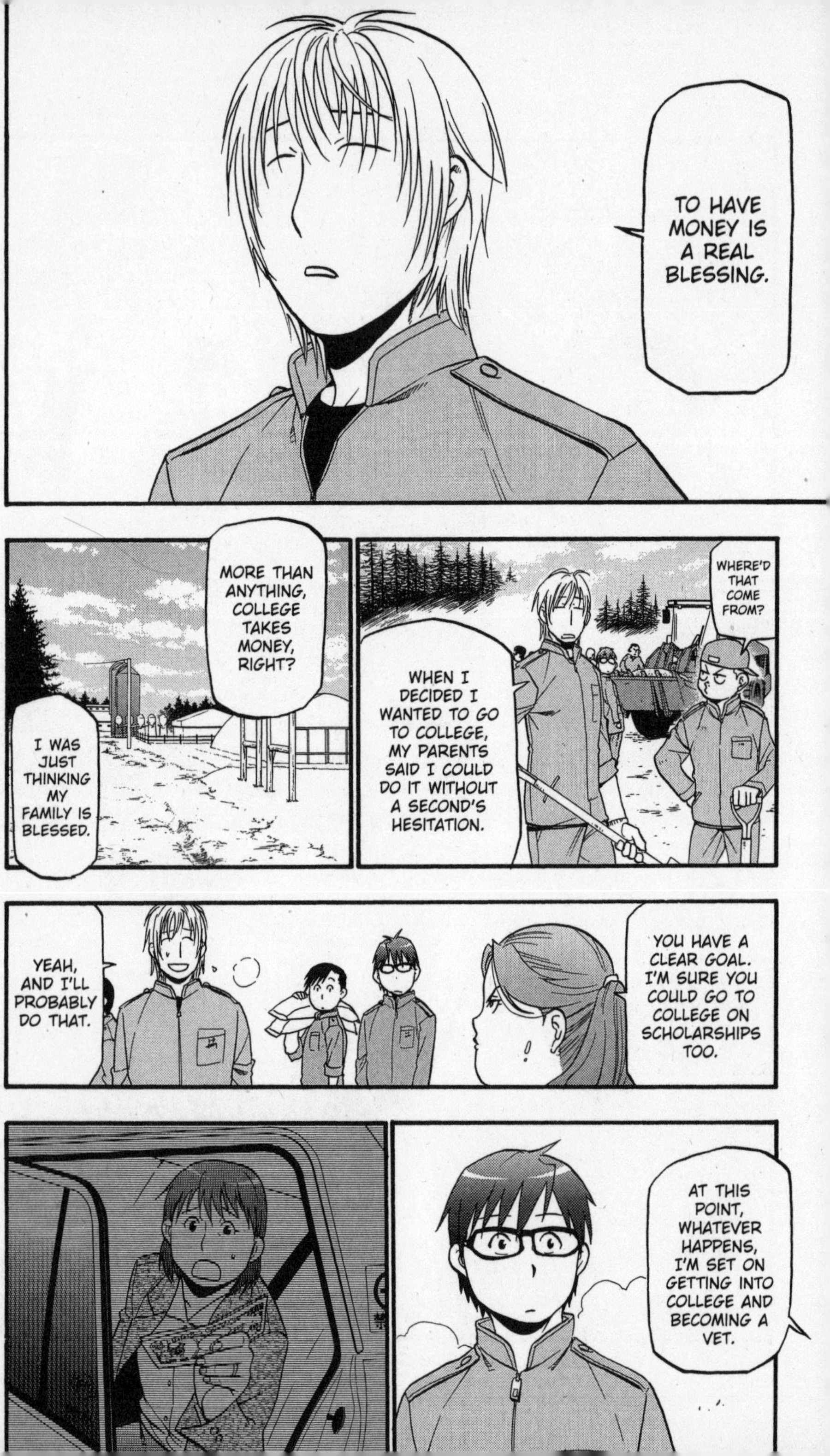
TO HAVE MONEY IS A REAL BLESSING.
WHERE'D THAT COME FROM?
WHEN I DECIDED I WANTED TO GO TO COLLEGE, MY PARENTS SAID I COULD DO IT WITHOUT A SECOND'S HESITATION.
MORE THAN ANYTHING, COLLEGE TAKES MONEY, RIGHT?
I WAS JUST THINKING MY FAMILY IS BLESSED.
YOU HAVE A CLEAR GOAL. I'M SURE YOU COULD GO TO COLLEGE ON SCHOLARSHIPS TOO.
YEAH, AND I'LL PROBABLY DO THAT.
AT THIS POINT, WHATEVER HAPPENS, I'M SET ON GETTING INTO COLLEGE AND BECOMING A VET.

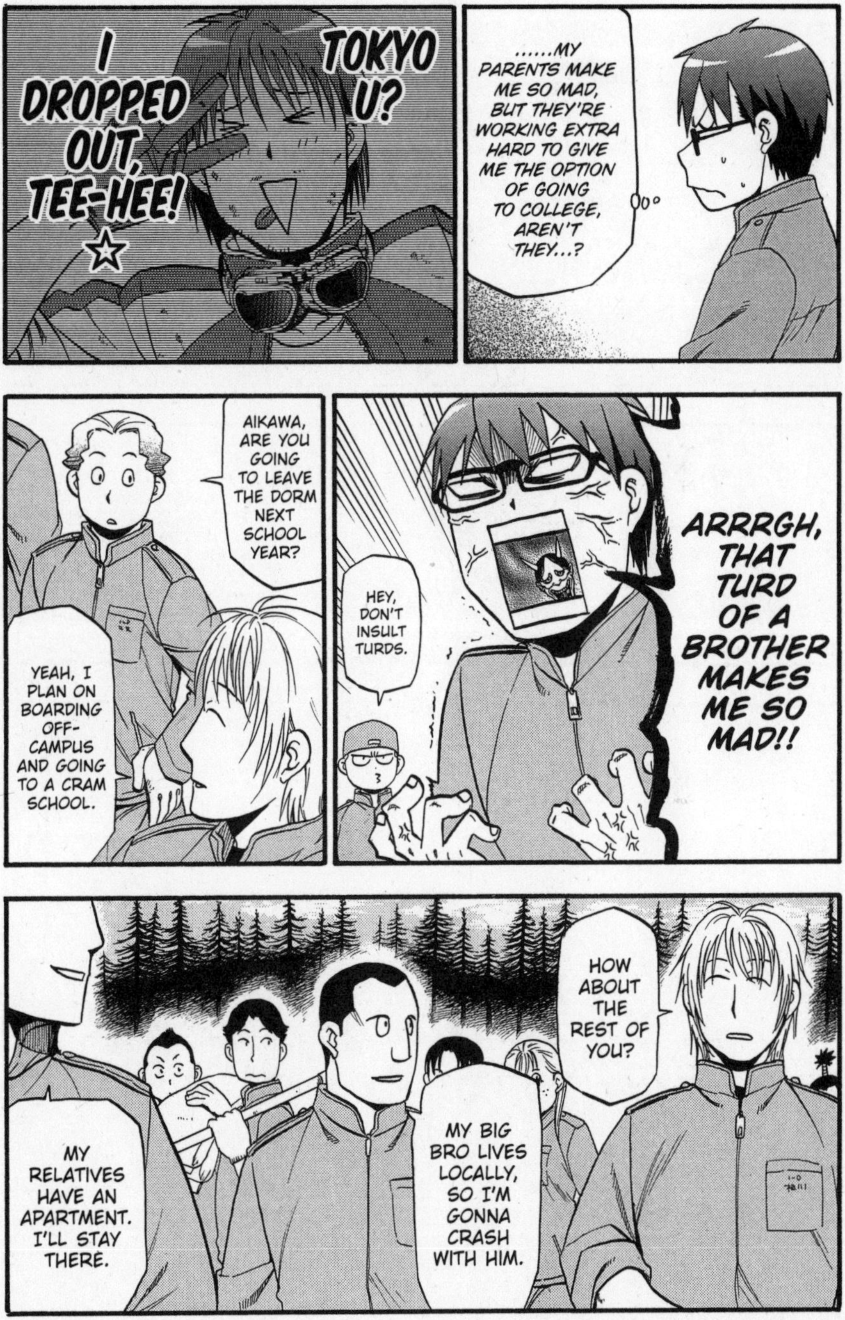
......MY PARENTS MAKE ME SO MAD, BUT THEY'RE WORKING EXTRA HARD TO GIVE ME THE OPTION OF GOING TO COLLEGE, AREN'T THEY...?
TOKYO U?
I DROPPED OUT, TEE-HEE! ☆
ARRRGH, THAT TURD OF A BROTHER MAKES ME SO MAD!!
HEY, DON'T INSULT TURDS.
AIKAWA, ARE YOU GOING TO LEAVE THE DORM NEXT SCHOOL YEAR?
YEAH, I PLAN ON BOARDING OFF-CAMPUS AND GOING TO A CRAM SCHOOL.
HOW ABOUT THE REST OF YOU?
MY BIG BRO LIVES LOCALLY, SO I'M GONNA CRASH WITH HIM.
MY RELATIVES HAVE AN APARTMENT. I'LL STAY THERE.

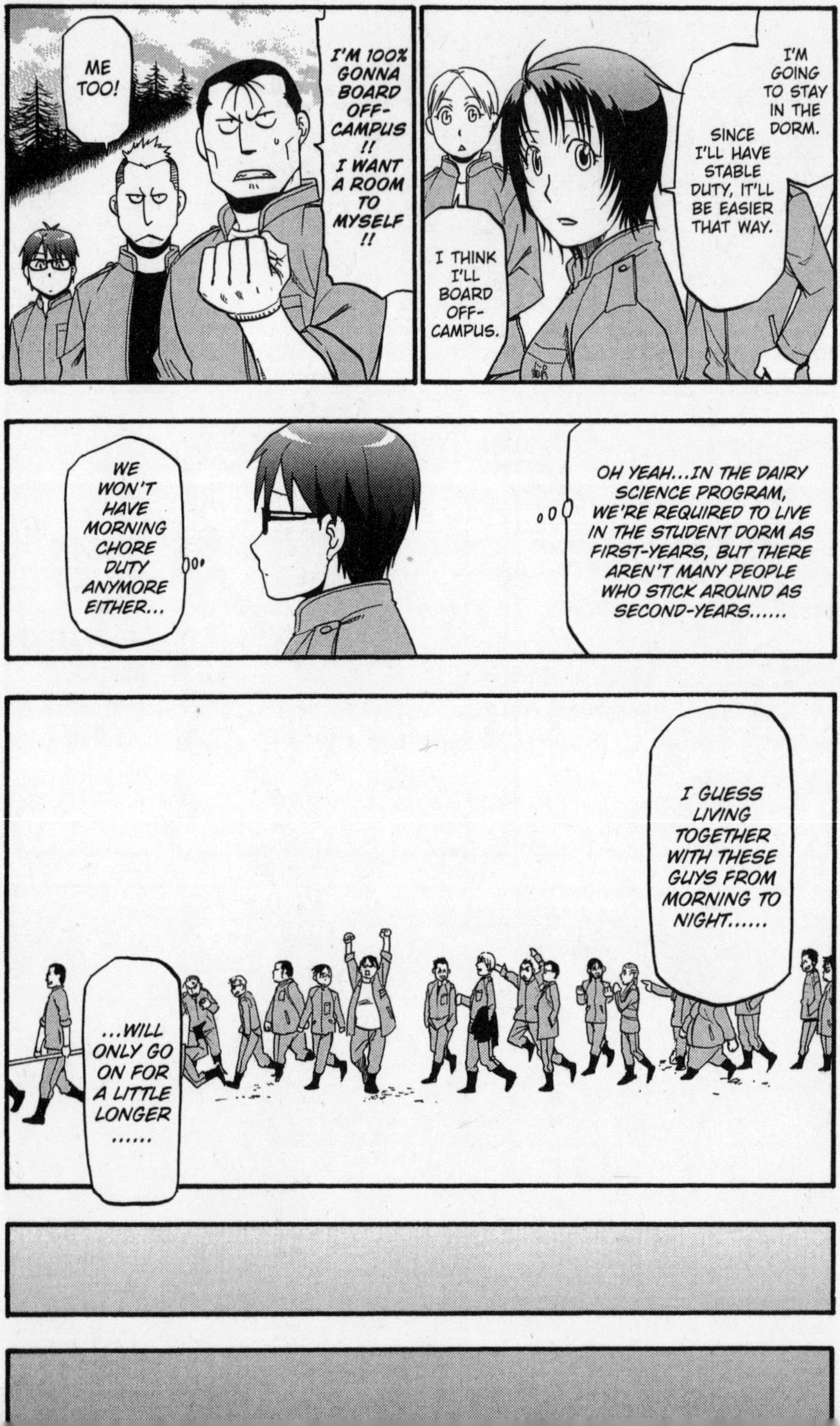
I'M GOING TO STAY IN THE DORM.
SINCE I'LL HAVE STABLE DUTY, IT'LL BE EASIER THAT WAY.
I THINK I'LL BOARD OFF-CAMPUS.
I'M 100% GONNA BOARD OFF-CAMPUS!! I WANT A ROOM TO MYSELF!!
ME TOO!
OH YEAH...IN THE DAIRY SCIENCE PROGRAM, WE'RE REQUIRED TO LIVE IN THE STUDENT DORM AS FIRST-YEARS, BUT THERE AREN'T MANY PEOPLE WHO STICK AROUND AS SECOND-YEARS......
WE WON'T HAVE MORNING CHORE DUTY ANYMORE EITHER...
I GUESS LIVING TOGETHER WITH THESE GUYS FROM MORNING TO NIGHT......
...WILL ONLY GO ON FOR A LITTLE LONGER......

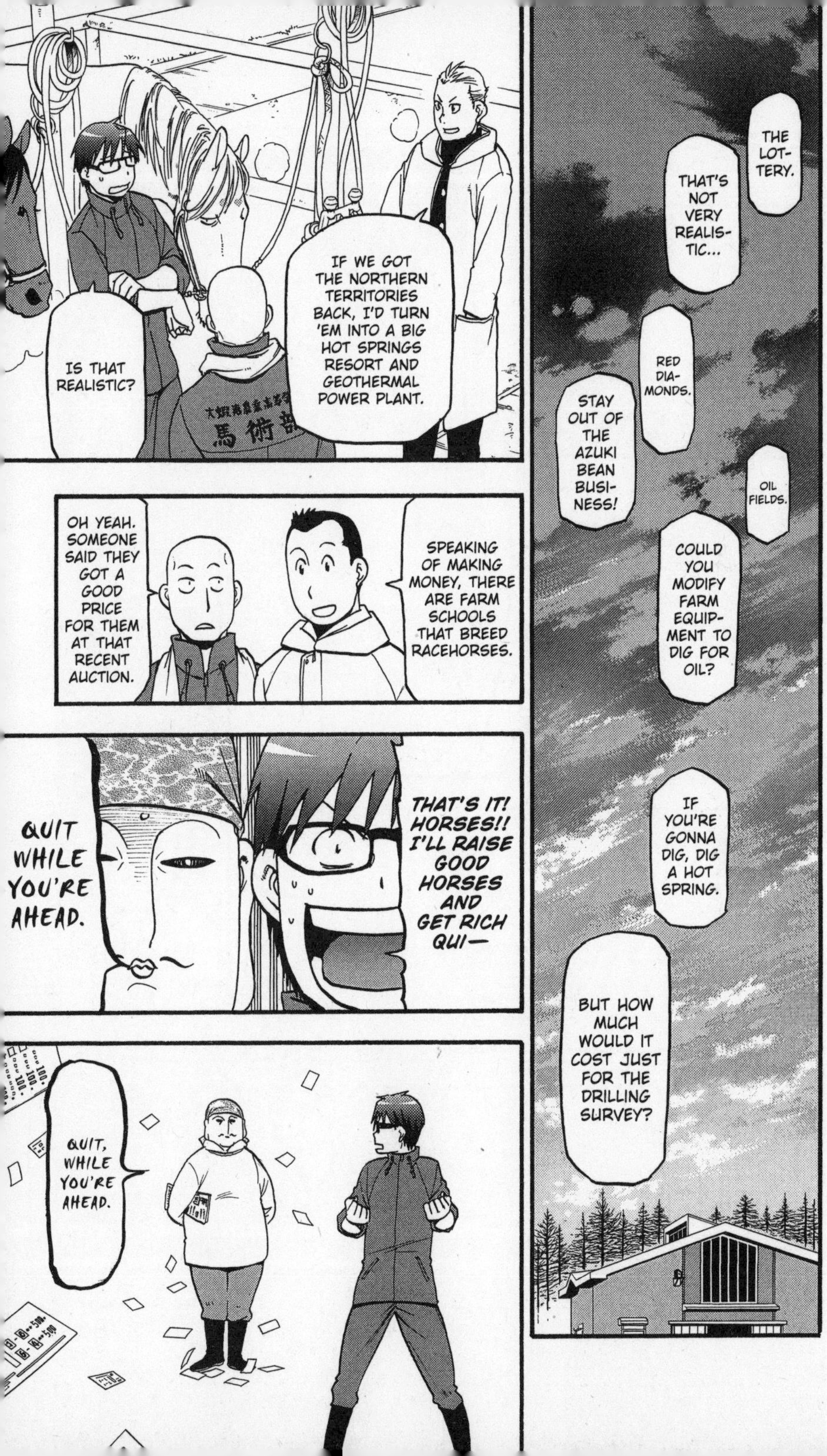
THE LOTTERY.
THAT'S NOT VERY REALISTIC...
RED DIAMONDS.
STAY OUT OF THE AZUKI BEAN BUSINESS!
OIL FIELDS.
COULD YOU MODIFY FARM EQUIPMENT TO DIG FOR OIL?
IF YOU'RE GONNA DIG, DIG A HOT SPRING.
BUT HOW MUCH WOULD IT COST JUST FOR THE DRILLING SURVEY?
IF WE GOT THE NORTHERN TERRITORIES BACK, I'D TURN 'EM INTO A BIG HOT SPRINGS RESORT AND GEOTHERMAL POWER PLANT.
馬術部
IS THAT REALISTIC?
SPEAKING OF MAKING MONEY, THERE ARE FARM SCHOOLS THAT BREED RACEHORSES.
OH YEAH. SOMEONE SAID THEY GOT A GOOD PRICE FOR THEM AT THAT RECENT AUCTION.
THAT'S IT! HORSES!! I'LL RAISE GOOD HORSES AND GET RICH QUI—
QUIT WHILE YOU'RE AHEAD.
QUIT, WHILE YOU'RE AHEAD.

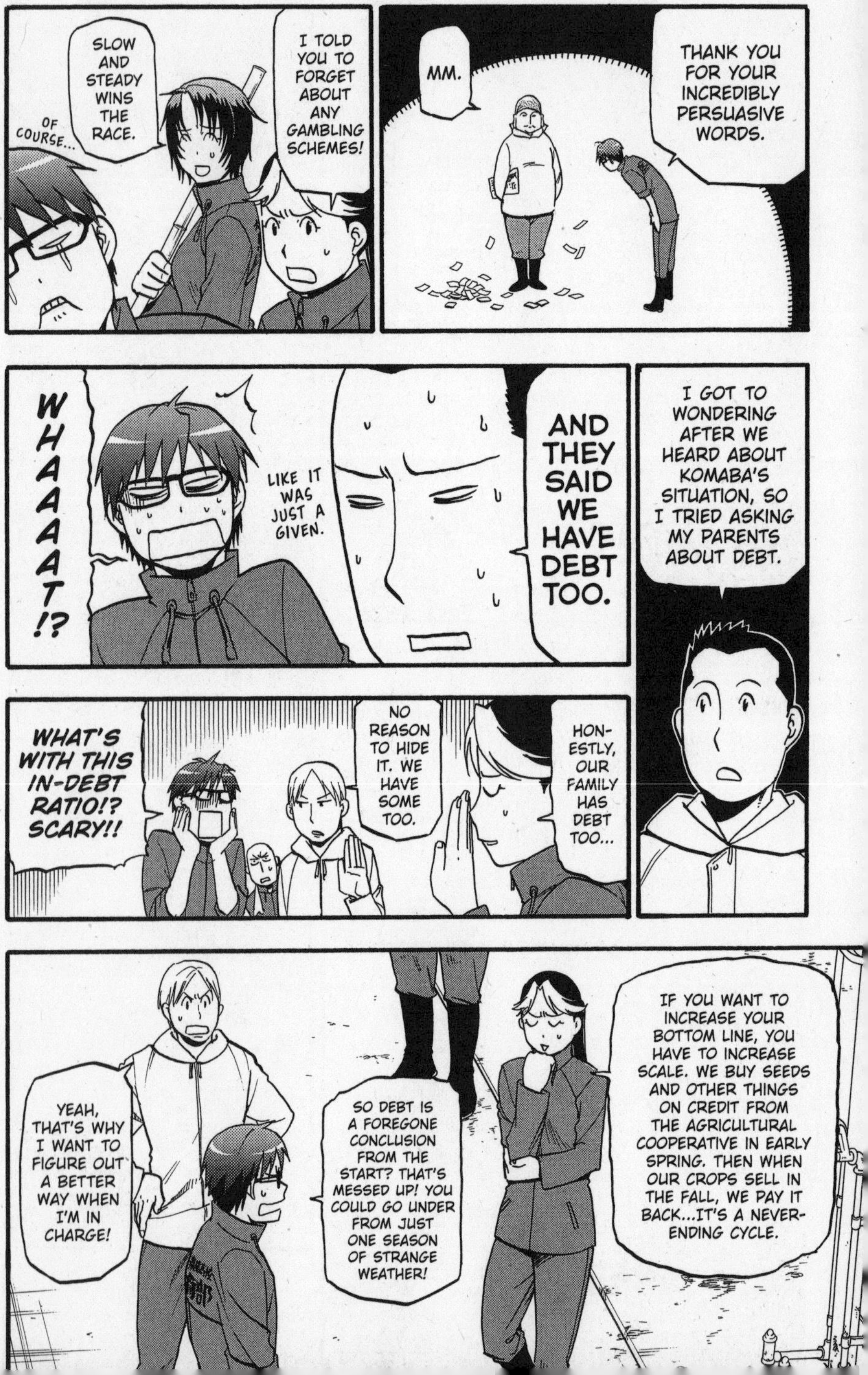
THANK YOU FOR YOUR INCREDIBLY PERSUASIVE WORDS.
MM.
I TOLD YOU TO FORGET ABOUT ANY GAMBLING SCHEMES!
SLOW AND STEADY WINS THE RACE.
OF COURSE...
I GOT TO WONDERING AFTER WE HEARD ABOUT KOMABA'S SITUATION, SO I TRIED ASKING MY PARENTS ABOUT DEBT.
AND THEY SAID WE HAVE DEBT TOO.
LIKE IT WAS JUST A GIVEN.
WHAAAAAT!?
HON-ESTLY, OUR FAMILY HAS DEBT TOO...
NO REASON TO HIDE IT. WE HAVE SOME TOO.
WHAT'S WITH THIS IN-DEBT RATIO!? SCARY!!
IF YOU WANT TO INCREASE YOUR BOTTOM LINE, YOU HAVE TO INCREASE SCALE. WE BUY SEEDS AND OTHER THINGS ON CREDIT FROM THE AGRICULTURAL COOPERATIVE IN EARLY SPRING. THEN WHEN OUR CROPS SELL IN THE FALL, WE PAY IT BACK...IT'S A NEVER-ENDING CYCLE.
SO DEBT IS A FOREGONE CONCLUSION FROM THE START? THAT'S MESSED UP! YOU COULD GO UNDER FROM JUST ONE SEASON OF STRANGE WEATHER!
YEAH, THAT'S WHY I WANT TO FIGURE OUT A BETTER WAY WHEN I'M IN CHARGE!

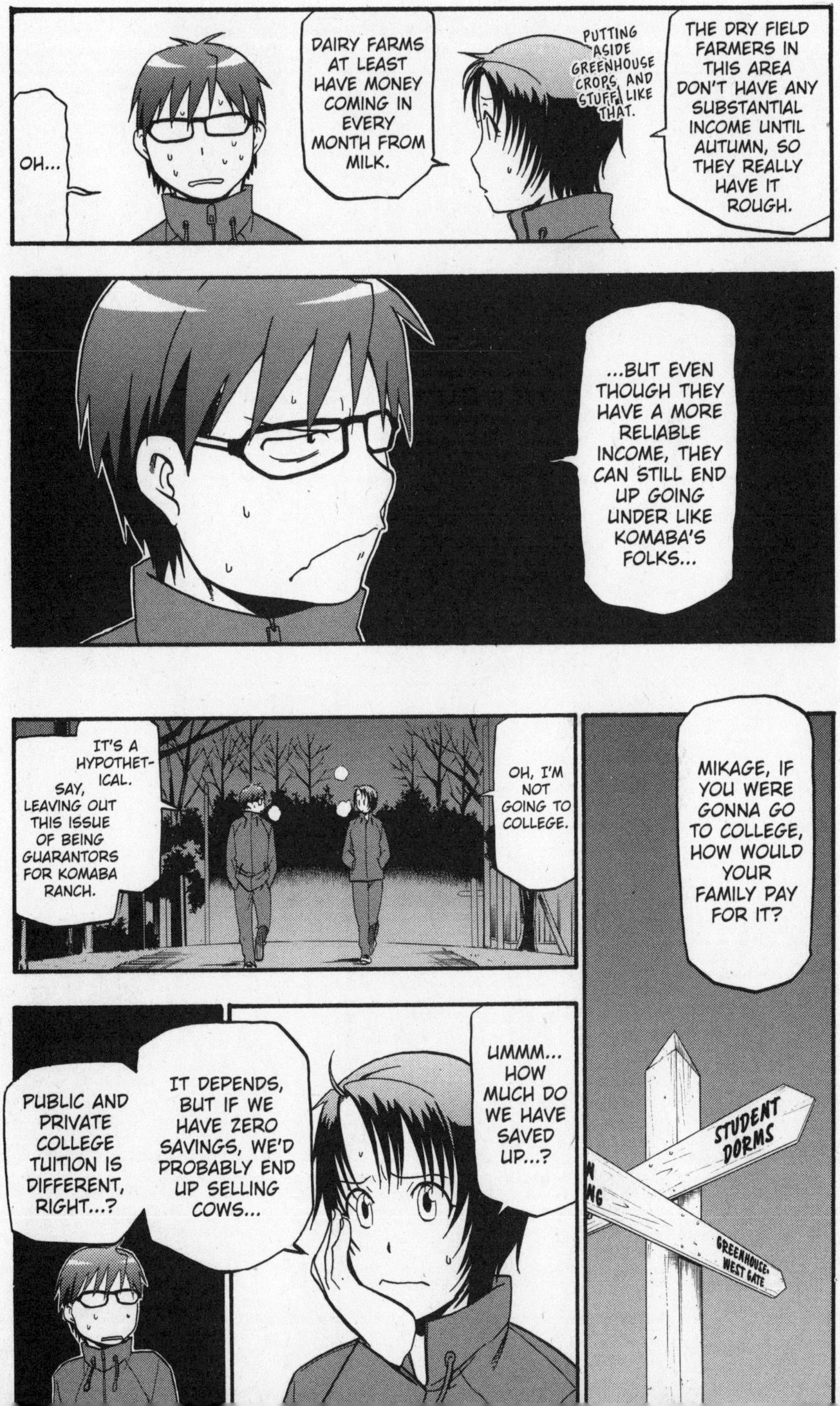
THE DRY FIELD FARMERS IN THIS AREA DON'T HAVE ANY SUBSTANTIAL INCOME UNTIL AUTUMN, SO THEY REALLY HAVE IT ROUGH.
PUTTING ASIDE GREENHOUSE CROPS AND STUFF LIKE THAT.
DAIRY FARMS AT LEAST HAVE MONEY COMING IN EVERY MONTH FROM MILK.
OH...
...BUT EVEN THOUGH THEY HAVE A MORE RELIABLE INCOME, THEY CAN STILL END UP GOING UNDER LIKE KOMABA'S FOLKS...
MIKAGE, IF YOU WERE GONNA GO TO COLLEGE, HOW WOULD YOUR FAMILY PAY FOR IT?
STUDENT DORMS
GREENHOUSE, WEST GATE
OH, I'M NOT GOING TO COLLEGE.
IT'S A HYPOTHETICAL.
SAY, LEAVING OUT THIS ISSUE OF BEING GUARANTORS FOR KOMABA RANCH.
UMMM... HOW MUCH DO WE HAVE SAVED UP...?
IT DEPENDS, BUT IF WE HAVE ZERO SAVINGS, WE'D PROBABLY END UP SELLING COWS...
PUBLIC AND PRIVATE COLLEGE TUITION IS DIFFERENT, RIGHT...?

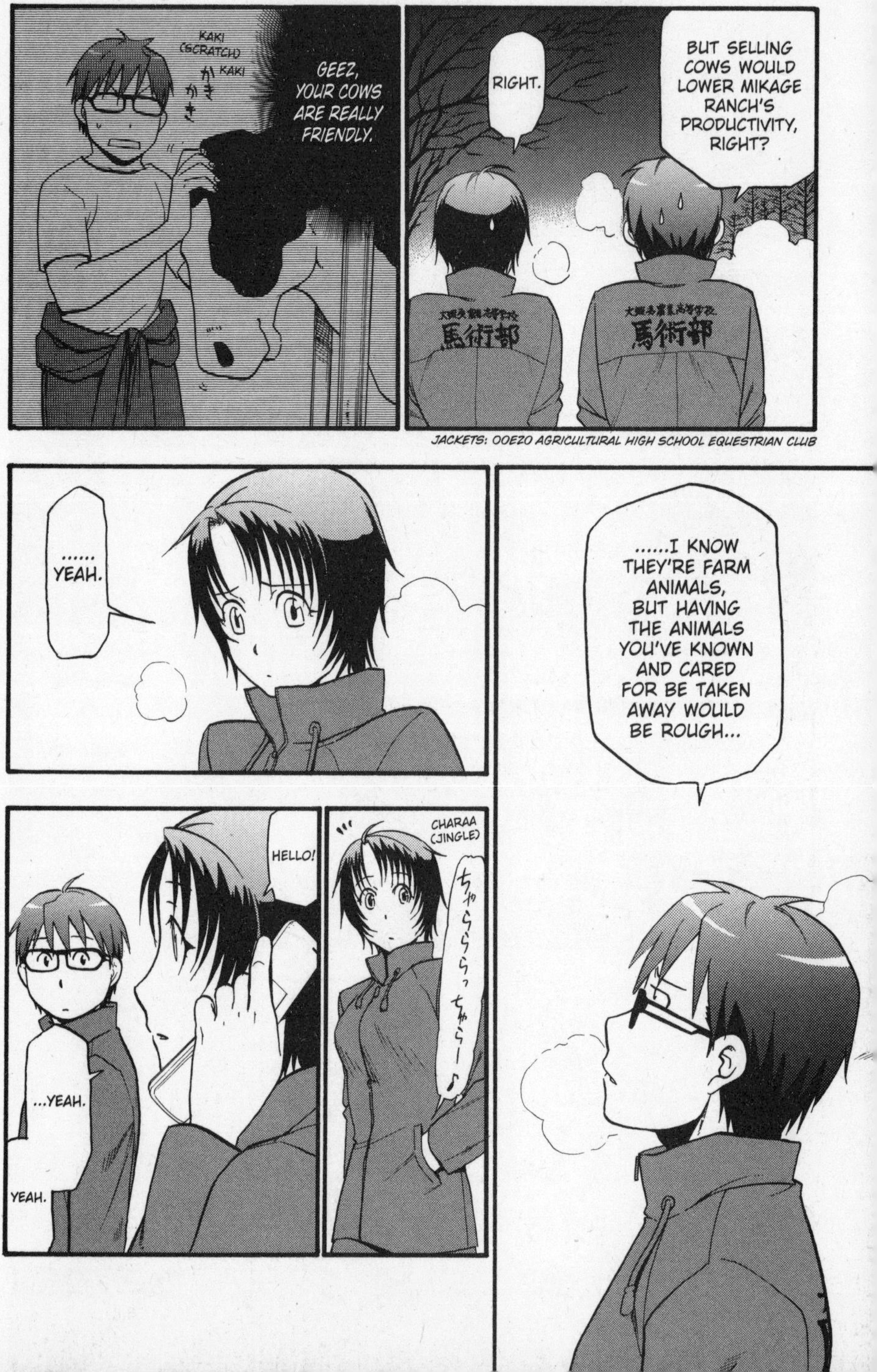
BUT SELLING COWS WOULD LOWER MIKAGE RANCH'S PRODUCTIVITY, RIGHT?
RIGHT.
馬術部
馬術部
KAKI (SCRATCH) KAKI
かきかき
GEEZ, YOUR COWS ARE REALLY FRIENDLY.
......I KNOW THEY'RE FARM ANIMALS, BUT HAVING THE ANIMALS YOU'VE KNOWN AND CARED FOR BE TAKEN AWAY WOULD BE ROUGH...
...... YEAH.
CHARAA (JINGLE)
ちゃらららっ ちゃらー♪
HELLO!
...YEAH.
YEAH.
JACKETS: OOEZO AGRICULTURAL HIGH SCHOOL EQUESTRIAN CLUB

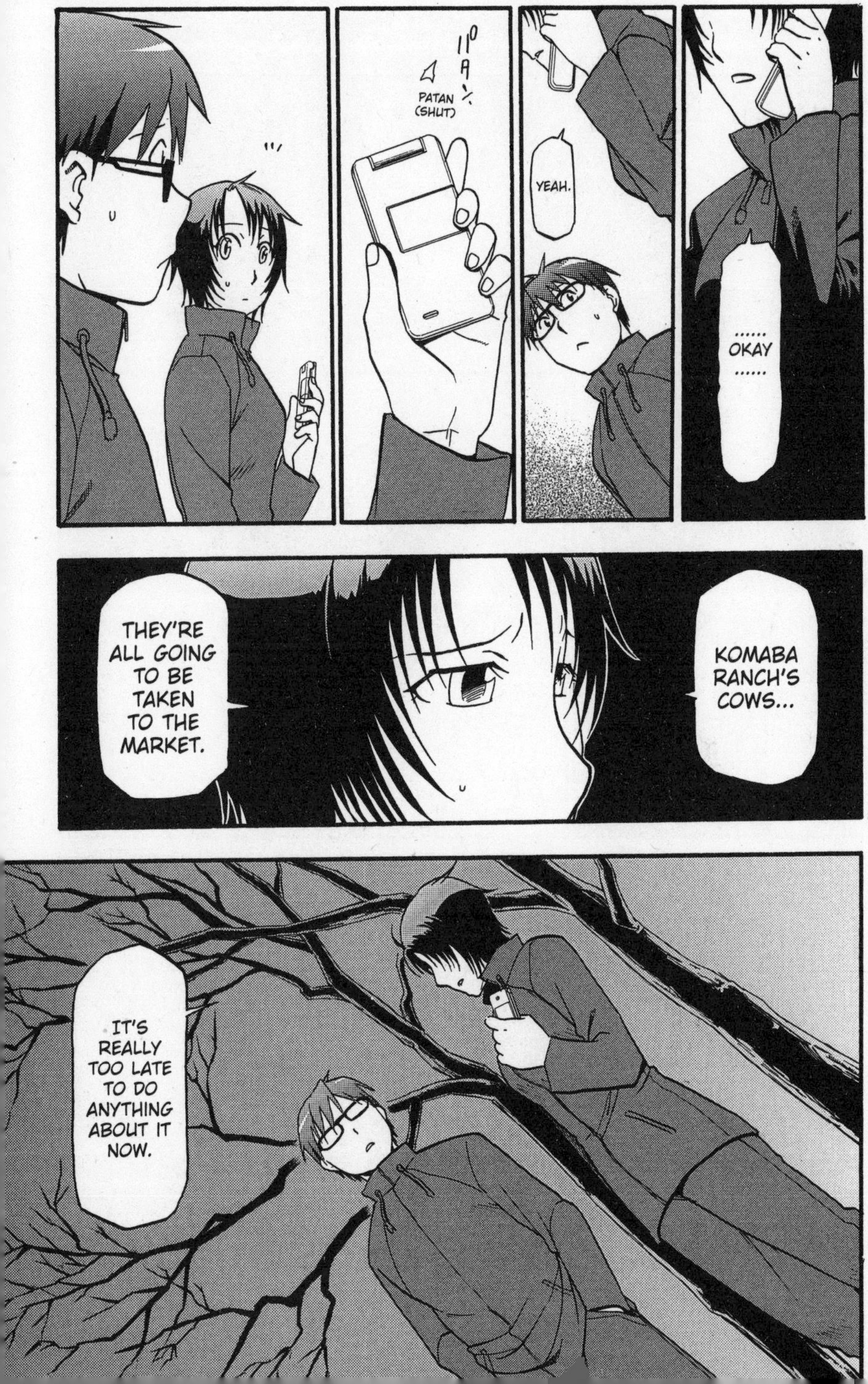
......OKAY......
YEAH.
PATAN (SHUT)
KOMABA RANCH'S COWS...
THEY'RE ALL GOING TO BE TAKEN TO THE MARKET.
IT'S REALLY TOO LATE TO DO ANYTHING ABOUT IT NOW.

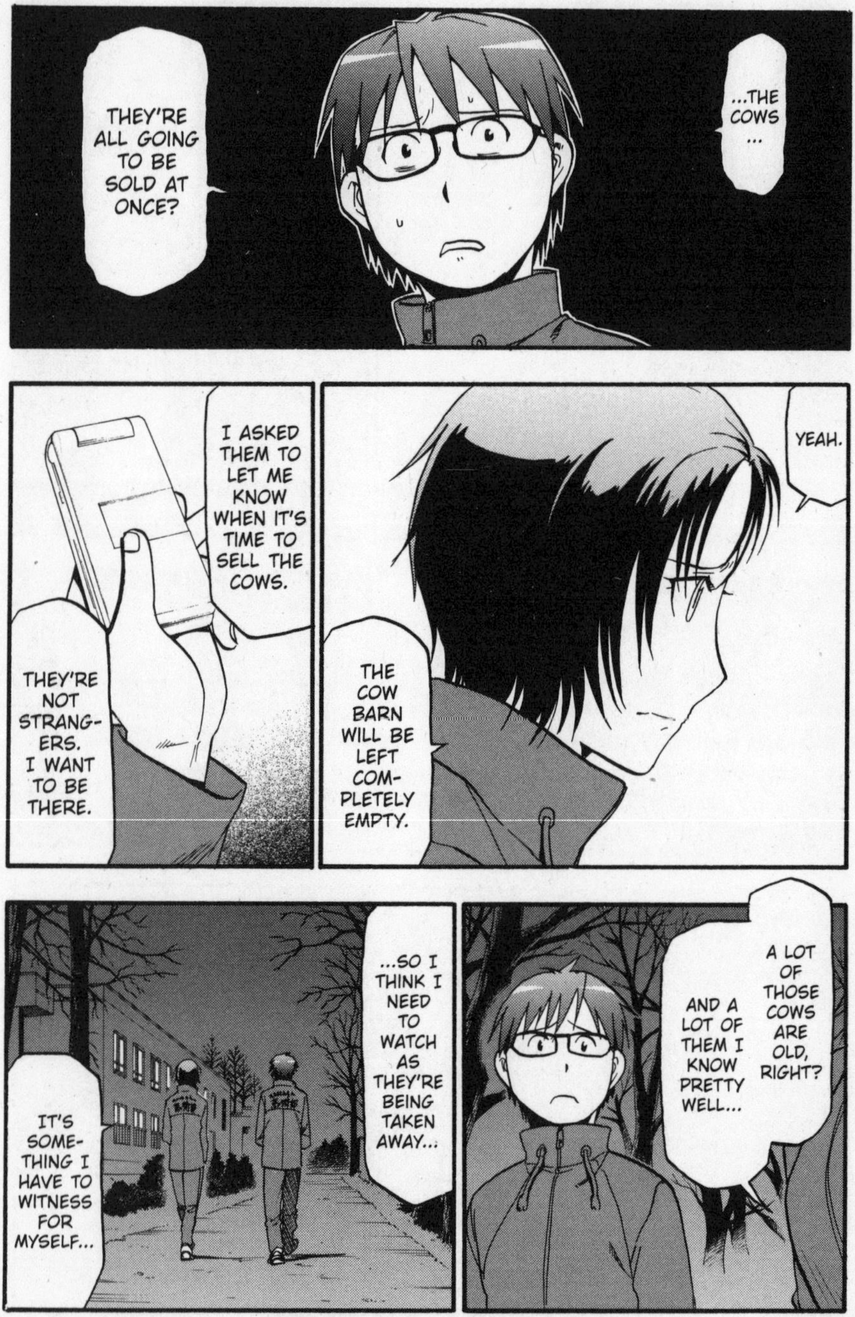
...THE COWS ...
THEY'RE ALL GOING TO BE SOLD AT ONCE?
YEAH.
THE COW BARN WILL BE LEFT COM-PLETELY EMPTY.
I ASKED THEM TO LET ME KNOW WHEN IT'S TIME TO SELL THE COWS.
THEY'RE NOT STRANG-ERS. I WANT TO BE THERE.
A LOT OF THOSE COWS ARE OLD, RIGHT?
AND A LOT OF THEM I KNOW PRETTY WELL...
...SO I THINK I NEED TO WATCH AS THEY'RE BEING TAKEN AWAY...
IT'S SOME-THING I HAVE TO WITNESS FOR MYSELF...

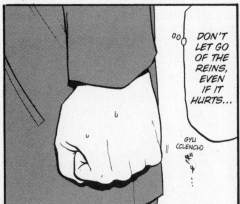

DON'T LET GO OF THE REINS, EVEN IF IT HURTS...

GYU (CLENCH)

WHEN THE COWS ARE TAKEN AWAY...I WANT TO BE THERE TOO.

HEY...

YEAH?

CAN I COME TOO?

CAN I GO WITH YOU?

C...

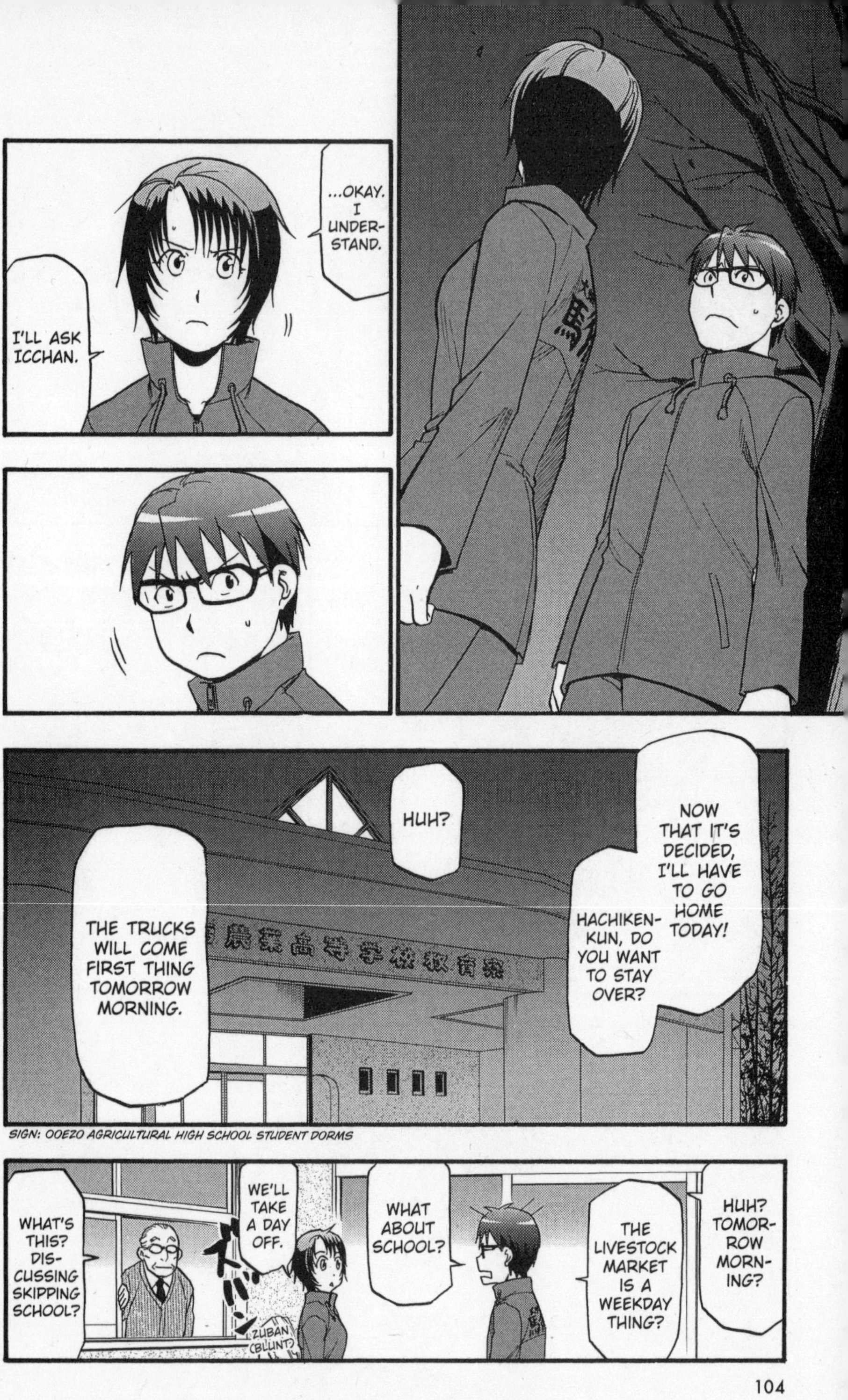
...OKAY. I UNDERSTAND.
I'LL ASK ICCHAN.
NOW THAT IT'S DECIDED, I'LL HAVE TO GO HOME TODAY!
HACHIKEN-KUN, DO YOU WANT TO STAY OVER?
HUH?
THE TRUCKS WILL COME FIRST THING TOMORROW MORNING.
SIGN: OOEZO AGRICULTURAL HIGH SCHOOL STUDENT DORMS
HUH? TOMORROW MORNING?
THE LIVESTOCK MARKET IS A WEEKDAY THING?
WHAT ABOUT SCHOOL?
WE'LL TAKE A DAY OFF.
ZUBAN (BLUNT)
WHAT'S THIS? DISCUSSING SKIPPING SCHOOL?

Silver Spoon

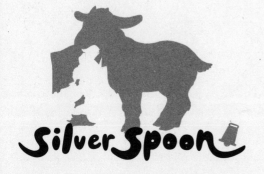

HORTICULTURE
TEACHER

HIROSHI TAIHEI

Chapter 67: Tale of Winter ④

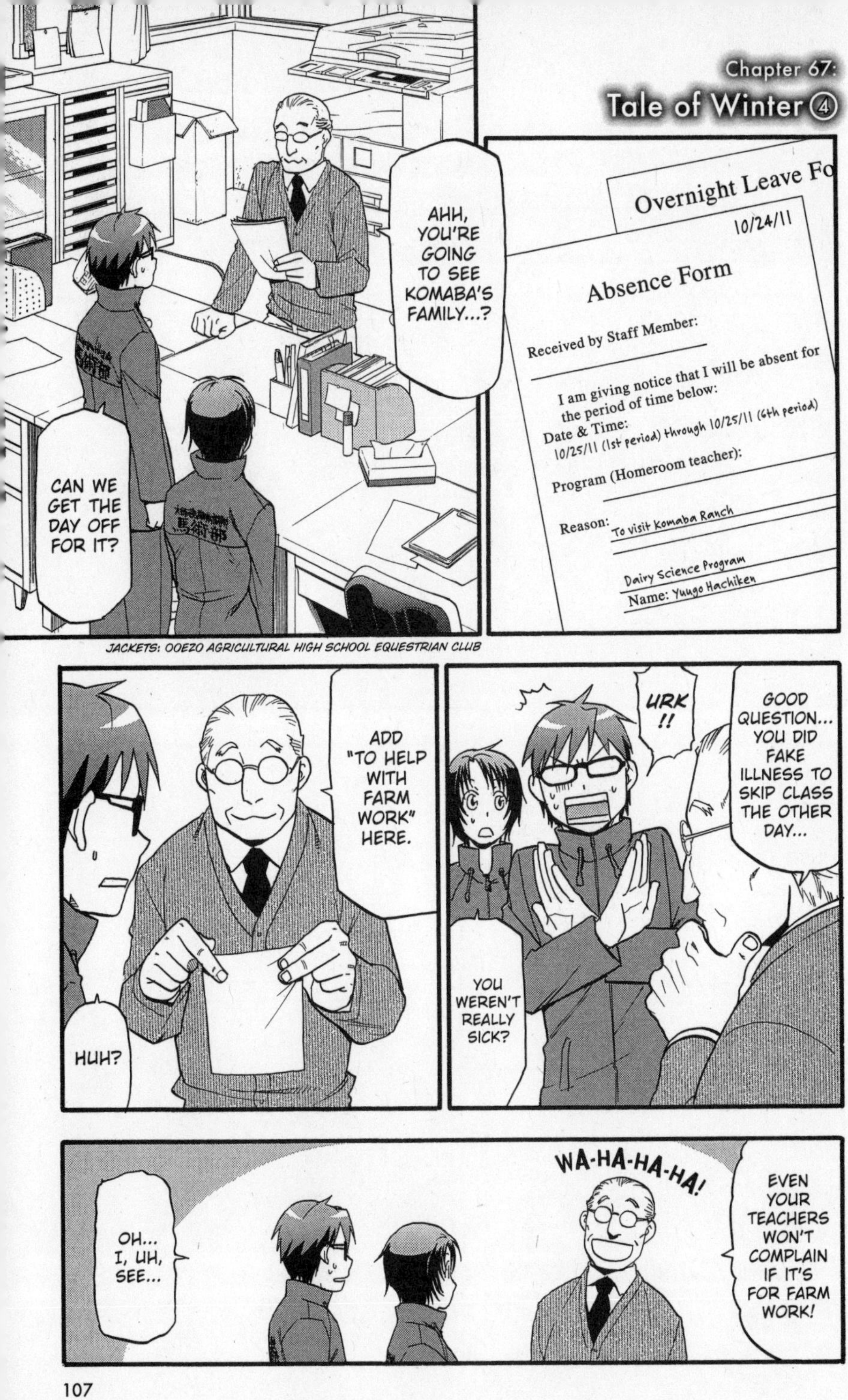

Overnight Leave Fo
10/24/11
Absence Form
Received by Staff Member:
I am giving notice that I will be absent for the period of time below:
Date & Time:
10/25/11 (1st period) through 10/25/11 (6th period)
Program (Homeroom teacher):
Reason: To visit Komaba Ranch
Dairy Science Program
Name: Yuugo Hachiken
AHH, YOU'RE GOING TO SEE KOMABA'S FAMILY...?
CAN WE GET THE DAY OFF FOR IT?
JACKETS: OOEZO AGRICULTURAL HIGH SCHOOL EQUESTRIAN CLUB
GOOD QUESTION... YOU DID FAKE ILLNESS TO SKIP CLASS THE OTHER DAY...
URK !!
YOU WEREN'T REALLY SICK?
ADD "TO HELP WITH FARM WORK" HERE.
HUH?
EVEN YOUR TEACHERS WON'T COMPLAIN IF IT'S FOR FARM WORK!
WA-HA-HA-HA!
OH... I, UH, SEE...

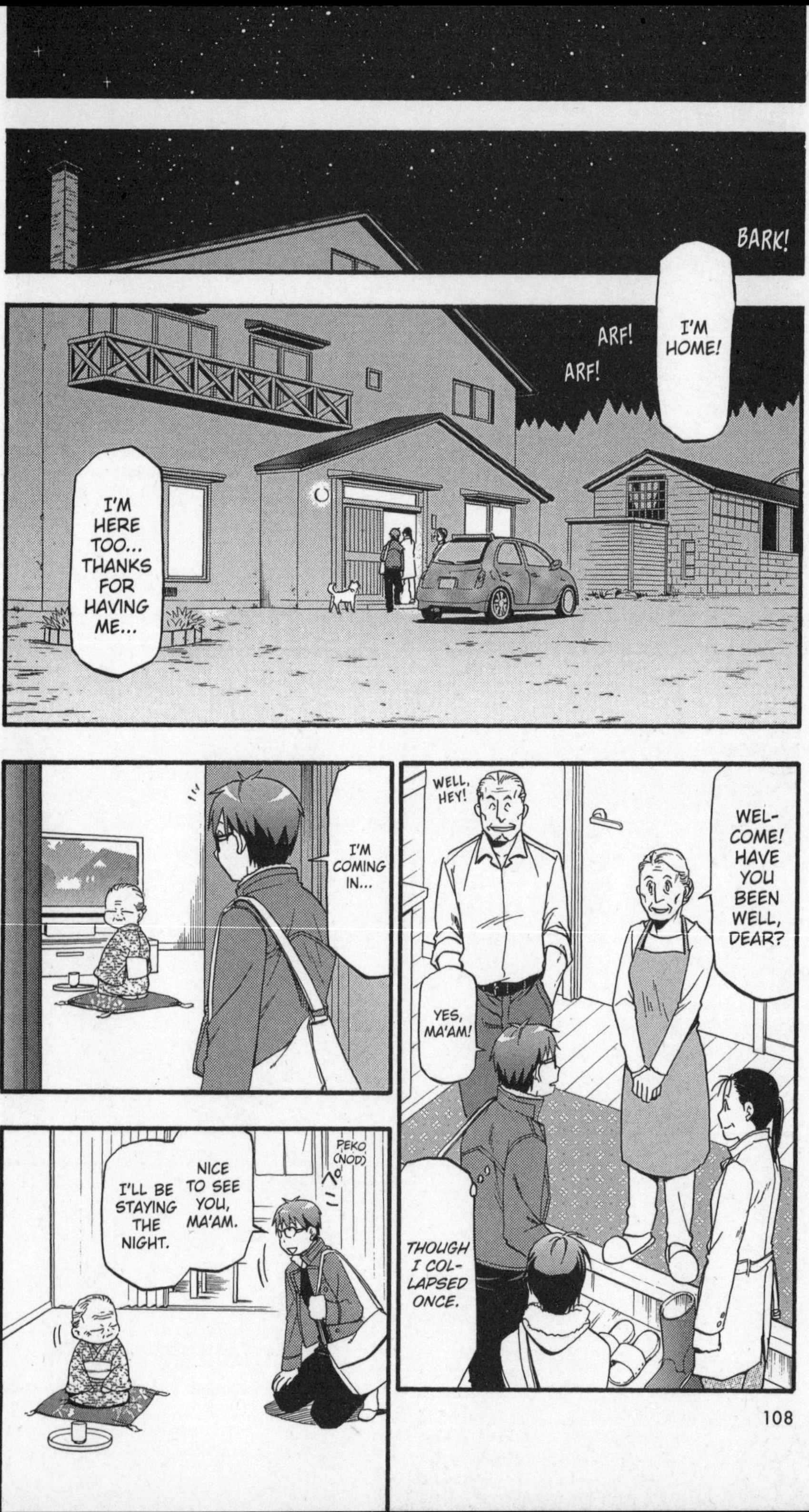
BARK!
I'M HOME!
ARF!
ARF!
I'M HERE TOO... THANKS FOR HAVING ME...
WEL-COME! HAVE YOU BEEN WELL, DEAR?
WELL, HEY!
YES, MA'AM!
THOUGH I COL-LAPSED ONCE.
I'M COMING IN...
PEKO (NOD)
NICE TO SEE YOU, MA'AM.
I'LL BE STAYING THE NIGHT.

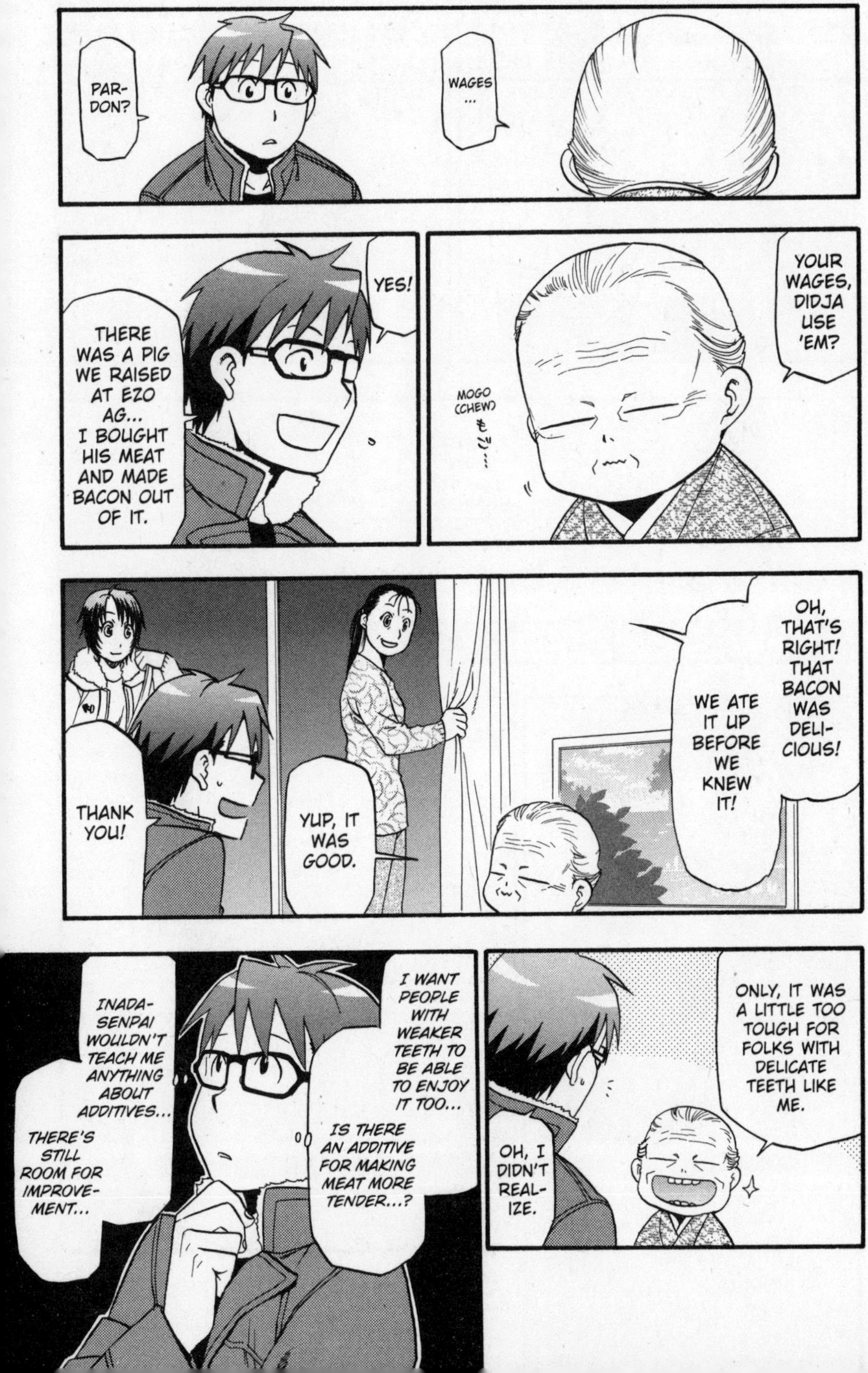
WAGES...
PARDON?
YOUR WAGES, DIDJA USE 'EM?
MOGO (CHEW)
もご…
YES!
THERE WAS A PIG WE RAISED AT EZO AG... I BOUGHT HIS MEAT AND MADE BACON OUT OF IT.
OH, THAT'S RIGHT! THAT BACON WAS DELICIOUS!
WE ATE IT UP BEFORE WE KNEW IT!
YUP, IT WAS GOOD.
THANK YOU!
ONLY, IT WAS A LITTLE TOO TOUGH FOR FOLKS WITH DELICATE TEETH LIKE ME.
OH, I DIDN'T REALIZE.
I WANT PEOPLE WITH WEAKER TEETH TO BE ABLE TO ENJOY IT TOO...
IS THERE AN ADDITIVE FOR MAKING MEAT MORE TENDER...?
INADA-SENPAI WOULDN'T TEACH ME ANYTHING ABOUT ADDITIVES...
THERE'S STILL ROOM FOR IMPROVEMENT...

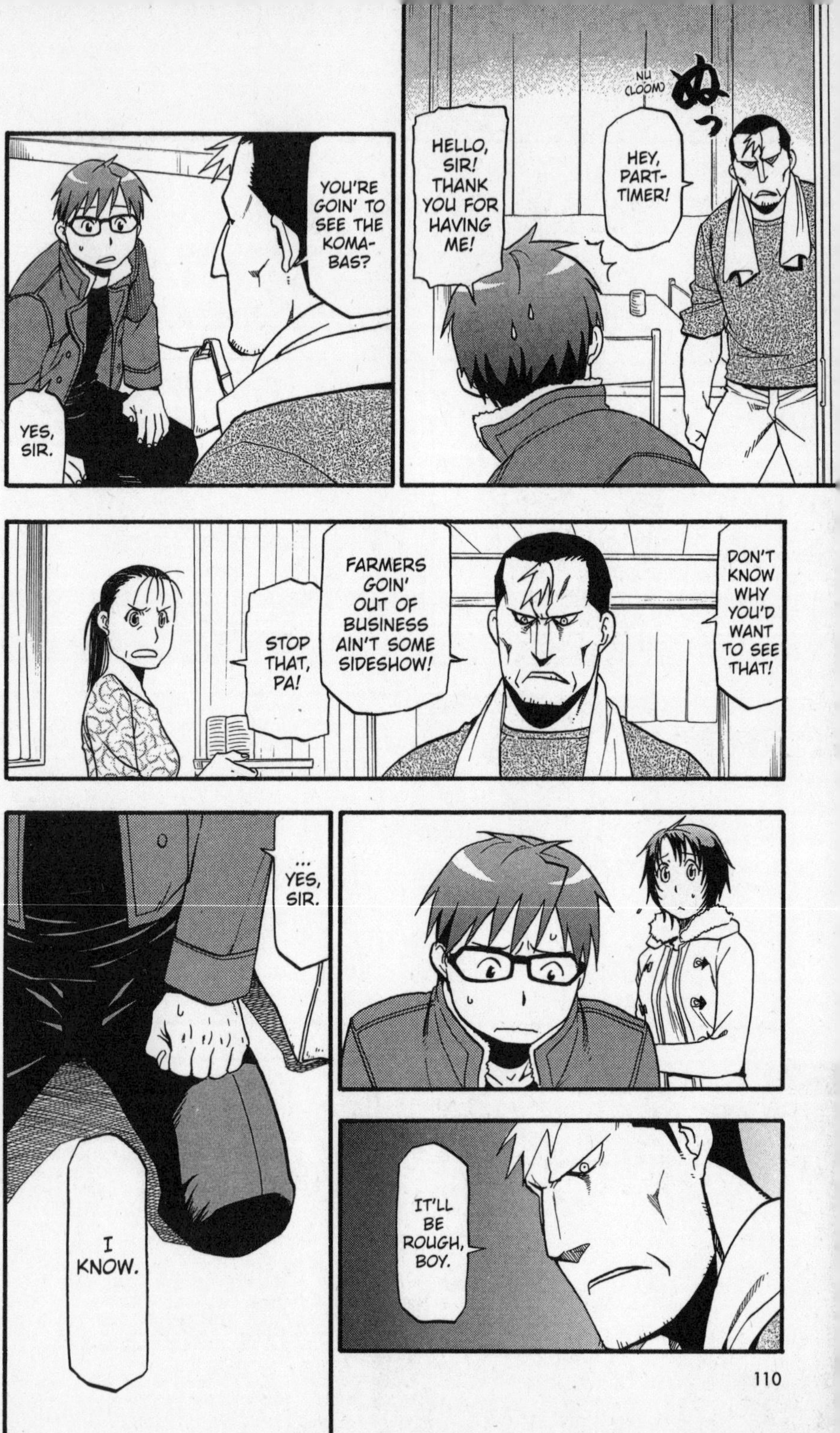
NU (LOOM)
ぬっ
HEY, PART-TIMER!
HELLO, SIR! THANK YOU FOR HAVING ME!
YOU'RE GOIN' TO SEE THE KOMA-BAS?
YES, SIR.
DON'T KNOW WHY YOU'D WANT TO SEE THAT!
FARMERS GOIN' OUT OF BUSINESS AIN'T SOME SIDESHOW!
STOP THAT, PA!
IT'LL BE ROUGH, BOY.
... YES, SIR.
I KNOW.

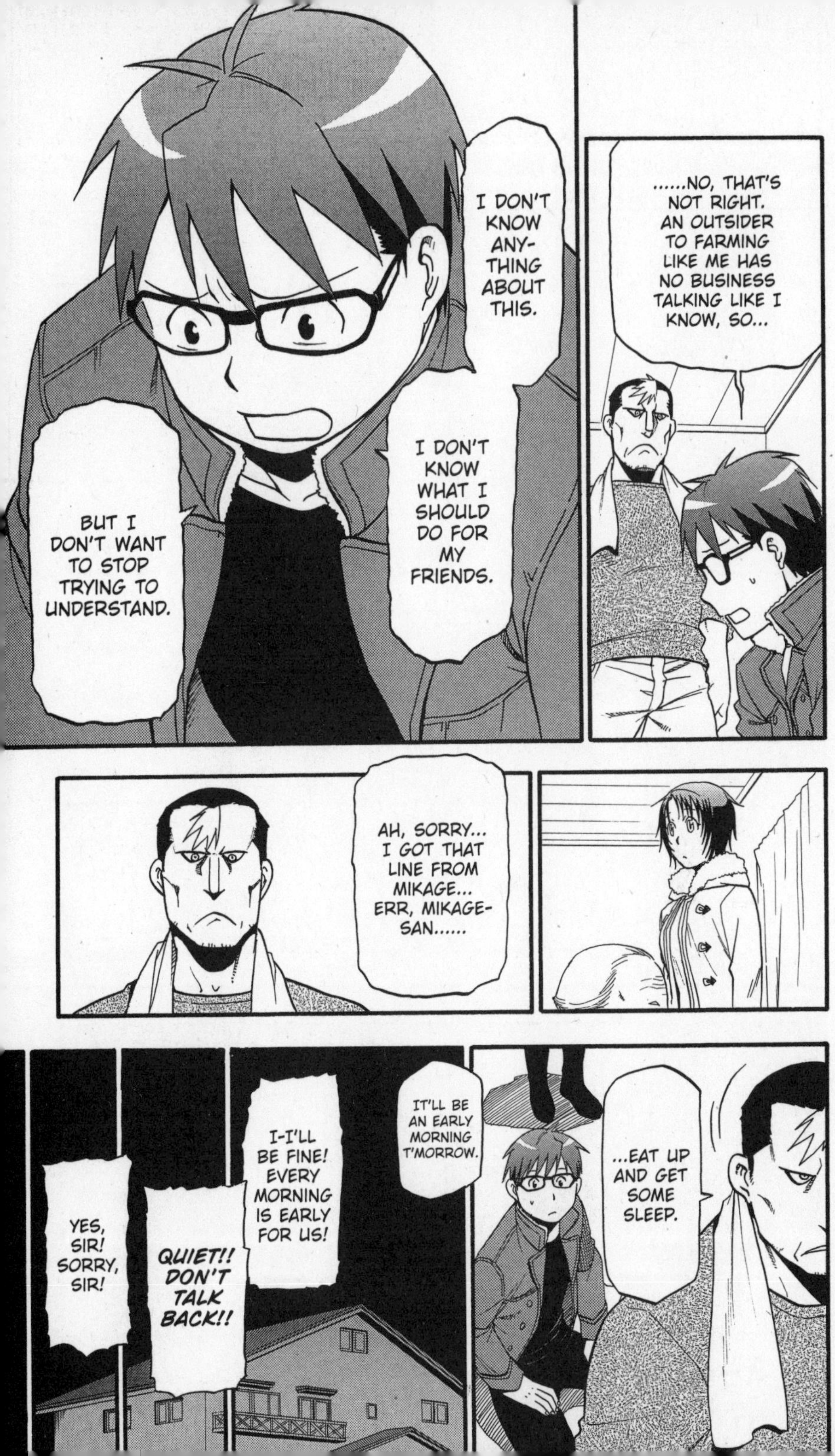
......NO, THAT'S NOT RIGHT. AN OUTSIDER TO FARMING LIKE ME HAS NO BUSINESS TALKING LIKE I KNOW, SO...
I DON'T KNOW ANY-THING ABOUT THIS.
I DON'T KNOW WHAT I SHOULD DO FOR MY FRIENDS.
BUT I DON'T WANT TO STOP TRYING TO UNDERSTAND.
AH, SORRY... I GOT THAT LINE FROM MIKAGE... ERR, MIKAGE-SAN......
...EAT UP AND GET SOME SLEEP.
IT'LL BE AN EARLY MORNING T'MORROW.
I-I'LL BE FINE! EVERY MORNING IS EARLY FOR US!
QUIET!! DON'T TALK BACK!!
YES, SIR! SORRY, SIR!

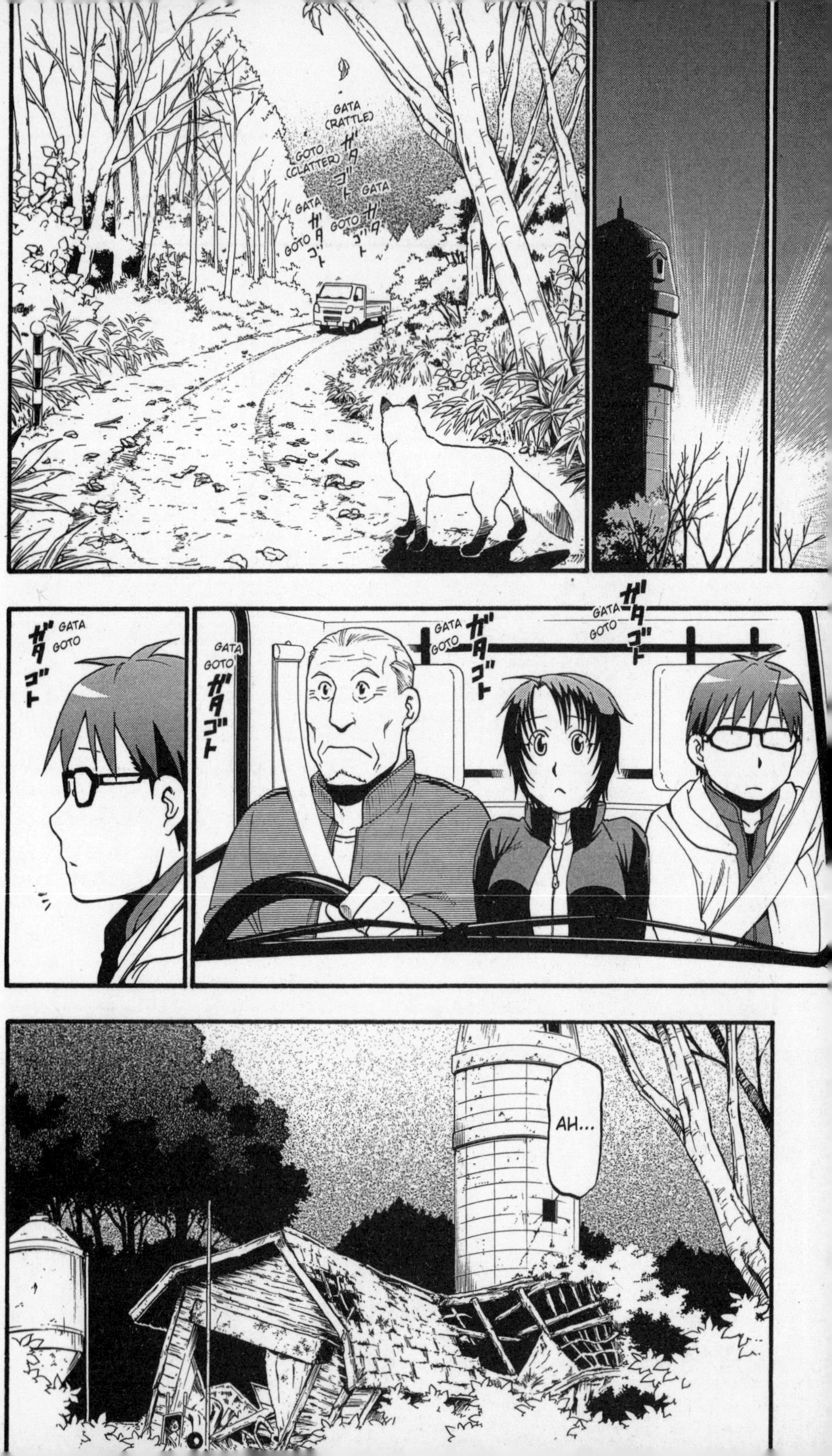
GATA (RATTLE) ガタ
GOTO (CLATTER) ゴト
GATA ガタ
GOTO ゴト
GATA ガタ
GOTO ゴト
GATA ガタ
GOTO ゴト
GATA ガタ
GOTO ゴト
GATA ガタ
GOTO ゴト
GATA ガタ
GOTO ゴト
AH...

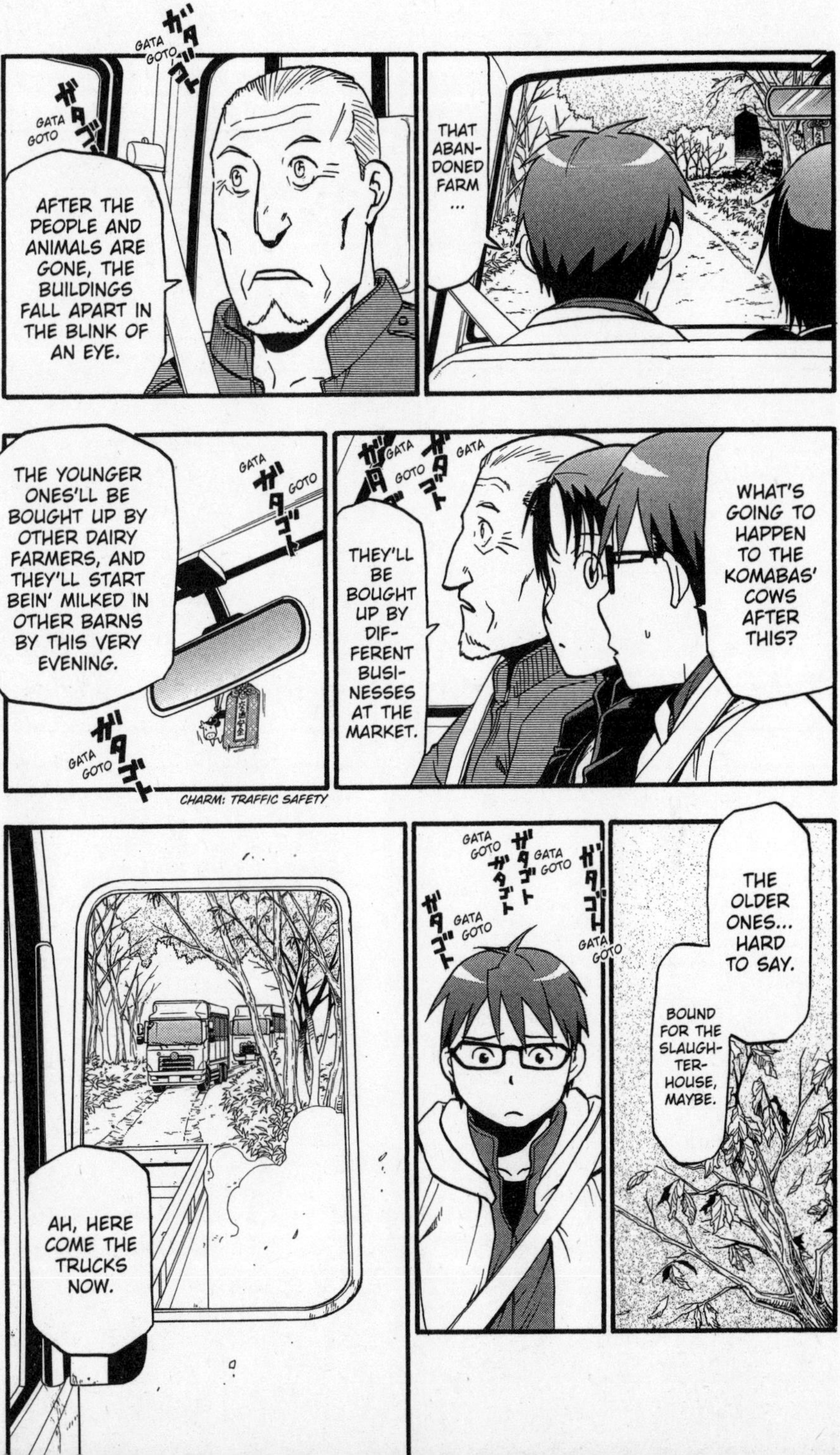
ガタゴト
GATA GOTO
THAT ABANDONED FARM...
ガタゴト
GATA GOTO
AFTER THE PEOPLE AND ANIMALS ARE GONE, THE BUILDINGS FALL APART IN THE BLINK OF AN EYE.
WHAT'S GOING TO HAPPEN TO THE KOMABAS' COWS AFTER THIS?
ガタゴト
GATA GOTO
ガタゴト
GATA GOTO
THEY'LL BE BOUGHT UP BY DIFFERENT BUSINESSES AT THE MARKET.
ガタゴト
GATA GOTO
THE YOUNGER ONES'LL BE BOUGHT UP BY OTHER DAIRY FARMERS, AND THEY'LL START BEIN' MILKED IN OTHER BARNS BY THIS VERY EVENING.
ガタゴト
GATA GOTO
CHARM: TRAFFIC SAFETY
THE OLDER ONES... HARD TO SAY.
BOUND FOR THE SLAUGHTERHOUSE, MAYBE.
ガタゴト
GATA GOTO
ガタゴト
GATA GOTO
ガタゴト
GATA GOTO
ガタゴト
GATA GOTO
AH, HERE COME THE TRUCKS NOW.

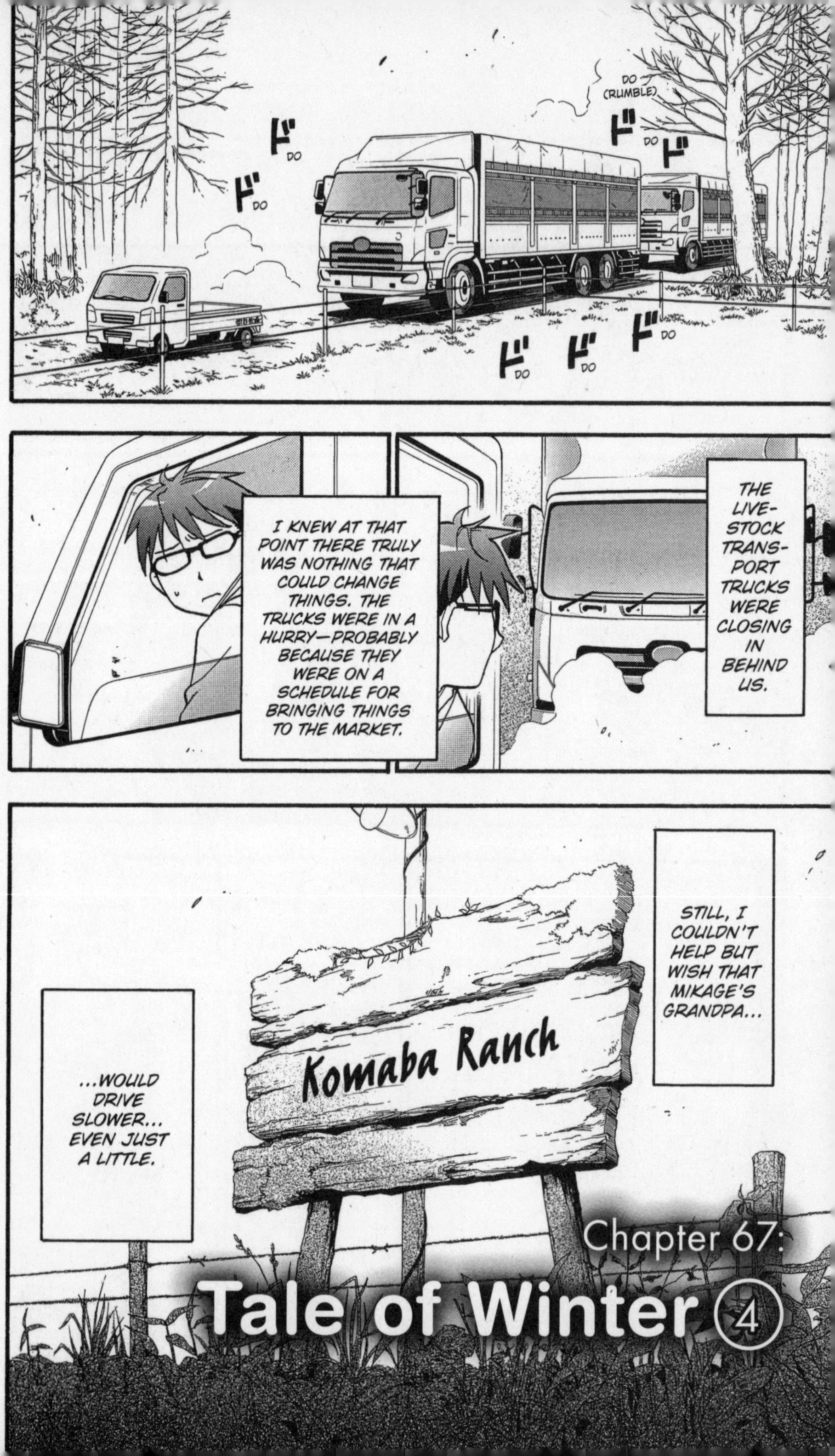
DO (RUMBLE)
ド DO
ド DO
ド DO
ド DO
ド DO
ド DO
ド DO
THE LIVE-STOCK TRANS-PORT TRUCKS WERE CLOSING IN BEHIND US.
I KNEW AT THAT POINT THERE TRULY WAS NOTHING THAT COULD CHANGE THINGS. THE TRUCKS WERE IN A HURRY—PROBABLY BECAUSE THEY WERE ON A SCHEDULE FOR BRINGING THINGS TO THE MARKET.
STILL, I COULDN'T HELP BUT WISH THAT MIKAGE'S GRANDPA...
Komaba Ranch
...WOULD DRIVE SLOWER... EVEN JUST A LITTLE.

Chapter 67: Tale of Winter ④

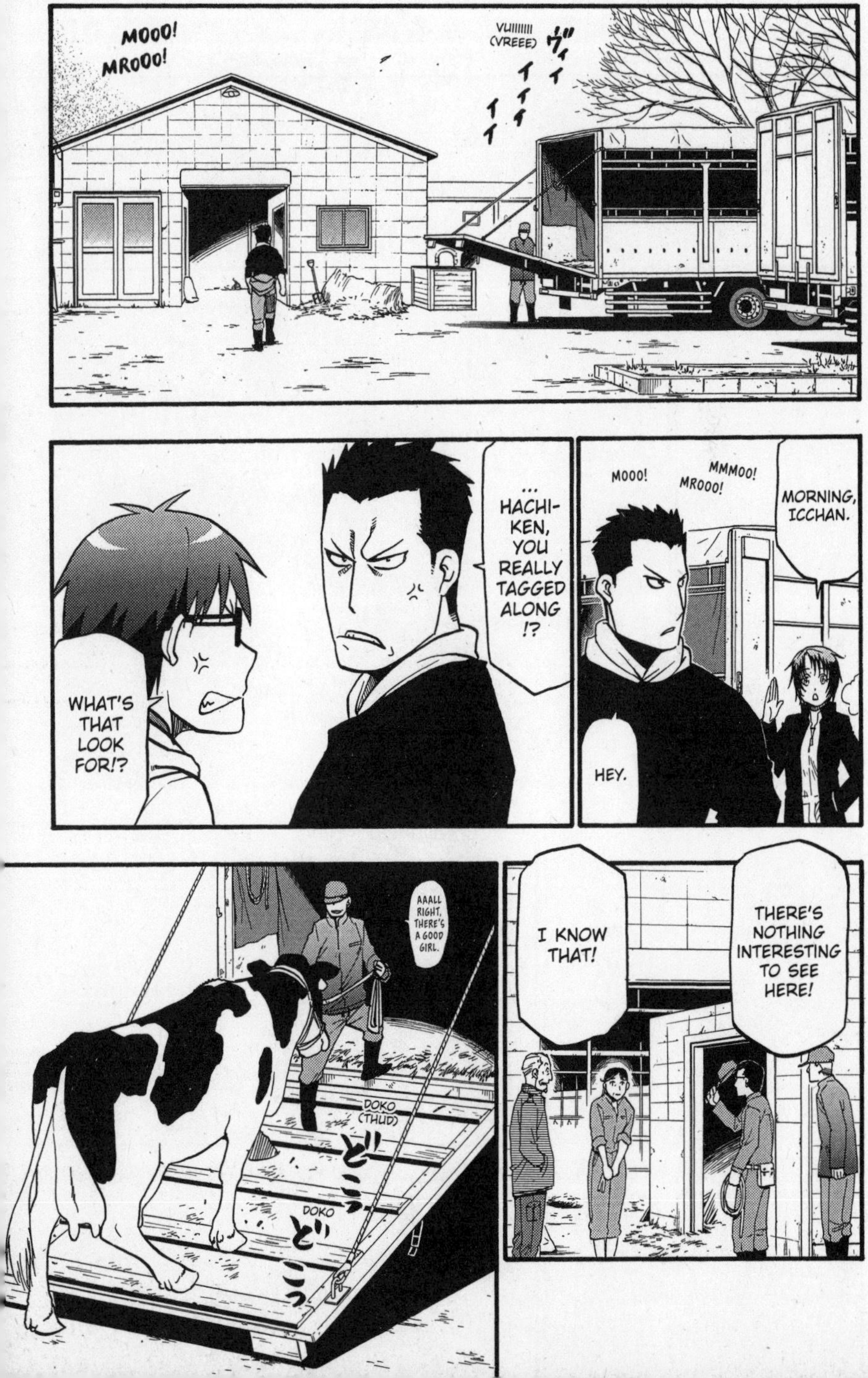
VUIIIIIIII
(VREEE)
ヴィイイイイイイ
MOOO!
MROOO!
MORNING, ICCHAN.
MMMOO!
MROOO!
MOOO!
HEY.
... HACHI-KEN, YOU REALLY TAGGED ALONG!?
WHAT'S THAT LOOK FOR!?
THERE'S NOTHING INTERESTING TO SEE HERE!
I KNOW THAT!
AAALL RIGHT, THERE'S A GOOD GIRL.
DOKO
(THUD)
どこ
DOKO
どこ

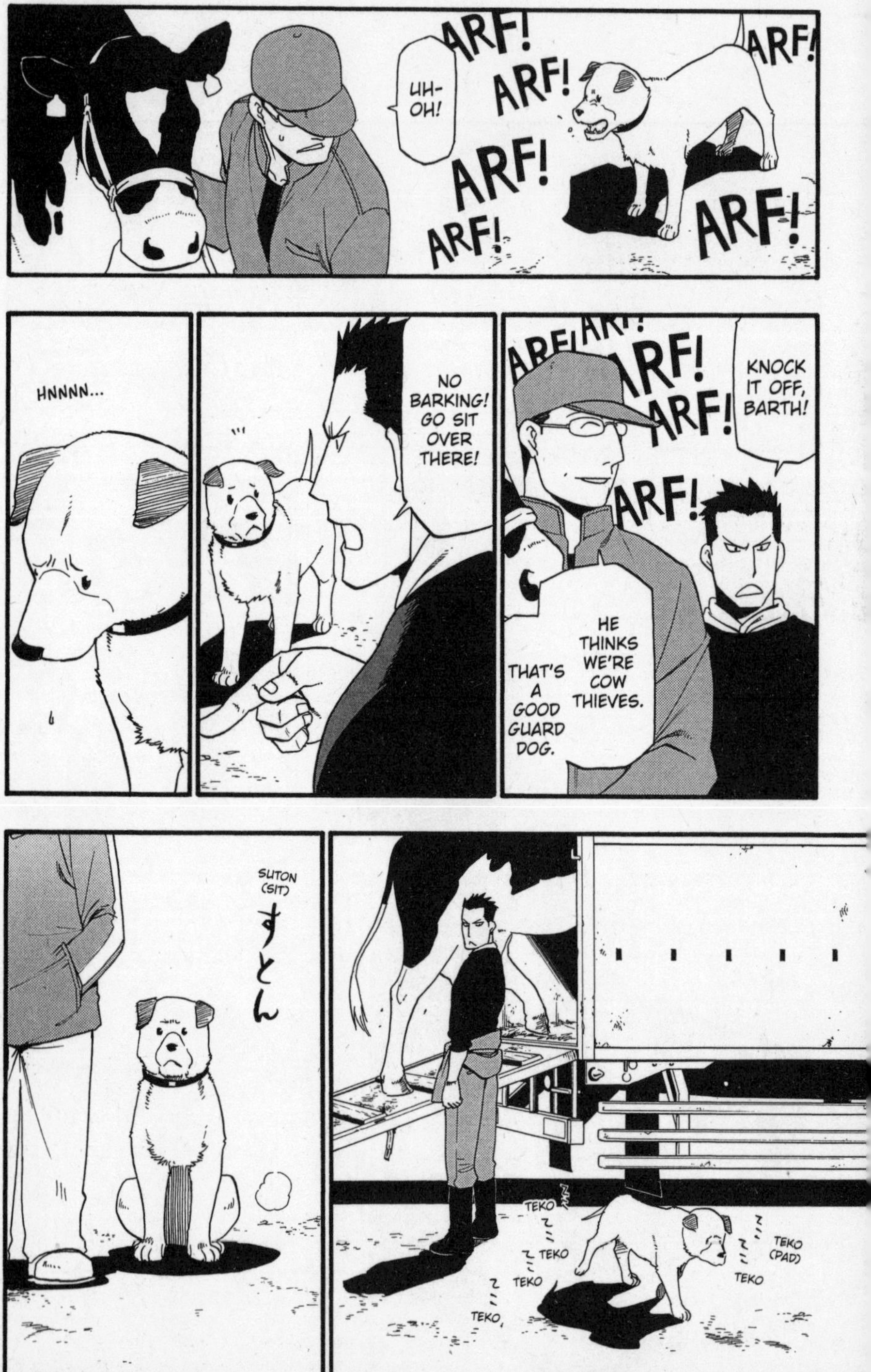
ARF!
ARF!
ARF!
UH-OH!
ARF!
ARF!
ARF!
KNOCK IT OFF, BARTH!
ARF!
ARF!
ARF!
ARF!
HE THINKS WE'RE COW THIEVES.
THAT'S A GOOD GUARD DOG.
NO BARKING! GO SIT OVER THERE!
HNNNN...
TEKO (PAD)
TEKO
TEKO
TEKO
TEKO
TEKO
SUTON (SIT)
すとん

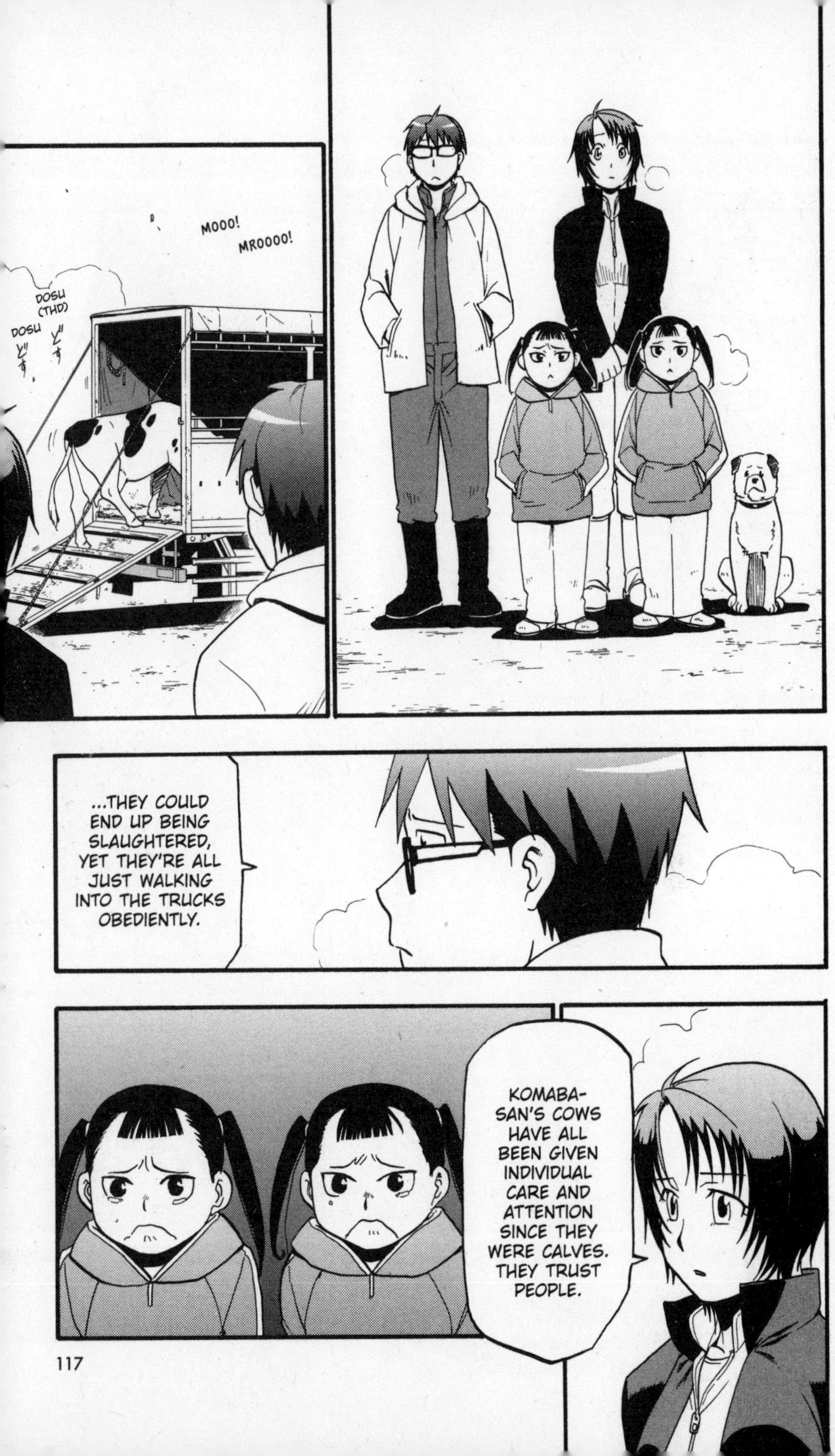
MOOO!
MROOOO!
DOSU (THD)
どす
DOSU
どす
...THEY COULD END UP BEING SLAUGHTERED, YET THEY'RE ALL JUST WALKING INTO THE TRUCKS OBEDIENTLY.
KOMABA-SAN'S COWS HAVE ALL BEEN GIVEN INDIVIDUAL CARE AND ATTENTION SINCE THEY WERE CALVES. THEY TRUST PEOPLE.

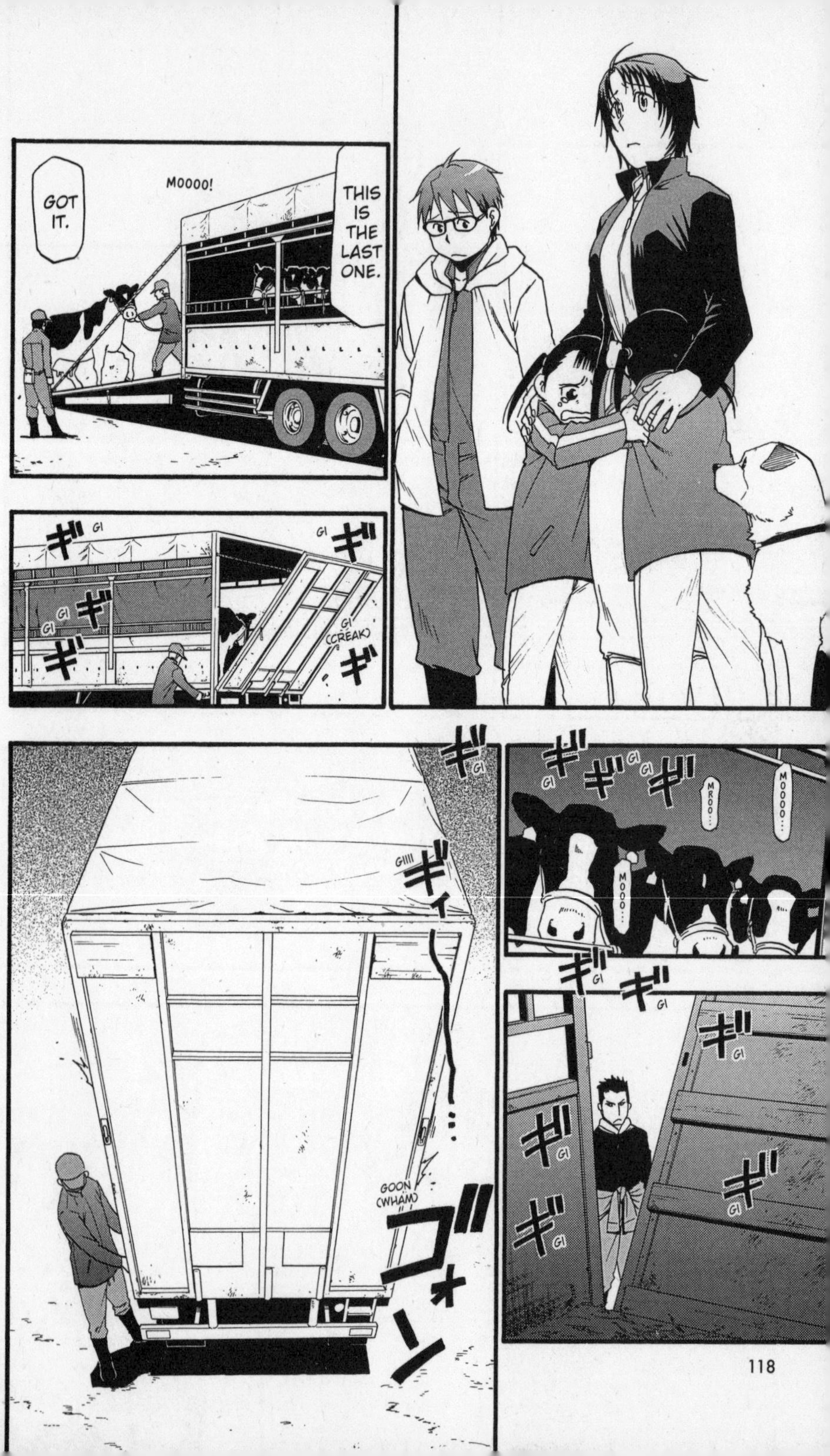
THIS IS THE LAST ONE.
MOOOO!
GOT IT.
ギ GI
ギ GI
ギ GI
ギ GI
ギ GI (CREAK)
ギ GI
ギ GI
ギ GI
MOOOO...
MROO...
MOOO...
ギ GI
ギ GI
ギ GI
ギ GI
ギ GI
ギ GI
ギ GI
ギィ GIIII
ゴォーン GOON (WHAM)

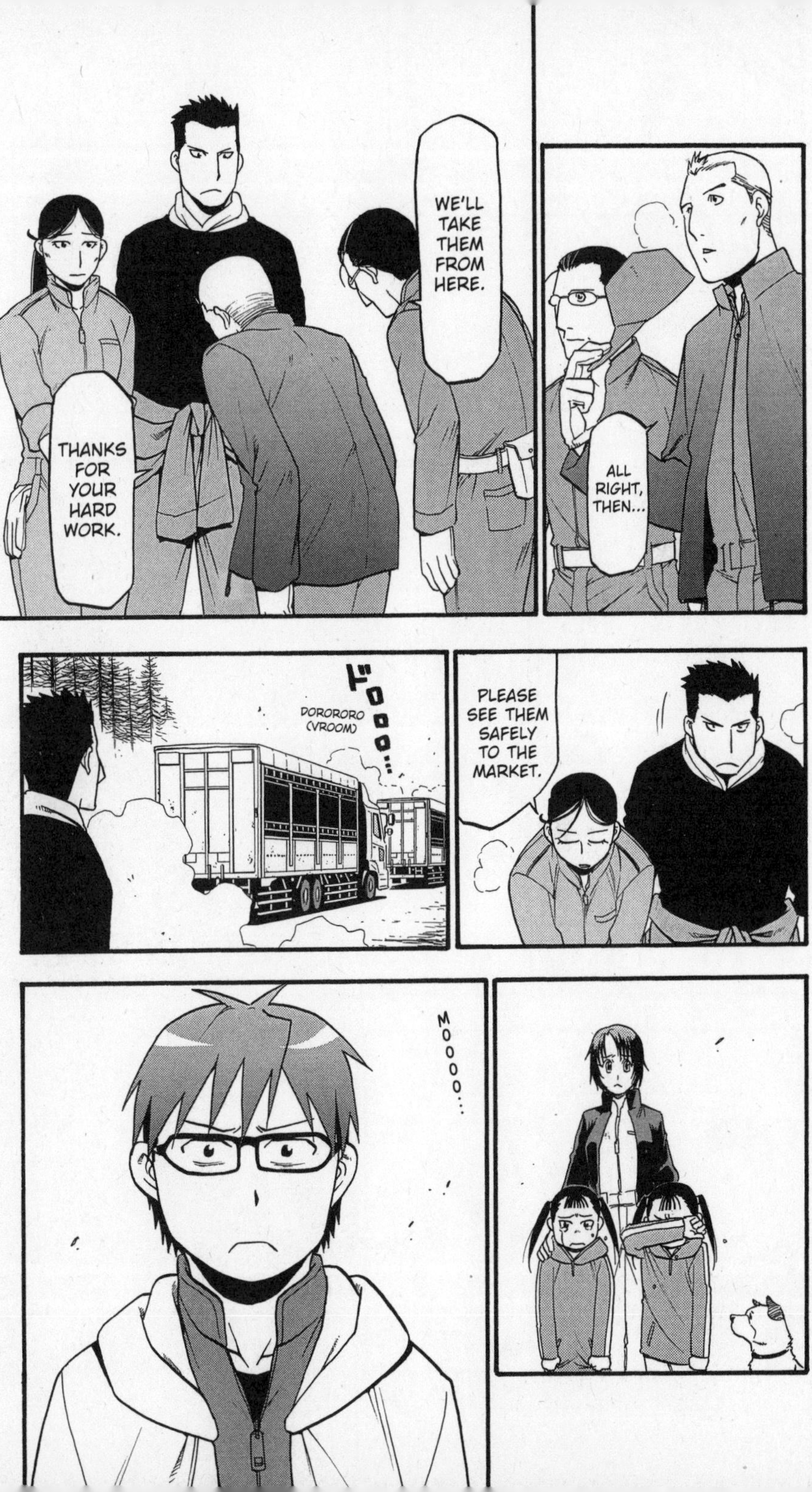
ALL RIGHT, THEN...
WE'LL TAKE THEM FROM HERE.
THANKS FOR YOUR HARD WORK.
PLEASE SEE THEM SAFELY TO THE MARKET.
ドロロロ…
DORORORO (VROOM)
MOOOOO...

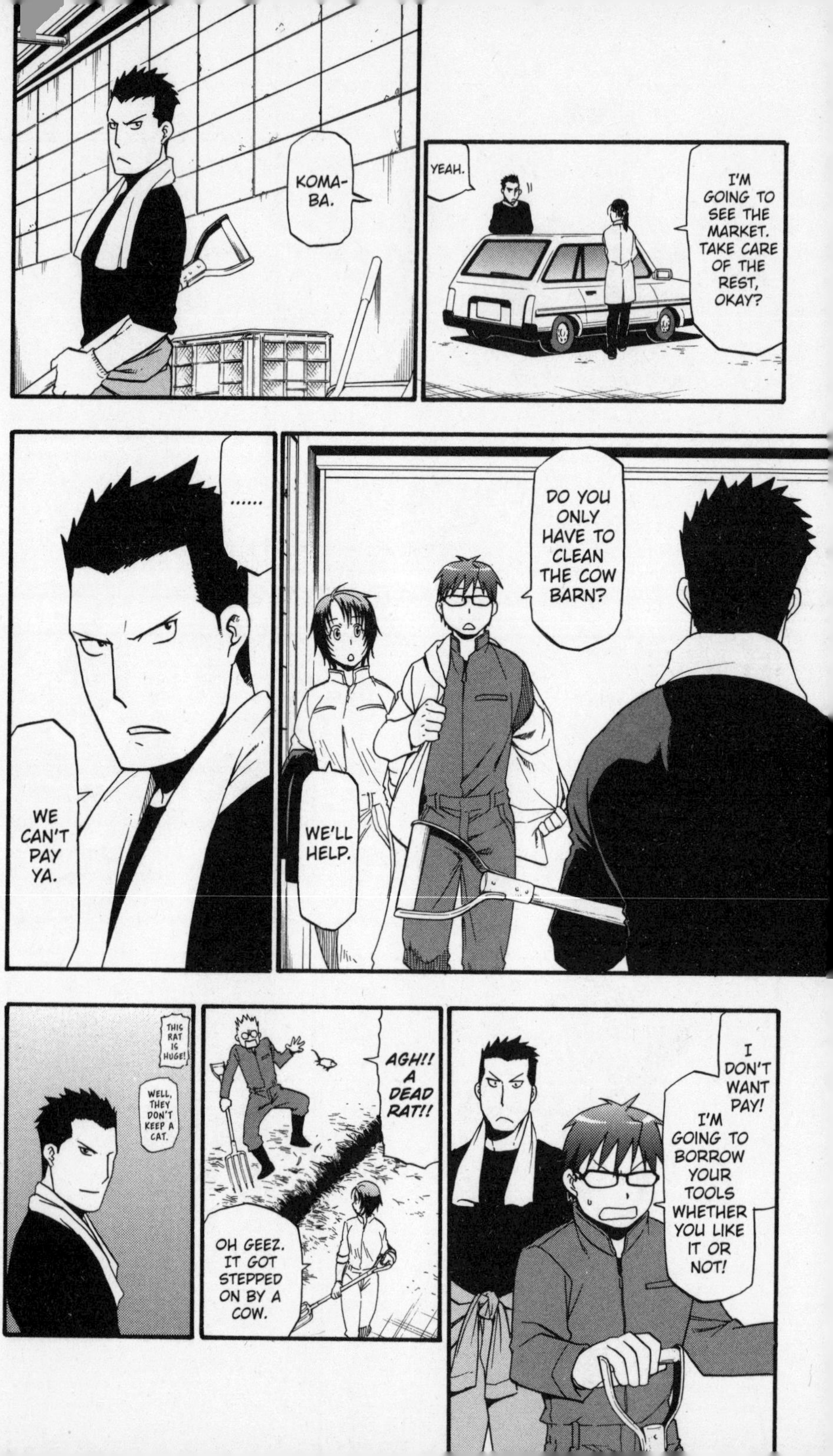
I'M GOING TO SEE THE MARKET. TAKE CARE OF THE REST, OKAY?
YEAH.
KOMA-BA.
DO YOU ONLY HAVE TO CLEAN THE COW BARN?
WE'LL HELP.
......
WE CAN'T PAY YA.
I DON'T WANT PAY!
I'M GOING TO BORROW YOUR TOOLS WHETHER YOU LIKE IT OR NOT!
AGH!! A DEAD RAT!!
OH GEEZ. IT GOT STEPPED ON BY A COW.
THIS RAT IS HUGE!
WELL, THEY DON'T KEEP A CAT.

CHARM: COW & HORSE HEALTH / OOEZO SHRINE PROTECTION / FARM ANIMAL PROSPERITY

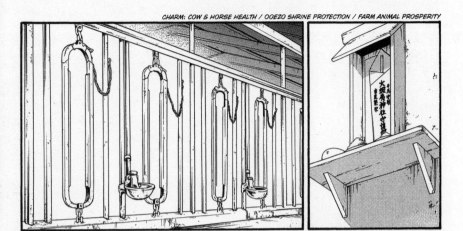

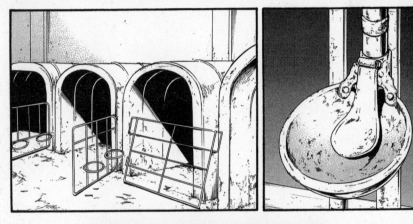

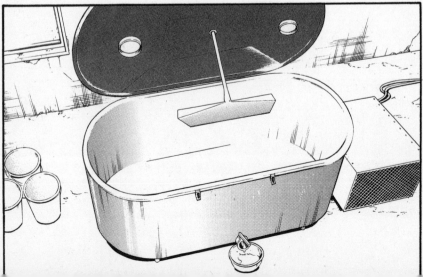

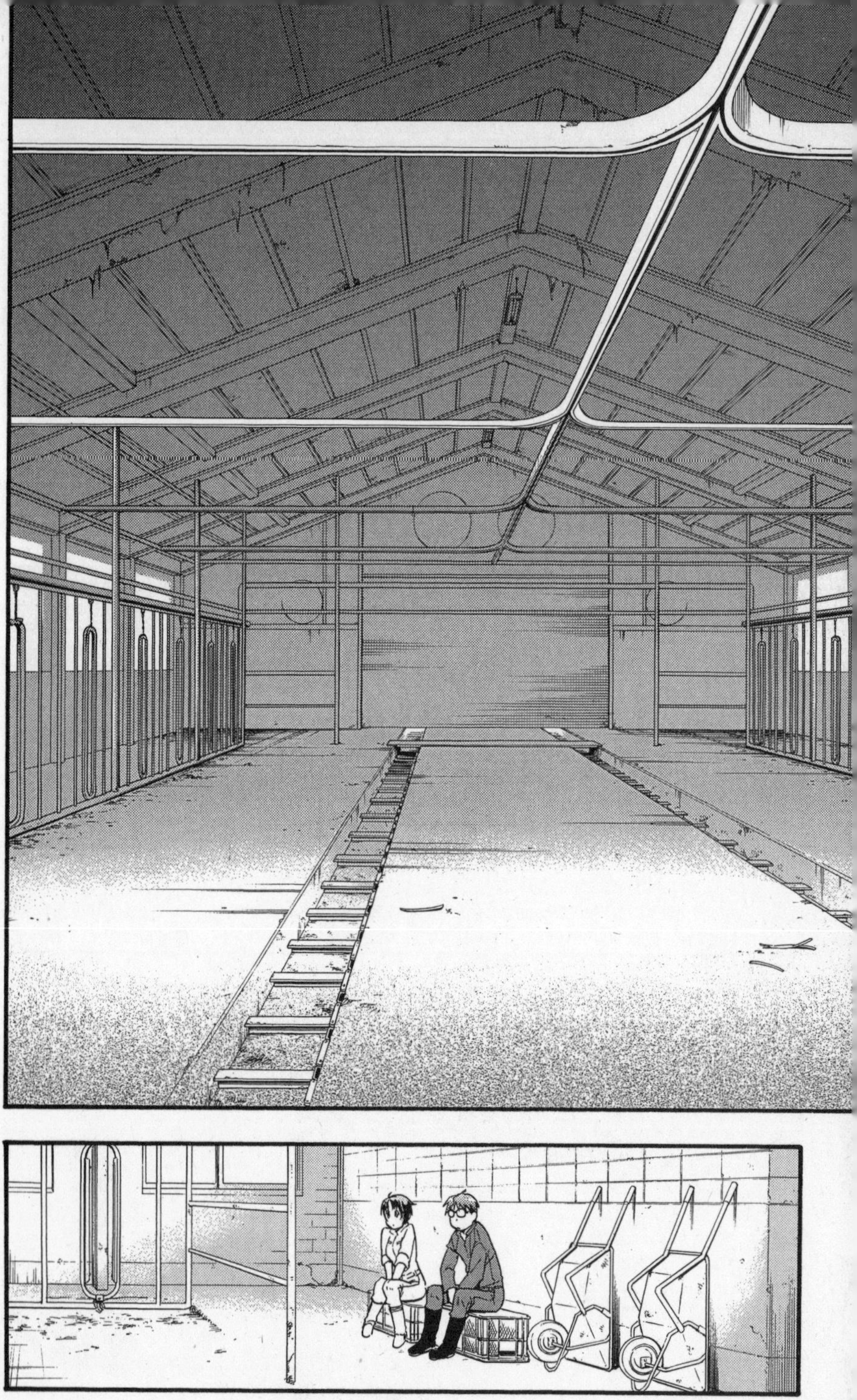

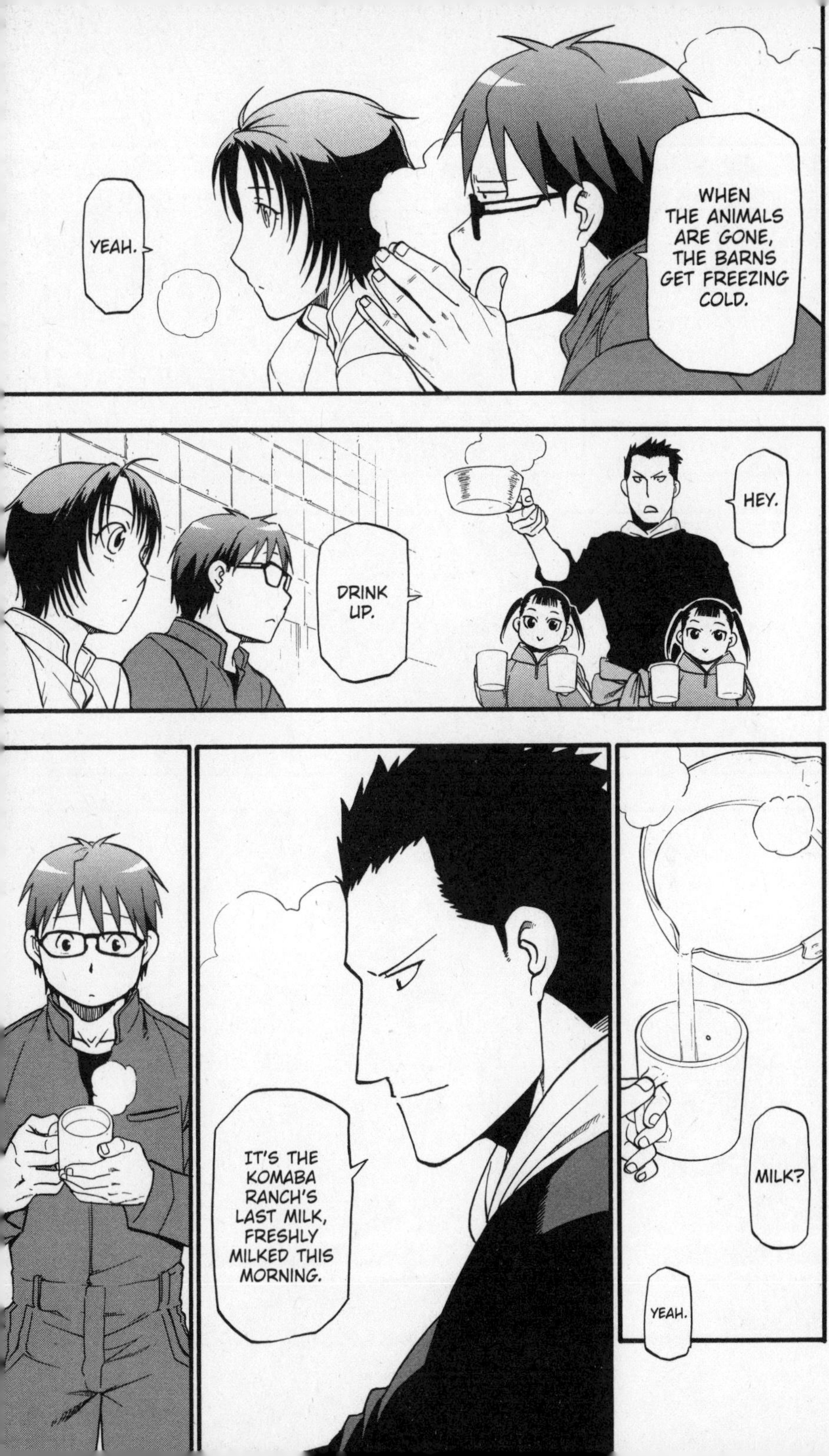
WHEN THE ANIMALS ARE GONE, THE BARNS GET FREEZING COLD.
YEAH.
HEY.
DRINK UP.
MILK?
YEAH.
IT'S THE KOMABA RANCH'S LAST MILK, FRESHLY MILKED THIS MORNING.

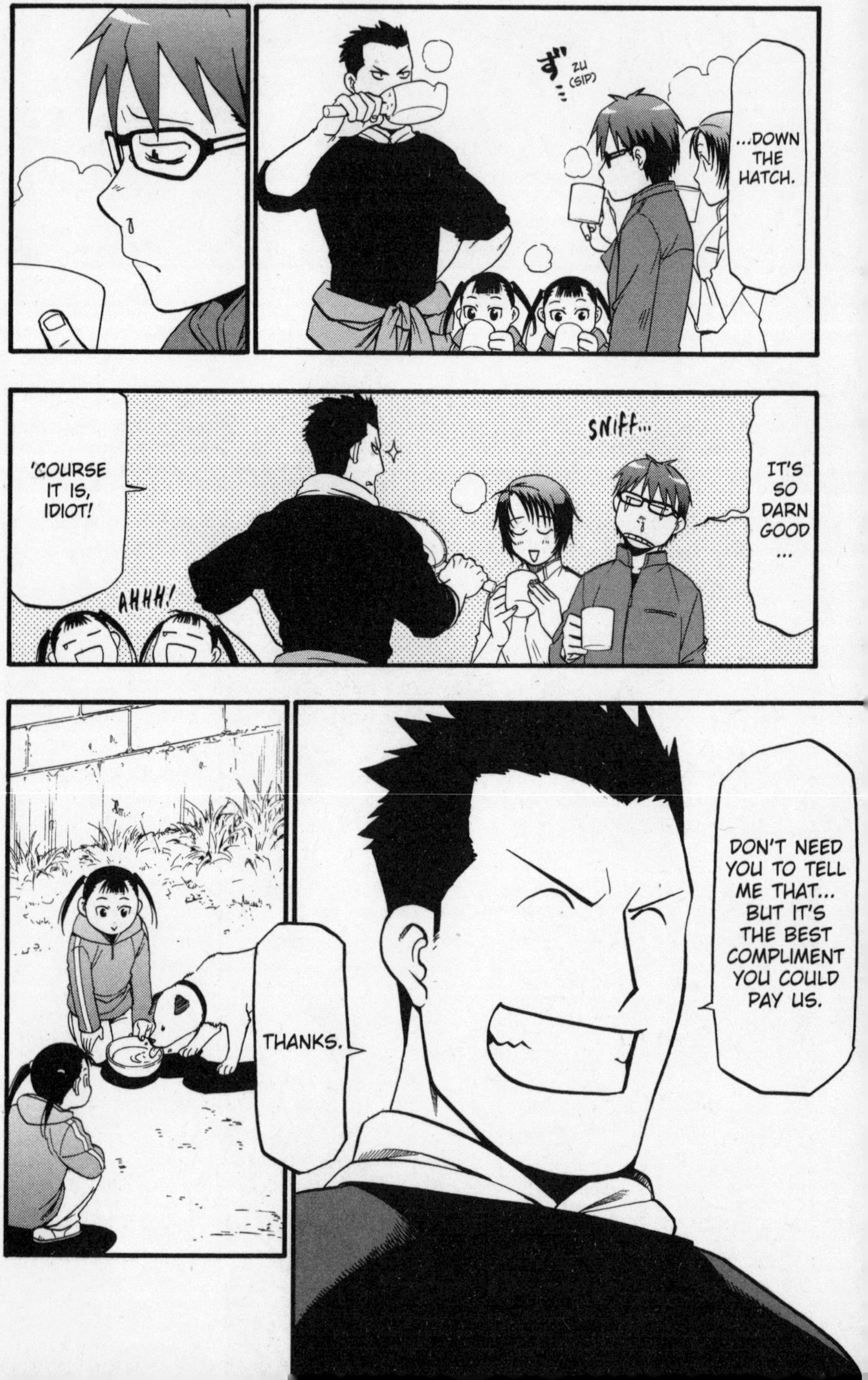
...DOWN THE HATCH.
ず
ZU (SIP)
IT'S SO DARN GOOD ...
SNIFF...
'COURSE IT IS, IDIOT!
AHHH!
DON'T NEED YOU TO TELL ME THAT... BUT IT'S THE BEST COMPLIMENT YOU COULD PAY US.
THANKS.

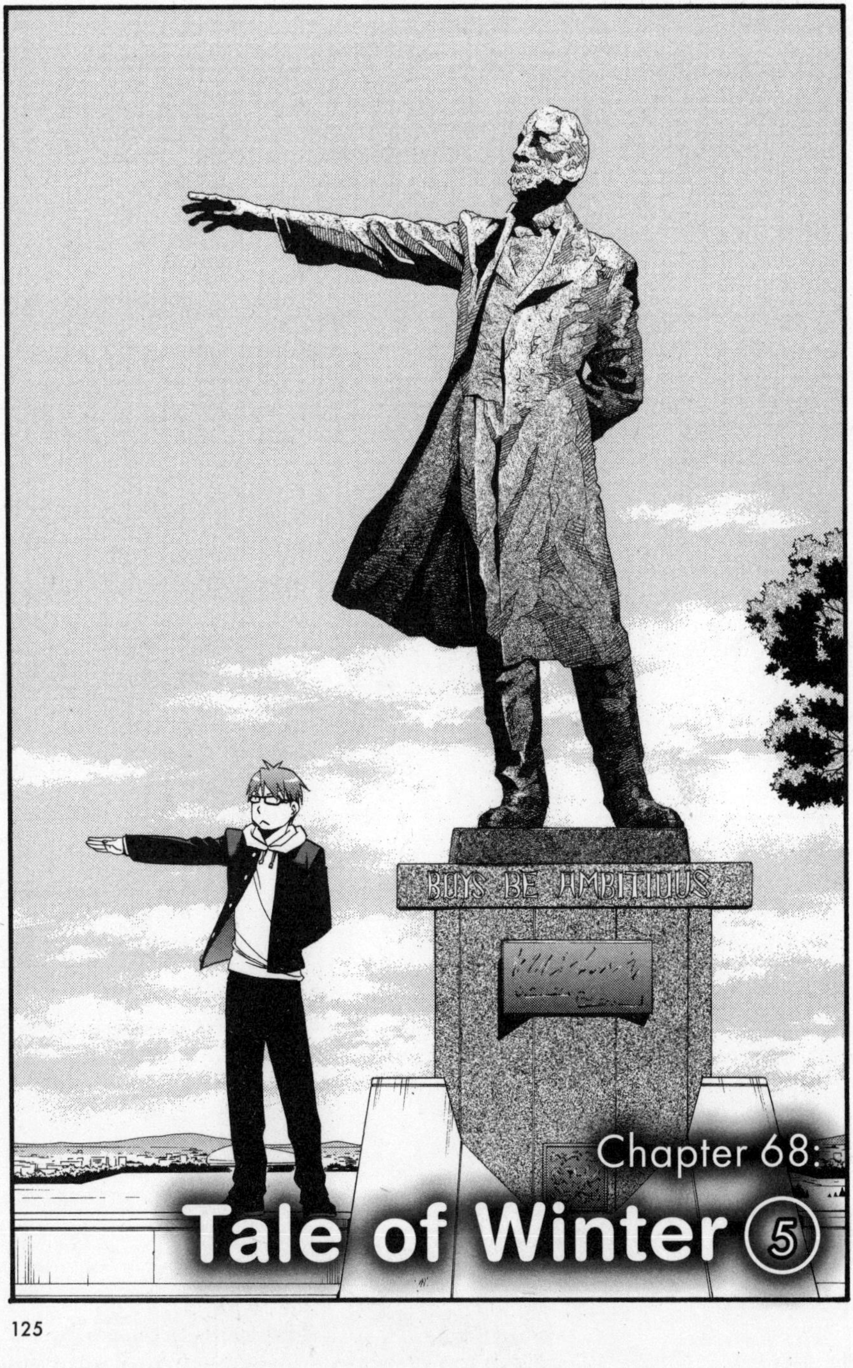
BOYS BE AMBITIOUS

Chapter 68: Tale of Winter ⑤

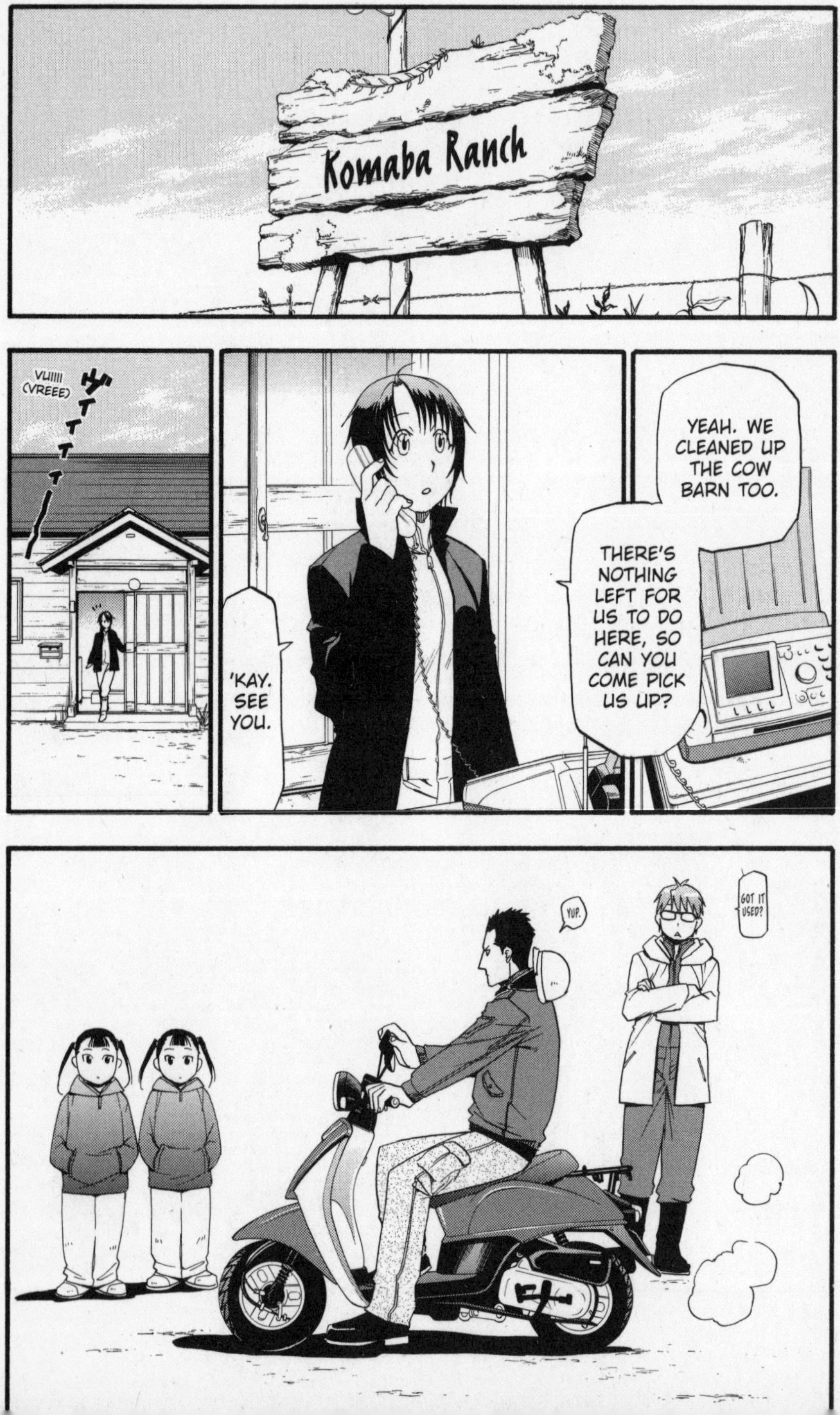
Komaba Ranch
YEAH. WE CLEANED UP THE COW BARN TOO.
THERE'S NOTHING LEFT FOR US TO DO HERE, SO CAN YOU COME PICK US UP?
'KAY. SEE YOU.
ヴィィィィー
VUIIII (VREEE)
GOT IT USED?
YUP.

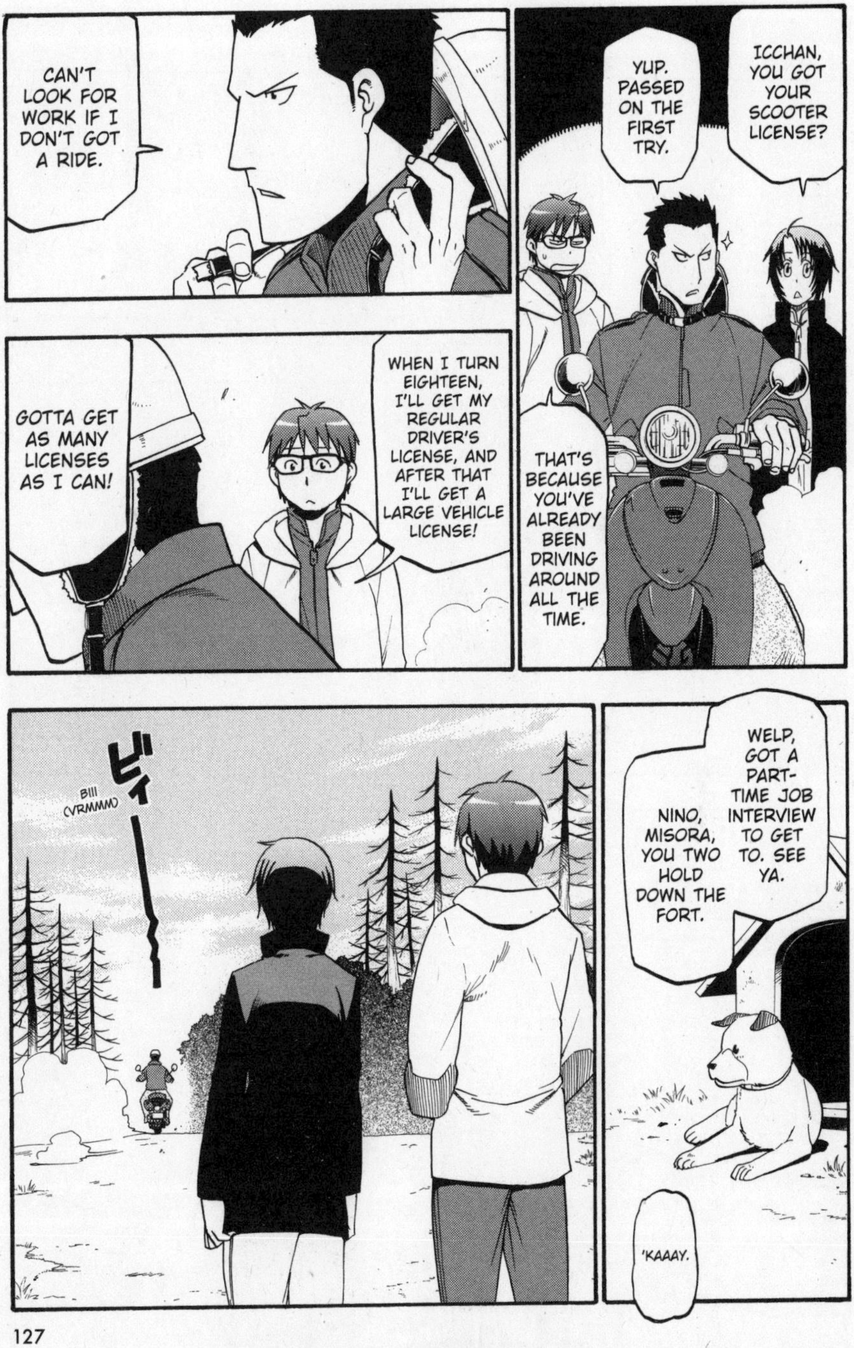
ICCHAN, YOU GOT YOUR SCOOTER LICENSE?
YUP. PASSED ON THE FIRST TRY.
THAT'S BECAUSE YOU'VE ALREADY BEEN DRIVING AROUND ALL THE TIME.
CAN'T LOOK FOR WORK IF I DON'T GOT A RIDE.
WHEN I TURN EIGHTEEN, I'LL GET MY REGULAR DRIVER'S LICENSE, AND AFTER THAT I'LL GET A LARGE VEHICLE LICENSE!
GOTTA GET AS MANY LICENSES AS I CAN!
WELP, GOT A PART-TIME JOB INTERVIEW TO GET TO. SEE YA.
NINO, MISORA, YOU TWO HOLD DOWN THE FORT.
'KAAAY.
ビィー
BIII (VRMMM)

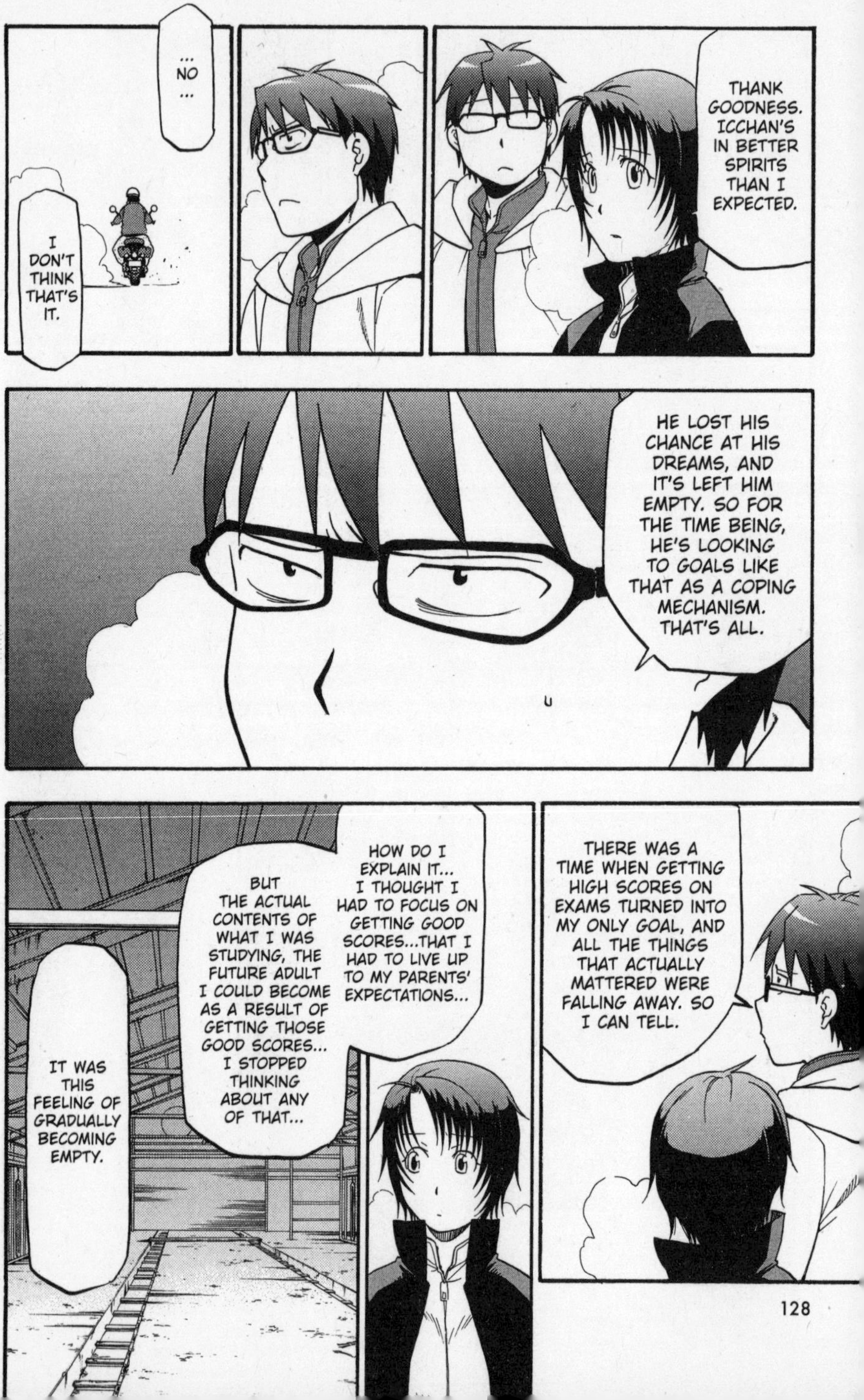
THANK GOODNESS. ICCHAN'S IN BETTER SPIRITS THAN I EXPECTED.
... NO ...
I DON'T THINK THAT'S IT.
HE LOST HIS CHANCE AT HIS DREAMS, AND IT'S LEFT HIM EMPTY. SO FOR THE TIME BEING, HE'S LOOKING TO GOALS LIKE THAT AS A COPING MECHANISM. THAT'S ALL.
THERE WAS A TIME WHEN GETTING HIGH SCORES ON EXAMS TURNED INTO MY ONLY GOAL, AND ALL THE THINGS THAT ACTUALLY MATTERED WERE FALLING AWAY. SO I CAN TELL.
HOW DO I EXPLAIN IT... I THOUGHT I HAD TO FOCUS ON GETTING GOOD SCORES...THAT I HAD TO LIVE UP TO MY PARENTS' EXPECTATIONS...
BUT THE ACTUAL CONTENTS OF WHAT I WAS STUDYING, THE FUTURE ADULT I COULD BECOME AS A RESULT OF GETTING THOSE GOOD SCORES... I STOPPED THINKING ABOUT ANY OF THAT...
IT WAS THIS FEELING OF GRADUALLY BECOMING EMPTY.

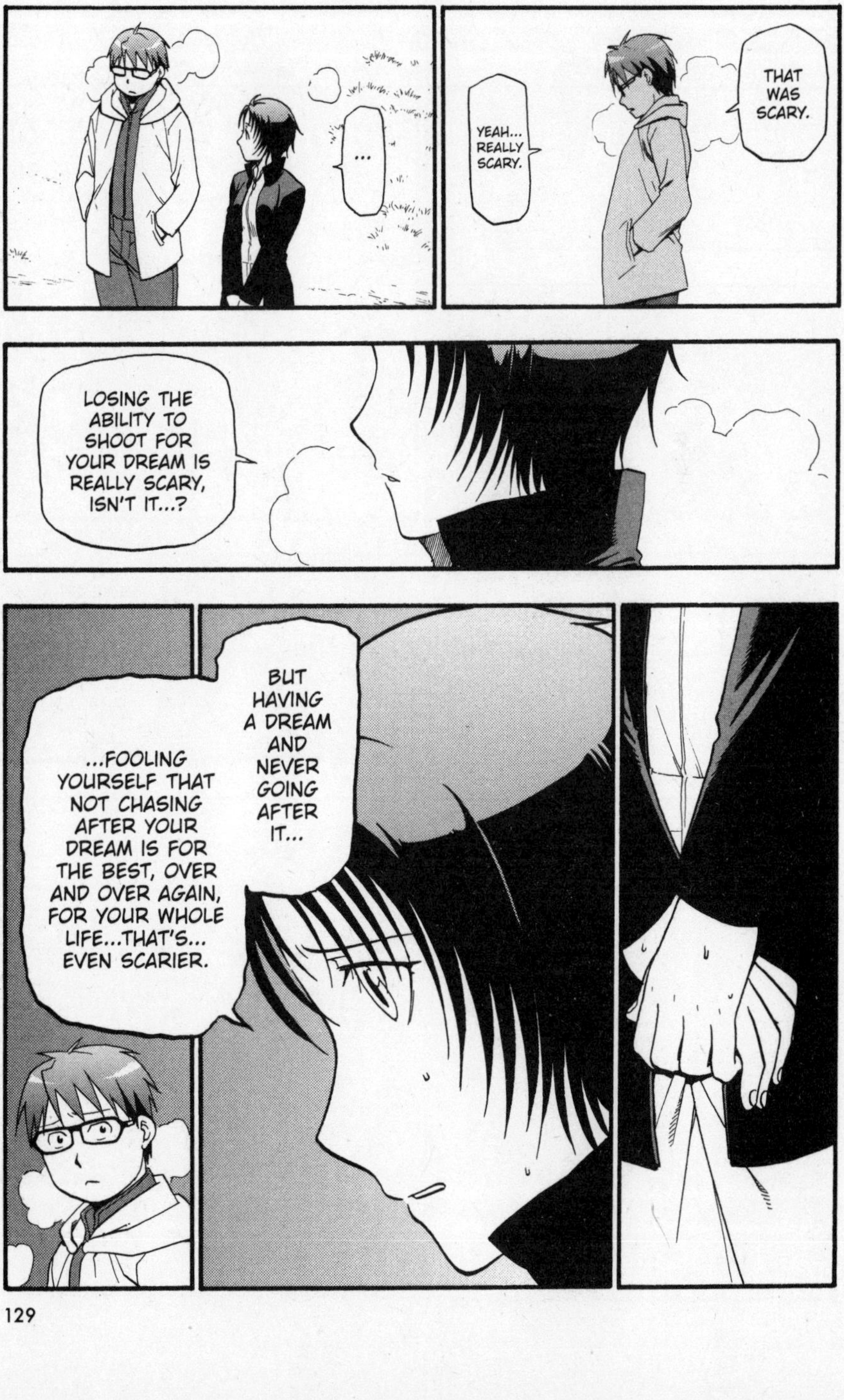
THAT WAS SCARY.
YEAH... REALLY SCARY.
...
LOSING THE ABILITY TO SHOOT FOR YOUR DREAM IS REALLY SCARY, ISN'T IT...?
BUT HAVING A DREAM AND NEVER GOING AFTER IT...
...FOOLING YOURSELF THAT NOT CHASING AFTER YOUR DREAM IS FOR THE BEST, OVER AND OVER AGAIN, FOR YOUR WHOLE LIFE...THAT'S... EVEN SCARIER.

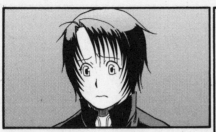

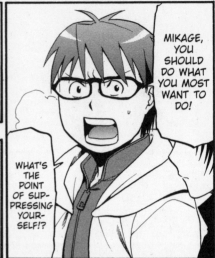

MIKAGE, YOU SHOULD DO WHAT YOU MOST WANT TO DO!
WHAT'S THE POINT OF SUP-PRESSING YOUR-SELF!?
...FOR THE WHOLE OF MY FIFTEEN YEARS... ALMOST SIXTEEN YEARS NOW......
...I'VE THOUGHT ONLY OF LIVING UP TO MY PARENTS' EXPECTATIONS. THAT'S WHAT I'VE TRIED TO DO.
HACHI-KEN-KUN... SORRY.
IT MIGHT BE A BOTHER, BUT...
...COULD YOU GIVE ME A LITTLE MORE COURAGE ...?

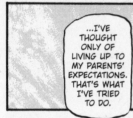

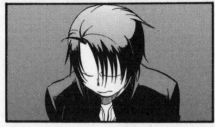

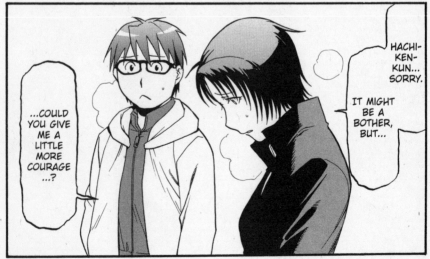

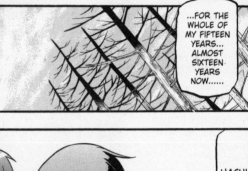

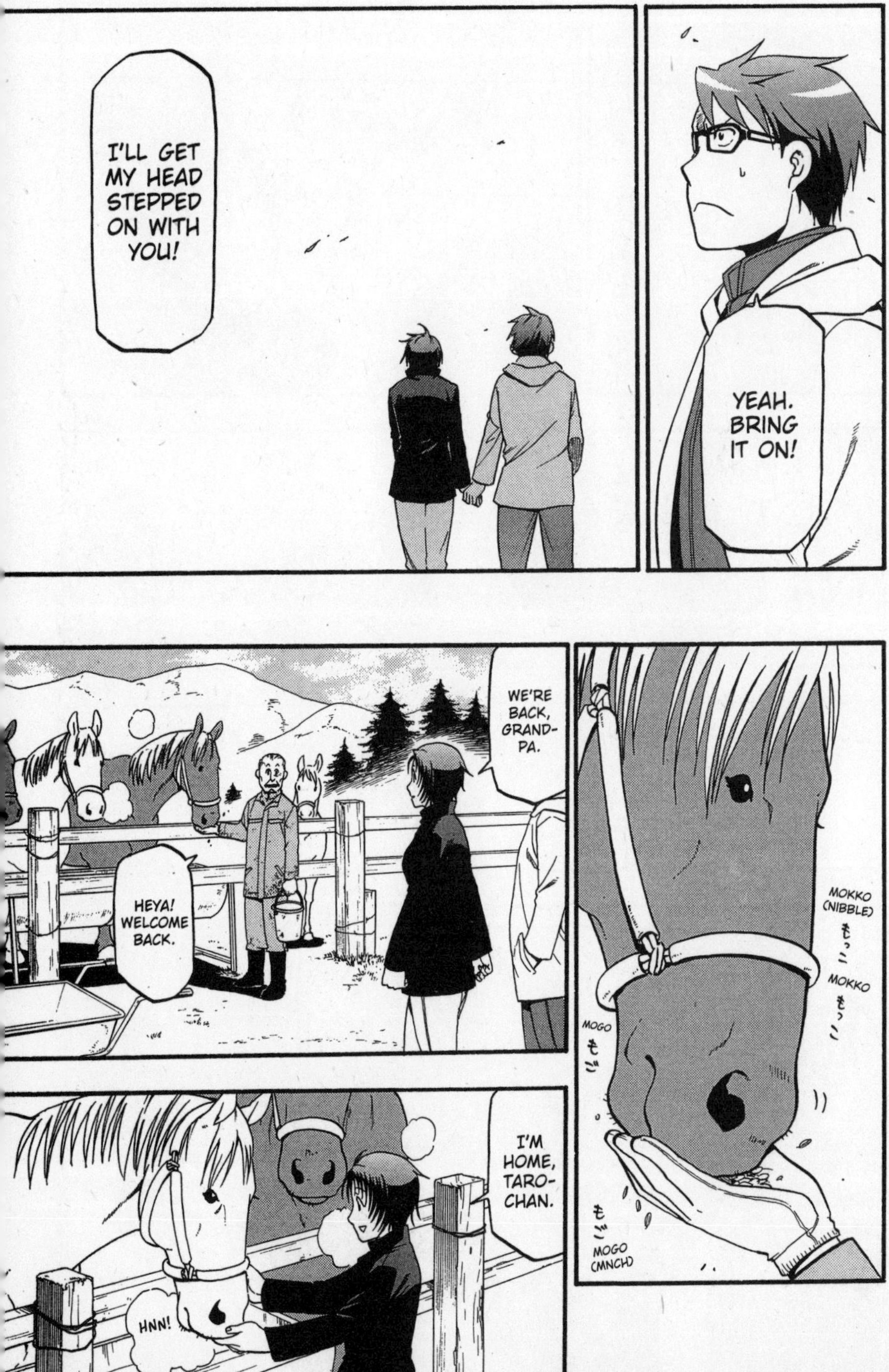
YEAH. BRING IT ON!
I'LL GET MY HEAD STEPPED ON WITH YOU!
MOKKO (NIBBLE)
もっこ
MOKKO
もっこ
MOGO
もご
もご
MOGO (MNCH)
WE'RE BACK, GRAND-PA.
HEYA! WELCOME BACK.
I'M HOME, TARO-CHAN.
HNN!

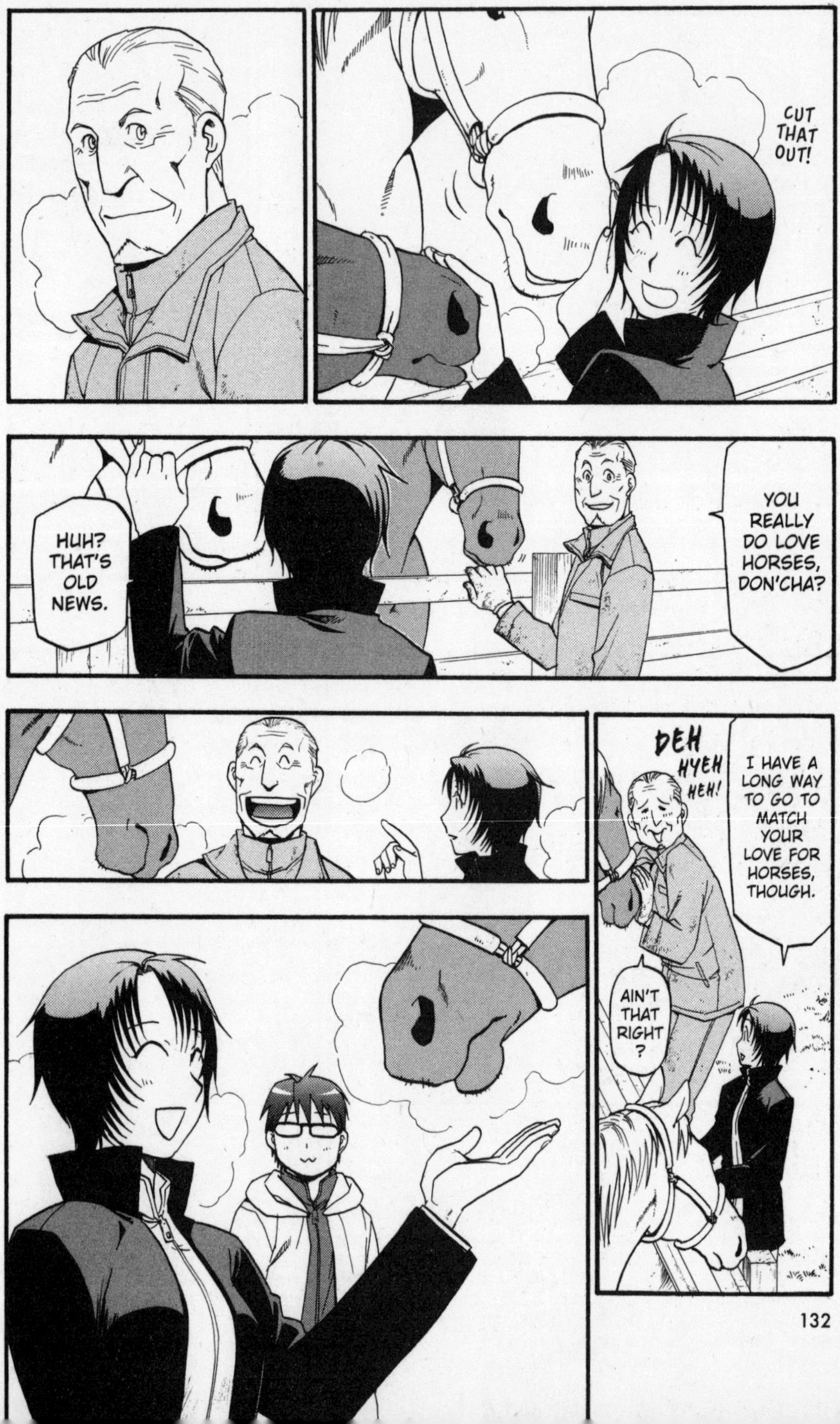
CUT THAT OUT!
YOU REALLY DO LOVE HORSES, DON'CHA?
HUH? THAT'S OLD NEWS.
I HAVE A LONG WAY TO GO TO MATCH YOUR LOVE FOR HORSES, THOUGH.
DEH HYEH HEH!
AIN'T THAT RIGHT?

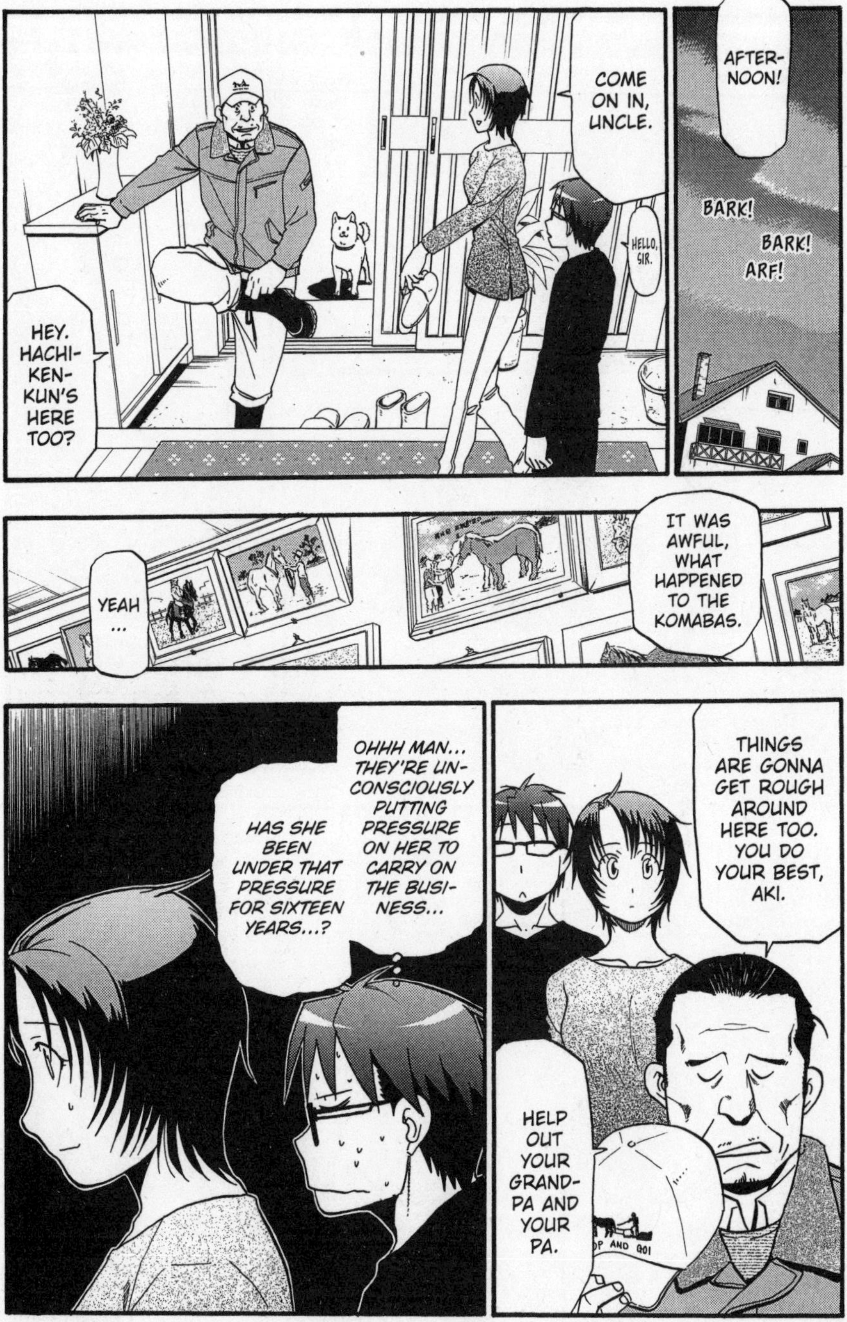
AFTER-NOON!
BARK!
BARK!
ARF!
COME ON IN, UNCLE.
HELLO, SIR.
HEY. HACHIKEN-KUN'S HERE TOO?
IT WAS AWFUL, WHAT HAPPENED TO THE KOMABAS.
YEAH ...
THINGS ARE GONNA GET ROUGH AROUND HERE TOO. YOU DO YOUR BEST, AKI.
HELP OUT YOUR GRANDPA AND YOUR PA.
OHHH MAN... THEY'RE UNCONSCIOUSLY PUTTING PRESSURE ON HER TO CARRY ON THE BUSINESS...
HAS SHE BEEN UNDER THAT PRESSURE FOR SIXTEEN YEARS...?

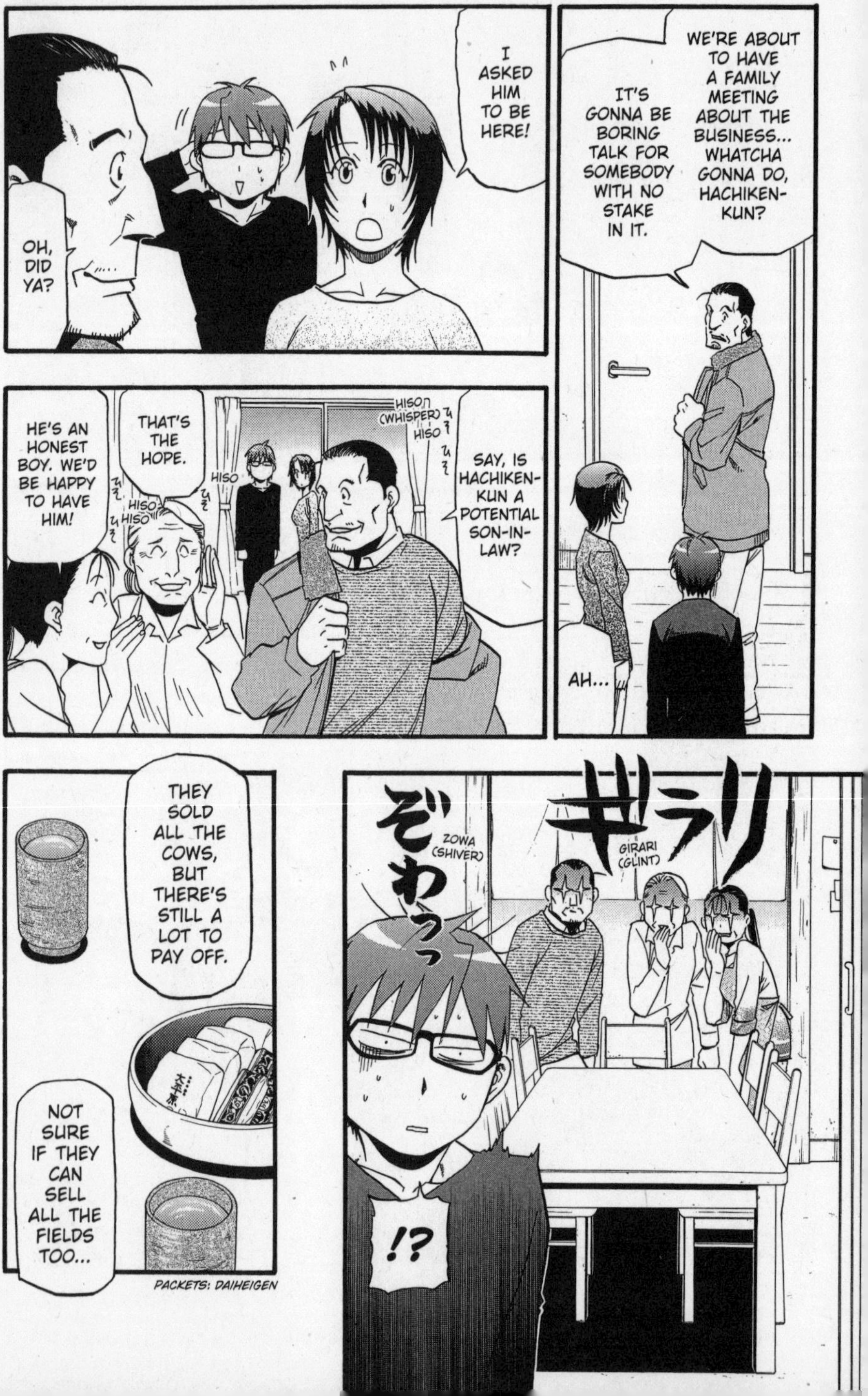
WE'RE ABOUT TO HAVE A FAMILY MEETING ABOUT THE BUSINESS... WHATCHA GONNA DO, HACHIKEN-KUN?
IT'S GONNA BE BORING TALK FOR SOMEBODY WITH NO STAKE IN IT.
AH...
I ASKED HIM TO BE HERE!
OH, DID YA?
SAY, IS HACHIKEN-KUN A POTENTIAL SON-IN-LAW?
HISO (WHISPER)
HISO
THAT'S THE HOPE.
HISO
HE'S AN HONEST BOY. WE'D BE HAPPY TO HAVE HIM!
HISO HISO
ギラリ
GIRARI (GLINT)
ぞわっ
ZOWA (SHIVER)
!?
THEY SOLD ALL THE COWS, BUT THERE'S STILL A LOT TO PAY OFF.
NOT SURE IF THEY CAN SELL ALL THE FIELDS TOO...
PACKETS: DAIHEIGEN

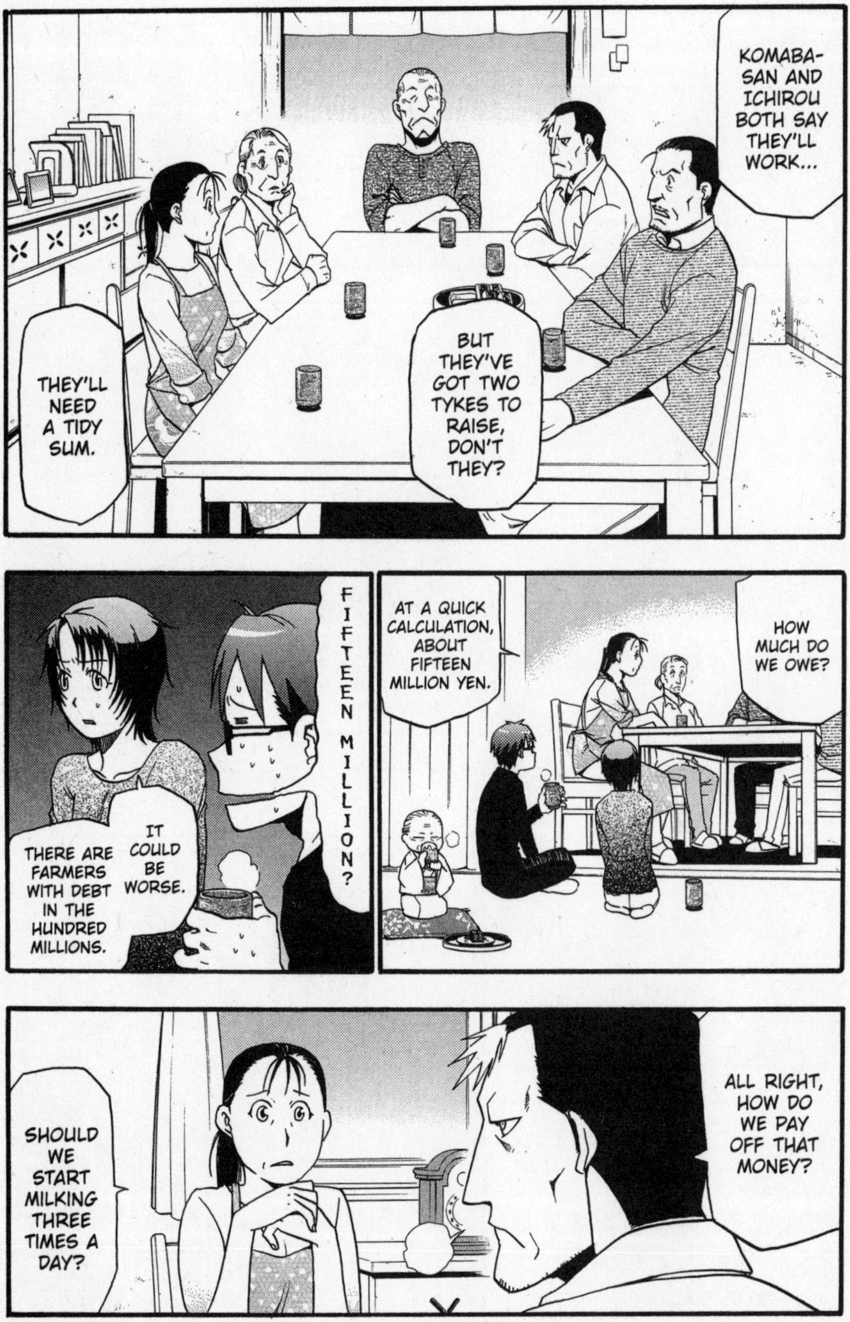
KOMABA-SAN AND ICHIROU BOTH SAY THEY'LL WORK...
BUT THEY'VE GOT TWO TYKES TO RAISE, DON'T THEY?
THEY'LL NEED A TIDY SUM.
HOW MUCH DO WE OWE?
AT A QUICK CALCULATION, ABOUT FIFTEEN MILLION YEN.
FIFTEEN MILLION?
IT COULD BE WORSE.
THERE ARE FARMERS WITH DEBT IN THE HUNDRED MILLIONS.
ALL RIGHT, HOW DO WE PAY OFF THAT MONEY?
SHOULD WE START MILKING THREE TIMES A DAY?

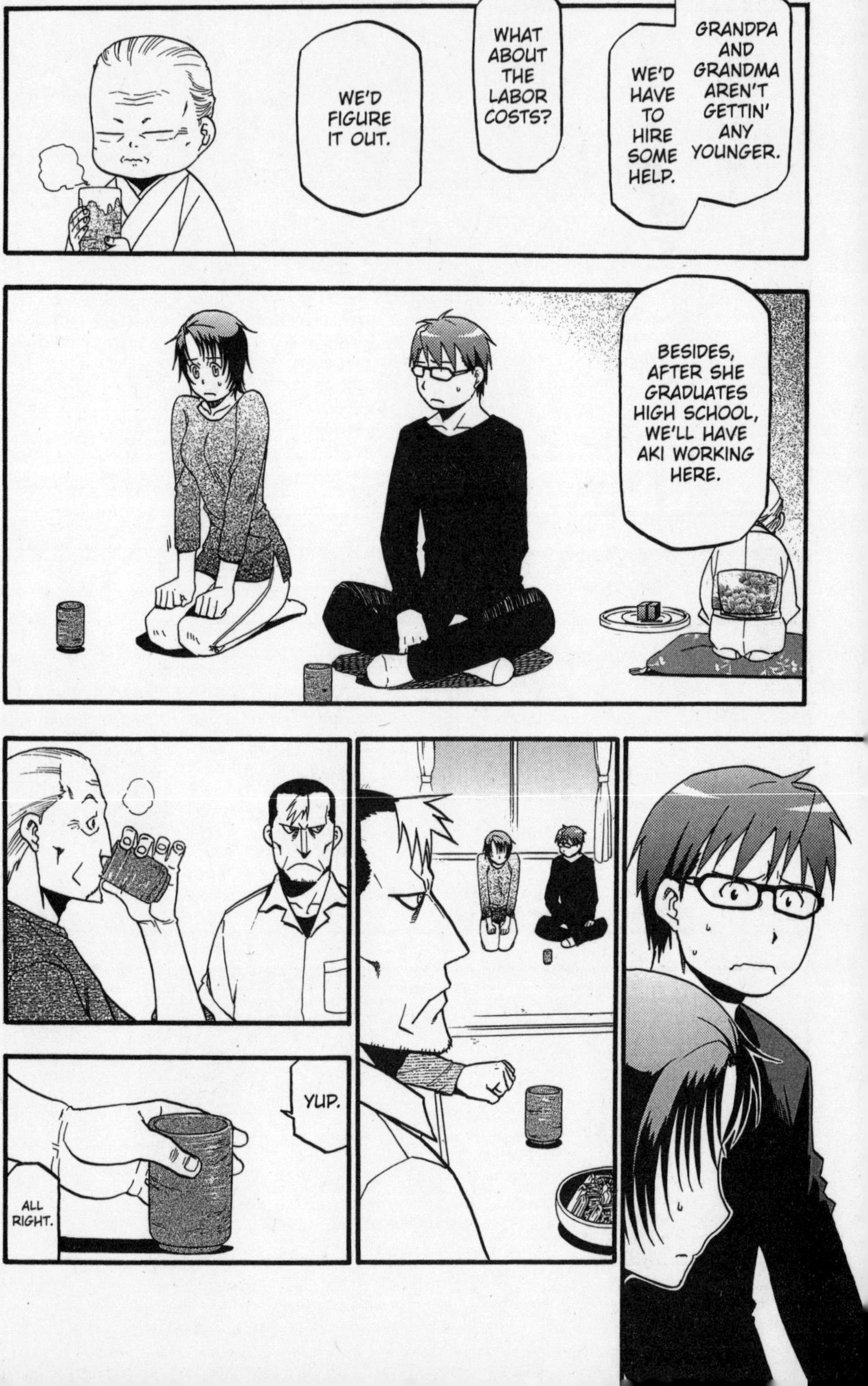
GRANDPA AND GRANDMA AREN'T GETTIN' ANY YOUNGER.
WE'D HAVE TO HIRE SOME HELP.
WHAT ABOUT THE LABOR COSTS?
WE'D FIGURE IT OUT.
BESIDES, AFTER SHE GRADUATES HIGH SCHOOL, WE'LL HAVE AKI WORKING HERE.
YUP.
ALL RIGHT.

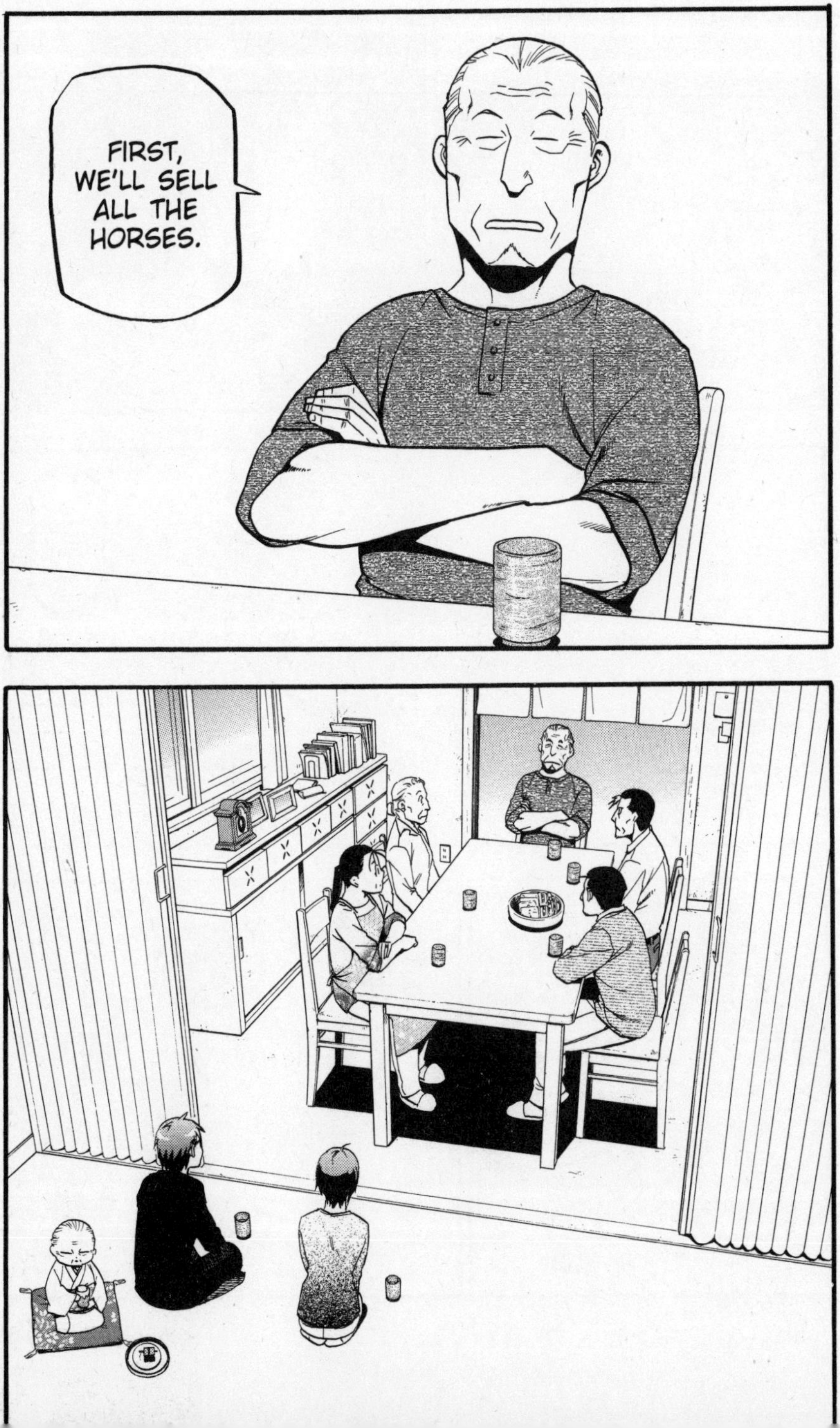
FIRST, WE'LL SELL ALL THE HORSES.

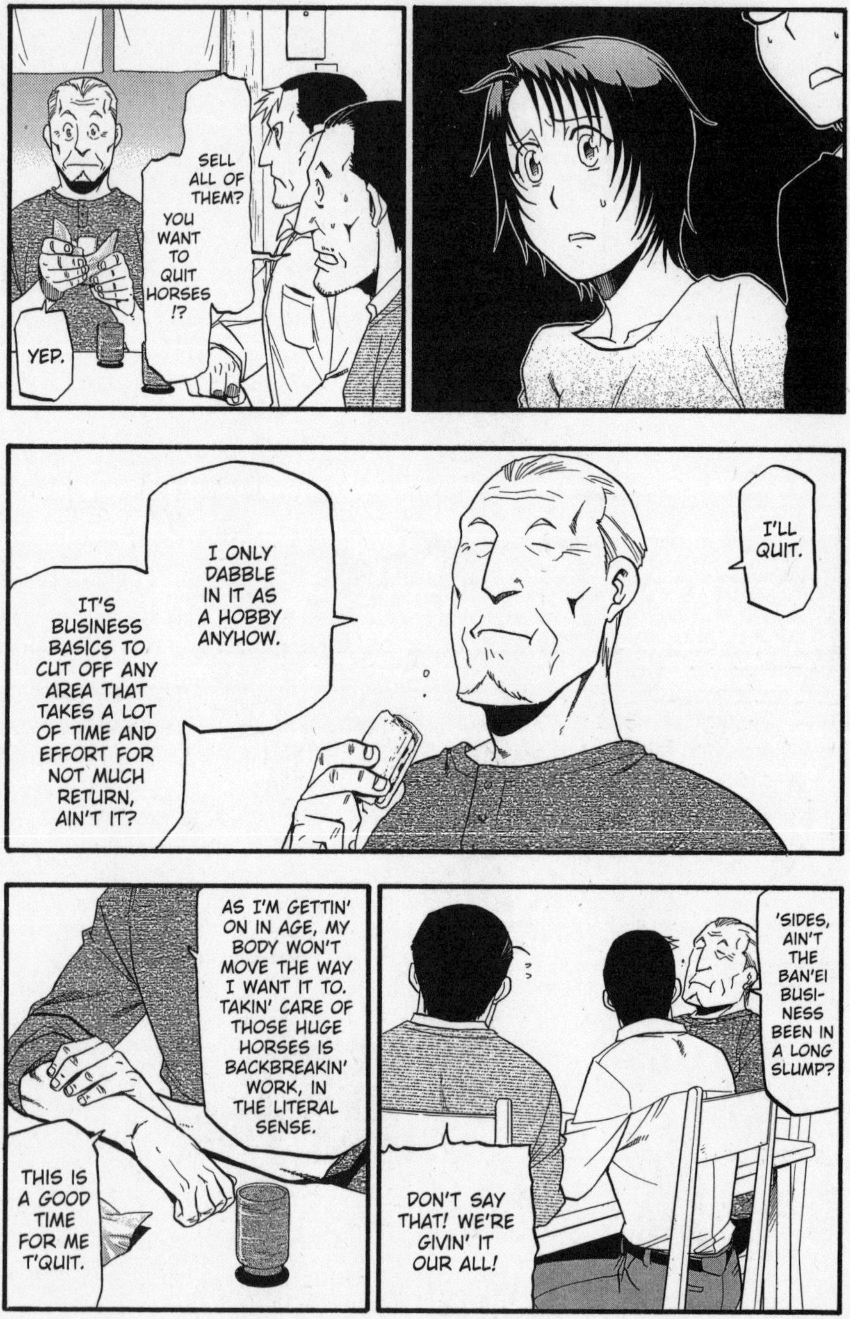
SELL ALL OF THEM? YOU WANT TO QUIT HORSES!?
YEP.
I'LL QUIT.
I ONLY DABBLE IN IT AS A HOBBY ANYHOW.
IT'S BUSINESS BASICS TO CUT OFF ANY AREA THAT TAKES A LOT OF TIME AND EFFORT FOR NOT MUCH RETURN, AIN'T IT?
'SIDES, AIN'T THE BAN'EI BUSINESS BEEN IN A LONG SLUMP?
DON'T SAY THAT! WE'RE GIVIN' IT OUR ALL!
AS I'M GETTIN' ON IN AGE, MY BODY WON'T MOVE THE WAY I WANT IT TO. TAKIN' CARE OF THOSE HUGE HORSES IS BACKBREAKIN' WORK, IN THE LITERAL SENSE.
THIS IS A GOOD TIME FOR ME T'QUIT.

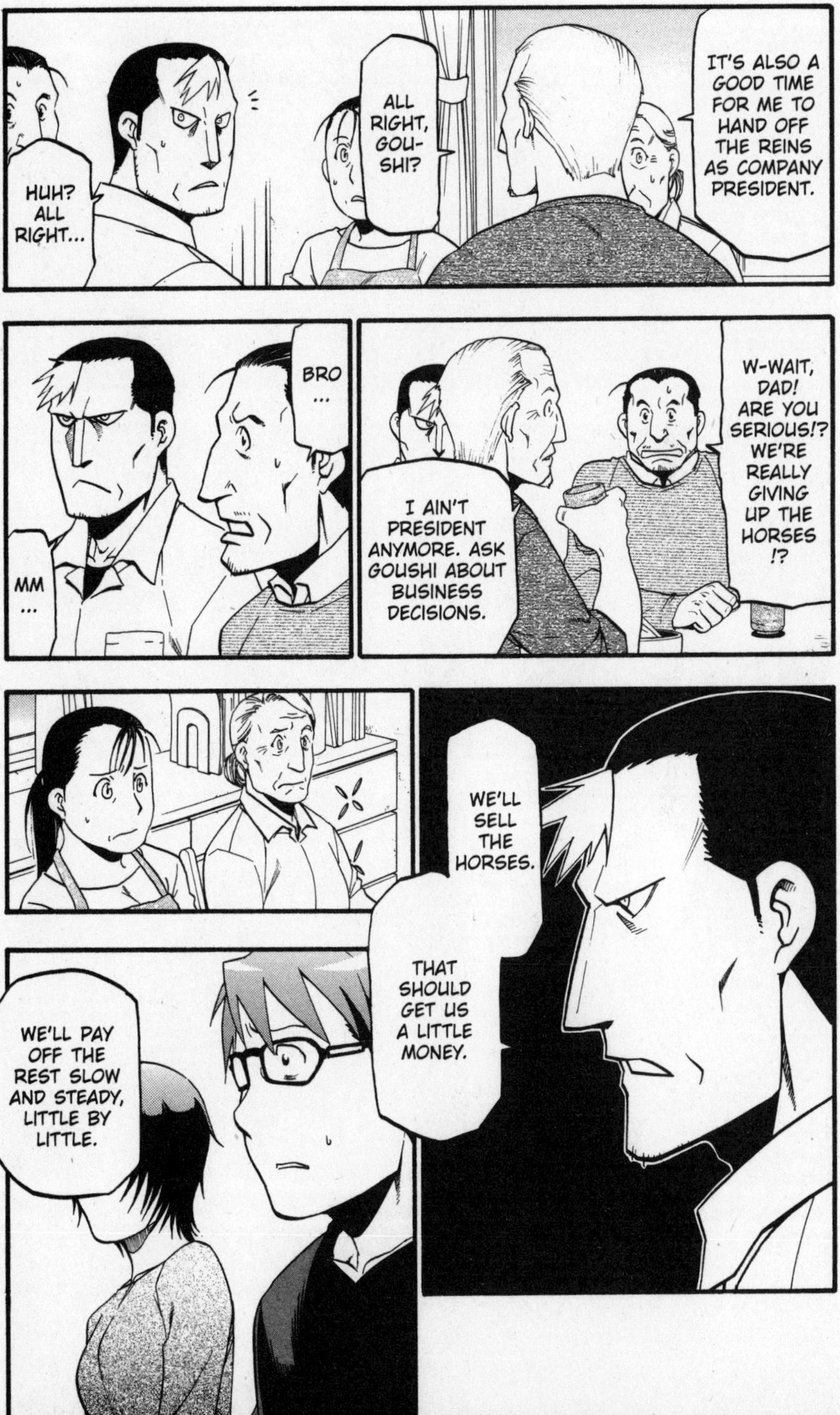
IT'S ALSO A GOOD TIME FOR ME TO HAND OFF THE REINS AS COMPANY PRESIDENT.
ALL RIGHT, GOU-SHI?
HUH? ALL RIGHT...
W-WAIT, DAD! ARE YOU SERIOUS!? WE'RE REALLY GIVING UP THE HORSES !?
I AIN'T PRESIDENT ANYMORE. ASK GOUSHI ABOUT BUSINESS DECISIONS.
BRO ...
MM ...
WE'LL SELL THE HORSES.
THAT SHOULD GET US A LITTLE MONEY.
WE'LL PAY OFF THE REST SLOW AND STEADY, LITTLE BY LITTLE.

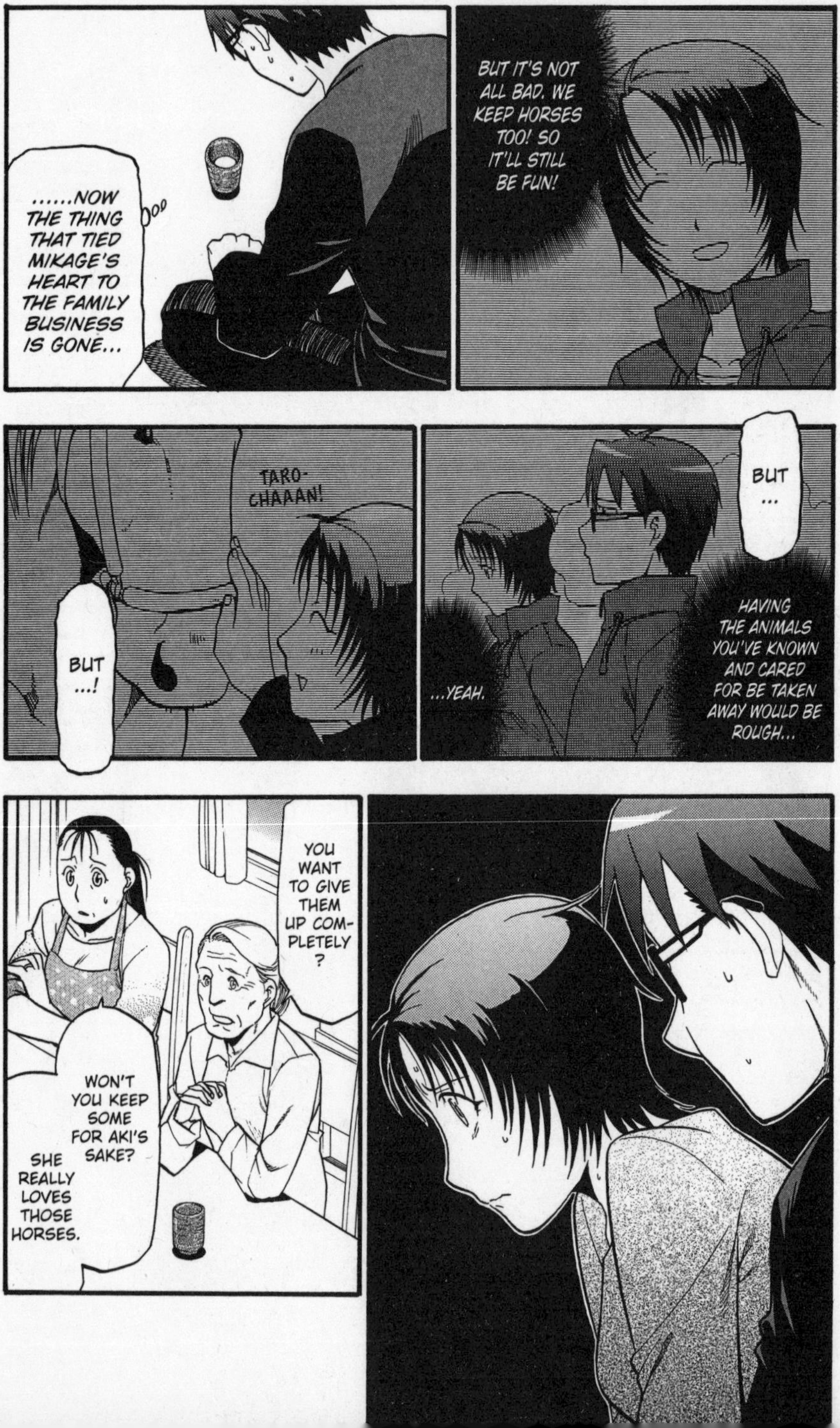
BUT IT'S NOT ALL BAD. WE KEEP HORSES TOO! SO IT'LL STILL BE FUN!
......NOW THE THING THAT TIED MIKAGE'S HEART TO THE FAMILY BUSINESS IS GONE...
BUT ...
HAVING THE ANIMALS YOU'VE KNOWN AND CARED FOR BE TAKEN AWAY WOULD BE ROUGH...
...YEAH.
TARO-CHAAAN!
BUT ...!
YOU WANT TO GIVE THEM UP COM-PLETELY?
WON'T YOU KEEP SOME FOR AKI'S SAKE?
SHE REALLY LOVES THOSE HORSES.

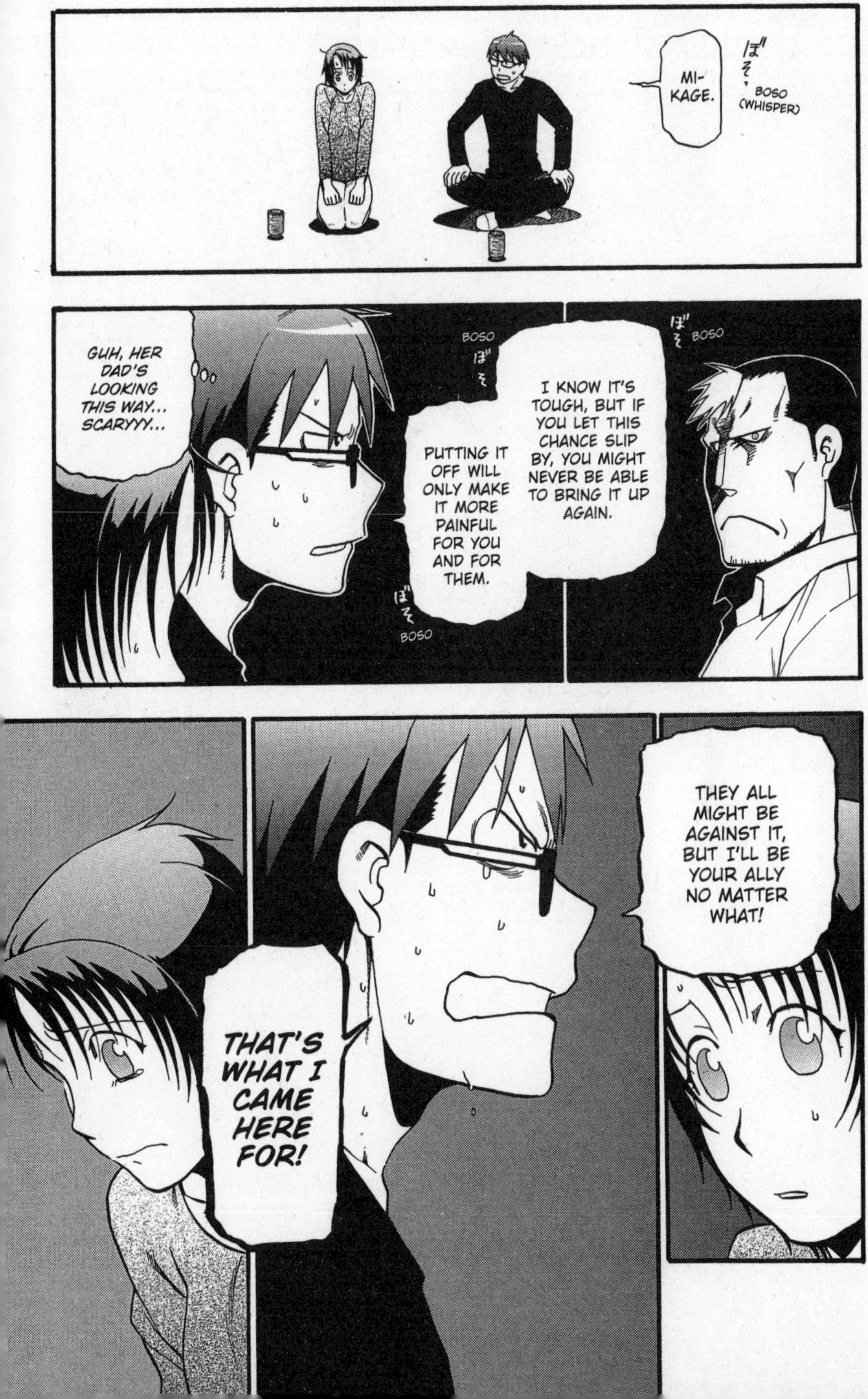

ぼそ
BOSO (WHISPER)
MI-KAGE.
ぼそ
BOSO
I KNOW IT'S TOUGH, BUT IF YOU LET THIS CHANCE SLIP BY, YOU MIGHT NEVER BE ABLE TO BRING IT UP AGAIN.
BOSO
ぼそ
PUTTING IT OFF WILL ONLY MAKE IT MORE PAINFUL FOR YOU AND FOR THEM.
ぼそ
BOSO
GUH, HER DAD'S LOOKING THIS WAY... SCARYYY...
THEY ALL MIGHT BE AGAINST IT, BUT I'LL BE YOUR ALLY NO MATTER WHAT!
THAT'S WHAT I CAME HERE FOR!

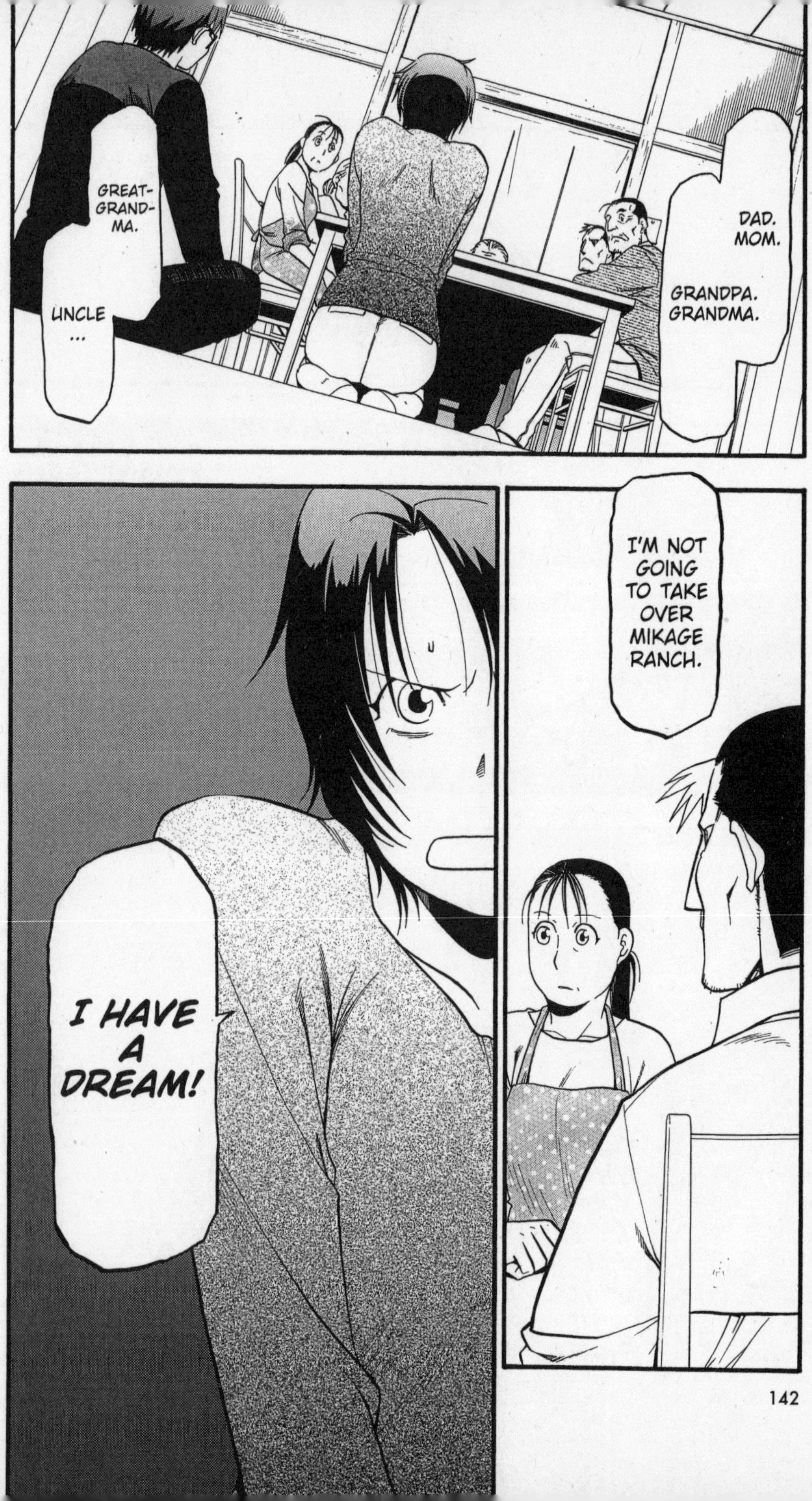
DAD. MOM.
GRANDPA. GRANDMA.
GREAT-GRAND-MA.
UNCLE ...
I'M NOT GOING TO TAKE OVER MIKAGE RANCH.
I HAVE A DREAM!

Silver Spoon

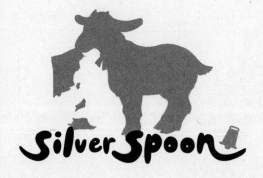

COW BARN
TEACHER

YASUKE KIYOKAWA

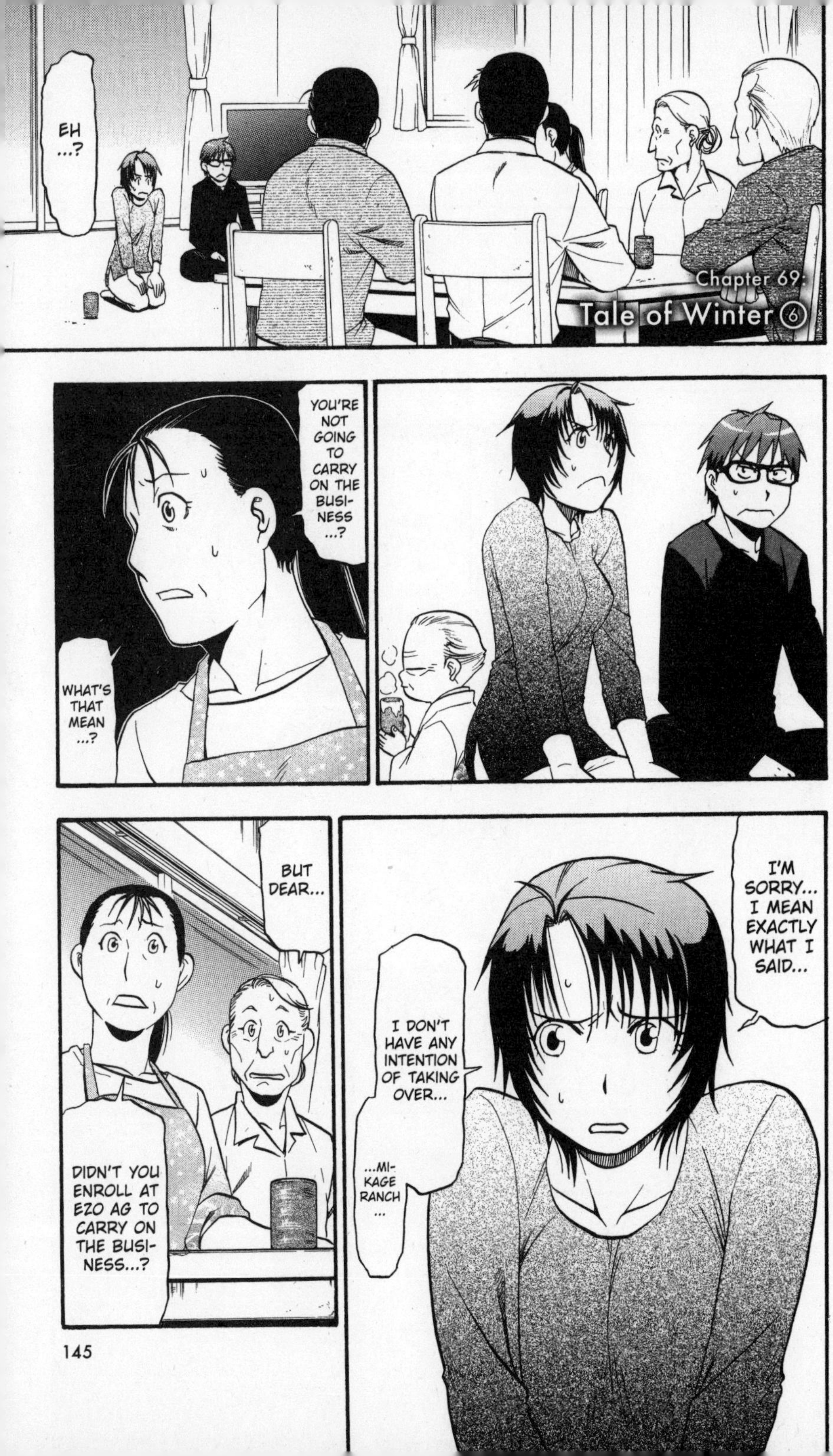
EH ...?
Chapter 69:
Tale of Winter ⑥
YOU'RE NOT GOING TO CARRY ON THE BUSINESS ...?
WHAT'S THAT MEAN ...?
I'M SORRY... I MEAN EXACTLY WHAT I SAID...
I DON'T HAVE ANY INTENTION OF TAKING OVER...
...MIKAGE RANCH ...
BUT DEAR...
DIDN'T YOU ENROLL AT EZO AG TO CARRY ON THE BUSINESS...?

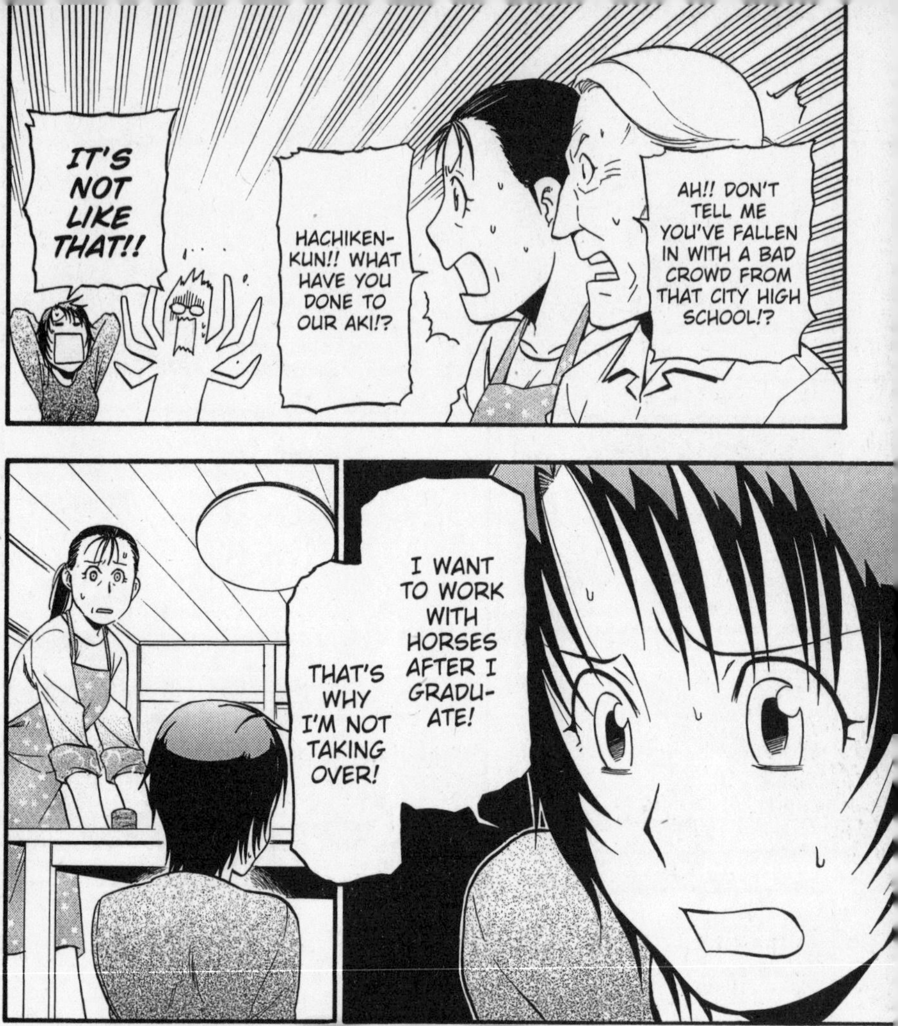
AH!! DON'T TELL ME YOU'VE FALLEN IN WITH A BAD CROWD FROM THAT CITY HIGH SCHOOL!?
HACHIKEN-KUN!! WHAT HAVE YOU DONE TO OUR AKI!?
IT'S NOT LIKE THAT!!
I WANT TO WORK WITH HORSES AFTER I GRADU-ATE!
THAT'S WHY I'M NOT TAKING OVER!

Chapter 69:

Tale of Winter ⑥

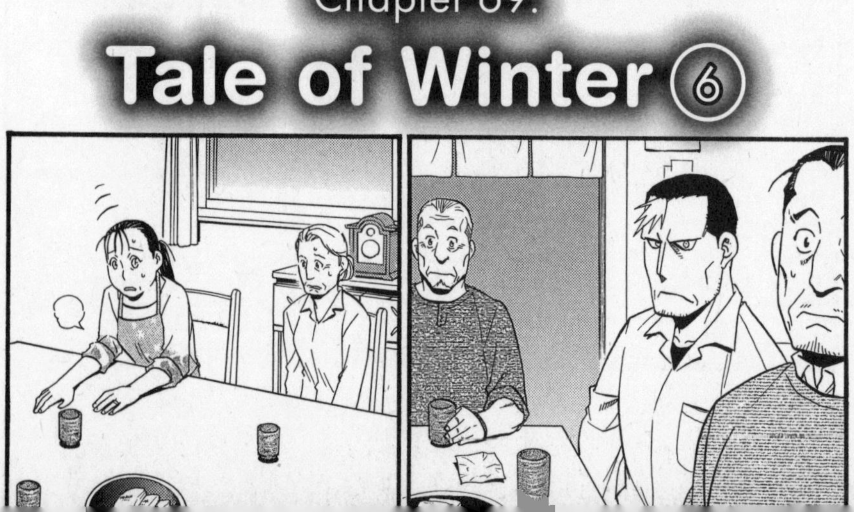

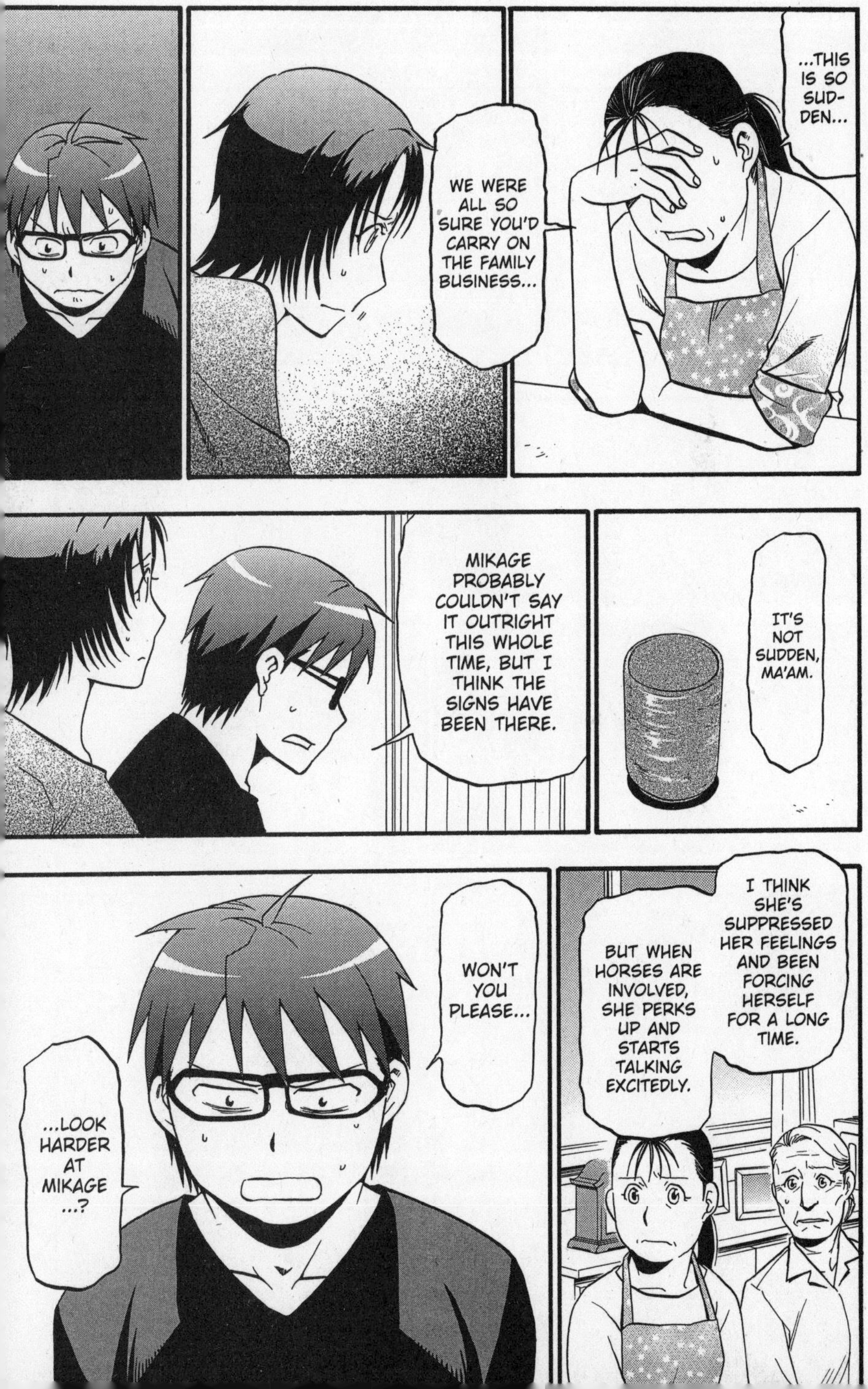
...THIS IS SO SUD-DEN...
WE WERE ALL SO SURE YOU'D CARRY ON THE FAMILY BUSINESS...
IT'S NOT SUDDEN, MA'AM.
MIKAGE PROBABLY COULDN'T SAY IT OUTRIGHT THIS WHOLE TIME, BUT I THINK THE SIGNS HAVE BEEN THERE.
I THINK SHE'S SUPPRESSED HER FEELINGS AND BEEN FORCING HERSELF FOR A LONG TIME.
BUT WHEN HORSES ARE INVOLVED, SHE PERKS UP AND STARTS TALKING EXCITEDLY.
WON'T YOU PLEASE...
...LOOK HARDER AT MIKAGE...?

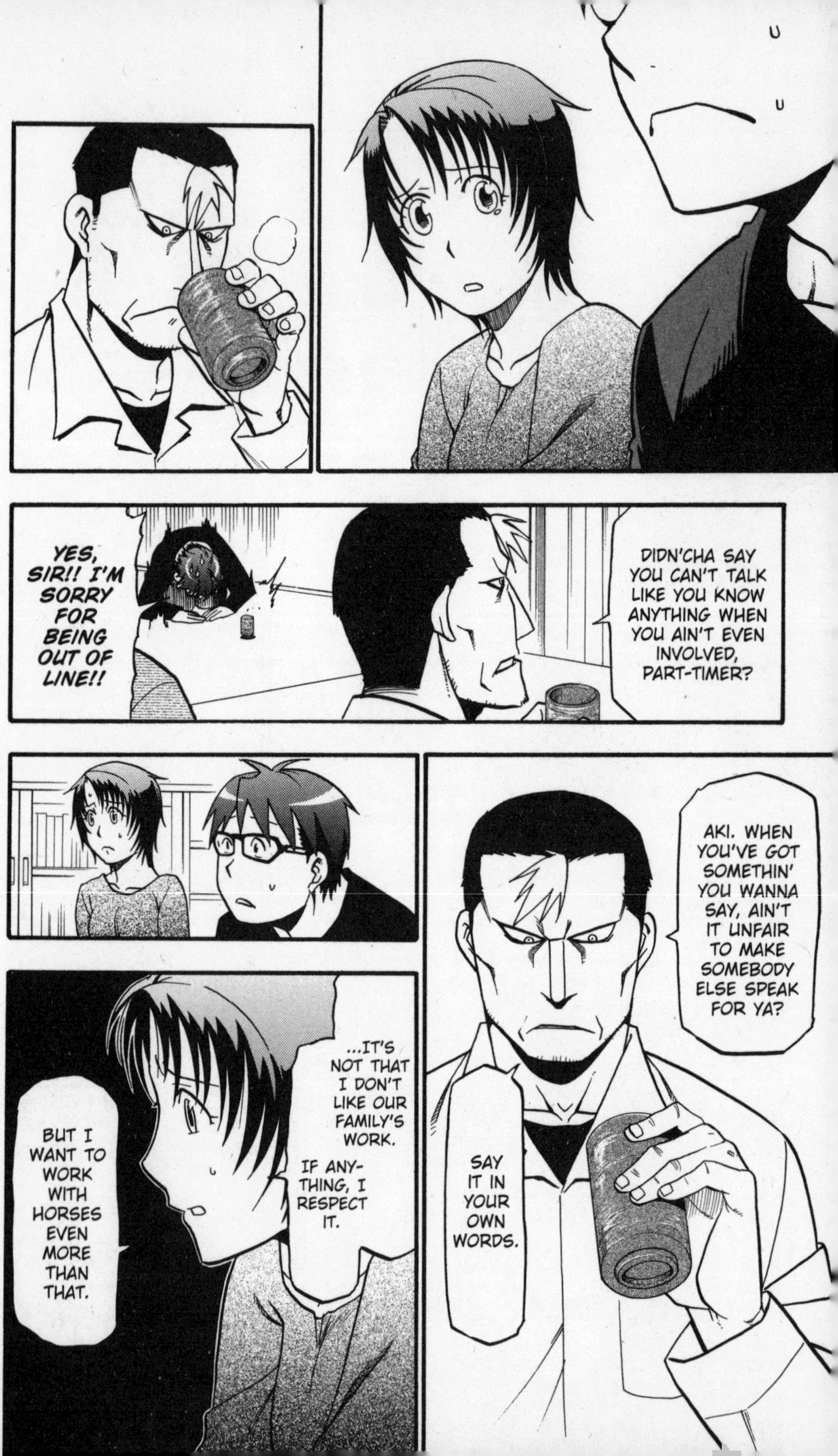
U
U
DIDN'CHA SAY YOU CAN'T TALK LIKE YOU KNOW ANYTHING WHEN YOU AIN'T EVEN INVOLVED, PART-TIMER?
YES, SIR!! I'M SORRY FOR BEING OUT OF LINE!!
AKI. WHEN YOU'VE GOT SOMETHIN' YOU WANNA SAY, AIN'T IT UNFAIR TO MAKE SOMEBODY ELSE SPEAK FOR YA?
SAY IT IN YOUR OWN WORDS.
...IT'S NOT THAT I DON'T LIKE OUR FAMILY'S WORK.
IF ANY-THING, I RESPECT IT.
BUT I WANT TO WORK WITH HORSES EVEN MORE THAN THAT.

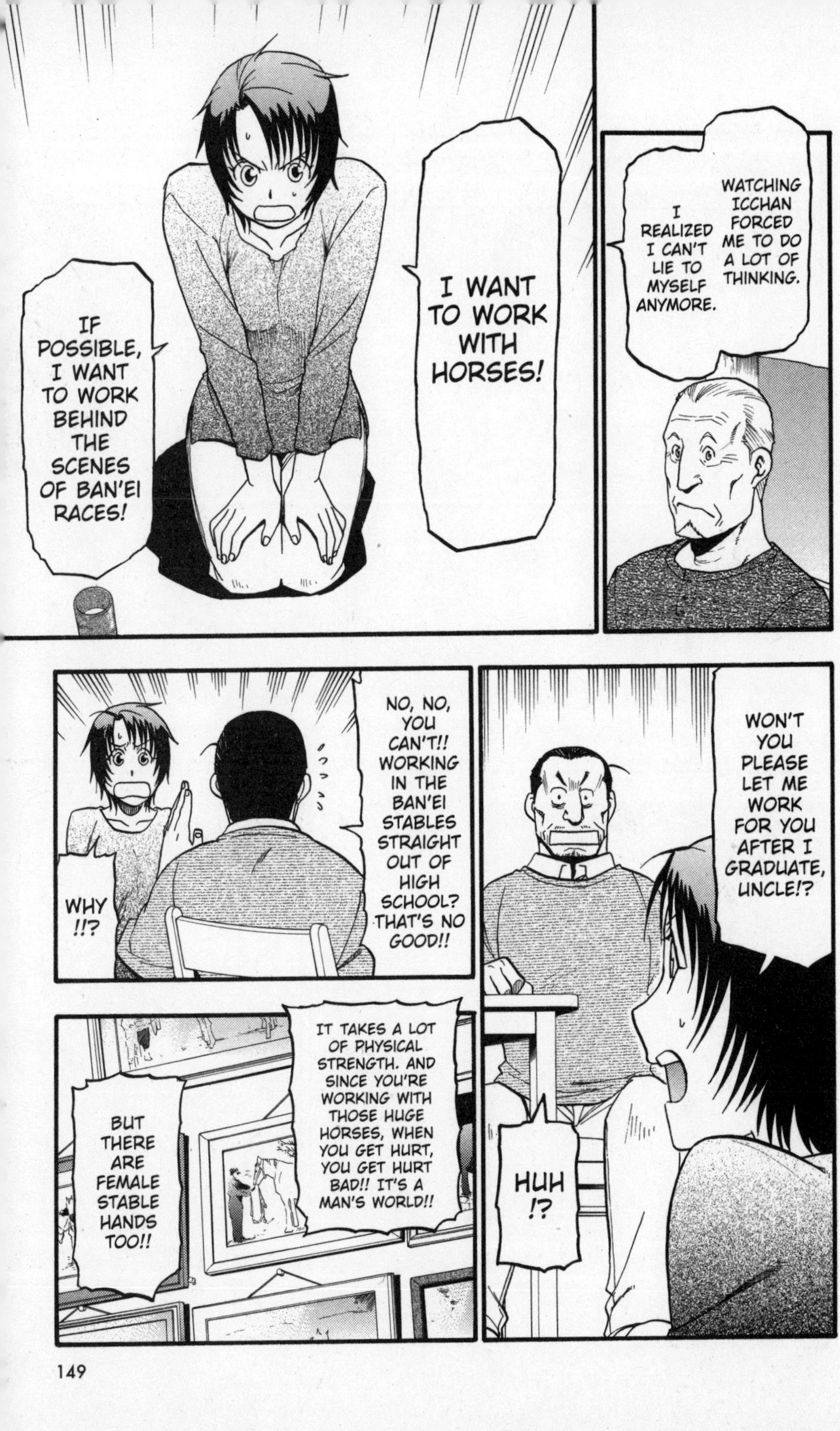
WATCHING ICCHAN FORCED ME TO DO A LOT OF THINKING.
I REALIZED I CAN'T LIE TO MYSELF ANYMORE.
I WANT TO WORK WITH HORSES!
IF POSSIBLE, I WANT TO WORK BEHIND THE SCENES OF BAN'EI RACES!
WON'T YOU PLEASE LET ME WORK FOR YOU AFTER I GRADUATE, UNCLE!?
HUH!?
NO, NO, YOU CAN'T!! WORKING IN THE BAN'EI STABLES STRAIGHT OUT OF HIGH SCHOOL? THAT'S NO GOOD!!
WHY!!?
IT TAKES A LOT OF PHYSICAL STRENGTH. AND SINCE YOU'RE WORKING WITH THOSE HUGE HORSES, WHEN YOU GET HURT, YOU GET HURT BAD!! IT'S A MAN'S WORLD!!
BUT THERE ARE FEMALE STABLE HANDS TOO!!

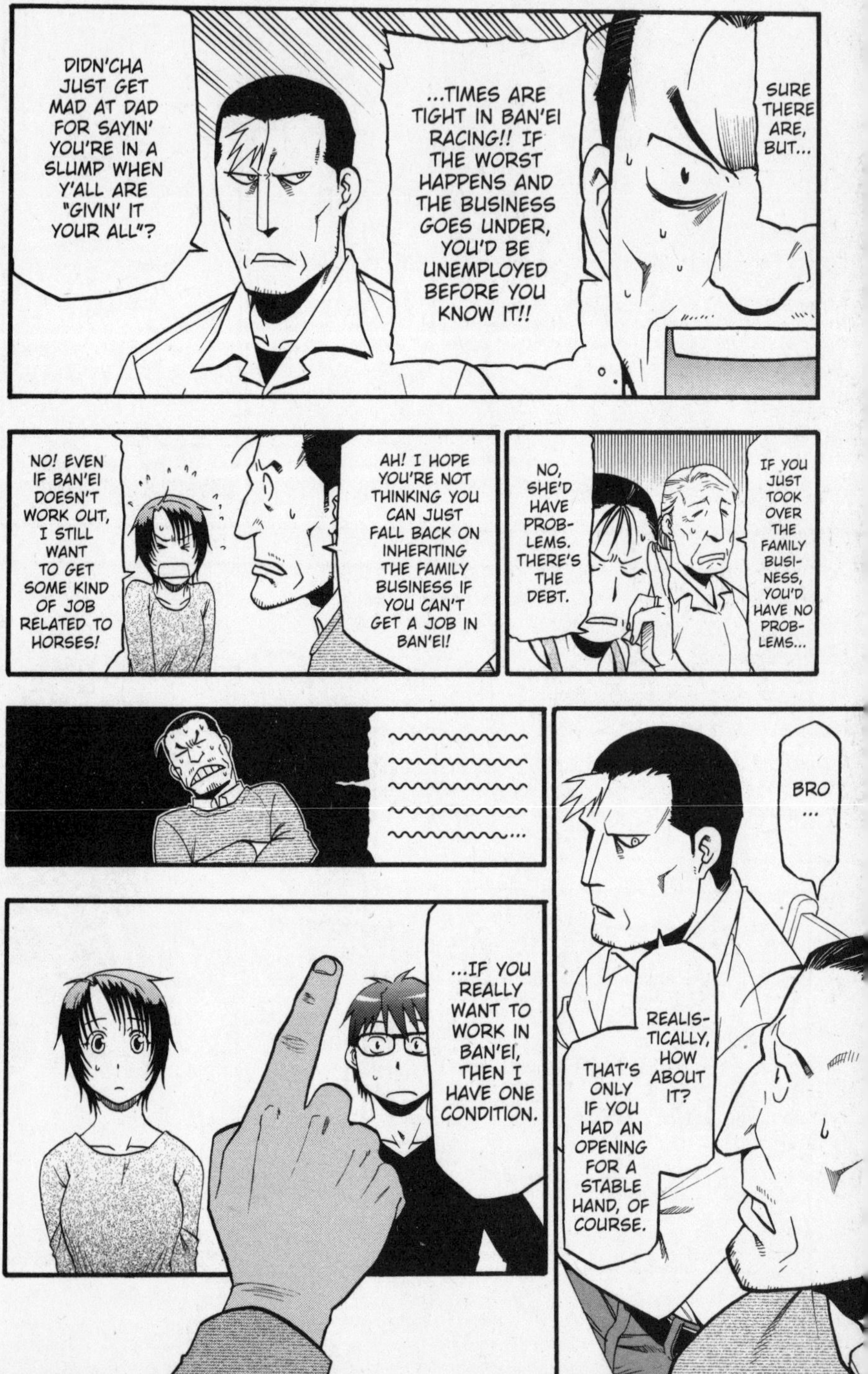
SURE THERE ARE, BUT...
...TIMES ARE TIGHT IN BAN'EI RACING!! IF THE WORST HAPPENS AND THE BUSINESS GOES UNDER, YOU'D BE UNEMPLOYED BEFORE YOU KNOW IT!!
DIDN'CHA JUST GET MAD AT DAD FOR SAYIN' YOU'RE IN A SLUMP WHEN Y'ALL ARE "GIVIN' IT YOUR ALL"?
IF YOU JUST TOOK OVER THE FAMILY BUSINESS, YOU'D HAVE NO PROBLEMS...
NO, SHE'D HAVE PROBLEMS. THERE'S THE DEBT.
AH! I HOPE YOU'RE NOT THINKING YOU CAN JUST FALL BACK ON INHERITING THE FAMILY BUSINESS IF YOU CAN'T GET A JOB IN BAN'EI!
NO! EVEN IF BAN'EI DOESN'T WORK OUT, I STILL WANT TO GET SOME KIND OF JOB RELATED TO HORSES!
BRO...
REALISTICALLY, HOW ABOUT IT?
THAT'S ONLY IF YOU HAD AN OPENING FOR A STABLE HAND, OF COURSE.
...IF YOU REALLY WANT TO WORK IN BAN'EI, THEN I HAVE ONE CONDITION.

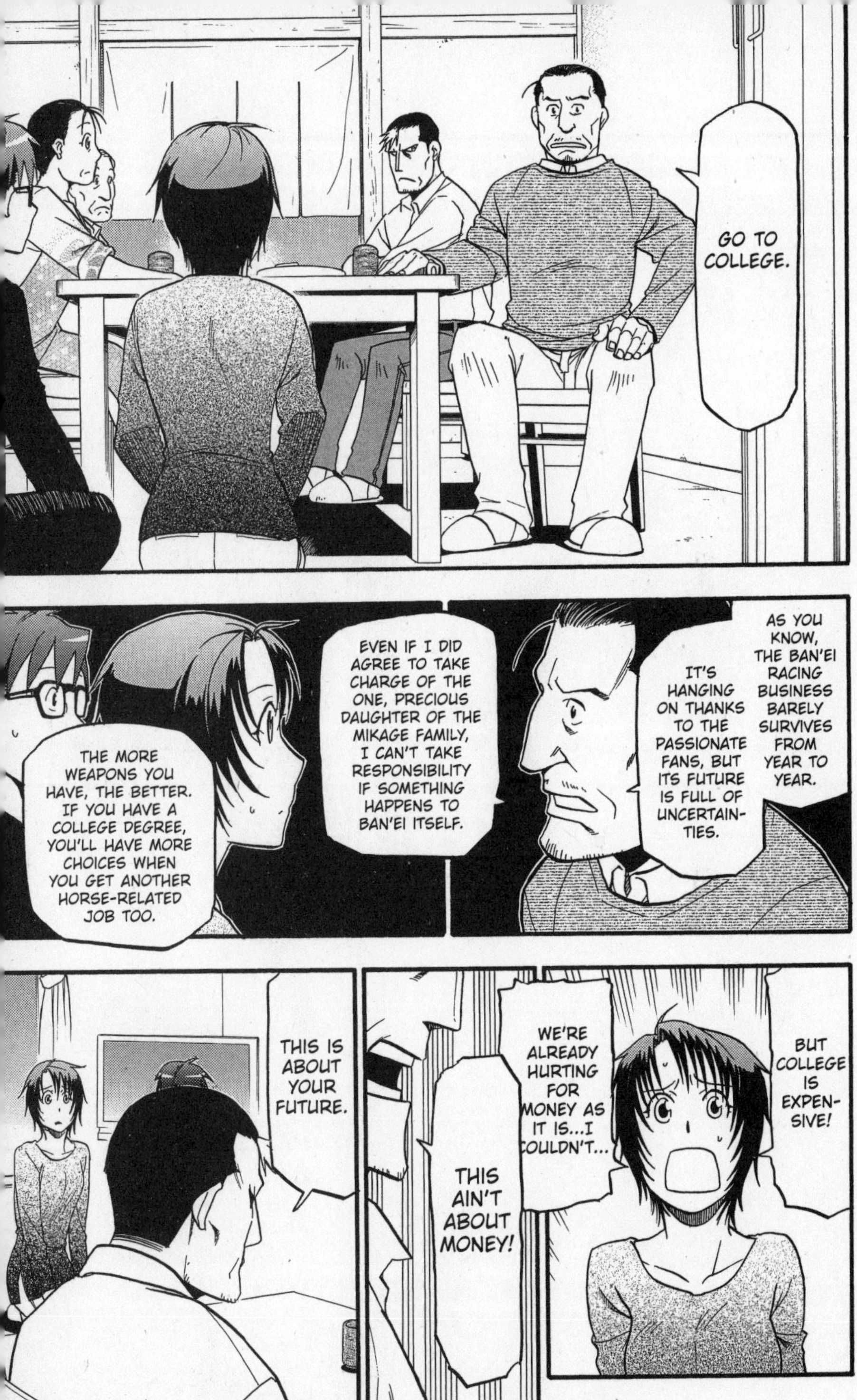
GO TO COLLEGE.
AS YOU KNOW, THE BAN'EI RACING BUSINESS BARELY SURVIVES FROM YEAR TO YEAR.
IT'S HANGING ON THANKS TO THE PASSIONATE FANS, BUT ITS FUTURE IS FULL OF UNCERTAINTIES.
EVEN IF I DID AGREE TO TAKE CHARGE OF THE ONE, PRECIOUS DAUGHTER OF THE MIKAGE FAMILY, I CAN'T TAKE RESPONSIBILITY IF SOMETHING HAPPENS TO BAN'EI ITSELF.
THE MORE WEAPONS YOU HAVE, THE BETTER. IF YOU HAVE A COLLEGE DEGREE, YOU'LL HAVE MORE CHOICES WHEN YOU GET ANOTHER HORSE-RELATED JOB TOO.
BUT COLLEGE IS EXPENSIVE!
WE'RE ALREADY HURTING FOR MONEY AS IT IS...I COULDN'T...
THIS AIN'T ABOUT MONEY!
THIS IS ABOUT YOUR FUTURE.

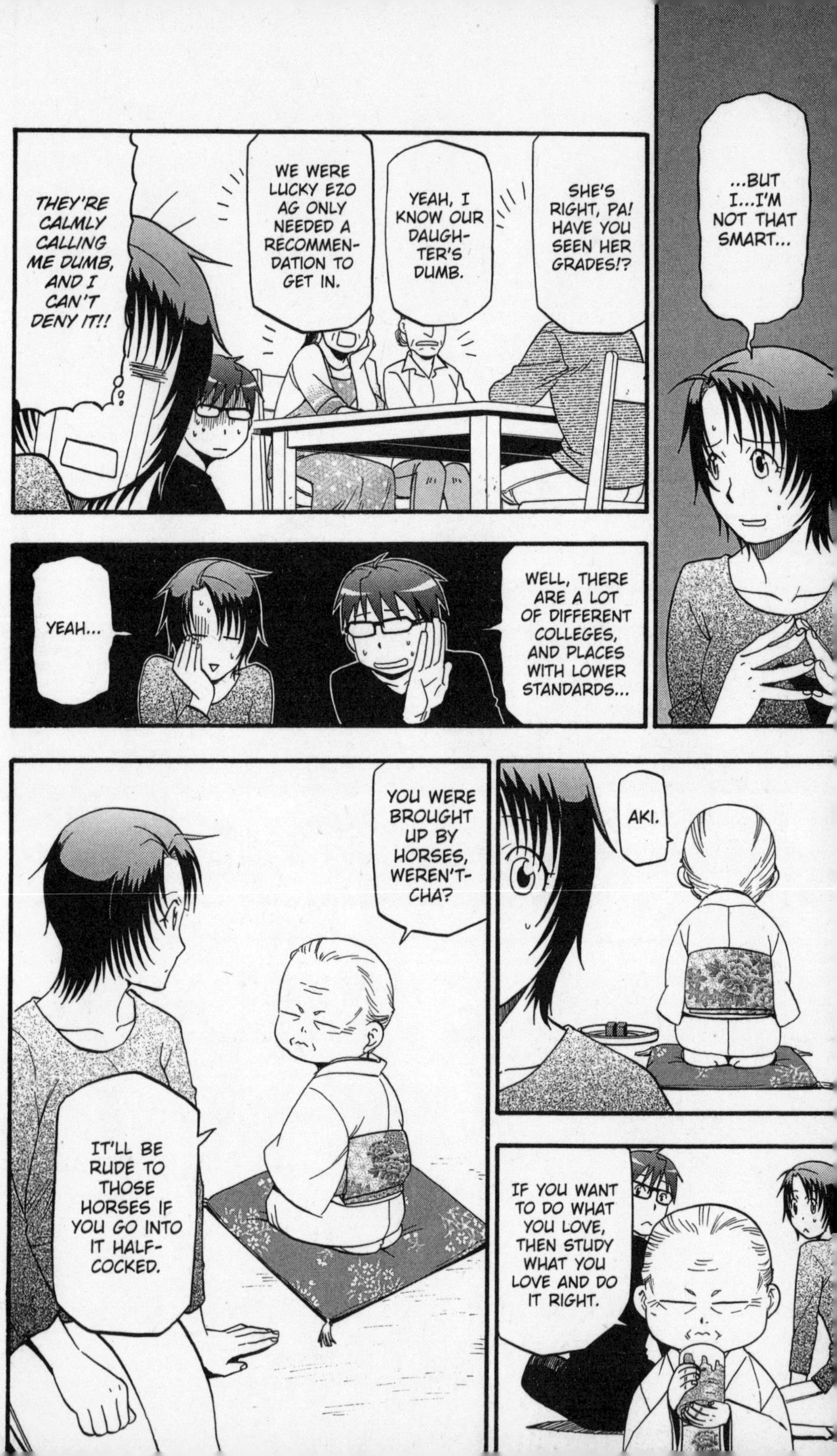
...BUT I...I'M NOT THAT SMART...
SHE'S RIGHT, PA! HAVE YOU SEEN HER GRADES!?
YEAH, I KNOW OUR DAUGH-TER'S DUMB.
WE WERE LUCKY EZO AG ONLY NEEDED A RECOMMEN-DATION TO GET IN.
THEY'RE CALMLY CALLING ME DUMB, AND I CAN'T DENY IT!!
WELL, THERE ARE A LOT OF DIFFERENT COLLEGES, AND PLACES WITH LOWER STANDARDS...
YEAH...
AKI.
IF YOU WANT TO DO WHAT YOU LOVE, THEN STUDY WHAT YOU LOVE AND DO IT RIGHT.
YOU WERE BROUGHT UP BY HORSES, WEREN'T-CHA?
IT'LL BE RUDE TO THOSE HORSES IF YOU GO INTO IT HALF-COCKED.

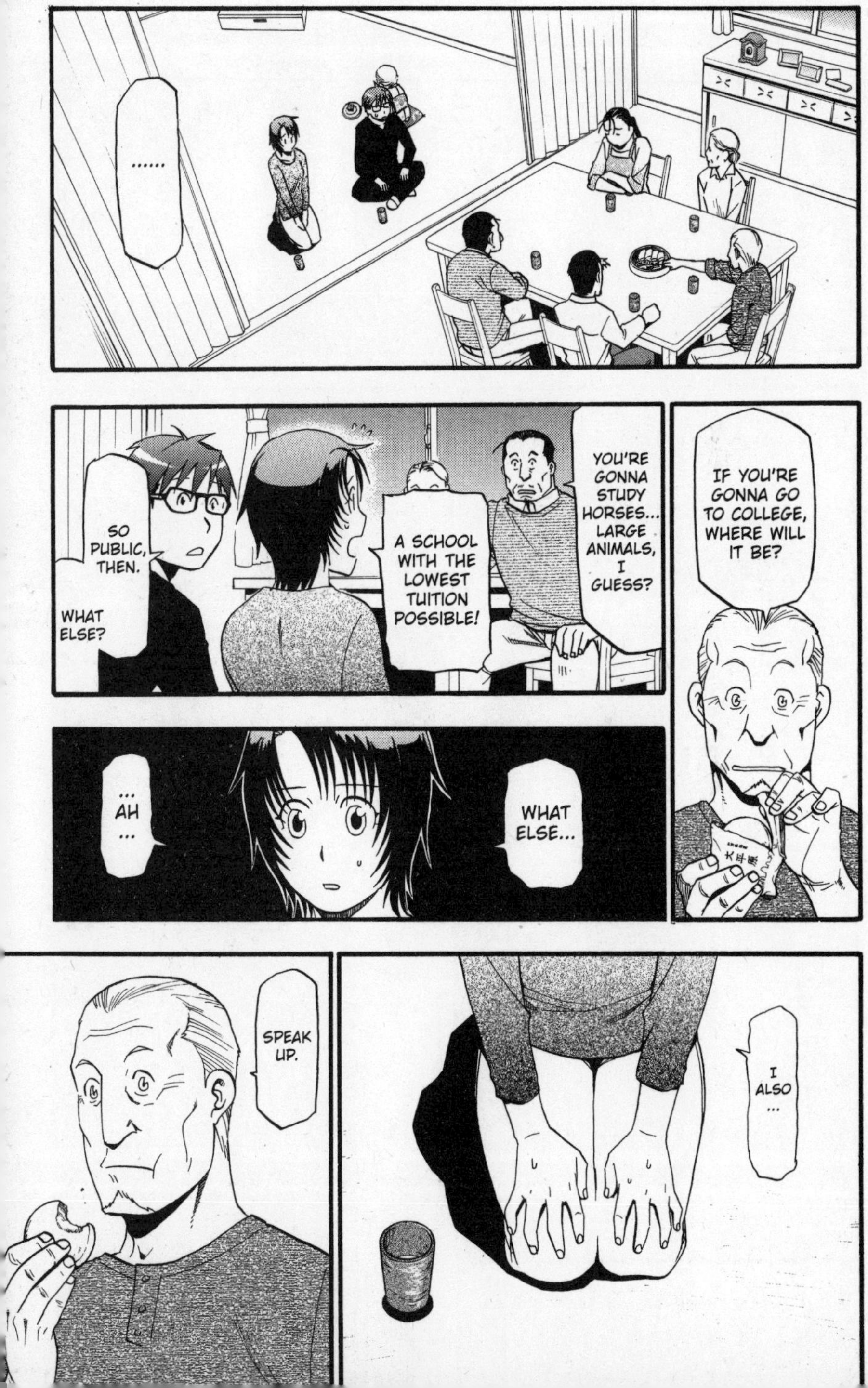
......
IF YOU'RE GONNA GO TO COLLEGE, WHERE WILL IT BE?
YOU'RE GONNA STUDY HORSES... LARGE ANIMALS, I GUESS?
A SCHOOL WITH THE LOWEST TUITION POSSIBLE!
SO PUBLIC, THEN.
WHAT ELSE?
WHAT ELSE...
... AH ...
I ALSO ...
SPEAK UP.

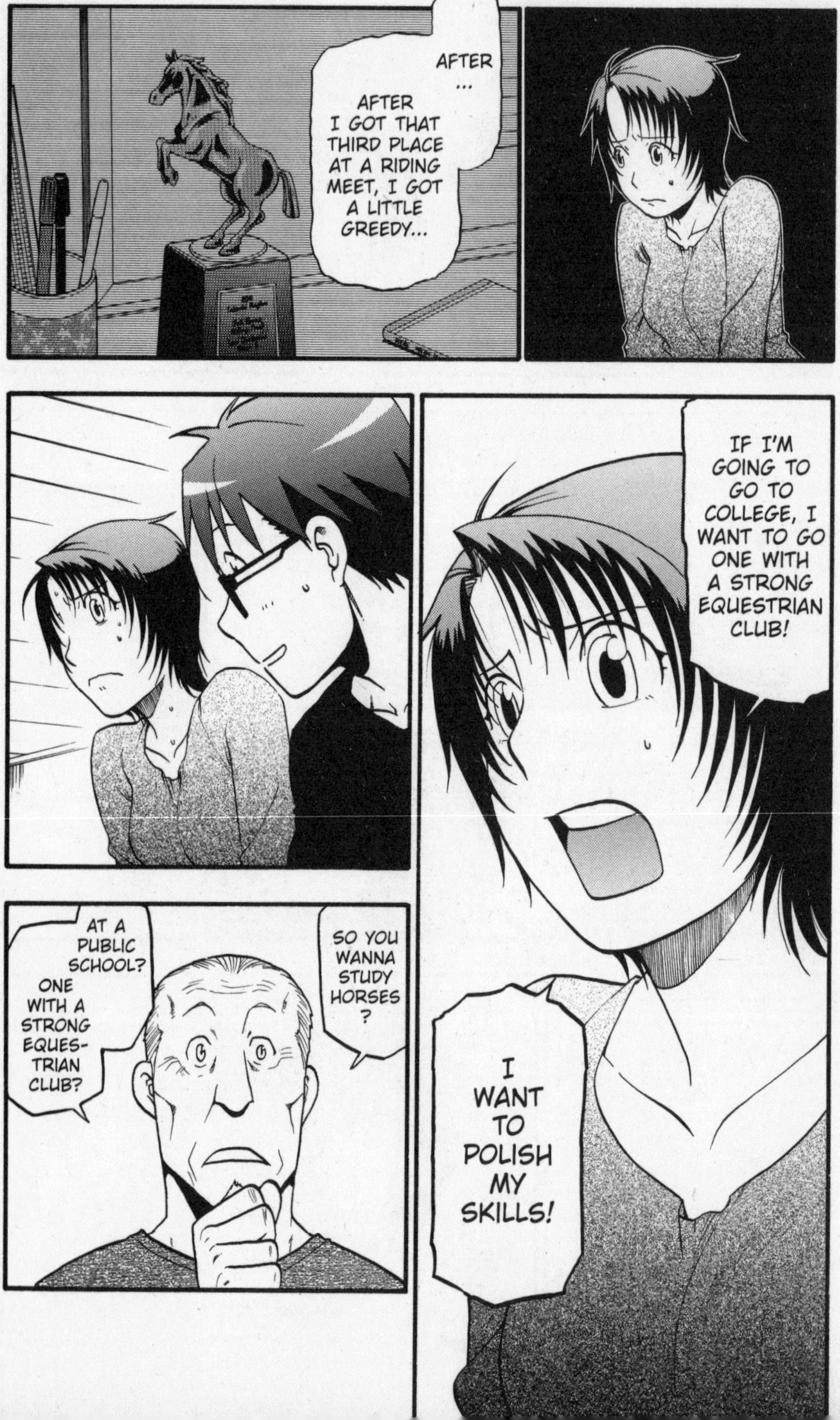
AFTER ...
AFTER I GOT THAT THIRD PLACE AT A RIDING MEET, I GOT A LITTLE GREEDY...
IF I'M GOING TO GO TO COLLEGE, I WANT TO GO ONE WITH A STRONG EQUESTRIAN CLUB!
I WANT TO POLISH MY SKILLS!
SO YOU WANNA STUDY HORSES?
AT A PUBLIC SCHOOL? ONE WITH A STRONG EQUES-TRIAN CLUB?

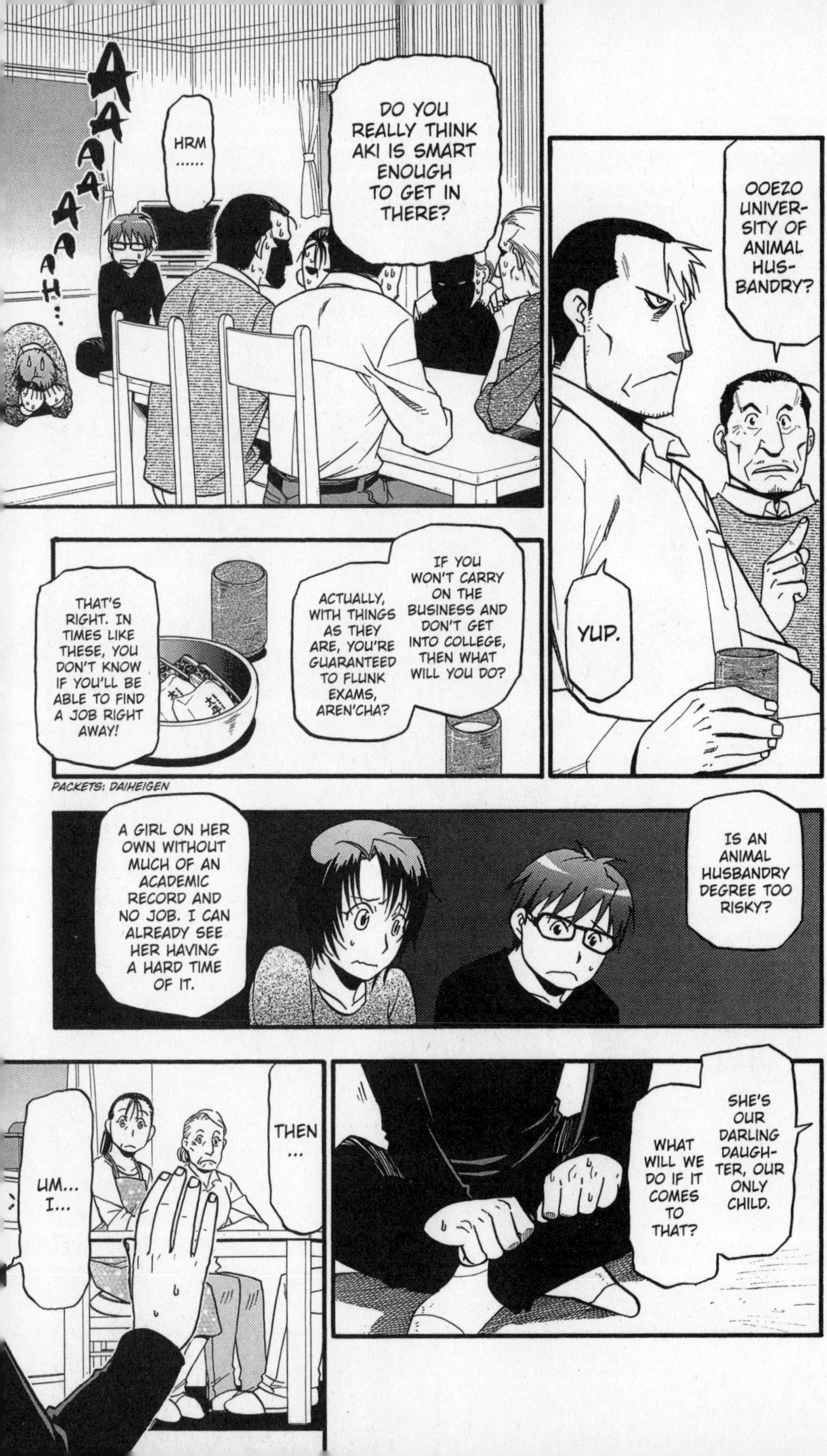
OOEZO UNIVERSITY OF ANIMAL HUSBANDRY?
YUP.
DO YOU REALLY THINK AKI IS SMART ENOUGH TO GET IN THERE?
HRM ......
AAAAAAAH...
IF YOU WON'T CARRY ON THE BUSINESS AND DON'T GET INTO COLLEGE, THEN WHAT WILL YOU DO?
ACTUALLY, WITH THINGS AS THEY ARE, YOU'RE GUARANTEED TO FLUNK EXAMS, AREN'CHA?
THAT'S RIGHT. IN TIMES LIKE THESE, YOU DON'T KNOW IF YOU'LL BE ABLE TO FIND A JOB RIGHT AWAY!
IS AN ANIMAL HUSBANDRY DEGREE TOO RISKY?
A GIRL ON HER OWN WITHOUT MUCH OF AN ACADEMIC RECORD AND NO JOB. I CAN ALREADY SEE HER HAVING A HARD TIME OF IT.
SHE'S OUR DARLING DAUGHTER, OUR ONLY CHILD.
WHAT WILL WE DO IF IT COMES TO THAT?
THEN ...
UM... I...

PACKETS: DAIHEIGEN

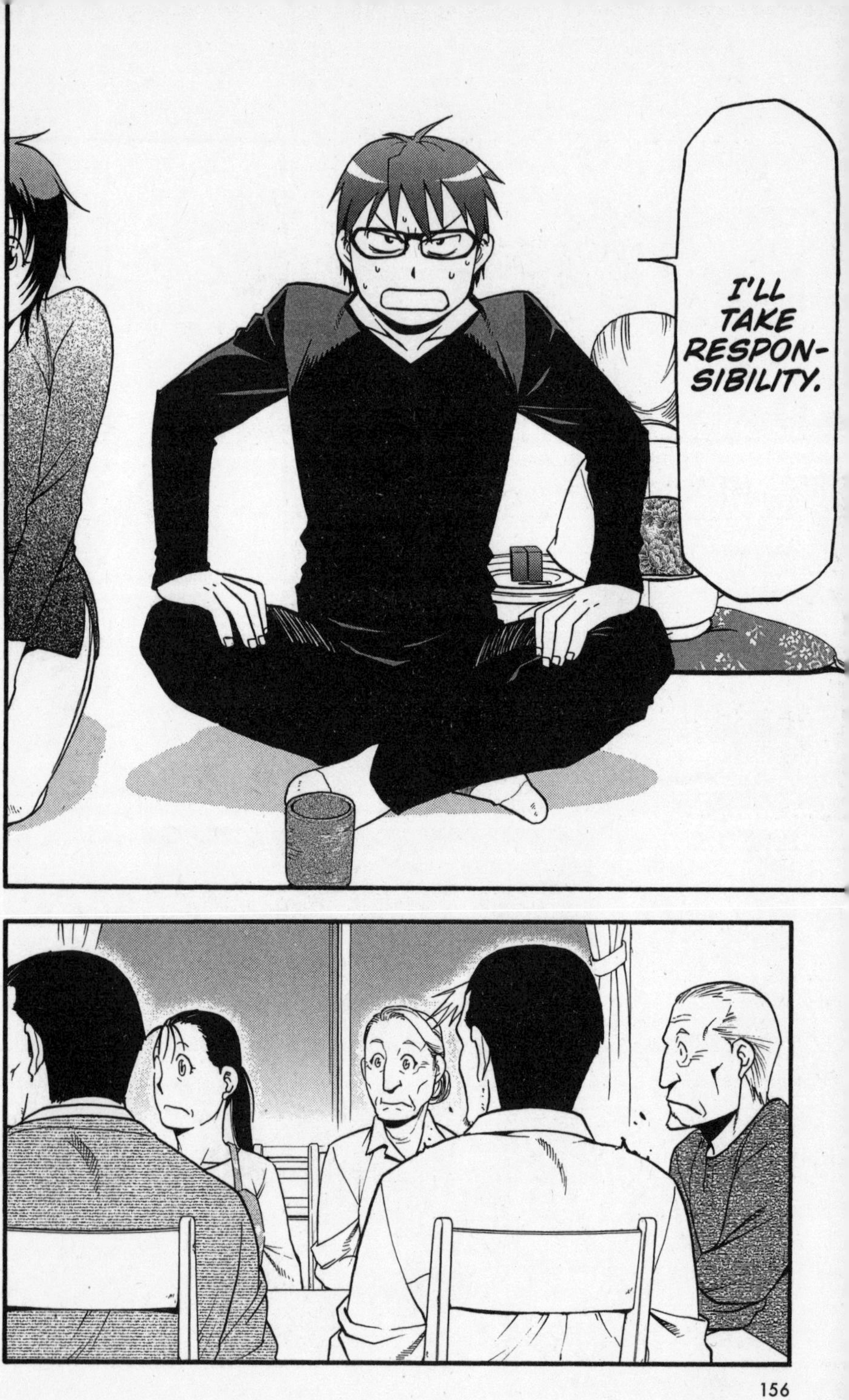
I'LL TAKE RESPONSIBILITY.

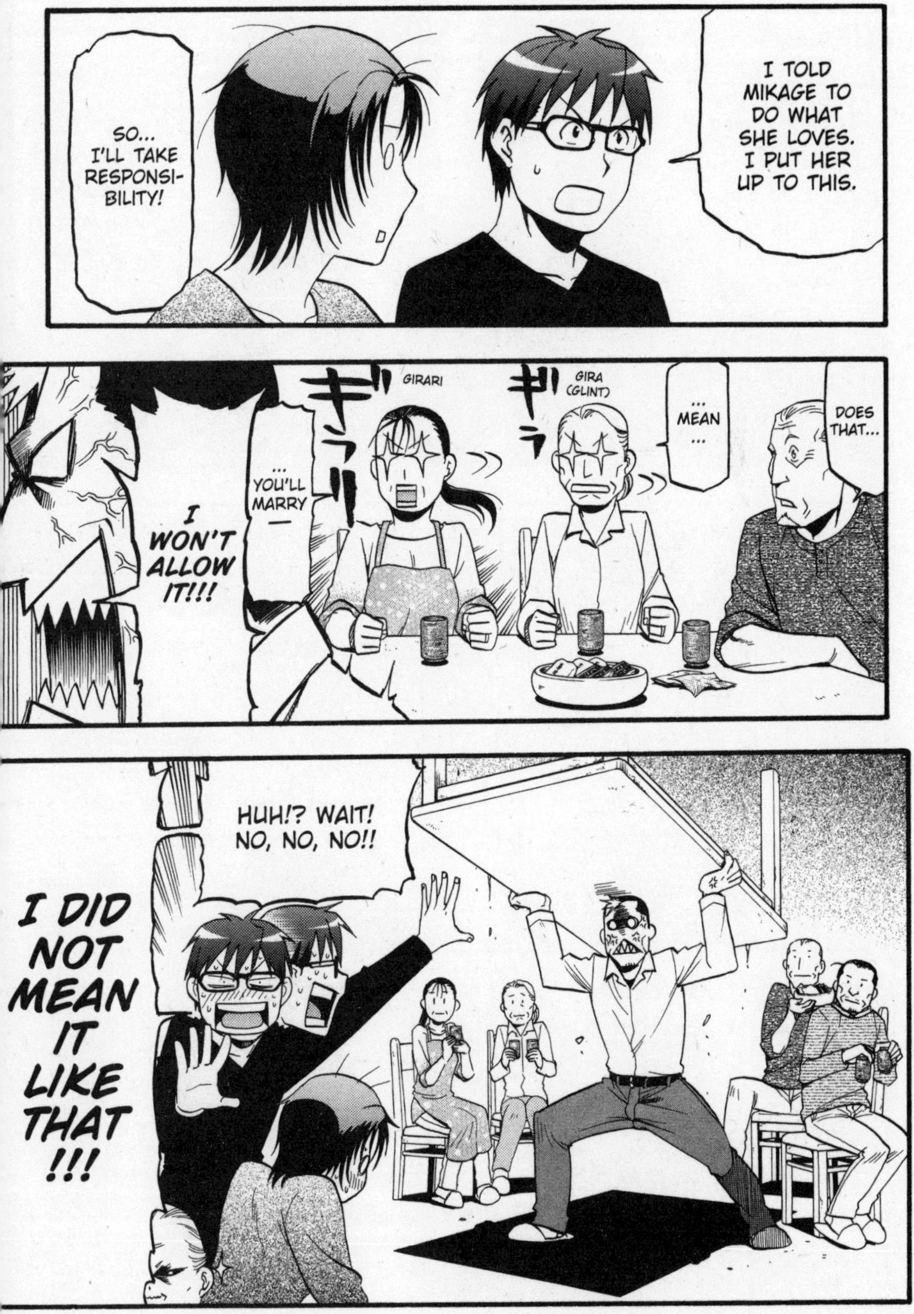
I TOLD MIKAGE TO DO WHAT SHE LOVES. I PUT HER UP TO THIS.
SO... I'LL TAKE RESPONSIBILITY!
DOES THAT...
... MEAN ...
ギラ
GIRA (GLINT)
ギラリ
GIRARI
... YOU'LL MARRY —
I WON'T ALLOW IT!!!
HUH!? WAIT! NO, NO, NO!!
I DID NOT MEAN IT LIKE THAT!!!

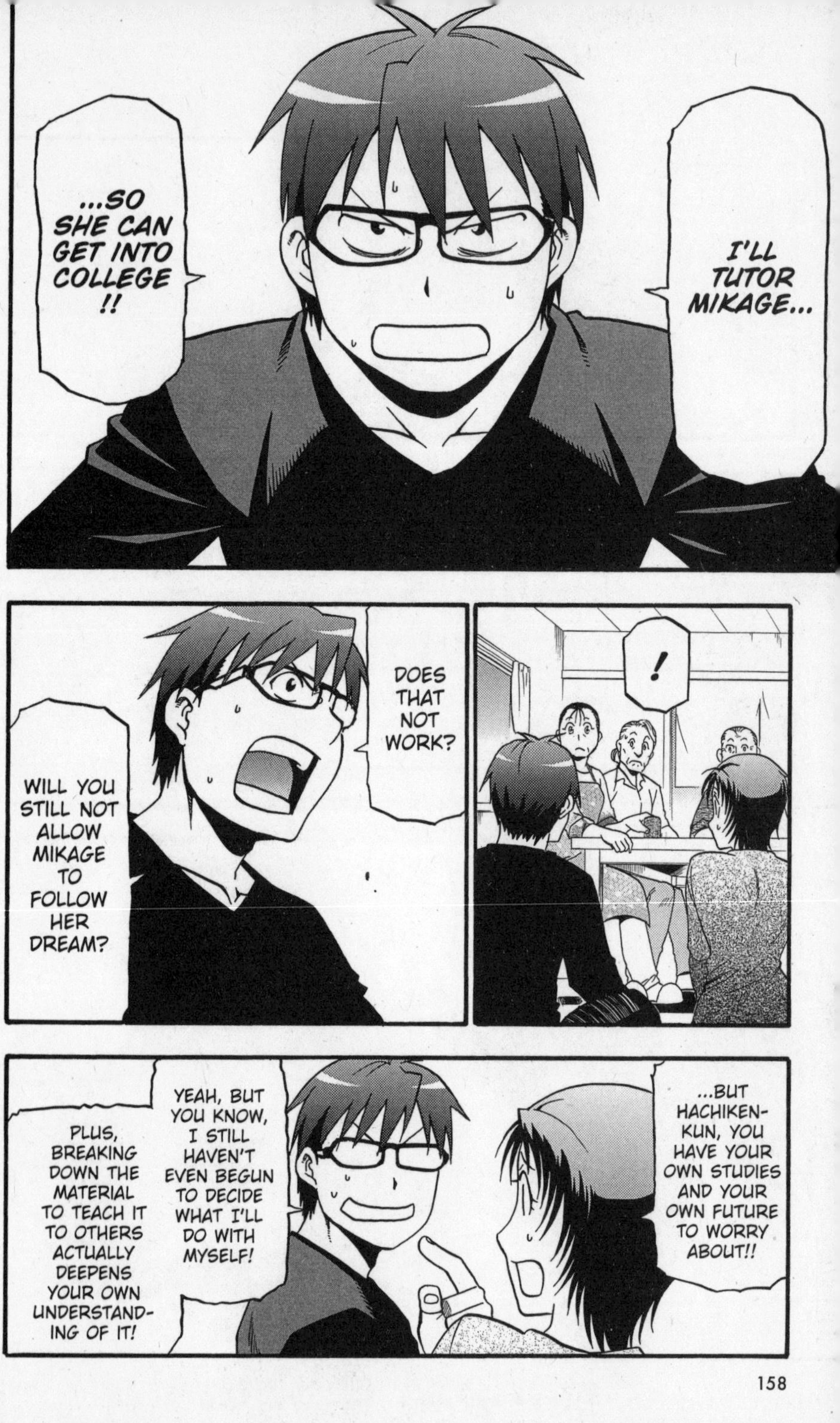
I'LL TUTOR MIKAGE...
...SO SHE CAN GET INTO COLLEGE !!
!
DOES THAT NOT WORK?
WILL YOU STILL NOT ALLOW MIKAGE TO FOLLOW HER DREAM?
...BUT HACHIKEN-KUN, YOU HAVE YOUR OWN STUDIES AND YOUR OWN FUTURE TO WORRY ABOUT!!
YEAH, BUT YOU KNOW, I STILL HAVEN'T EVEN BEGUN TO DECIDE WHAT I'LL DO WITH MYSELF!
PLUS, BREAKING DOWN THE MATERIAL TO TEACH IT TO OTHERS ACTUALLY DEEPENS YOUR OWN UNDERSTANDING OF IT!

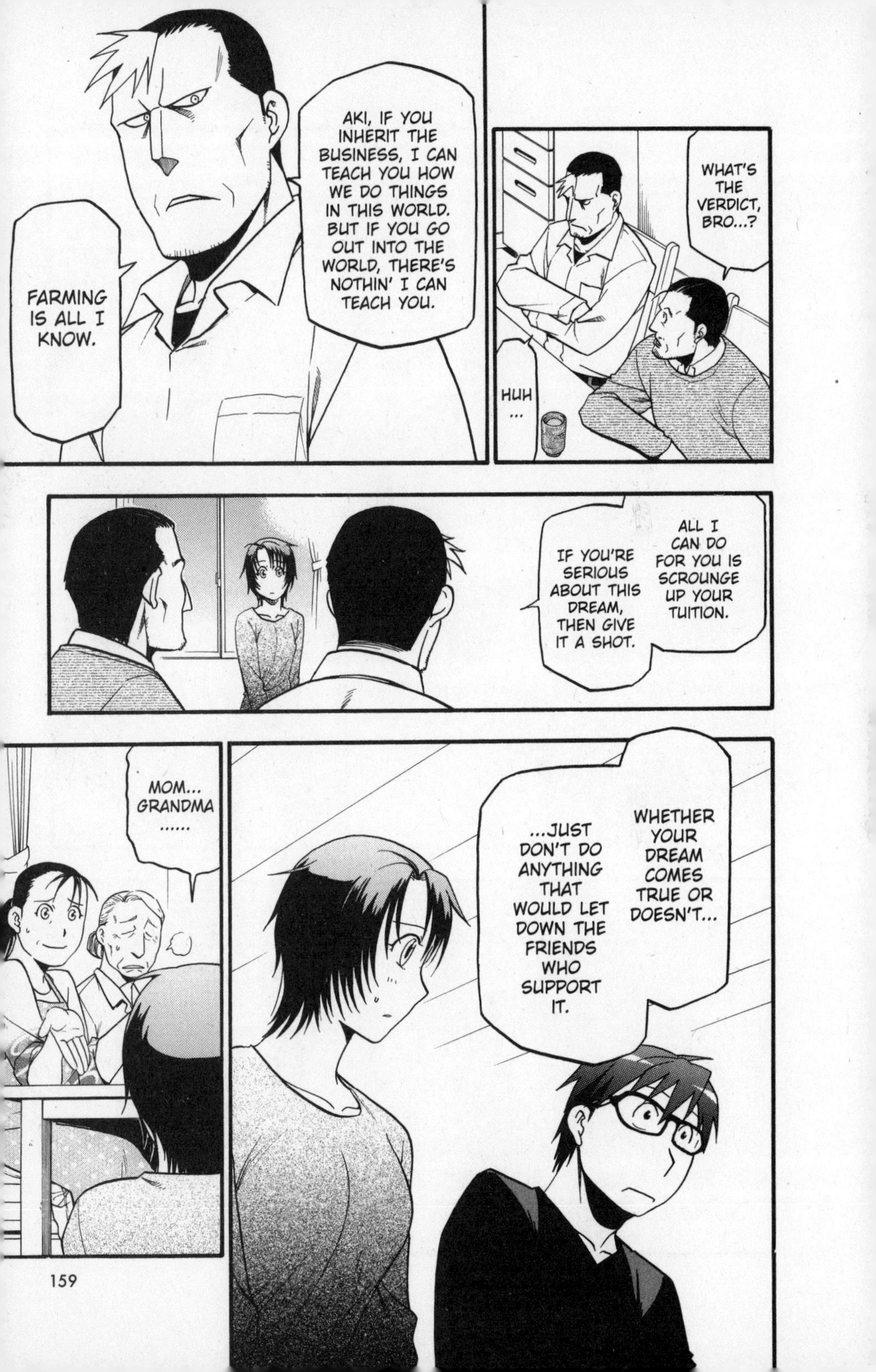
WHAT'S THE VERDICT, BRO...?
HUH...
AKI, IF YOU INHERIT THE BUSINESS, I CAN TEACH YOU HOW WE DO THINGS IN THIS WORLD. BUT IF YOU GO OUT INTO THE WORLD, THERE'S NOTHIN' I CAN TEACH YOU.
FARMING IS ALL I KNOW.
ALL I CAN DO FOR YOU IS SCROUNGE UP YOUR TUITION.
IF YOU'RE SERIOUS ABOUT THIS DREAM, THEN GIVE IT A SHOT.
WHETHER YOUR DREAM COMES TRUE OR DOESN'T...
...JUST DON'T DO ANYTHING THAT WOULD LET DOWN THE FRIENDS WHO SUPPORT IT.
MOM... GRANDMA ......

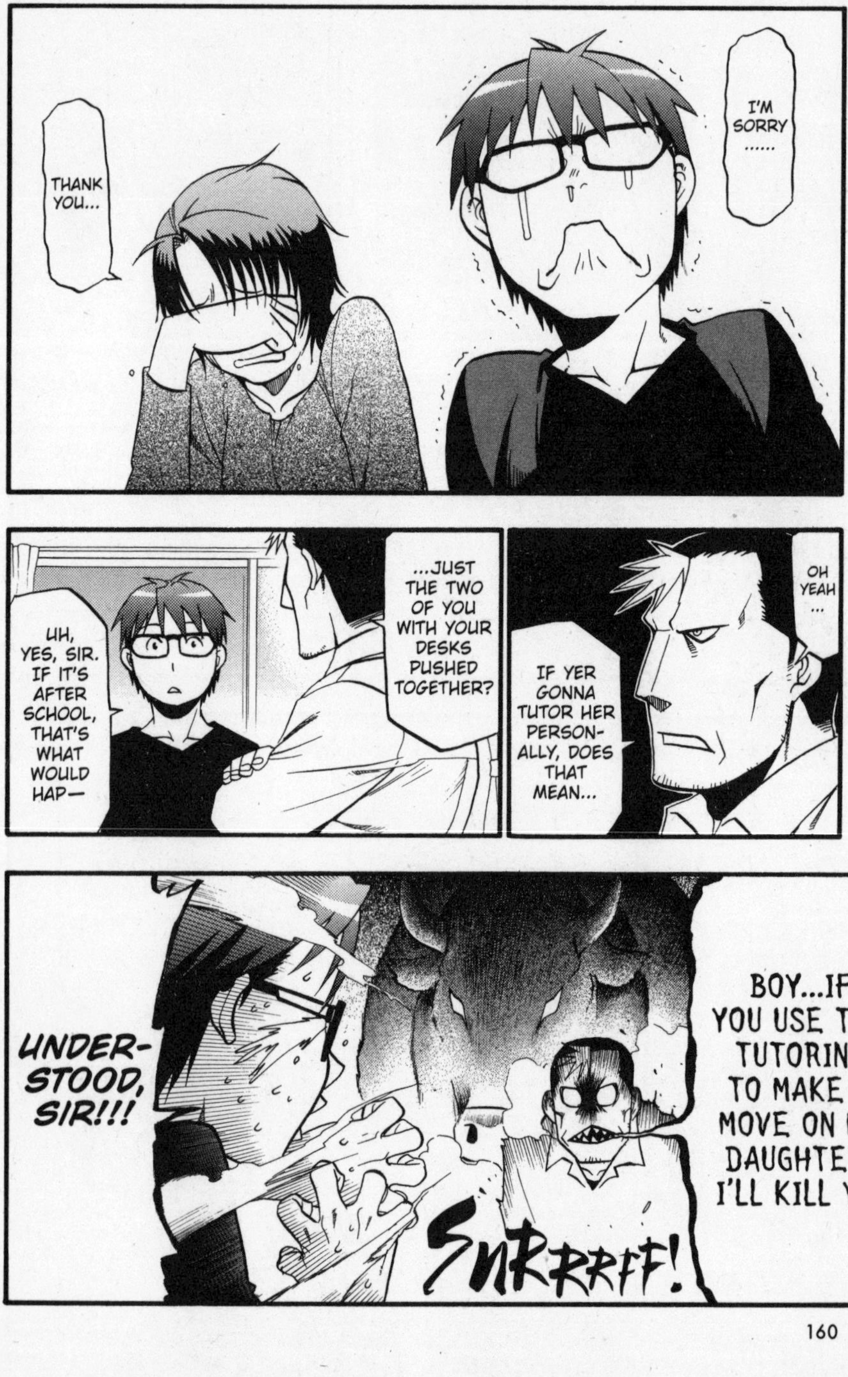
I'M SORRY ......
THANK YOU...
OH YEAH ...
IF YER GONNA TUTOR HER PERSON-ALLY, DOES THAT MEAN...
...JUST THE TWO OF YOU WITH YOUR DESKS PUSHED TOGETHER?
UH, YES, SIR. IF IT'S AFTER SCHOOL, THAT'S WHAT WOULD HAP—
BOY...IF YOU USE THE TUTORING TO MAKE A MOVE ON MY DAUGHTER, I'LL KILL YA.
SNRRRFF!
UNDER-STOOD, SIR!!!

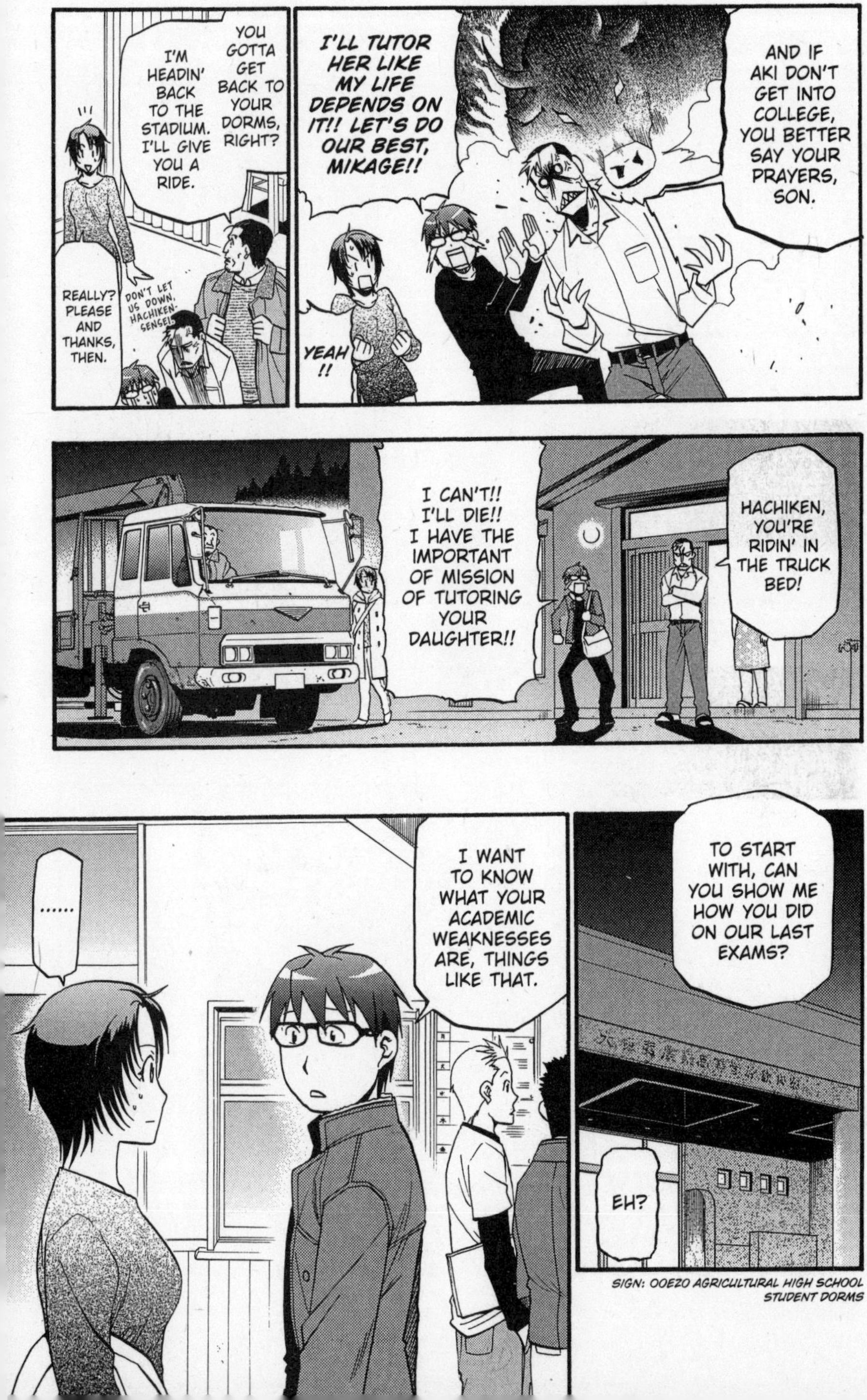
AND IF AKI DON'T GET INTO COLLEGE, YOU BETTER SAY YOUR PRAYERS, SON.
I'LL TUTOR HER LIKE MY LIFE DEPENDS ON IT!! LET'S DO OUR BEST, MIKAGE!!
YEAH!!
YOU GOTTA GET BACK TO YOUR DORMS, RIGHT?
I'M HEADIN' BACK TO THE STADIUM. I'LL GIVE YOU A RIDE.
DON'T LET US DOWN, HACHIKEN-SENSEI.
REALLY? PLEASE AND THANKS, THEN.
HACHIKEN, YOU'RE RIDIN' IN THE TRUCK BED!
I CAN'T!! I'LL DIE!! I HAVE THE IMPORTANT OF MISSION OF TUTORING YOUR DAUGHTER!!
TO START WITH, CAN YOU SHOW ME HOW YOU DID ON OUR LAST EXAMS?
EH?
SIGN: OOEZO AGRICULTURAL HIGH SCHOOL STUDENT DORMS
I WANT TO KNOW WHAT YOUR ACADEMIC WEAKNESSES ARE, THINGS LIKE THAT.
......

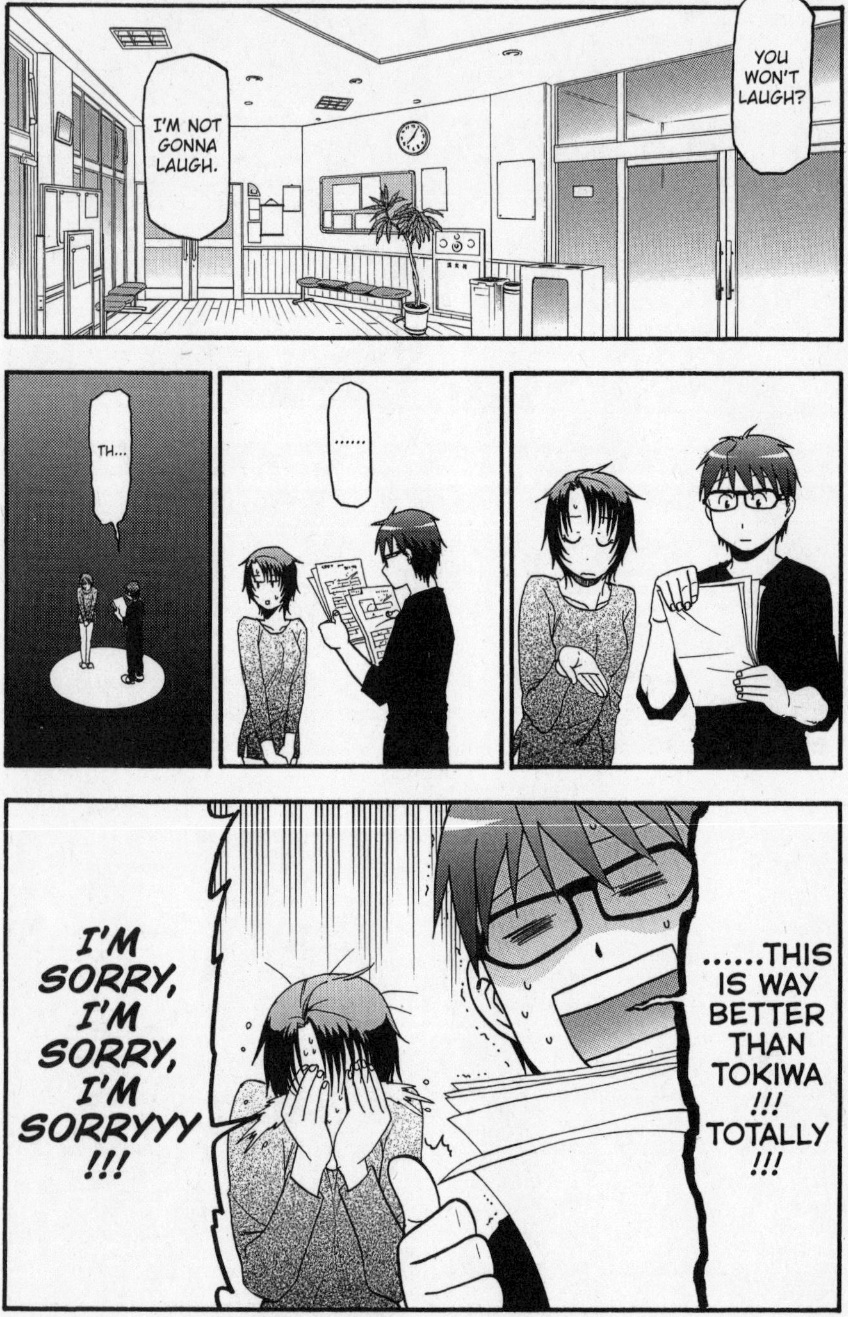
YOU WON'T LAUGH?
I'M NOT GONNA LAUGH.
......
TH...
......THIS IS WAY BETTER THAN TOKIWA!!! TOTALLY!!!
I'M SORRY, I'M SORRY, I'M SORRYYY!!!

Silver Spoon

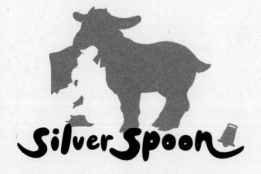

PHYS ED.
TEACHER

GOU TODOROKI

Chapter 70:
Tale of Winter ⑦

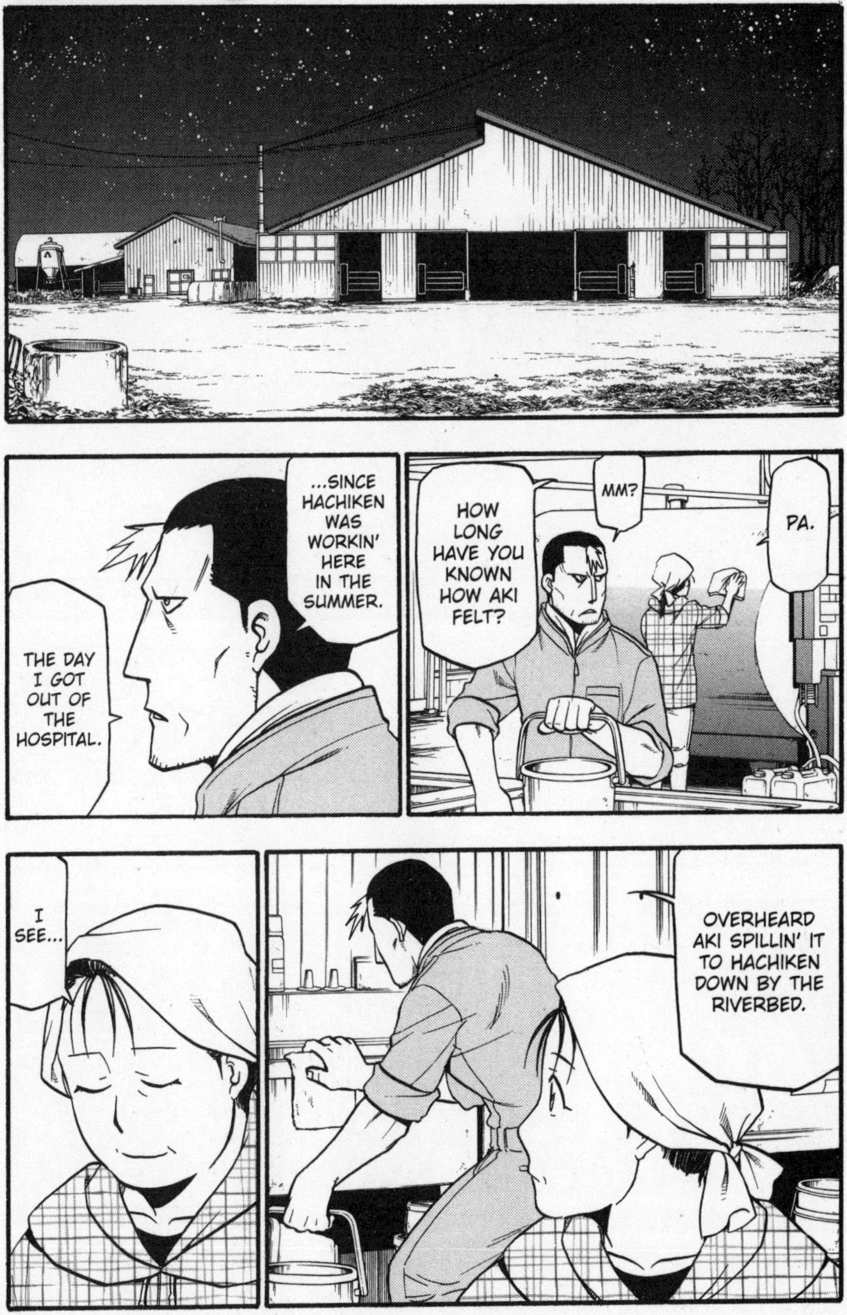
PA.
MM?
HOW LONG HAVE YOU KNOWN HOW AKI FELT?
...SINCE HACHIKEN WAS WORKIN' HERE IN THE SUMMER.
THE DAY I GOT OUT OF THE HOSPITAL.
OVERHEARD AKI SPILLIN' IT TO HACHIKEN DOWN BY THE RIVERBED.
I SEE...

OUR AKI HAS FOUND FRIENDS SHE CAN SPEAK HER MIND TO AT EZO AG.

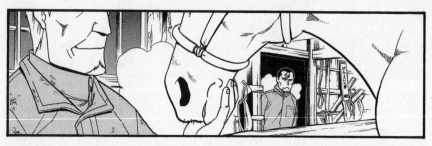

HOW MUCH WILL WE GET ALL TOLD IF WE SELL 'EM?

DAD...

THESE HORSES...

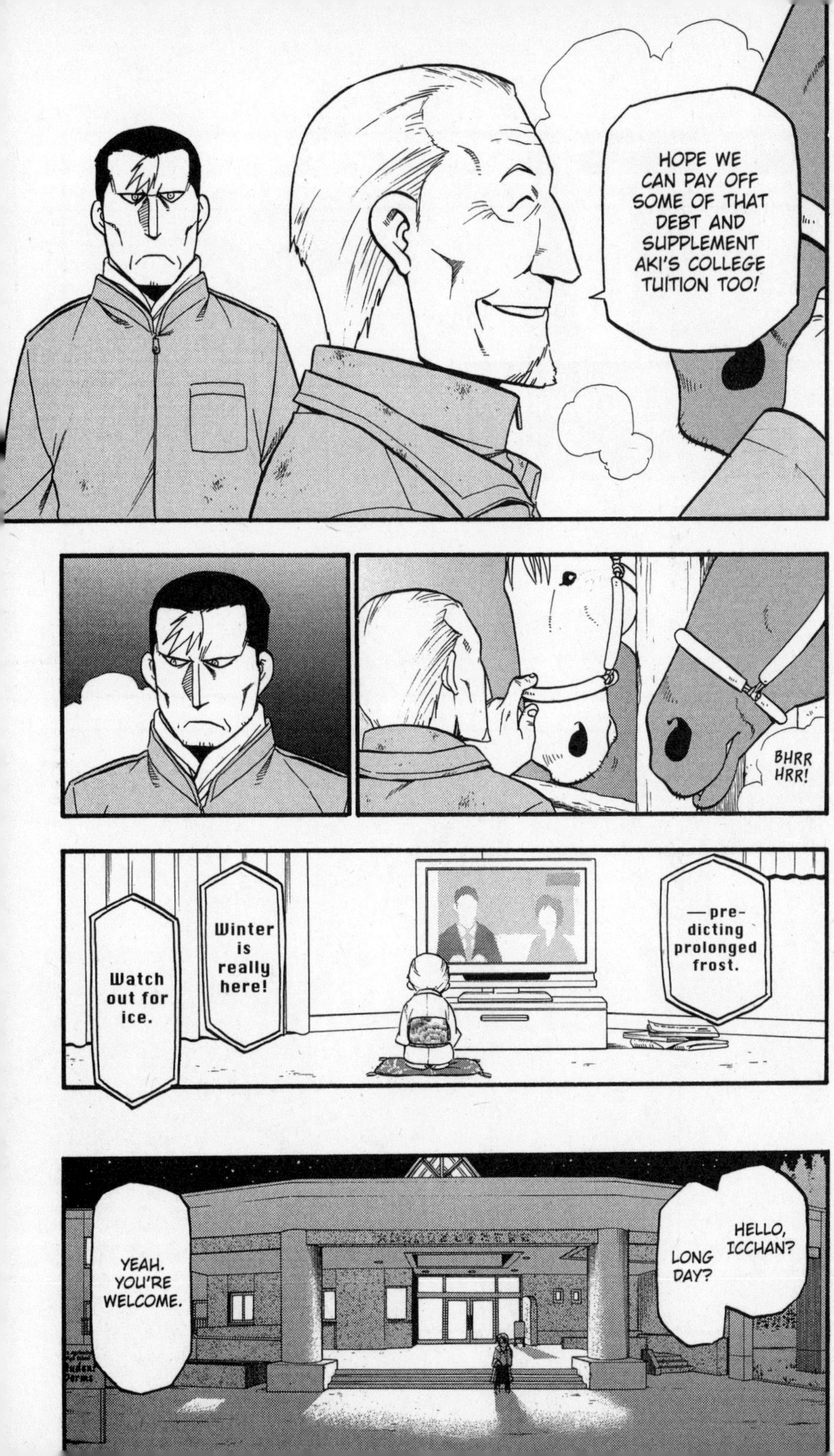
HOPE WE CAN PAY OFF SOME OF THAT DEBT AND SUPPLEMENT AKI'S COLLEGE TUITION TOO!
BHRR HRR!
—pre-dicting prolonged frost.
Winter is really here!
Watch out for ice.
HELLO, ICCHAN?
LONG DAY?
YEAH. YOU'RE WELCOME.

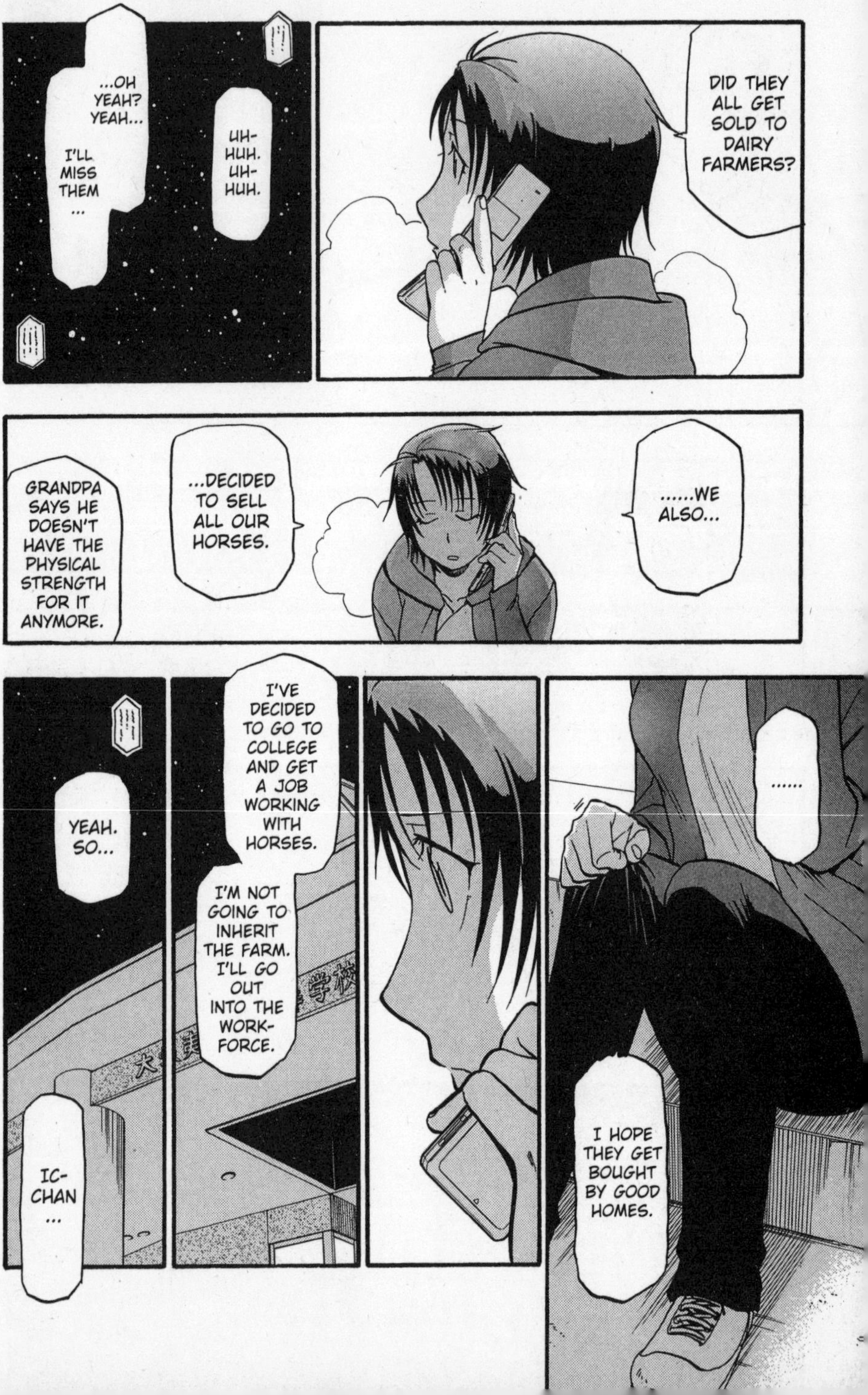
DID THEY ALL GET SOLD TO DAIRY FARMERS?
UH-HUH. UH-HUH.
...OH YEAH? YEAH... I'LL MISS THEM ...
......WE ALSO...
...DECIDED TO SELL ALL OUR HORSES.
GRANDPA SAYS HE DOESN'T HAVE THE PHYSICAL STRENGTH FOR IT ANYMORE.
......
I HOPE THEY GET BOUGHT BY GOOD HOMES.
I'VE DECIDED TO GO TO COLLEGE AND GET A JOB WORKING WITH HORSES.
I'M NOT GOING TO INHERIT THE FARM. I'LL GO OUT INTO THE WORK-FORCE.
YEAH. SO...
IC-CHAN ...

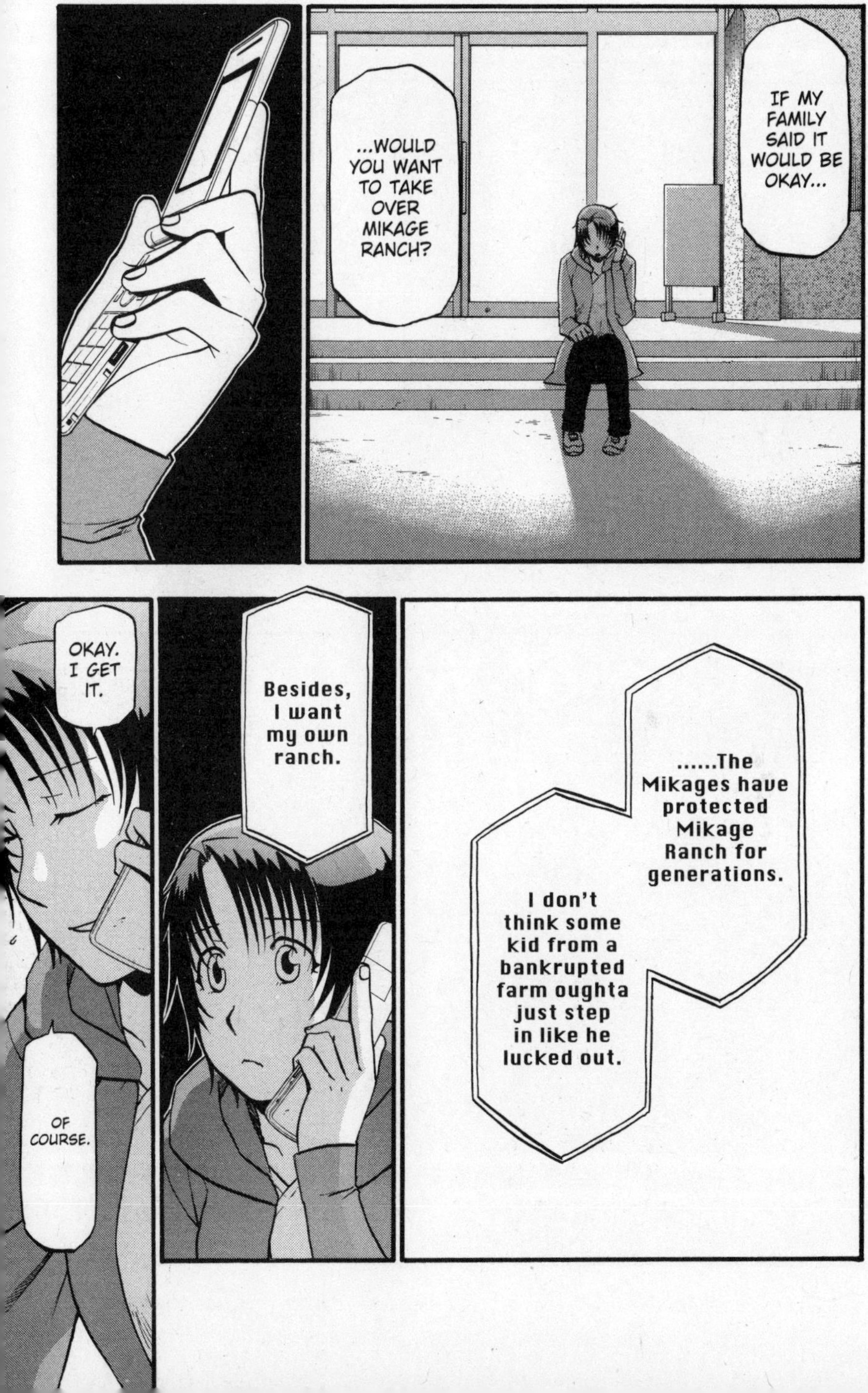
IF MY FAMILY SAID IT WOULD BE OKAY...
...WOULD YOU WANT TO TAKE OVER MIKAGE RANCH?
......The Mikages have protected Mikage Ranch for generations.
I don't think some kid from a bankrupted farm oughta just step in like he lucked out.
Besides, I want my own ranch.
OKAY. I GET IT.
OF COURSE.

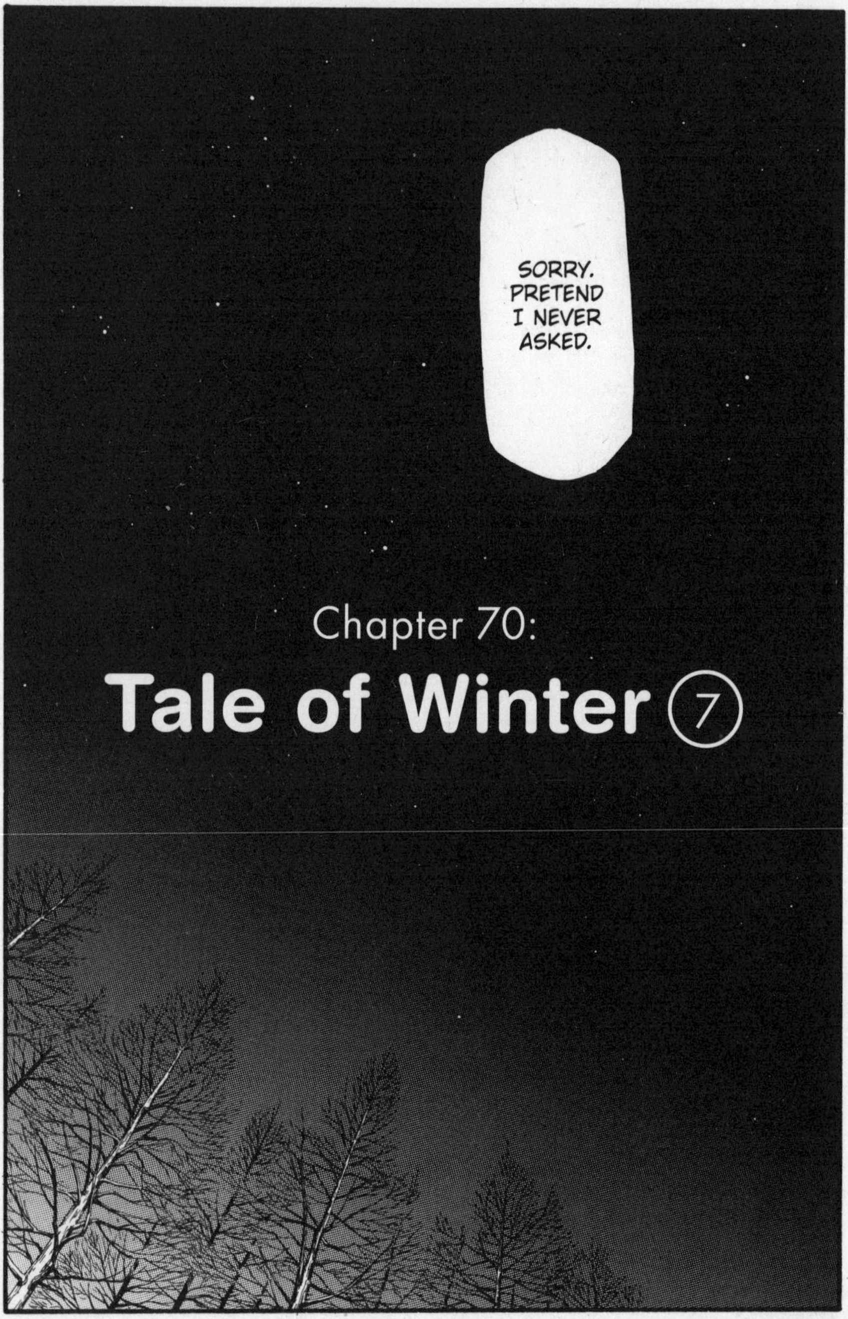
SORRY. PRETEND I NEVER ASKED.

Chapter 70:
Tale of Winter ⑦

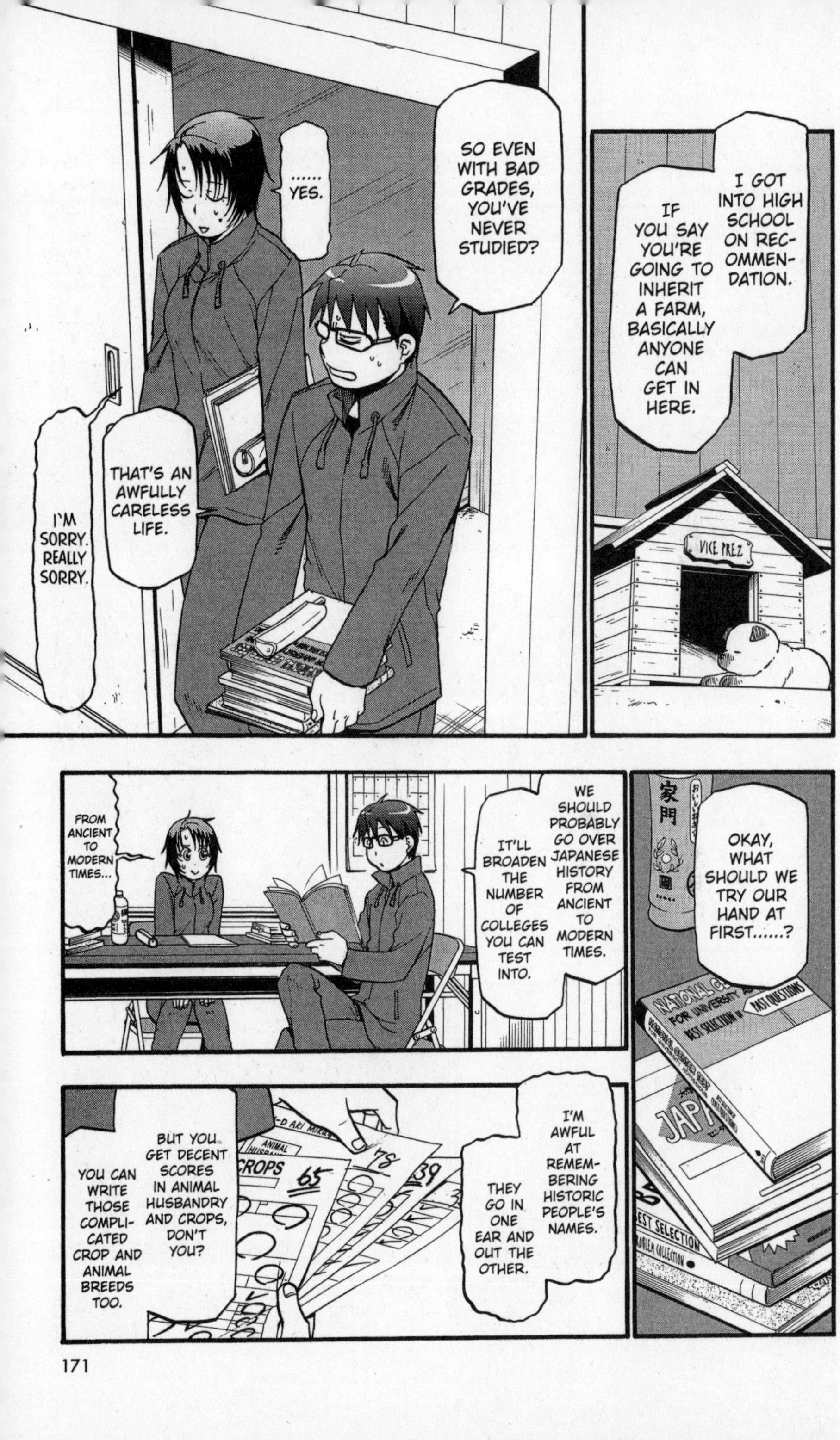
I GOT INTO HIGH SCHOOL ON RECOMMENDATION.
IF YOU SAY YOU'RE GOING TO INHERIT A FARM, BASICALLY ANYONE CAN GET IN HERE.
VICE PREZ
SO EVEN WITH BAD GRADES, YOU'VE NEVER STUDIED?
......YES.
THAT'S AN AWFULLY CARELESS LIFE.
I'M SORRY. REALLY SORRY.
OKAY, WHAT SHOULD WE TRY OUR HAND AT FIRST......?
PAST QUESTIONS
WE SHOULD PROBABLY GO OVER JAPANESE HISTORY FROM ANCIENT TO MODERN TIMES.
IT'LL BROADEN THE NUMBER OF COLLEGES YOU CAN TEST INTO.
FROM ANCIENT TO MODERN TIMES...
I'M AWFUL AT REMEMBERING HISTORIC PEOPLE'S NAMES.
THEY GO IN ONE EAR AND OUT THE OTHER.
CROPS 65
BUT YOU GET DECENT SCORES IN ANIMAL HUSBANDRY AND CROPS, DON'T YOU?
YOU CAN WRITE THOSE COMPLICATED CROP AND ANIMAL BREEDS TOO.

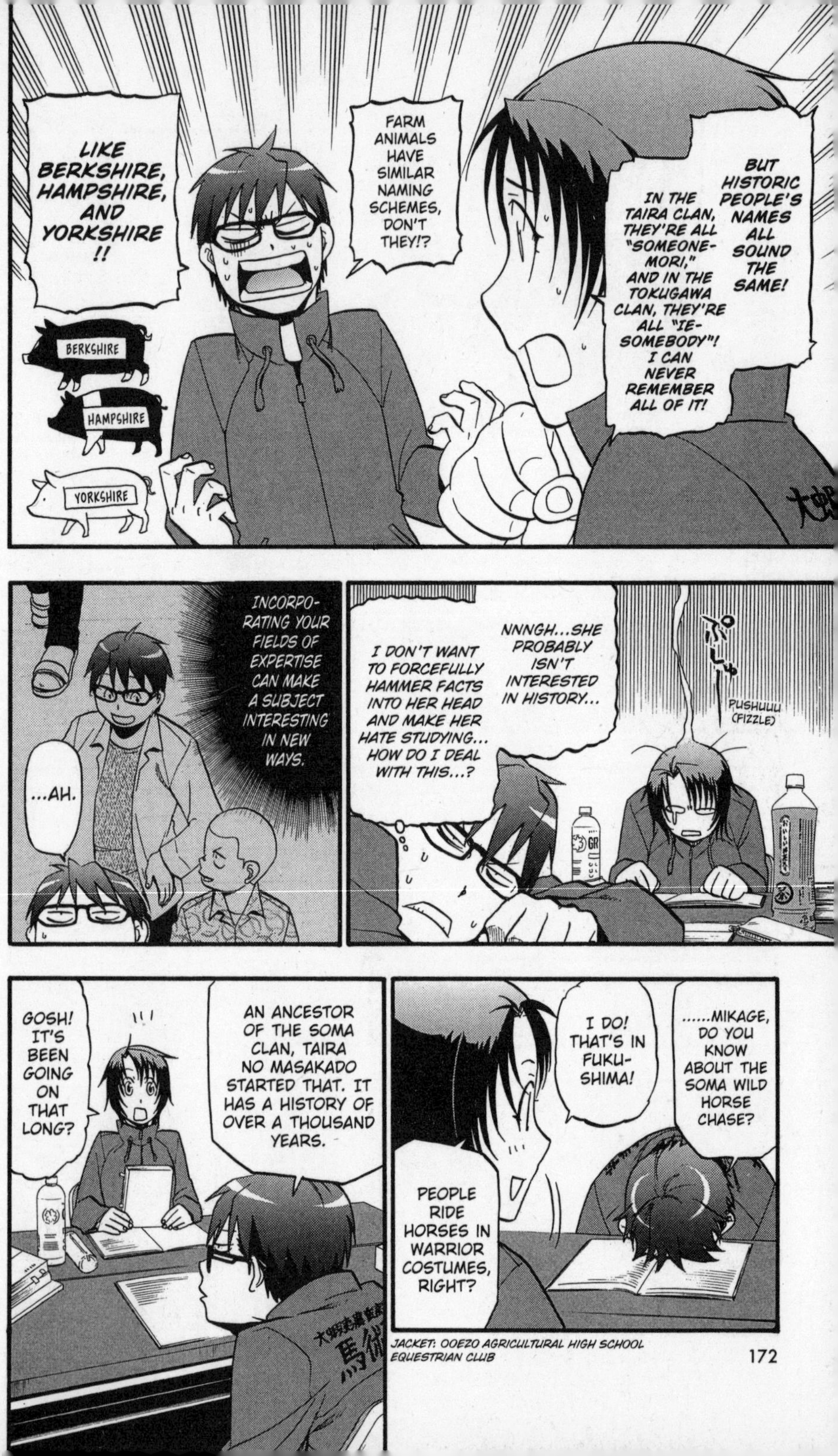
BUT HISTORIC PEOPLE'S NAMES ALL SOUND THE SAME!
IN THE TAIRA CLAN, THEY'RE ALL "SOMEONE-MORI," AND IN THE TOKUGAWA CLAN, THEY'RE ALL "IE-SOMEBODY"! I CAN NEVER REMEMBER ALL OF IT!
FARM ANIMALS HAVE SIMILAR NAMING SCHEMES, DON'T THEY!?
LIKE BERKSHIRE, HAMPSHIRE, AND YORKSHIRE !!
BERKSHIRE
HAMPSHIRE
YORKSHIRE
PUSHUUU (FIZZLE)
NNNGH...SHE PROBABLY ISN'T INTERESTED IN HISTORY...
I DON'T WANT TO FORCEFULLY HAMMER FACTS INTO HER HEAD AND MAKE HER HATE STUDYING... HOW DO I DEAL WITH THIS...?
INCORPORATING YOUR FIELDS OF EXPERTISE CAN MAKE A SUBJECT INTERESTING IN NEW WAYS.
...AH.
......MIKAGE, DO YOU KNOW ABOUT THE SOMA WILD HORSE CHASE?
I DO! THAT'S IN FUKUSHIMA!
PEOPLE RIDE HORSES IN WARRIOR COSTUMES, RIGHT?
AN ANCESTOR OF THE SOMA CLAN, TAIRA NO MASAKADO STARTED THAT. IT HAS A HISTORY OF OVER A THOUSAND YEARS.
GOSH! IT'S BEEN GOING ON THAT LONG?
JACKET: OOEZO AGRICULTURAL HIGH SCHOOL EQUESTRIAN CLUB

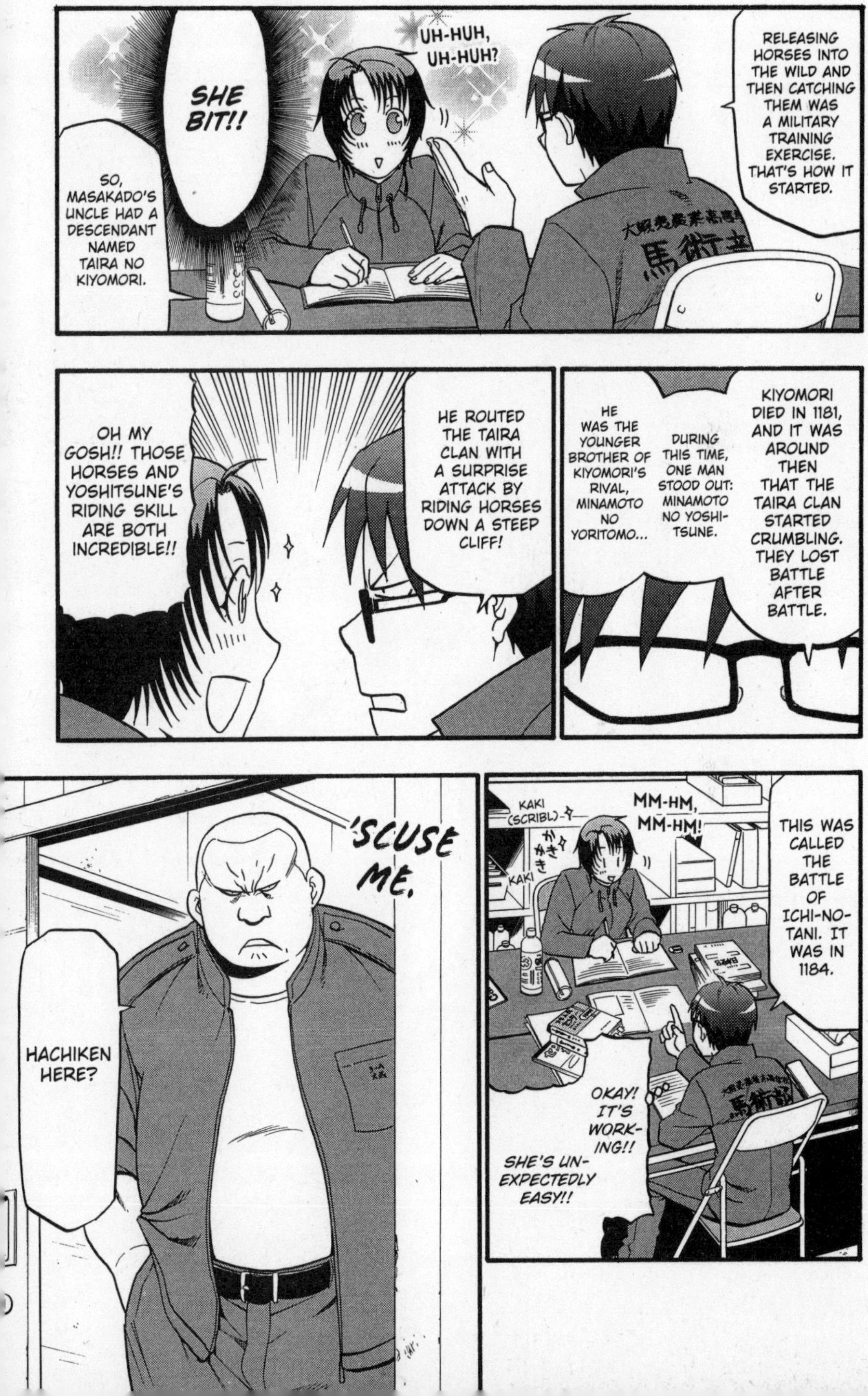
RELEASING HORSES INTO THE WILD AND THEN CATCHING THEM WAS A MILITARY TRAINING EXERCISE. THAT'S HOW IT STARTED.
UH-HUH, UH-HUH?
SHE BIT!!
SO, MASAKADO'S UNCLE HAD A DESCENDANT NAMED TAIRA NO KIYOMORI.
KIYOMORI DIED IN 1181, AND IT WAS AROUND THEN THAT THE TAIRA CLAN STARTED CRUMBLING. THEY LOST BATTLE AFTER BATTLE.
DURING THIS TIME, ONE MAN STOOD OUT: MINAMOTO NO YOSHI-TSUNE.
HE WAS THE YOUNGER BROTHER OF KIYOMORI'S RIVAL, MINAMOTO NO YORITOMO...
HE ROUTED THE TAIRA CLAN WITH A SURPRISE ATTACK BY RIDING HORSES DOWN A STEEP CLIFF!
OH MY GOSH!! THOSE HORSES AND YOSHITSUNE'S RIDING SKILL ARE BOTH INCREDIBLE!!
THIS WAS CALLED THE BATTLE OF ICHI-NO-TANI. IT WAS IN 1184.
MM-HM, MM-HM!
KAKI (SCRIBL)
KAKI
OKAY! IT'S WORK-ING!!
SHE'S UN-EXPECTEDLY EASY!!
'SCUSE ME.
HACHIKEN HERE?

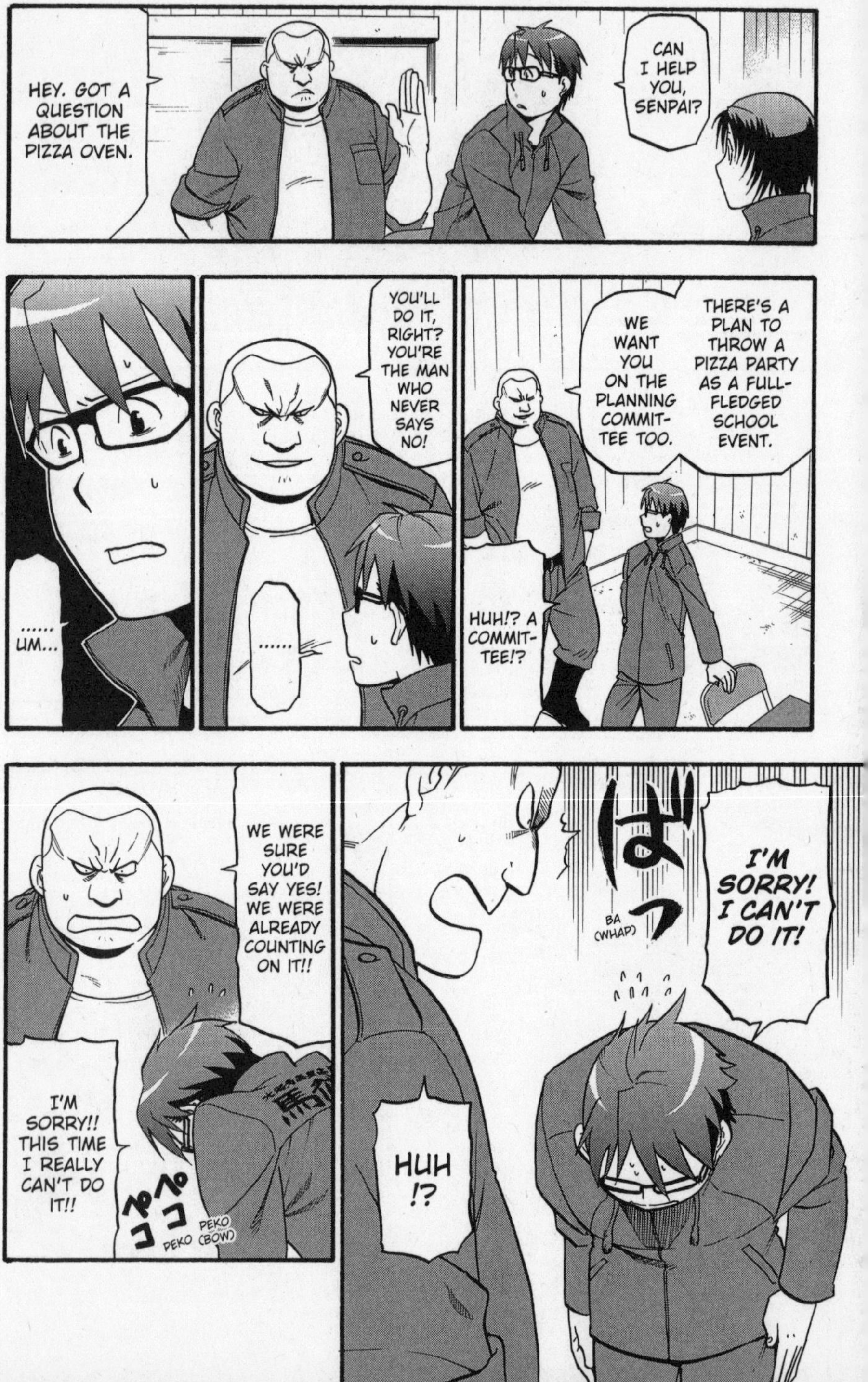
CAN I HELP YOU, SENPAI?
HEY. GOT A QUESTION ABOUT THE PIZZA OVEN.
THERE'S A PLAN TO THROW A PIZZA PARTY AS A FULL-FLEDGED SCHOOL EVENT.
WE WANT YOU ON THE PLANNING COMMIT-TEE TOO.
HUH!? A COMMIT-TEE!?
YOU'LL DO IT, RIGHT? YOU'RE THE MAN WHO NEVER SAYS NO!
......
...... UM...
I'M SORRY! I CAN'T DO IT!
ぱっ
BA (WHAP)
HUH !?
WE WERE SURE YOU'D SAY YES! WE WERE ALREADY COUNTING ON IT!!
I'M SORRY!! THIS TIME I REALLY CAN'T DO IT!!
ペコペコ
PEKO PEKO (BOW)

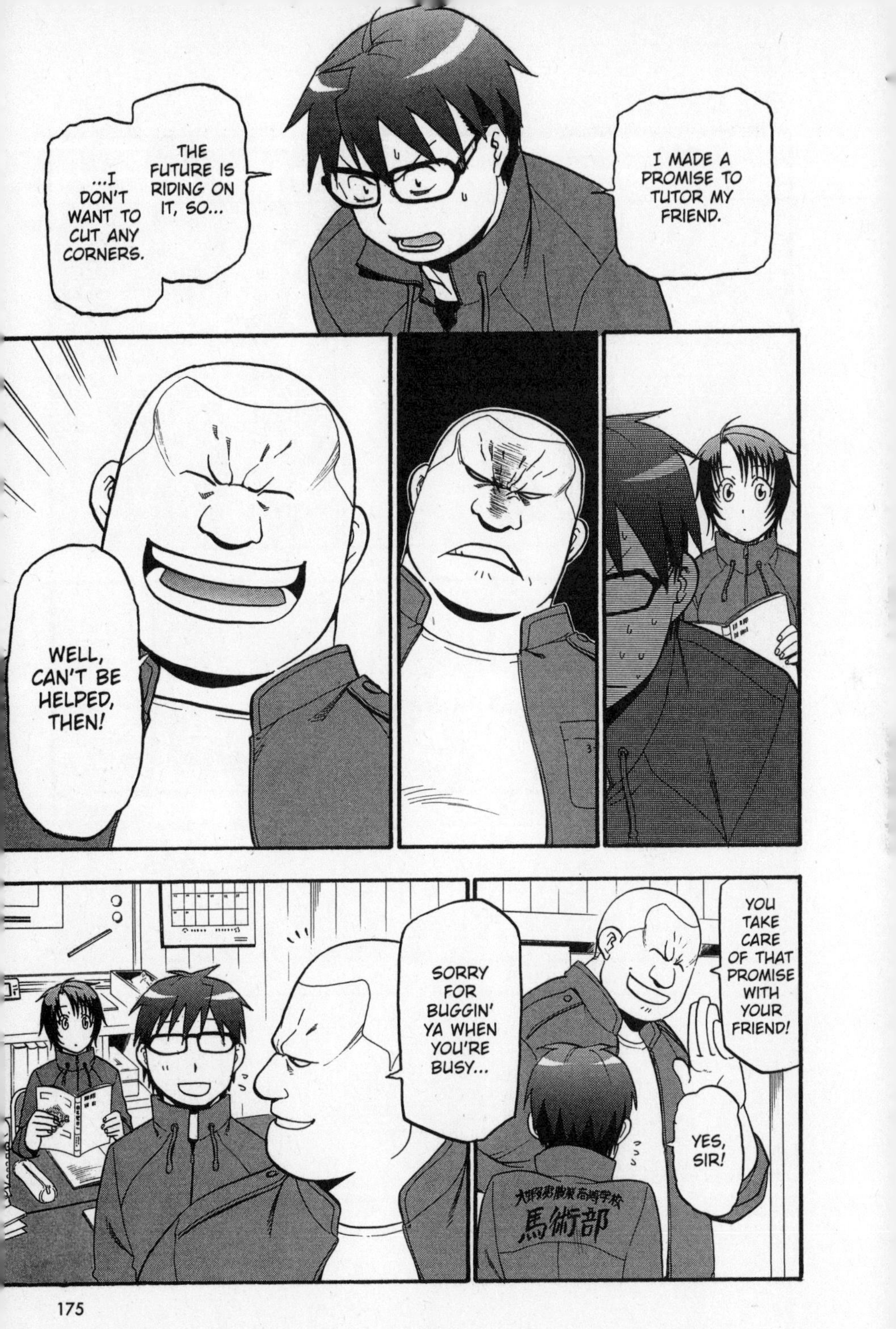
I MADE A PROMISE TO TUTOR MY FRIEND.
THE FUTURE IS RIDING ON IT, SO...
...I DON'T WANT TO CUT ANY CORNERS.
WELL, CAN'T BE HELPED, THEN!
YOU TAKE CARE OF THAT PROMISE WITH YOUR FRIEND!
YES, SIR!
馬術部
SORRY FOR BUGGIN' YA WHEN YOU'RE BUSY...

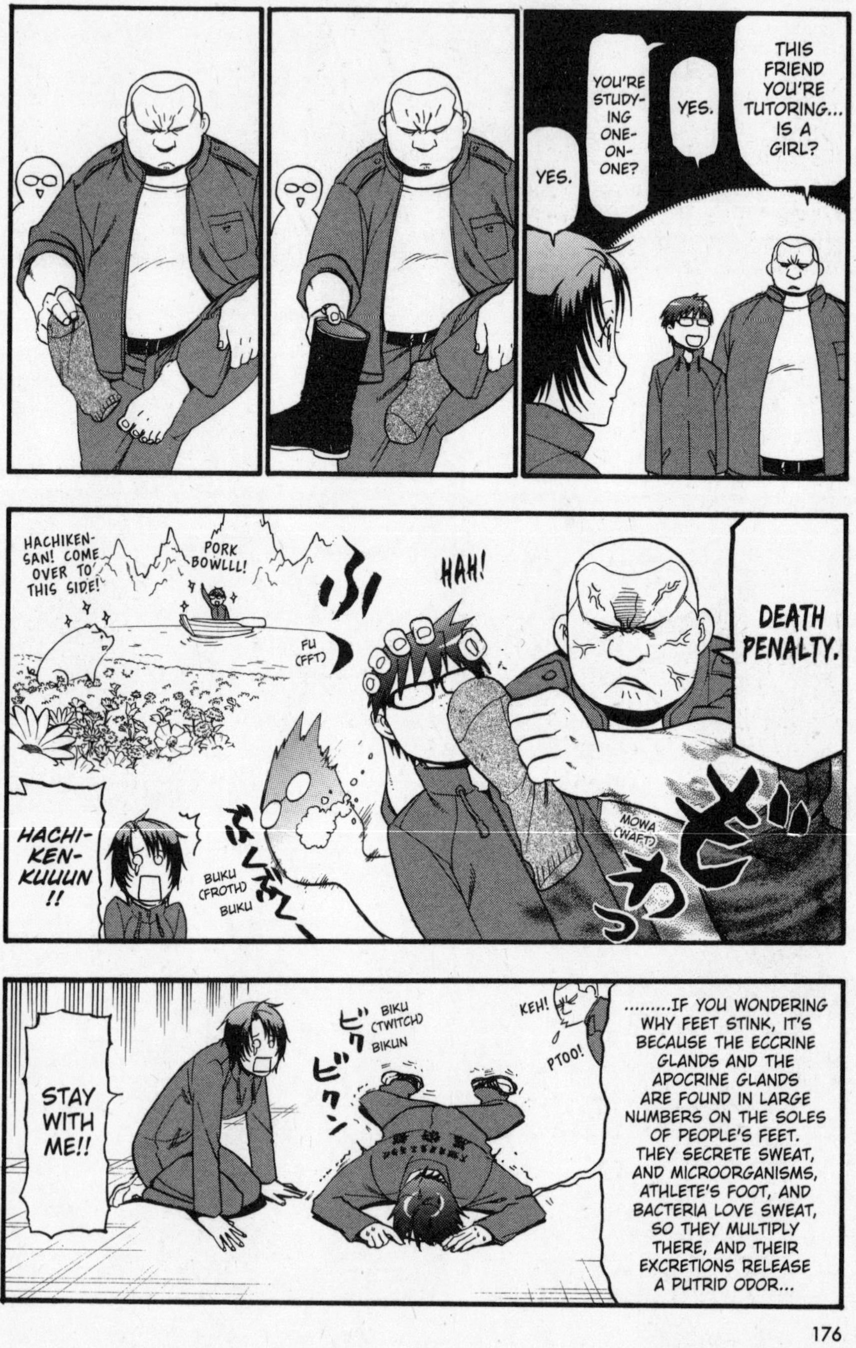
THIS FRIEND YOU'RE TUTORING... IS A GIRL?
YES.
YOU'RE STUDYING ONE-ON-ONE?
YES.
DEATH PENALTY.
HAH!
MOWA (WAFT)
FU (FFT)
PORK BOWLLL!
HACHIKEN-SAN! COME OVER TO THIS SIDE!
BUKU (FROTH) BUKU
HACHIKEN-KUUUN!!
.........IF YOU WONDERING WHY FEET STINK, IT'S BECAUSE THE ECCRINE GLANDS AND THE APOCRINE GLANDS ARE FOUND IN LARGE NUMBERS ON THE SOLES OF PEOPLE'S FEET. THEY SECRETE SWEAT, AND MICROORGANISMS, ATHLETE'S FOOT, AND BACTERIA LOVE SWEAT, SO THEY MULTIPLY THERE, AND THEIR EXCRETIONS RELEASE A PUTRID ODOR...
KEH!
PTOO!
BIKU (TWITCH) BIKUN
STAY WITH ME!!

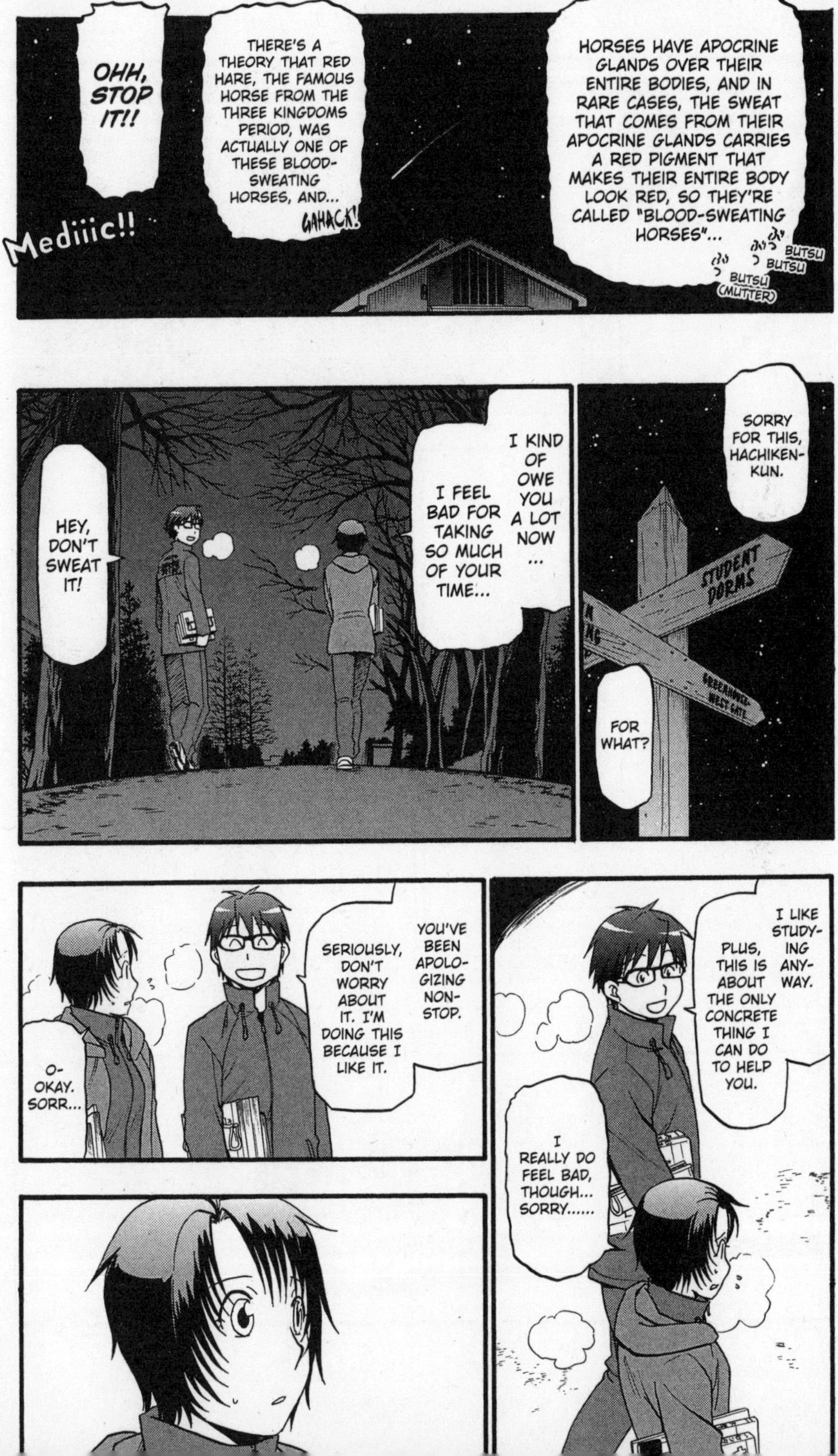
HORSES HAVE APOCRINE GLANDS OVER THEIR ENTIRE BODIES, AND IN RARE CASES, THE SWEAT THAT COMES FROM THEIR APOCRINE GLANDS CARRIES A RED PIGMENT THAT MAKES THEIR ENTIRE BODY LOOK RED, SO THEY'RE CALLED "BLOOD-SWEATING HORSES"...
BUTSU
BUTSU
BUTSU (MUTTER)
THERE'S A THEORY THAT RED HARE, THE FAMOUS HORSE FROM THE THREE KINGDOMS PERIOD, WAS ACTUALLY ONE OF THESE BLOOD-SWEATING HORSES, AND...
GAHACK!
OHH, STOP IT!!
Mediiic!!
SORRY FOR THIS, HACHIKEN-KUN.
STUDENT DORMS
FOR WHAT?
I KIND OF OWE YOU A LOT NOW ...
I FEEL BAD FOR TAKING SO MUCH OF YOUR TIME...
HEY, DON'T SWEAT IT!
I LIKE STUDYING ANYWAY.
PLUS, THIS IS ABOUT THE ONLY CONCRETE THING I CAN DO TO HELP YOU.
I REALLY DO FEEL BAD, THOUGH... SORRY......
YOU'VE BEEN APOLOGIZING NON-STOP.
SERIOUSLY, DON'T WORRY ABOUT IT. I'M DOING THIS BECAUSE I LIKE IT.
O-OKAY. SORR...

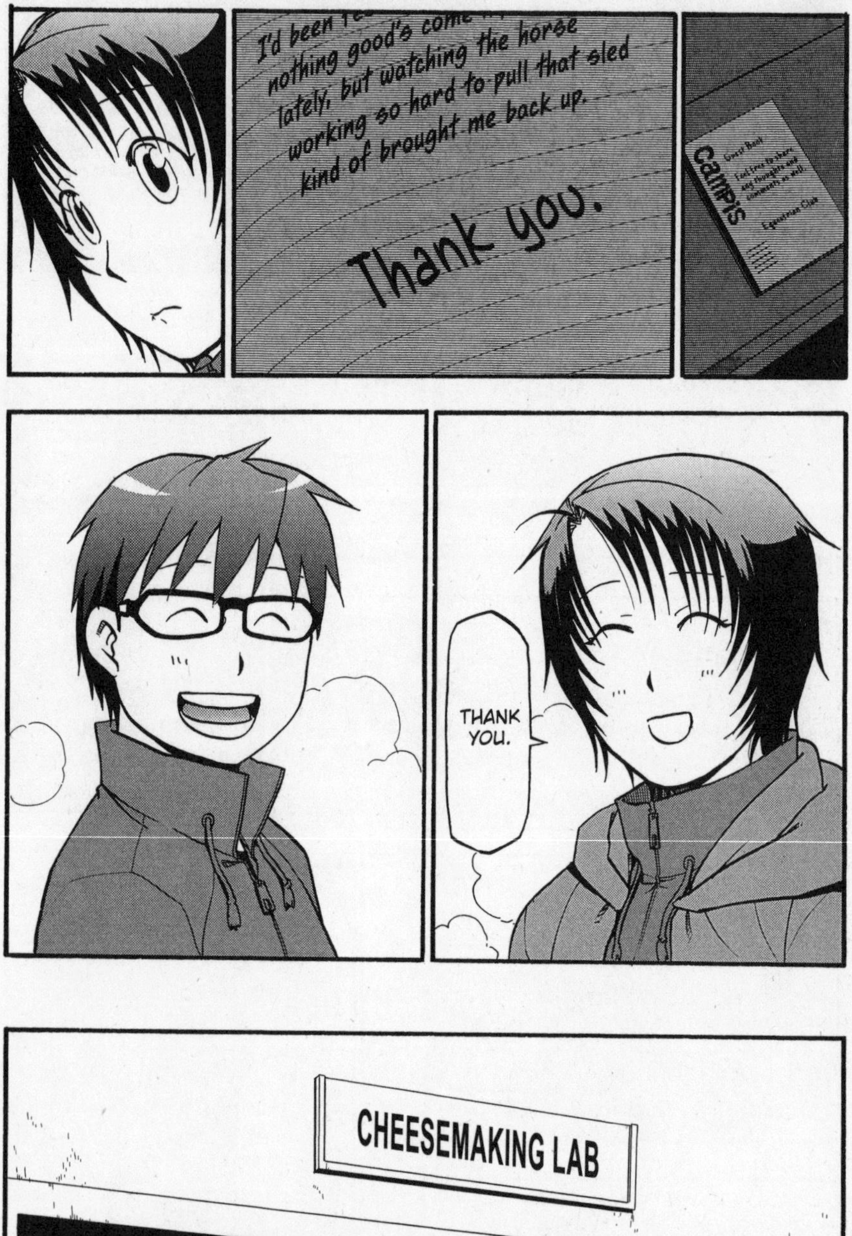
Campis
Guest Book
Feel free to share any thoughts and comments as well.
Equestrian Club
I'd been
nothing good's come
lately, but watching the horse
working so hard to pull that sled
kind of brought me back up.
Thank you.
THANK YOU.
CHEESEMAKING LAB

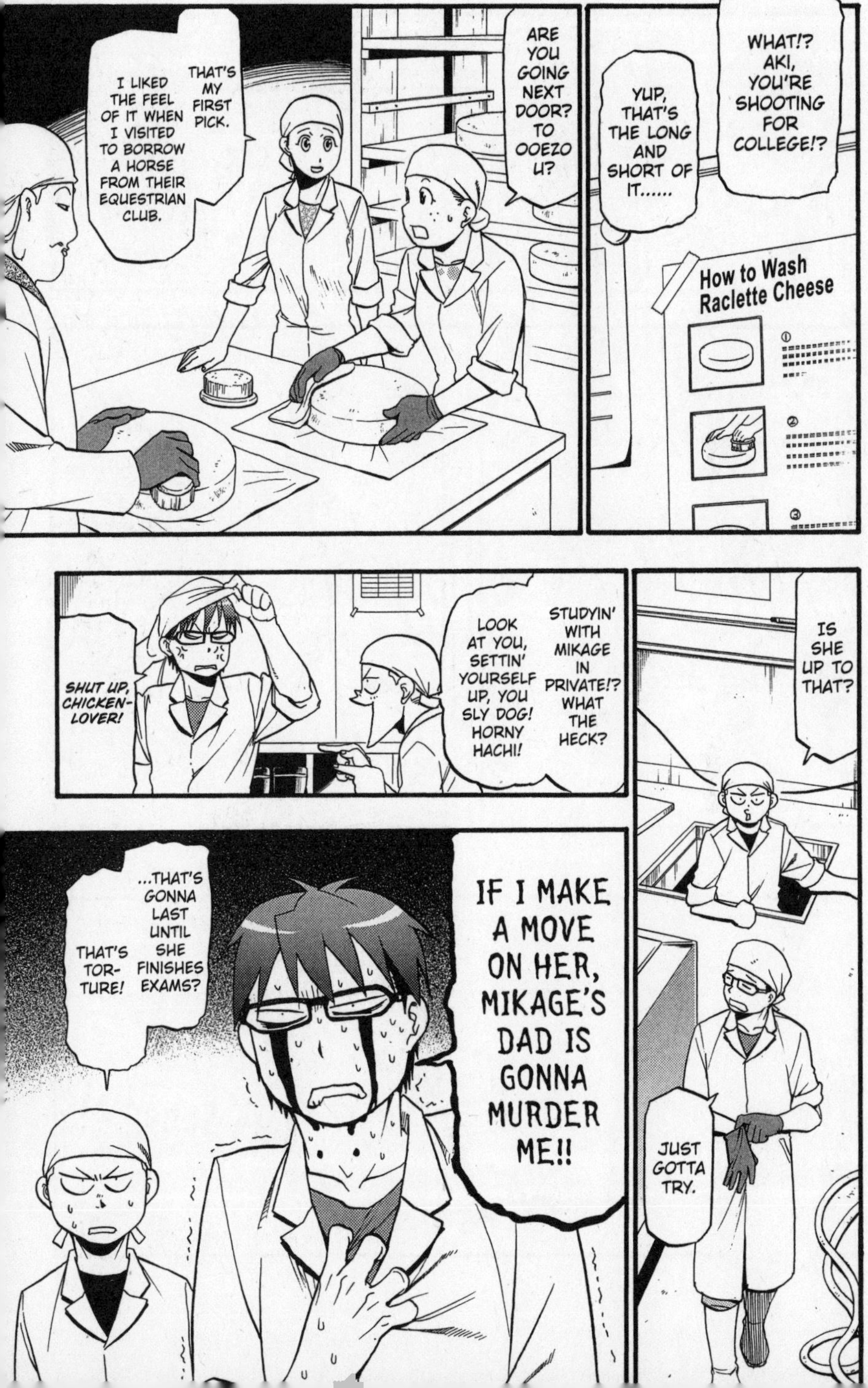
WHAT!? AKI, YOU'RE SHOOTING FOR COLLEGE!?
YUP, THAT'S THE LONG AND SHORT OF IT......
How to Wash Raclette Cheese
ARE YOU GOING NEXT DOOR? TO OOEZO U?
THAT'S MY FIRST PICK.
I LIKED THE FEEL OF IT WHEN I VISITED TO BORROW A HORSE FROM THEIR EQUESTRIAN CLUB.
IS SHE UP TO THAT?
JUST GOTTA TRY.
STUDYIN' WITH MIKAGE IN PRIVATE!? WHAT THE HECK?
LOOK AT YOU, SETTIN' YOURSELF UP, YOU SLY DOG! HORNY HACHI!
SHUT UP, CHICKEN-LOVER!
IF I MAKE A MOVE ON HER, MIKAGE'S DAD IS GONNA MURDER ME!!
...THAT'S GONNA LAST UNTIL SHE FINISHES EXAMS?
THAT'S TOR-TURE!

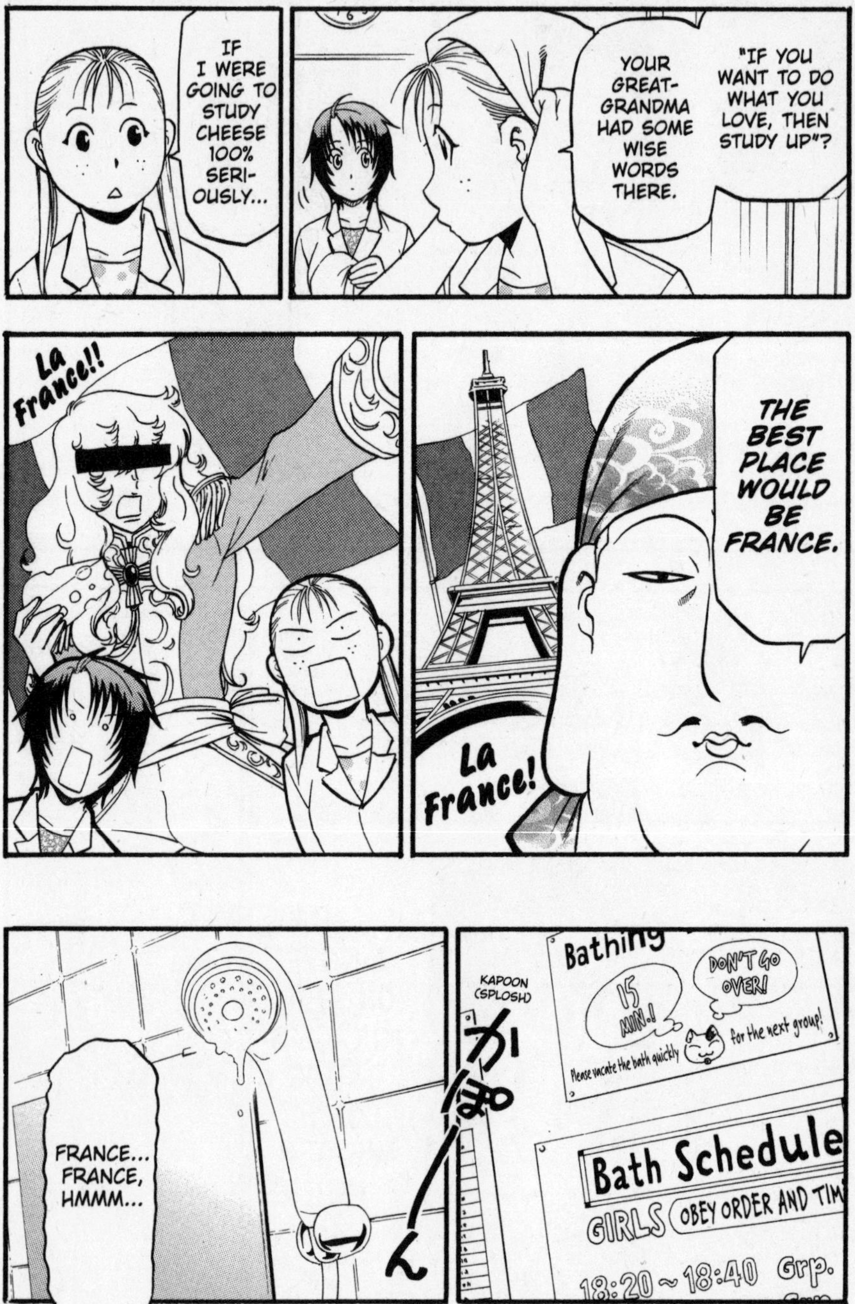
"IF YOU WANT TO DO WHAT YOU LOVE, THEN STUDY UP"?
YOUR GREAT-GRANDMA HAD SOME WISE WORDS THERE.
IF I WERE GOING TO STUDY CHEESE 100% SERI-OUSLY...
THE BEST PLACE WOULD BE FRANCE.
La France!
La France!!
Bathing
DON'T GO OVER!
15 MIN.!
Please vacate the bath quickly for the next group!
KAPOON (SPLOSH)
かぽーん
Bath Schedule
GIRLS
OBEY ORDER AND TIM
18:20 ~ 18:40 Grp.
FRANCE... FRANCE, HMMM...

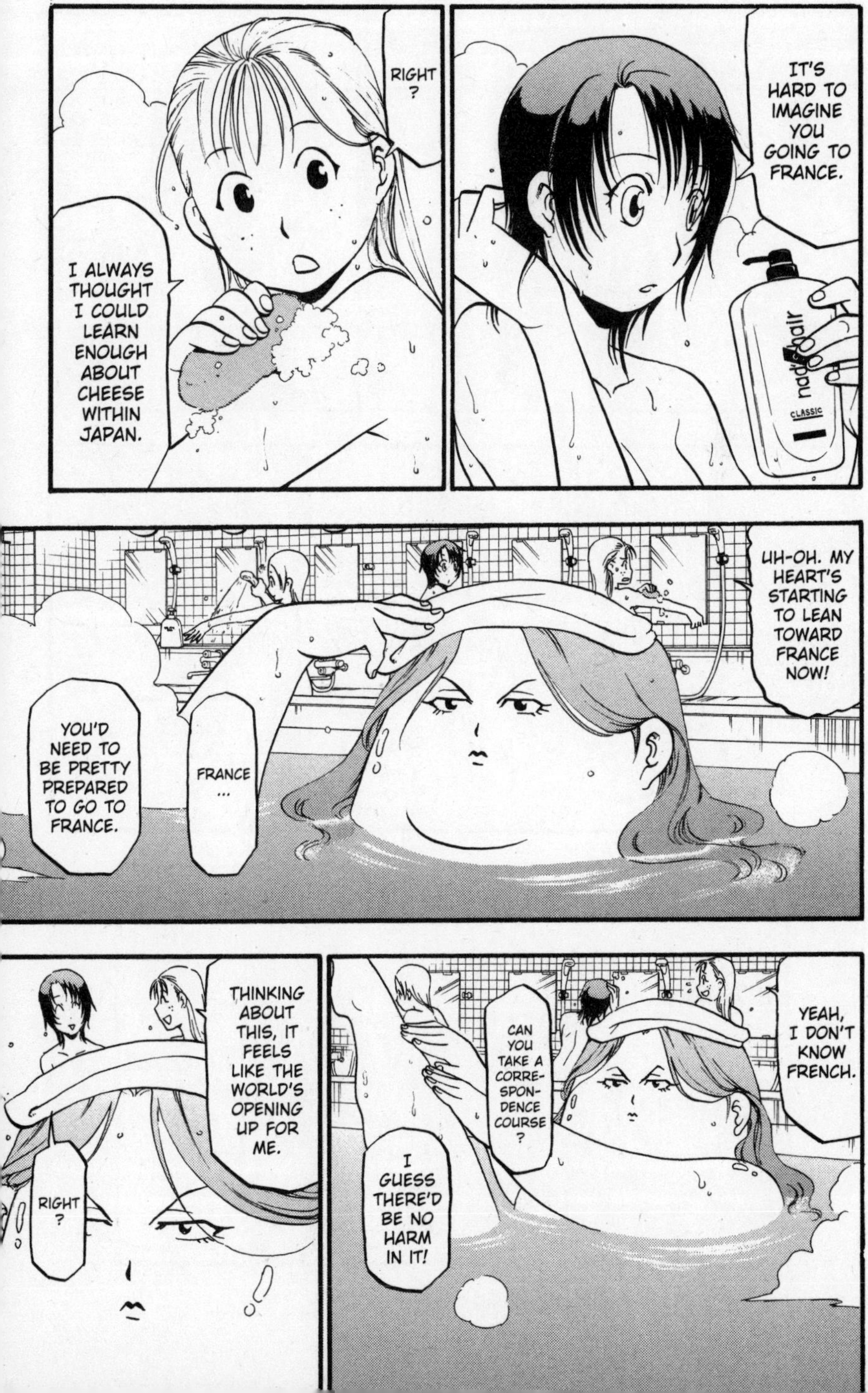
IT'S HARD TO IMAGINE YOU GOING TO FRANCE.
RIGHT?
I ALWAYS THOUGHT I COULD LEARN ENOUGH ABOUT CHEESE WITHIN JAPAN.
UH-OH. MY HEART'S STARTING TO LEAN TOWARD FRANCE NOW!
FRANCE...
YOU'D NEED TO BE PRETTY PREPARED TO GO TO FRANCE.
YEAH, I DON'T KNOW FRENCH.
CAN YOU TAKE A CORRE-SPON-DENCE COURSE?
I GUESS THERE'D BE NO HARM IN IT!
THINKING ABOUT THIS, IT FEELS LIKE THE WORLD'S OPENING UP FOR ME.
RIGHT?

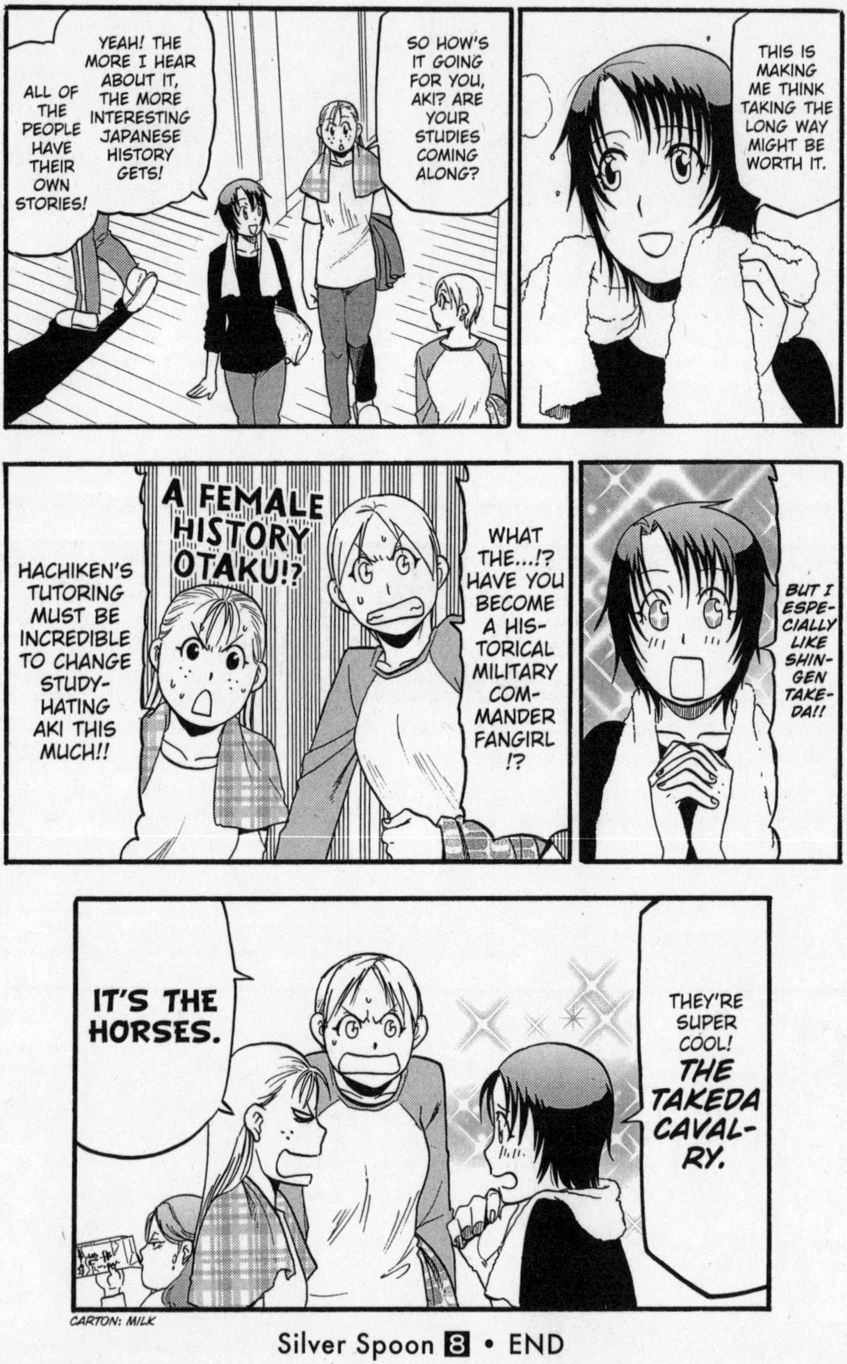
THIS IS MAKING ME THINK TAKING THE LONG WAY MIGHT BE WORTH IT.
SO HOW'S IT GOING FOR YOU, AKI? ARE YOUR STUDIES COMING ALONG?
YEAH! THE MORE I HEAR ABOUT IT, THE MORE INTERESTING JAPANESE HISTORY GETS!
ALL OF THE PEOPLE HAVE THEIR OWN STORIES!
BUT I ESPECIALLY LIKE SHINGEN TAKEDA!!
WHAT THE...!? HAVE YOU BECOME A HISTORICAL MILITARY COMMANDER FANGIRL!?
A FEMALE HISTORY OTAKU!?
HACHIKEN'S TUTORING MUST BE INCREDIBLE TO CHANGE STUDY-HATING AKI THIS MUCH!!
THEY'RE SUPER COOL! THE TAKEDA CAVALRY.
IT'S THE HORSES.

CARTON: MILK

Silver Spoon 8 • END

Silver Spoon

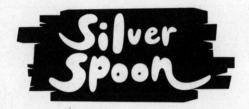

Days Off

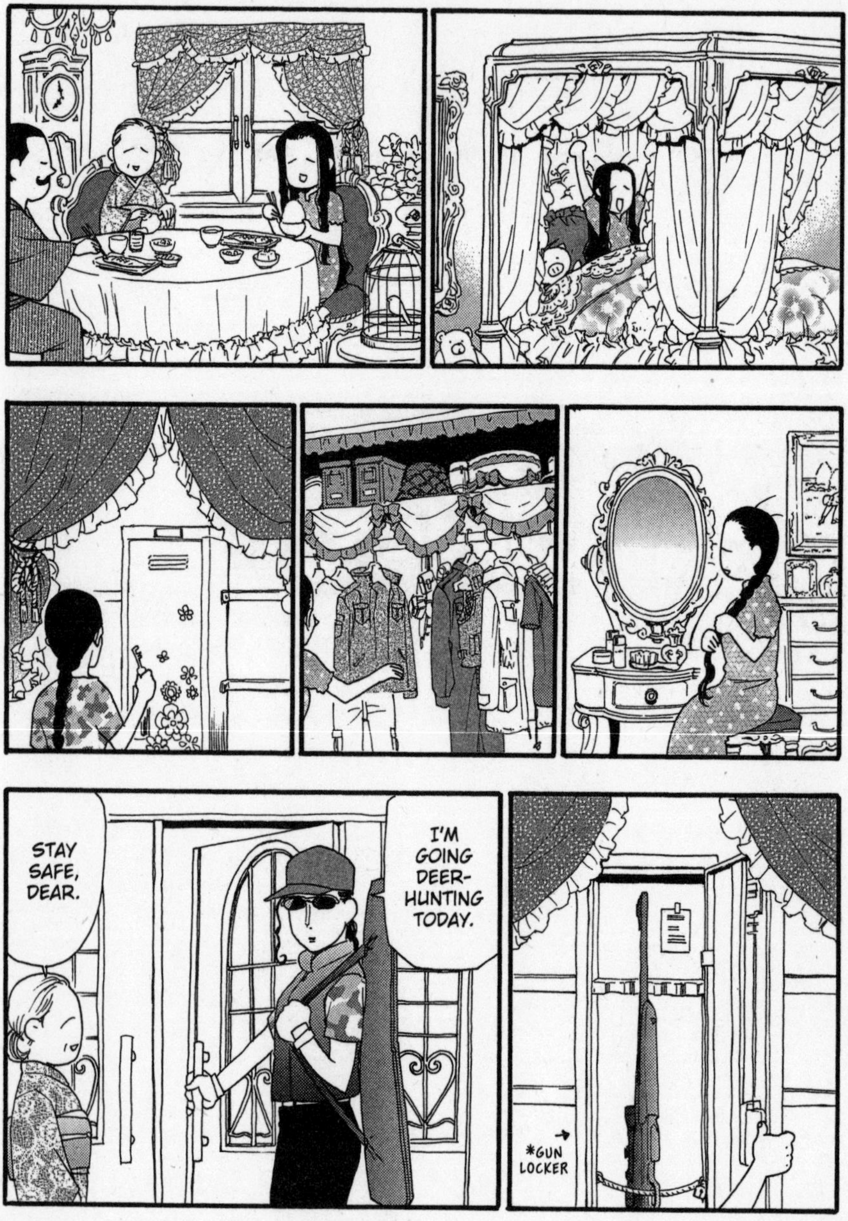
*GUN LOCKER
I'M GOING DEER-HUNTING TODAY.
STAY SAFE, DEAR.

Cow Shed Diaries:
Tale of the Three Super Saiy●ns & the Farmers

AT THE VENUE FOR THE SHOGAKUKAN MANGA AWARDS
GREETINGS, GREETINGS, GREETINGS, AND MORE GREETINGS.
MY SON
I WAS RUSHING AROUND, WHEN NEXT THING I KNEW...
HUH? WHERE'D MY SON GO?
GONE.
KAZUHIRO FUJITA-SENSEI
MY SON
RUMIKO TAKAHASHI-SENSEI
MITSURU ADACHI-SENSEI
SOOOOOON!!

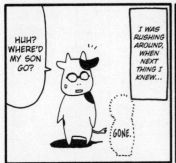

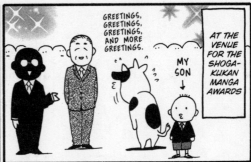

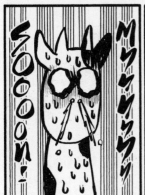

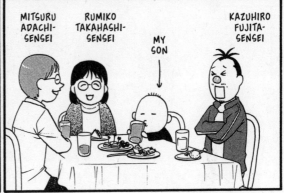

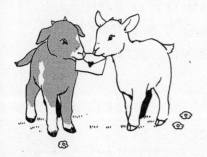

Silver Spoon 8!

The eighth volume unfolds!!
I hope to see you in the next volume as well.

あらかわひろむ
Hiromu Arakawa

~ Special Thanks ~

All of my assistants,
Everyone who helped with collecting material, interviews, and consulting,
My editor, Takashi Tsubouchi,

AND YOU!!

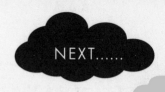

NEXT......

IF THERE'S ANYTHING I CAN DO, JUST LET ME KNOW.
I'LL DO ANY-THING.
ANYTHING
AT... HOME ......
CAN YOU HANDLE PRACTICE LIKE THAT?
I'M OKAY.
I'LL ...
... FEED THIS TO MY PAR-ENTS ......
GO (WHOOSH)

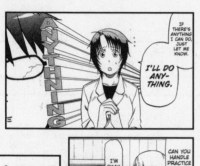

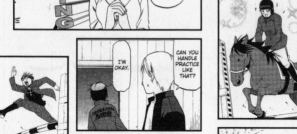

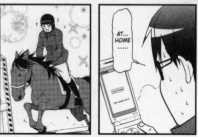

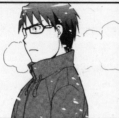

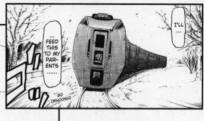

Where do people come from,
and where are they going...?
Hachiken faces his roots.
For Aki's sake...
No, not just that.
He does it for his own sake.
Running away wasn't a mistake.
Life isn't a one-way street.

KAW!
KAW!
KAW!
...I'VE ONLY BEEN HERE ONCE, FOR THE ENTRANCE CEREMONY, BUT...
...THIS REALLY IS A SCHOOL... RIGHT?
とりゃっ
COME AN' GET IT!
AH ...
TRY IT WITH SALT!
HUH? YOU MEAN WITH LEMON JUICE AND SOY SAUCE!!
HAH!? NO, SEVEN SPICE BLEND!!
GINGER SOY SAUCE !!
WITH MAYO, SOY SAUCE, AND CHILI PEPPER. IT GOES GREAT WITH BEER THAT WAY!!
DID SOMEONE SAY "BEER" ?
GARABAAN (SLAM)
SNOW ......
LOOKS LIKE THE SNOW WILL PILE UP...
WAKU (GIDDY)
WAKU

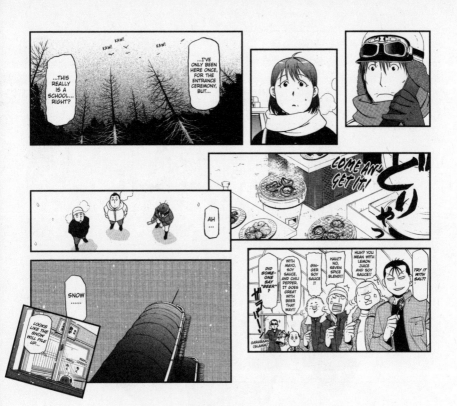

Learning that lesson has enabled him to change. He doesn't dislike the person he is now.

Silver Spoon volume 9, coming soon!!

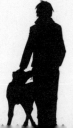

to be continued......

Silver Spoon

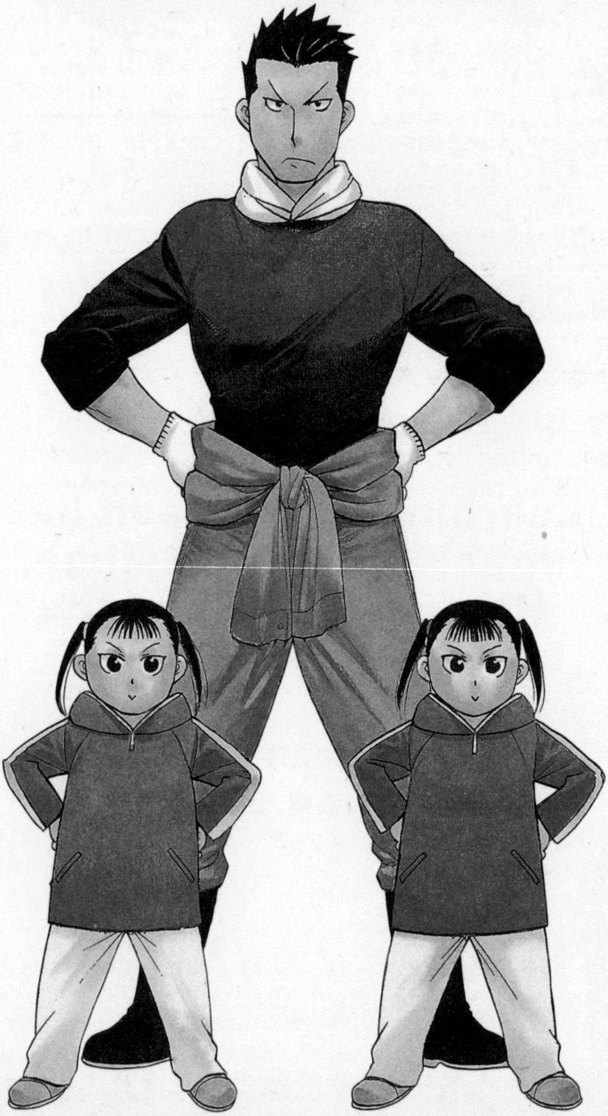

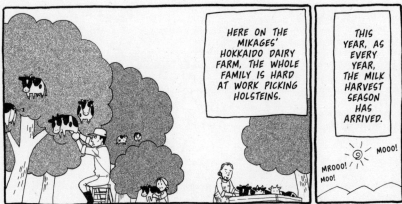

THIS YEAR, AS EVERY YEAR, THE MILK HARVEST SEASON HAS ARRIVED.
MOOO!
MROOO!
MOO!
HERE ON THE MIKAGES' HOKKAIDO DAIRY FARM, THE WHOLE FAMILY IS HARD AT WORK PICKING HOLSTEINS.
THE MILK SQUEEZED OUT BY THE VILLAGE GIRLS' BARE FEET...
...WILL SPEND AN ENTIRE YEAR AGING BEFORE IT IS DELIVERED TO THE PUBLIC'S DINING TABLES.
SINCE WE HAD A COOL SUMMER THIS YEAR, WE GOT SOME GREAT MILK!
THE MILK HARVEST WILL REACH ITS PEAK THIS VERY WEEK.
DAIRY FARMER MIKAGE-SAN

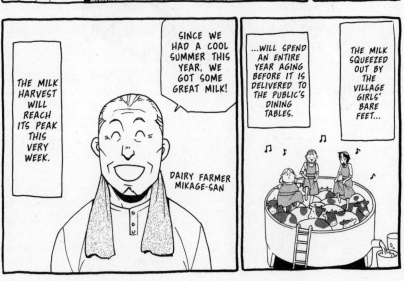

Translation Notes

Common Honorifics

no honorific: Indicates familiarity or closeness; if used without permission or reason, addressing someone in this manner would constitute an insult.

-san: The Japanese equivalent of Mr./Mrs./Miss. If a situation calls for politeness, this is the fail-safe honorific.

-sama: Conveys great respect; may also indicate the social status of the speaker is lower than that of the addressee.

-kun: Used most often when referring to boys, this honorific indicates affection or familiarity. Occasionally used by older men among their peers, but it may also be used by anyone referring to a person of lower standing.

-chan: An affectionate honorific indicating familiarity used mostly in reference to girls; also used in reference to cute persons or animals of either gender.

-sensei: A respectful term for teachers, artists, or high-level professionals.

-niisan, nii-san, aniki, etc.: A term of endearment meaning "big brother" that may be more widely used to address any young man who is like a brother, regardless of whether he is related or not.

-neesan, nee-san, aneki, etc.: The female counterpart of the above, nee-san means "big sister."

Currency Conversion

While conversion rates fluctuate, an easy estimate for Japanese Yen conversion is ¥100 to 1 USD.

Page 8

Natto is a sticky, smelly snack made from fermented soybeans.

Yakiniku, sometimes referred to as "Japaense barbecue," is a style of grilling bite-sized pieces of meat and vegetables on a small tabletop grill.

Page 45

The god of poverty (*binbougami*) refers to a particular spirit from Japanese folklore that possesses a person or their house and brings them bad fortune and poverty.

Page 51

In Japanese, Hachiken's advisor outfit is captioned with a play on "The Ambush from Ten Sides," a strategy employed in the Battle of Cangting that left ten brigades lying in wait as an ambush. Instead of from ten sides, Hachiken's ambush is from "eight houses" (or "hachiken," playing on the number "eight" in Hachiken's name).

Page 97

The Northern Territories (or the Kuril Islands) are part of an ongoing sovereignty dispute between Japan and Russia. Located north of Hokkaido, they were annexed by Russia after World War II.

Page 125

Hachiken is imitating the statue of Dr. William S. Clark (1826–1886), an American professor who was invited to Japan to establish an agricultural college in Hokkaido. "Boys, be ambitious," were his parting words to his Japanese students, and the motto is well-known throughout Japan.

Page 172

The Taira clan (also sometimes referred to as the Heike or Heishi from the Chinese pronunciation of the clan name) was a major samurai clan first founded in 825 and was one of the most influential clans in Japanese politics during the Heian period (794–1185). The Tokugawa clan, a line of feudal lords, rose to power near the end of the Warring States period (1467–1600) and ruled until the end of the Edo period (1603–1868). The Soma clan was a samurai clan and a minor regional power. The Soma Wild Horse Chase began as a military tournament and continues today as a three-day festival.

Page 180
The character pictured in panel four is from the classic shoujo manga *The Rose of Versailles* (which takes place in France). Oscar is a woman who was raised as a man to follow in her father's footsteps as captain of the palace guards.

Page 182
Shingen Takeda (1521–1573) was an aggressive and skilled military leader and one of the feudal lords who fought for control of Japan during the Warring States period. Ultimately, his cavalry was destroyed by Oda Nobunaga's gunmen.

Page 185
Arakawa's son is sitting with three well-known manga artists. Kazuhiro Fujita debuted in 1989 and is most famous for *Ushio and Tora*. Rumiko Takahashi debuted in 1978, is one of Japan's most successful manga artists, and created the huge international hits *Ranma ½* and *Inuyasha*. Mitsuru Adachi debuted in 1970 and is known for his romantic comedies and baseball manga; *Touch* and *Cross Game* are two of his major works.

MATH
Aki Mika

Silver Spoon

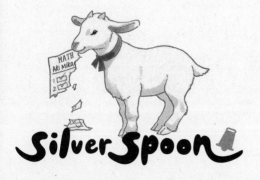

Silver Spoon 8

HIROMU ARAKAWA

Translation: **Amanda Haley** Lettering: **Abigail Blackman**

GIN NO SAJI SILVER SPOON Vol. 8
by Hiromu ARAKAWA
© 2011 Hiromu ARAKAWA
All rights reserved.
Original Japanese edition published by SHOGAKUKAN.
English translation rights in the United States of America, Canada, the United Kingdom, Ireland, Australia and New Zealand arranged with SHOGAKUKAN through Tuttle-Mori Agency, Inc.

English translation © 2019 by Yen Press, LLC

Yen Press
1290 Avenue of the Americas
New York, NY 10104

Visit us at yenpress.com
facebook.com/yenpress
twitter.com/yenpress
yenpress.tumblr.com
instagram.com/yenpress

First Yen Press Edition: April 2019

Yen Press is an imprint of Yen Press, LLC.
The Yen Press name and logo are trademarks of Yen Press, LLC.

The publisher is not responsible for websites (or their content) that are not owned by the publisher.

Library of Congress Control Number: 2017959207

ISBN: 978-1-9753-2763-7

10 9 8 7 6 5 4 3 2 1

WOR

Printed in the United States of America